Cine-Ethics

This volume looks at the significance and range of ethical questions that pertain to various film practices. Diverse philosophical traditions provide useful frameworks to discuss spectators' affective and emotional engagement with film, which can function as a moral ground for one's connection to others and to the world outside the self. These traditions encompass theories of emotion, phenomenology, the philosophy of compassion, and analytic and continental ethical thinking and environmental ethics. This anthology is one of the first volumes to open a dialogue among these diverse methodologies. Contributors bring to the forefront some of the assumptions implicitly shared between these theories and forge a new relationship between them to explore the moral engagement of the spectator and the ethical consequences of both producing and consuming films.

Jinhee Choi is senior lecturer in film studies at King's College London, UK.

Mattias Frey is senior lecturer in film studies at the University of Kent, UK.

Routledge Advances in Film Studies

Cine-Ethics

Ethical Dimensions of Film Theory,
Practice, and Spectatorship

Edited by Jinhee Choi and Mattias Frey

NEW YORK AND LONDON

First published 2014
by Routledge
711 Third Avenue, New York, NY 10017

and by Routledge
2 Park Square, Milton Park, Abingdon, Oxfordshire OX14

First issued in paperback 2016

*Routledge is an imprint of the Taylor & Francis Group,
an informa business*

Library of Congress Cataloging-in-Publication Data

Cine-ethics : ethical dimensions of film theory, practice and spectatorship /
   edited by Jinhee Choi and Mattias Frey.
     pages cm — (Routledge advances in film studies ; 29)
   Includes bibliographical references and index.
  1. Motion pictures—Philosophy. 2. Motion pictures—Moral and
ethical aspects. I. Choi, Jinhee editor of compilation. II. Frey, Mattias
editor of compilation.
  PN1995.C4848 2013
  791.43′684—dc23
  2013020407

ISBN 13: 978-1-138-23385-0 (pbk)
ISBN 13: 978-0-415-82125-4 (hbk)

Typeset in Sabon
by Apex CoVantage, LLC

Contents

Figures

Animal-Borne Imaging, Sam Easterson, 1998–2008

Introduction

Jinhee Choi and Mattias Frey

Interdisciplinarity has been one of film studies' major strengths. In the last decade, philosophical inquiry—and ethical inquiry in particular—has emerged as a central focus for film scholars, philosophers, and students alike. This has to do not only with a search for new methodologies suitable for studying contemporary film and media practices, but also with rethinking the previously dominant film theories and methodologies in light of the relationship between the self and others—especially spectators' moral engagement and the ethical consequences of producing and consuming films.

Classical film theories were concerned with the ontological and epistemological status of the then new medium. Medium specificity—i.e., how film's materiality and mechanism differ from other artistic forms—has been the basis for film aesthetics, derived from, and distinctive to, the medium. In contrast, 1970s structuralist and psychoanalytical film theories were preoccupied primarily with epistemological and ideological concerns. The principal research questions sought to understand how the spectator assesses and appreciates the world depicted and asked to what extent mainstream film styles (such as Hollywood continuity editing) could be considered ideologically conservative by not foregrounding the illusory and constructed nature of their representations.

The ethical turn, on the other hand, stresses the particular affective nature of film spectatorship. Spectators' perceptual and sensorial engagement with film is considered as ethical in and of itself, not merely as a moral ground to connect to reality and others outside the self. Numerous approaches have emerged to forge a new relationship between film and ethics, as demonstrated in *Ethics at the Cinema*,[1] *Film and Ethics: Foreclosed Encounters*,[2] and *World Cinema and the Ethics of Realism*,[3] to name a few recent scholarly works. However, these titles diverge not only in terms of the methodologies they employ, but also in how they explore the scope of "ethical" parameters. Indeed, even as film studies and philosophy have begun to explore each other, institutional differences over the very objects of their inquiry remain.

In traditional aesthetics (in the Anglo-American analytic tradition), the relationship between ethics and aesthetics revolves around the sustainability of ethical criticism—in other words, whether the moral attitude manifest in a work of art (e.g., a racist or fascist viewpoint represented and endorsed in a work of art) should or should not affect the aesthetic appreciation and judgment of the work. Autonomism and moralism (or ethicism) of various degrees have been proposed.[4] The former asserts that art maintains its autonomy, and thus should not be evaluated in terms of nonaesthetic criteria, such as moral, political, and social concerns; the latter advocates a stronger correlation between moral and aesthetic values for some art forms and genres.

In film studies, "ethics" has been defined in looser ways, including not only the examination of ethical perspectives manifest in individual films, but more importantly, the ethical dimension of film as a medium. Various philosophical traditions, which developed more or less independently, provide useful frameworks to discuss ethical issues of film—theories of emotion, phenomenology, the philosophy of compassion, and continental thinking including the writings of Gilles Deleuze, Emmanuel Levinas, Alain Badiou, and Jacques Rancière. Despite the diverse schools of thoughts within philosophy-informed film studies, there seems to be a general move toward prioritizing singularity over universality, affectivity over rationality, and ethics of the particular over ethics of moral imperatives. However, there are three major ways of seeing the relationship between film and its ethical functions: the revisionist, the perceptionist, and the cognitivist perspective. Each of these offers a particular negotiation of the two traditional realms within ethics—goodness and morality.

1. THE REVISIONIST PERSPECTIVE

Revisionists such as Levinas, Badiou, and D. N. Rodowick reconsider the realms of ethics, relating ethics to ontology, metaphysics, and epistemology in a new way. Levinas, for instance, claims that ethics (of the other) precedes ontology (of the self) because the self's relationship with the other logically precedes the formation of subjectivity; he thereby asserts the primacy of the other over the self. The singularity or particularity of the self, according to Levinas, is not an outcome of the active formation of subjectivity within one's own consciousness, but a result of passivity, receptivity, and sensibility—being addressed and affected by the other external to oneself, that is, "alterity."[5]

In contrast, Badiou replaces the realm of ethics with that of metaphysics and epistemology. "Ethics," according to Badiou, should concern a "faithful" truth-seeking process.[6] "Truth," claims Badiou, is contingent on a particular situation, where "an event" intervenes into, and interferes with, the situation. The event demands a novel conception ("name") to articulate what has been lacking ("the void") or unaddressed ("the unknown") within the previous frameworks of institutionalized knowledge.[7] One's ethical responsibility is then to be "faithful" to a situation, which emanates *a* truth, rather than *the* truth. In this line of thought, ethics reconfigures the traditional range of ethical issues by assuming the tasks that once belonged to ontology and epistemology. Stanley Cavell's ontology of film—and, in particular, Rodowick's ethical reading of it—adds another strand of such a revisionist approach.

Cavell's ontology of film has earned a new currency as of late,[8] especially amidst the recent proliferation of the term *ethics* in film studies discourse. In the work reprinted here, Rodowick invokes Cavell's film theory as a way to demonstrate how "aesthetic questions of medium specificity have continually turned into ethical questions."[9] Rodowick unearths an ethical dimension embedded in Cavell's film theory and observes how "Cavell is less interested in how photographs represent, picture or mean than in how they place us subjectively. Thus projection, or 'the phenomenological facts of viewing' is coextensive with the subjective condition of modernity, imagined here as a filmic way of encountering the world."[10]

For Cavell, film's characteristic presence and absence of the world viewed and the spectator address the conditions of the modern subject. At the root of modern philosophy—especially in the idealist tradition of John Locke, George Berkeley, and David Hume, and even in the rationalist tradition of René Descartes—exists an epistemological skepticism regarding the existence of external reality. Through photographic mechanical reproduction, however, film points to the possibility that a world exists outside one's subjectivity. Because the spectator was absent in the world filmed, the medium provides material evidence of reality outside one's subjectivity; that is, film's mechanical processes prevent it from being an invented creation of the mind.[11] In Cavell's words, "photography satisfied a wish . . . the human wish, intensifying in the West since the Reformation, to escape subjectivity and metaphysical isolation—a wish for the power to reach this world, having for so long tried, at last hopelessly, to manifest fidelity to another."[12] In contrast to Noël Carroll (who identifies Cavell as a realist), Rodowick underlines "ontological restlessness" manifest in this wish, foregrounding the subject's "desire" to confirm the existence of reality.[13]

In Rodowick's reconstruction of Cavell, film not only addresses the modern subject's epistemological or existential concerns but also provides an ethical solution to the dilemma of modern subjectivity. Throughout his discussion of Cavell, Rodowick emphasizes the subject's desire to "connect to" or "regain access to" the world despite the spatial and temporal gaps inherent in the medium. In what way does film enable the subject to rebuild a connection to the world and embody a collectivity that exceeds the realm of subjectivity? Rodowick elaborates on Cavell's ontology of film:

> In our views of the world, we are presented a situation wherein humanity is returned to (visible) nature in sharing the same duration with it. . . . In response to the skeptical attitude, which sets the perceiving subject at a distance from nature, in film humanity and nature are of

one substance and held in a common duration—they are expressed as having a common Being.[14]

By "duration" Rodowick does not merely refer to screen time, but to a temporal experience by which the viewer (re)experiences the past or the world passing in the present tense—a virtual time in which the skeptical subject and the world viewed share the same mode of existence, or "partake of the same ontological substance"—what Rodowick/Cavell calls "reality."[15]

The ethics of film that Rodowick reads in Cavell's ontology of film needs further dissecting. To what extent should the medium's capacity to (re)present the profilmic world be necessarily considered ethical? Rodowick appeals to two notions—self-examination and transformation[16]—which might help us see Cavell's ontology as a cine-ethics. If, as William Frankena notes, "the moderns conceive of a specifically moral way to live . . . [which] is largely a matter of our relations to our fellow human beings,"[17] the modern subject's lack of ontological conviction of the world outside one's subjectivity deprives the subject of a possibility to engage with others. According to Rodowick, "the modern ethical dilemma is how to regain contact with this world, to overcome our distance from it and restore its knownness to us"[18]—preconditions necessary for the subject's moral responsibility and commitment. Rodowick interprets Cavell's ontology of film as having less to do with identifying constituents of the medium than appreciating its capability to *express* the modern dilemma (self-examination) as well as *overcome* it (transformation). Rodowick ties the ethical dimension of Cavell's film theory to his moral perfectionism, which seeks transcendence of the modern condition "in anticipation of a better, future existence."[19] The aim of moral perfectionism, in general, can be understood as the protection and promotion of "good" human life; film helps the subject perfect oneself by transcending the ontological, epistemic impasse through the virtual experience of the world (the past).

Rodowick's rehearsal of Cavell's theory highlights film as the site for an ethical encounter between the self, reality, and others. However, one may ask to what extent the cinematic connection posited between the self and reality (and thus others) can be substantiated. In Cavell's ontology of film, the role of absence is just as vital as presence—it is the world present *to* us, not vice versa. The magic of film, Cavell claims, lies in its capacity to lift the burden of responsibility, relieving the spectator from the burden of acting on the situation.[20] "Viewing a movie makes this condition automatic, takes the responsibility for it out of our hands . . . Not because they are escapes into fantasy, but because they are reliefs from private fantasy and its responsibilities; from the fact that the world is already drawn by fantasy."[21] It is not just because of the fictional nature of the diegetic world that the spectator is exempted from responsibility. It also has to do with the mechanical reproduction of the profilmic world, which is displaced both temporally and spatially, and thus prevents the spectator from participating in it. The magic of film, according to Cavell, functions "not by literally presenting us with the world, but by permitting us to view it unseen. This is not a wish for a power over creation (as Pygmalion's was), but a wish not to need power, not to have to bear its burden."[22] For Cavell, "a screen *is* a barrier," which "screens me from the world it holds" and "screens that world from me."[23]

Film *is* philosophical for Cavell, because its self-reflexive dimension carries an existential significance. Film is philosophy or, as some philosophers contend, it invites philosophical reflection. It is a matter of debate whether ontological acknowledgement of the other (otherness) suffices to grant film theory or film philosophy an ethical dimension, however. Certainly, ethics *in* cinema, as will be explored in this volume, extends the scope further and includes not only what film is, but how film is made, distributed, and consumed. In general, Rodowick's explorations of ethical dimensions inherent in film ontology resemble the strategy of other revisionists, such as Levinas and Badiou, who reorient philosophy by prioritizing ethics over other areas of philosophical inquiry.

2. THE MORAL PERCEPTIONIST PERSPECTIVE

In her book *Carnal Thoughts*, Vivian Sobchack broaches the relationship between ethics and aesthetics: "Central to any understanding of the connection between ethics and aesthetics," lies "the question of the limit between the body and the world."[24] Like Cavell, the idea of "connection" also plays a key role in Sobchack's delineation of the ethical foundation of the filmic medium. However, Sobchack's interest lies in the examination of how the spectator's sensorial affective engagement (sense-ability) and response (response-ability) to the profilmic world yields an ethical responsibility unto others.

Sobchack, along with Martha Nussbaum, can be considered moral perceptionists: They foreground sensorial, perceptual, and perceptive engagement with a medium—rather than conscious, self-reflexive engagement—as the basis of morality. Lawrence A. Blum delimits moral perception as something that "cannot be identified with moral judgment. In a given situation, moral perception comes on the scene before moral judgment; moral perception can lead to moral action outside the operation of judgment entirely; and, more generally, perception can involve moral capacities not encompassed by moral judgment."[25] Neither Sobchack nor Nussbaum objects to the idea that moral perception can lead to more conscious moral understanding and reflection. They only negate the stronger claim that acute responsive feelings require moral standards and principles, or need to reach moral judgment, in order to be viewed as moral engagement.[26] Nussbaum underscores how a "morality of perception" cultivates our capacity to see and care for particulars as themselves, not as instances of the universal.[27] In other words, an acute sensitivity to engage affectively with characters is in and of itself worthy; the value of which should not be judged by universal moral principles.

According to Sobchack, the phenomenological experience of film viewing consists both in subjective bodily experience and its objective representation—i.e., one that includes both sensibility and intelligibility. A film engages a precognitive, primordial state, in which both the subject's sensual and crossmodal activities make sense of a range of inputs *"without a thought."*[28] Tactility manifest in films such as Jane Campion's *The Piano* (1993) can be transmitted to the viewer through various sensory modes, without the viewer's sense of touch being fully activated. Sensory modes communicate and cooperate to provide the viewer the carnal knowledge, and the viewer's lived body (or the body-subject) functions as a site for these modes to operate simultaneously.

The role of sensorial experience is not only to channel information about the profilmic world, but also to enrich the subject's relationship with the world as a material being. Sobchack writes:

> In being actively devoted to (rather than passively suffering) the embracing and enfolding of the world's—and one's own—objectivity, the body subject experiences not a diminution of subjectivity but its sensual and sensible expansion—and an enhanced awareness of what it is to be material . . . It allows us to understand in a primordial way the general pervasion in existence of material *sense-ability.*[29]

The subject's sense perception of, and reaction to, the external world (including film) not only reinforces the subject as a material being (the body-subject), but also helps the subject to be aware of the possibility of being an object (the body-object).

Unlike Cavell, who views the screen as a barrier, Sobchack construes it as flesh—"the common existential ground of both body and world" or "the manner in which subject and object inhabit each other by participating in a common condition of embodied sense."[30] The reversibility of subject and object within this common ground is what provides the material, corporeal foundation for the possibility of recognizing—and caring for—material objects external to ourselves.[31] Finding oneself deeply affected by a film or passionately caring for characters is an ethical investment, in which one becomes "unselfish and radically decentered."[32]

> The mutual origin of aesthetic sensibility and ethical responsibility lies in the subjective realization of our own objectivity, in the passion of our own material. Aesthetics and ethics thus emerge first and corporeally as sense-ability and response-ability—by virtue of the inherent structure of the lived body-subject's transcendent consciousness of its own objective immanence, and in the experienced sense (both corporeal and self-conscious) of what it is to exist, at once, and as a sensible body-object and a sensate body-subject.[33]

Sobchack is careful not to reduce the significance of the world or other body-subjects as extensions of one's subjectivity. Self-interests can be expanded to include those of others and the external world, but not merely as the object of one's own subjectivity. "Inter-objectivity"—a term coined by Sobchack—underlies the affective engagement, which is neither centered on the subject nor remains only on the level of self-understanding. This represents a move toward "communal attunement," in Nussbaum's idiom.[34]

Sobchack's phenomenology may invite criticism in terms of the way she distinguishes between and links various levels and meanings of sensibility and responsibility, both in their prereflective and reflective forms. Perceptual acuteness and sensitivity are not achieved independent of cognitive operations; as Hume observes, one's knowledge and training can refine one's perceptual sensitivity and receptivity.[35] Furthermore, despite the ontological reversibility (although not replaceability) between subject and object in Sobchack's phenomenology, there still remains unidirectionality in the interaction between subject and object in the diegetic world. Characters can affect us emotionally, but not vice versa. Nevertheless, Sobchack's phenomenological approach fleshes out the relationship between ethics and aesthetics, and the ethical relationship between the self and others. In other words, one's sensorial and affective engagement with film and others not only provides a ground for aesthetic appreciation (sensibility) and moral behavior (responsibility) on a conscious level; it is also valuable in and of itself.

3. THE COGNITIVIST PERSPECTIVE

Some film scholars turn to affects and ethics to counterbalance the "disembodied, transcendental subject," a notion of spectatorship posited in the structuralist-psychoanalytic theories of the 1970s.[36] According to the ideas advanced by the latter, the subject is not a viewer of flesh and blood, but rather a textually inscribed position that a viewer may or may not take up during actual screening. Mainstream films are often designed to elicit emotions; they manipulate viewers to react in accordance with the intended effects. For the film theorists of the 1970s, the terms *moral* or *moral criticism* have been tainted with severe ideological connotations to mean a reinforcement of the dominant political ideology and the taste and culture of white, middle-class men.

The presuppositions of such film theories were challenged and gradually abandoned with the emergence of cultural studies and cognitivism, which rejected a deterministic relationship between film/film style and the audience's response/agency. Increasing attention has been paid to the affective engagement, which was once viewed as an impediment to the viewer's (political) consciousness of film both as an institution and the apparatus.

Cognitive theory has contributed to such a shift, highlighting the fact that affective or emotional engagement with fiction/film is not completely irrational, given the cognitive constituent of emotion. Emotion is not opposite to cognition, but instead involves a propositional attitude directed toward the object of an emotion.[37]

The irrationality of emotion, although not as politically charged as in film studies, has been a long-standing challenge in philosophical aesthetics since Plato and philosophers of art have explored both the mechanism and value of appreciating fiction. For example, Colin Radford's famous essay, "How Can We Be Moved By the Fate of Anna Karenina?,"[38] interrogates this concern for emotional responses to fiction, and charts various ways in which emotional responses to fiction can be viewed. He proposes that we are fully aware that characters in fiction do not exist, but cannot help but feel for their plights and fates. He entertains various ways to solve this "paradox," yet acknowledges the inconsistency and incoherence involved in emotional response to fiction. It is natural—as well as sensible—that we respond to fictional characters as we do, even if the puzzle still remains as to whether it diverges from everyday emotion.

Various attempts have been made to resolve this paradox. Some interlocutors classify emotions directed toward fiction as different from everyday emotions (i.e., make-believe emotions),[39] while others show the continuity between emotions directed toward real people in real-life situations and those directed toward fiction.[40] It is beyond the scope of this introduction to delineate in detail the cognitivist debates advanced in the last two decades; emotional engagement with fiction bears relevance to the ethical inquiry of film—above all, how one connects to, and cares for, others.

Film theories of a cognitivist bent, such as those advanced by Carroll, Gregory Currie, Murray Smith, Carl Plantinga, and Torben Grodel, draw on findings in cognitive psychology, biology, and neuroscience to illuminate how we engage with film on an emotional level. In this regard, cognitivists depart from the first two approaches discussed earlier—the revisionist and the moral perceptionist—in their effort to empirically ground their theories and test their hypotheses. Nevertheless, cognitivist interests are narrower in that they have often focused on character engagement as inflected by narrative structure; scholars working in this vein do so despite their acknowledgement that film elicits responses broader than cognitively imbued emotions.[41]

Carroll, one of the leading cognitivists in aesthetics and film studies, assimilates emotions elicited by fiction with those emotional responses in real life. Despite the fact that emotions felt watching film are caused by thoughts (entertained unassertively) of (rather than beliefs in) the objects of emotions, film triggers the same kind of emotions as those we experience in everyday life. For example, entertaining the thought that the Christmas gifts one has ordered may not arrive on time can give rise to as much frustration as the actual incident. Some behavioral differences may accompany the respective emotions, but one must nonetheless note that everyday emotion can be caused by both belief and imagination. In fact, film has a capacity to invoke more powerful emotions thanks to its prefocused emotive structure—i.e., the structure designed to activate certain types of emotions from the spectator—and the spectator's care (or pro-attitude) for characters.[42] How film emotions can further one's moral understanding or yield ethical commitments is addressed more extensively by other theorists;[43] Carroll himself addresses the topic in this volume.

Not all emotions—whether in response to real-life or fictional scenarios—are triggered by conscious assessments or moral judgments. At times they occur almost automatically, prior to forming any cognitively mediated judgment about the object. In his discussion of how popular novels and mainstream films might morally orient and change viewers' perception of social phenomenon, Carroll adopts Ronald DeSousa's idea of "paradigm scenarios"—the perceptual as well as cognitive patterns and conditions that set off emotional responses. Carroll argues that the viewer tends to assimilate a new emotional situation to existing paradigms and that popular media deploy moral "calibration" (Jesse Prinz's term) to morally redeem (or condemn) character types or marginal groups. In changing the viewer's moral perception, its narratives would have to provide perceptual cues and scenarios that would help the viewer shift from paradigm scenarios previously associated with a character or an event to more favorably conceived ones.

Cognitivists examine the process of emotional alignment with characters and its potential contribution to the moral understanding of others. Regardless of the lengthy debates on both their stipulated processes (such as make-believe or simulated)[44] and the dominant mode between the two in engaging with fiction, empathy and sympathy come to the fore in discussing possible moral dimension of consuming fiction, including film. Alex Neill neatly sums up the difference between empathy and sympathy as feeling *with* versus feeling *for*.[45] Both are "other-directed" emotions, but may be nonetheless distinguished. In feeling empathy, one shares the same type of emotions as the object of one's emotion; in feeling sympathy, one responds to the object's emotional state, yet forms a different type of emotional response. Squeaky noise coming from an attic, whose source is unknown to both a character and the viewer, could prompt the viewer to share an ominous mood *with* the character; if the range of the viewer's knowledge is greater than the character, the viewer may feel fear *for* the character, anticipating how the narrative might unfold.

Focus on empathy, in both its cognitive and precognitive forms, opens up possibilities for phenomenological and cognitive approaches to converge fruitfully, as Jane Stadler demonstrates in this volume. Both phenomenologists and cognitivists acknowledge that motor and affective mimicry, which might be considered as universal, precognitive forms of empathic response, could be rendered in the viewer through such film techniques as close-up, texture, editing pace, and camera movement.[46] Mimicry is the mirroring of physiological or affective states of the other in a weakened form, without consciously emulating them. Babies often mimic the facial expressions of their caretakers and, during a boxing match, fans may mimic the muscular actions of a boxer, dodging the blows of an opponent without any conscious intention of doing so. As Stadler notes, compassion for characters is often embodied in precognitive mimicries *and* cognitively imbued empathic responses. Insisting on the saliency and value of only one form of empathic response—either purely affective or cognitively mediated response—would indeed limit our understanding of the moral engagement with film through multiple layers of perceptual, affective, and cognitive experiences.

These three perspectives—revisionist, moral perceptionist, and cognitivist—neither represent the entire body of scholarly literature on ethics in film studies, nor do they exhaust the methodologies employed in *Cine-Ethics*. However, an examination of these prominent approaches helps us to understand the context for the disciplinary turn to ethics, and the extent to which these approaches converge (or diverge) in their theoretical preoccupations and concerns. Unlike the previously published volumes on cinema and ethics, which engage with relatively few theorists, *Cine-Ethics* is one of the first volumes to open up a dialogue between diverse methodologies including both continental and analytic traditions. The chapters pick up on these theories as tools for the fruitful analysis of particular films; moreover, these ideas will be challenged and contested in light of contemporary film practices.

Cine-Ethics further extends its discussion to encompass the various modes and trends of film practices—such as documentary, extreme cinema, and employment of images of nature—which require ethical commitments of both filmmakers and consumers and thus engender ethical scrutiny. The essays collected here are not merely ethical critiques of particular filmmaking or filmmakers, but moreover reflect upon, and critically assess, the rhetoric of ethics and morality employed in film production and promotion. Ethics is championed (by some) over morality; the latter has been denounced as a set of ideologically acculturated norms that lacks the self-reflexivity attributed to the former.[47] However, as briefly noted in this introduction, historically the scope of ethics is broader than the critical assessment of imposed morality or moral principles, and concerns a range of both normative and non-normative questions including goodness, right action, ethical beliefs, and knowledge. The very distinction between ethics and morality should be revisited against how it functions in promoting auteurs, films, or specific film styles with an eye on the moral agency and performativity of filmmakers, and on claims to its relevance in judging their artistic achievement. Finally, this volume further pays proper attention to nonhuman subjects and objects such as animals and environments, which have previously been neglected or deemed beyond the scope of film studies' ethical considerations.

* * *

The chapters of the first section, entitled "The Ethical Self and Others," examine and expand on the contemporary methodologies employed in the ethical inquiry into film spectatorship and engagement. In his discussion of Cavell, Rodowick examines how the viewer regains contact with the pro-filmic world despite its spatial and temporal displacement. Rodowick treats the metaphysical and ethical dilemma that Cavell locates in film by focusing on how cinema enables the viewer to recognize the "deep connectedness with a way of being in the world."[48] Jane Stadler bridges the moral philosophy of Nussbaum and the phenomenology advanced by Sobchack in her analysis of *The Diving Bell and the Butterfly* (dir. Julian Schnabel, 2007). Carroll reconsiders the question of emotional engagement and the extent to which fiction appeals to pre-established paradigm scenarios for moral changes in the viewer. Alasdair King complements the first three contributions by turning to Deleuze, another major interlocutor in the debate over cinematic ethics. Nevertheless, King redirects his attention from Deleuzian time (well explored in secondary literature) to examine how Deleuze elucidates an ethics of cinematic space.

Each of the subsequent sections focuses on a contemporary film practice that demands ethical consideration: documentary, extreme cinema, and images of nature, respectively. "Documentary and the Ethical" presents four essays on the documentary and closely related modes of filmmaking. Jinhee Choi critically assesses South Korean provocateur Kim Ki-duk's self-portrait *Arirang* (2011). Focusing on Kim's philosophical contemplations on his filmmaking, Choi discusses the extent to which Kim is unable to embrace the vulnerability inherent in both the self and one's relationship with the other. Robert Clift's essay scrutinizes the mockumentary *Borat* (dir. Larry Charles, 2006) in light of the notion of "deauthorized performances," which violates the ethical code of documentary practice. Annelies van Noortwijk investigates, using the rubric of *ars vitae* ("life as a work of art"), the oeuvre of Heddy Honigmann, which portrays ordinary people who suffer under extraordinary circumstances such as poverty, war, and exile. Vince Bohlinger explores the possibility—as well as limitation—of self-reflexivity manifest in autobiographical Iranian cinema, Mohsen Makhmalbaf's *A Moment of Innocence* (1996) and *The Apple* (dir. Samira Makhmalbaf, 1998), the latter of which is based on a real-life incident of child abuse.

In the next section, "Exploitation and the Extreme," Mattias Frey and other contributors examine both commercial exploitation cinema and extreme cinema, a production and aesthetic strategy found in contemporary "art-house" films. Focusing on the public statements and criticism of Catherine Breillat, Michael Haneke, Michael Winterbottom and others, Frey's discursive study of extreme cinema explores filmmakers' festival antics and ethical pretensions, performances that codetermine the films' reception as art rather than exploitation. Under the heading of "immoralism," Trevor Ponech discusses another perennial provocateur at the Cannes Film Festival: Lars von Trier. Drawing on debates of moralism in the analytic tradition and advancing the thesis of "partial intentionalism," Ponech examines von Trier's controversial themes and public persona to argue that evaluating artworks must attend to real artists' acts of moral agency; morally troubling or reprehensible thinking can mesh with the work's creative design, its artistically evaluable features, and the artist's achievements in making the work. James Middleton provides a case study of the spectatorship fostered in the *Saw* series (2004–2010), one of the most successful horror-"torture porn" franchises of the last decade. Characterizing the spectatorship elicited in the series as "intimate-distance," Middleton underscores the film's thematization of the war-on-terror ideology as well as its allegory of the conditions of post-9/11 US citizenship.

"Ethics and the Images of Nature" is dedicated to film practices that employ the images of nature and by animals. Drawing on the diagnoses of psychologists and experiments conducted by health practitioners, Mette Hjort discusses the ethical role of nature images (including representations of nature in film) in countering such symptoms as biophobia (the fear of nature) found in urban dwellers in Hong Kong and in promoting public wellbeing. Finally, Ruth Erickson deliberates on the ethics of animal-borne imaging (images captured via cameras attached to animals) and how it fosters a new form of sensory experience and spectatorial identification.

NOTES

1. Ward Jones and Samantha Vice, eds., *Ethics at the Cinema* (New York: Oxford University Press, 2011).
2. Lisa Downing and Libby Saxton, *Film and Ethics: Foreclosed Encounters* (Oxon: Routledge, 2009).
3. Lucia Nagib, *World Cinema and the Ethics of Realism* (New York and London: Continuum, 2011).
4. Noël Carroll, "Moderate Moralism," *British Journal of Aesthetics* 36.3 (1996): 223–238. Berys Gaut, "The Ethical Criticism of Art," in *Aesthetics and Ethics: Essays at the Intersection,* ed. Jerrold Levinson (Cambridge: Cambridge University Press, 1998), 182–203.
5. Emmanuel Levinas, *Otherwise than Being or Beyond Essence,* trans. Alphonso Lingis (The Hague: Martinus Njhoff Publishers, 1981), 14–16.
6. Alain Badiou, *Ethics: An Essay on the Understanding of Evil* (London: Verso, 2001), 41.
7. Ibid., 44–52.
8. See, for example, Colin Davis, *Critical Excess: Overreading in Derrida, Deleuze, Zizek, and Cavell* (Stanford: Stanford University Press, 2010); D.N. Rodowick, "An Elegy for Theory," *October* 121 (2007): 99–110; Espen Hammer, *Stanley Cavell: Skepticism, Subjectivity and the Ordinary* (Oxford and Malden, MA: Blackwell Publishing, 2002); William Rothman and Marian Keane, *Reading Cavell's "The World Viewed: A Philosophical Perspective on Film* (Detroit: Wayne State University Press, 2000); Stephen Mulhall, *Stanley Cavell: Philosophy's Recounting of the Ordinary* (Oxford and New York: Oxford University Press, 1994).
9. D. N. Rodowick, *The Virtual Life of Film* (Cambridge, MA: Harvard University Press, 2007), 73.
10. Ibid.

11. Certainly, this is not full proof of the existence of reality because one might argue that the idea or belief that the spectator's watching a film can be a creation of the mind.

12. Stanley Cavell, *The World Viewed* (New York: Viking Press, 1971), 21.

13. Rodowick, *The Virtual Life of Film,* 63.

14. Ibid.

15. Ibid.

16. D. N. Rodowick, "An Elegy for Theory," *October* 122 (2007): 91–110. Reprinted in *The Film Theory Reader: Debates and Arguments,* ed. Marc Furstenau (Oxon: Routledge, 2010), 24–37 (the following discussion cites the page number of the latter).

17. William K. Frankena, *Thinking about Morality* (Ann Arbor: University of Michigan Press, 1980), 11.

18. Rodowick, *The Virtual Life of Film,* 70.

19. Rodowick, "An Elegy for Theory," in *The Film Theory Reader,* 35.

20. Ibid., 54.

21. Ibid., 102.

22. Ibid., 40.

23. Ibid., 24.

24. Vivian Sobchack, *Carnal Thoughts: Embodiment and Moving Image Culture* (Berkeley: University of California Press, 2004), 286.

25. Lawrence A. Blum, *Moral Perception and Particularity* (Cambridge: Cambridge University Press, 1994), 31.

26. Martha C. Nussbaum, "Perceptive Equilibrium: Literary Theory and Ethical Theory," in *Love's Knowledge: Essays on Philosophy and Literature* (New York: Oxford University Press, 1990), 168–194.

27. Ibid., 184.

28. Sobchack, *Carnal Thoughts,* 71.

29. Ibid., 290.

30. Ibid., 286.

31. Ibid., 288.

32. Ibid., 290.

33. Ibid., 310.

34. Nussbaum, "Perceptive Equilibrium: Literary Theory and Ethical Theory," 173.

35. David Hume, "Of the Standard of Taste," in *Essays: Moral, Political and Literary,* ed. Eugene F. Miller (Indianapolis: Liberty Fund, 1985), 236.

36. Jean-Louis Baudry, "Ideological Effects of the Basic Cinematographic Apparatus," in *Narrative, Apparatus, Ideology,* ed. Philip Rosen (New York: Columbia University Press, 1986), 286–298. Christian Metz, *Psychoanalysis and the Cinema: The Imaginary Signifier* (Bloomington: Indiana University Press, 1982). The original French versions were published in 1970 and 1975, respectively.

37. Noël Carroll, "Film, Rhetoric, and Ideology," in *Theorizing The Moving Image* (Cambridge: Cambridge University Press, 1996), 175–189; *A Philosophy of Mass Art* (Oxford: Oxford University Press, 1998).

38. Colin Radford and Michael Weston, "How Can We Be Moved By the Fate of Anna Karenina?," *Proceedings of the Aristotelian Society,* Supplementary Volumes 49 (1975): 67–93.

39. Kendall Walton, *Mimesis as Make-Believe: On the Foundations of the Representational Arts* (Cambridge, MA: Harvard University Press, 1993).

40. Noël Carroll, *The Philosophy of Horror: Paradoxes of the Heart* (London: Routledge, 1990).

41. Carl Plantinga, *Moving Viewers: American Film and the Spectator's Experience* (Berkeley: University of California Press, 2009).
42. Noël Carroll, "Film, Emotion, Genre," in *Philosophy of Film and Motion Pictures: An Anthology,* ed. Noël Carroll and Jinhee Choi (Malden, MA: Blackwell, 2006), 217–233. Originally appeared in *Passionate Views,* ed. Carl Plantinga and Greg M. Smith (Baltimore: Johns Hopkins University Press, 1999), 21–47.
43. Joseph H. Kupper, "Film Criticism and Virtue Theory," in *Philosophy of Film and Motion Pictures,* ed. Noël Carroll and Jinhee Choi (Malden, MA: Blackwell, 2006), 335–346. Dan Flory, "Spike Lee and the Sympathetic Racist," in *Thinking through Cinema: Film as Philosophy,* ed. Murray Smith and Thomas E. Wartenberg (Malden, MA: Blackwell, 2006), 67–80.
44. Walton, *Mimesis as Make-Believe*; Gregory Currie, *Image and Mind: Film, Philosophy, and Cognitive Science* (Cambridge: Cambridge University Press, 1995).
45. Alex Neill, "Empathy and (Fiction) Film," in *Post-Theory: Reconstructuring Film Studies,* ed. Noël Carroll and David Bordwell (Madison: University of Wisconsin Press, 1996), 175–176.
46. Murray Smith, *Engaging Characters: Fiction, Emotion and the Cinema* (Oxford: Clarendon Press, 1995), 96–102. Jennifer Barker, *The Tactile Eye: Touch and the Cinematic Experience* (Berkeley: University of California Press, 2009), 73–74.
47. Michele Aaron, *Spectatorship: the Power of Looking On* (London: Wallflower, 2007), 116.
48. Rodowick, *The Virtual Life of Film,* 69.

Part I

The Ethical Self and Others

1   A World Past*

D. N. Rodowick

The camera has been praised for extending the senses; it may, as the world goes, deserve more praise for confining them, leaving room for thought.

—Stanley Cavell, *The World Viewed*

The concept of automatism in its broader senses informs Cavell's notions of filmic ontology in fascinating ways. In raising the concept of ontology, Cavell refers to a set of conditions ("*a succession of automatic world projections*") that leads us to intuit a thing as being a film rather than possibly something else (a theatrical presentation, a video, etc.). In this sense, he defines "world" as "the ontological facts of photography and its subjects."[1] But this intuition derives less from a formal definition of the object than from the experience of our quotidian encounters with it. While the subtitle of *The World Viewed* is *An Ontology of Film*, this indicates neither an essence of the medium nor an attempt to find its timeless and integral being or teleological direction. It expresses, rather, our being or being in the world, not necessarily as film spectators, but rather as a condition expressed in photography and cinema as such. This is a manifestation of a mind recognizing something that has already happened to itself; namely, the "fall into skepticism, together with its efforts to recover itself, events recorded variously in Descartes and Hume and Kant and Emerson and Nietzsche and Heidegger and Wittgenstein."[2] Philosophy has prepared the way for photography, then, and the shift in picturing it inspires. Like Roland Barthes in *Camera Lucida,* Cavell is less interested in the representation, picture, or meaning of photographs than in how they place us subjectively. Thus *projection,* or "the phenomenological facts of viewing,"[3] is coextensive with the subjective condition of modernity, imagined here as a filmic way of encountering the world.

If photographs interest us subjectively, if their mode of existence calls for thinking in a certain way, it is because their conceptual structure provokes certain conundrums of being or to being—thus Cavell's characterization of photography as making us "ontologically restless." It is important to follow his wording closely: "A photograph does not present us with 'likenesses' of things; it presents us, *we want to say,* with the things themselves. But wanting to say that may well make us ontologically restless".[4] (emphasis added). Wanting to say that we are present to the objects themselves does not mean we believe or even wish to assert this. For the fundamental perplexity of photographs does not derive simply from the problem of representation, but rather from the curious sentiment that things absent in time can be present in space, a paradox of presence and absence that ordinary language has trouble resolving. Furthermore, there is another, equally powerful side to this puzzle: Film presents a world from which the viewer is absent, from which its temporal absence screens necessarily, yet with which the viewer hopes to reconnect or rejoin. Here Cavell, alone with Gilles Deleuze in recent scholarship, proposes not just an ontology but an ethics of cinema.

Part of the strangeness of photographs, according to Cavell, is that "we are not accustomed to seeing things that are invisible, or not present to us, not present with us; or we are not accustomed to acknowledging that we do (except in dreams). Yet this seems, ontologically, to be what is happening when we look at a photograph: we see things that are not present."[5] Although these things are present to us as pictures, they are usually no longer present either spatially or historically—they have receded from us both geographically and temporally. The frame of the photograph, then, solicits a divided perception, and this division is spatial and temporal as well as historical—the present perceptual conviction of a past existence in time.

It bears reemphasis that, rightly or wrongly, our conviction of past presence in photographs is independent of being able to recognize or identify space in the image. If there is mimesis in photography, it is not spatial. Rather, it is the confounding perception that things absent in time can be present in space. Think of the puzzling image of the "duck-rabbit," evoked by Wittgenstein and others—this is a paradox of spatial recognition, of identifying linguistically two contradictory things as being presented by the same space. The photograph, however, is a paradox of temporal perception. The advent of photography in the nineteenth century confounded a culture that habitually associated sight or views with spatial (and temporal) presence. The fact of perceiving implied the co-presence in space of the observer and observed; perception here meant identification by sight, even if the original sensation was acoustic or olfactory. Sight and space were indelibly associated. This is partially what Walter Benjamin meant by the concept of aura and its subsequent decline in photographic culture.

The ontological strangeness of photography does not derive only from the picturing of objects absent in space. If this were the case, the criterion of spatial recognition, or representability, would be more important. Real-time displays such as surveillance video or even live television are much less uncanny than photographs. Here co-presence in time fills up, as it were, absences in space. Like other forms of observation at a distance, this absence is felt as a gap that could be overcome. Stranger still for the modern sensibility was the uneasy sense of an image that gave it *time,* or the very idea that time could be given as a *perception.* To see at a distance in space was commonplace by the nineteenth century, but to see at a distance in time was so confounding that it took nearly a hundred years to comprehend it. (Siegfried Kracauer's 1927 essay on photography is perhaps the first deep philosophical exploration of this idea.) Photographic picturing presents us with existences in which we are inclined to believe, but in a temporal distance that is unbridgeable. This is why, in its deepest sense, photographic perception is historical rather than actual.

This sense of historical distance from what is pictured is not explicitly part of Cavell's argument. Yet, this belief in past existence, that we could be present to photographed objects if it were not for time, contributes strongly to feeling ourselves screened from the world thus presented, to our being held before it in a state of anonymous and invisible viewing. Part of Cavell's originality, though, is recognizing that not only is the spectator held at a distance from the photographed world, but this world, too, is screened from the viewer. What we feel in photographs is equally *our* absence from the view presented, that this view is screened for us, and from us, in time. The experience invoked here is in no way an identification of image and nature, as in the writings of Bazin, nor is it exactly physical reality, as Siegfried Kracauer would have it in his late works. Neither physical reality nor profilmic space accounts for the referentiality of photographs, but rather *space past*. Space is inescapably and complexly temporal in photography in a way that painting is not. Photographs do not just picture the already-happened; in making existential claims on our acts of viewing, they picture *history*. And in doing so, they encourage us to reflect on our own ontological situatedness in space—time.

Through his concept of ontology, then, Cavell argues that photographs and films express not only a variable mode of existence for themselves (the medium defined by its automatisms), but also our current, and perhaps changing, mode of existence. In other words, the condition of viewing in photography and film expresses the situation of the modern subject. Moreover, they also express a displacement of the subject, or even a kind of de-subjectivization or the dissolution of this subject in the anticipation of something else. This happens, first, by relieving us of the burden of perception by automating it ("a succession of automatic world pictures"). Photography and film "overcome" subjectivity not only in removing the human agent from the task of reproduction, but also in relieving it from the task or responsibility for perceiving in giving it a series of automated views. This is another way of saying that film's automatism is also our automatism; or to reinvoke Spinoza, that in the modern era our spiritual automatisms have had a cinematic character. The quality of succession not only automates movement in the film image—it is at the heart of the mechanical nature of cinema—but also catches us up in a peculiar temporality, a passing present of uniform instants over which we have little control. In so doing, it not only produces a world in movement; it relieves us from the burdens of perception in the production and projection of manufactured views.

20 D. N. Rodowick

"Photographs are not hand-made," Cavell writes; "they are manufactured. And what is manufactured is an image of the world. The inescapable fact of mechanism or automatism in the making of these images is that feature Bazin points to as [satisfying], once and for all and in its very essence, our obsession with realism."[6] This realism, however, insofar as Cavell uses the term, has nothing to do with the making or apprehension of likenesses. It is a matter of metaphysical contact with the world from which we have become separated: "So far as photography satisfied a wish, it satisfied a wish not confined to painters, but the human wish, intensifying since the Reformation, to escape subjectivity and metaphysical isolation—a wish for the power to reach this world, having for so long tried, at last hopelessly, to manifest fidelity to another."[7] In this manner, for Cavell cinema appears in response to a long and complex trajectory in the history of philosophy. The rediscovery of Pyrrhonism, or classical skepticism, during the Renaissance, and the decline of theological dogmatism in the wake of the Reformation and Enlightenment philosophy, had three consequences for the emerging subject of modernity. That God was in all of us gave society and collectivity a reason from which the modern subject of scientific empiricism became detached. Confined to itself or within itself, the individual subject then bore responsibility for the epistemological and moral consequences of this isolation. And because God was no longer in the world to give it meaning, whatever meaning nature could give to the individual had to be found in its isolated perceptions. Finally, the individual was equally wrested from nature in her or his perceptions because humanity and nature no longer shared the same metaphysical context.

Cinema responds to this dilemma as a kind of machine for metaphysics with a distinct place in the complex history of skeptical thought. In one way, in conveying the impression that all we can know of the world is that we have perceptions of it, film embodies the modern skeptical attitude. This is why, for Cavell, film responds to a specific and profound desire: to view the world as it was, but anonymously and unseen. Here the screen functions as neither medium nor support, but rather as a barrier as much conceptual as physical—it is a philosophical situation embodied in photography and film themselves comprising our present (but perhaps passing) ontology as a self divided from the world by the window of perception. The history of skepticism is complex, however, and this desire also expresses a longing to maintain or regain contact with this world *through* our perceptions of it. "What we wish to see in this way is the world itself—that is to say, everything," Cavell concludes. "Nothing less than that is what modern philosophy has told us (whether for Kant's reasons, or for Locke's, or Hume's) is metaphysically beyond our reach or (as Hegel or Marx or Kierkegaard or Nietzsche might rather put it) beyond our reach metaphysically."[8] This is a strange desire, indeed. For in feeling that our hold on the world was confined to our perceptions of it, we began to invent machines for perceiving the whole of the world.

The comparison with painting is again informative. What separates painting and photography in the history of philosophy as it were, is the fall into and return from skepticism. "[What] painting wanted," Cavell argues:

> In wanting connection with reality, was a sense of *presentness*—not exactly a conviction of the world's presence to us, but our presence to it. At some point the unhinging of our consciousness from the world interposed our subjectivity between us and our presentness to the world. Then our subjectivity became what is present to us, individuality became isolation. The route to conviction in reality was through the acknowledgment of that endless presence of self . . . To maintain conviction in our connection with reality, to maintain our presentness, painting accepts the recession of the world. Photography maintains the presentness of the world by accepting our absence from it. The reality in a photograph is present to me while I am not present to it; and a world I know, and see, but to which I am nevertheless not present (through no fault of my subjectivity), is a world past.[9]

A world past. It is not just physical reality or profilmic space that constitutes the referentiality of photographs, but more importantly, it is a physical presence strongly indicative of space past. "Before" representation, or being taken to represent, this space expresses a causal and counterfactually dependent relation with the past as a unique and nonrepeatable duration; hence Roland Barthes's suggestion that the space of the photograph is copiable and thus repeatable, while its temporal expression is singular—"What the Photograph reproduces to infinity has occurred only once: the Photograph mechanically repeats what could never be repeated existentially."[10] To recognize the ontological presentness of painting, that it is fully disclosed before us in time and space, meant acknowledging its autonomous state of being as well as our own autonomy in confronting it. The deeper lesson of photography for philosophy is understanding not only how the skeptical attitude is expressed in photographic looking, but also how photography returns the world to us while nonetheless holding perception at a distance.

That we wish to see everything in this way means that film responds to a moral condition, a way of being in the world that film manages to express for us as a generalized, cultural perception. For Cavell, the "reality" of film is the actuality of this metaphysical dilemma; there is no other relation of photography or film to reality. The succession of automated world projections is our condition of perceiving as such to the extent that we are modern subjects; or, as Cavell puts it, film is a moving image of skepticism. The skeptical attitude, of which photography is one manifestation, expresses a realization "of human distance from the world, or some withdrawal of the world, which philosophy interprets as a limitation in our capacity for knowing the world . . . It is perhaps the principal theme of *The World Viewed* that the advent of photography expresses this distance as the modern fate to relate to the world by viewing it, taking views of it, as from behind the self."[11] As spiritual automata, what film produces is an ontological condition for the human subject,

> [not] by literally presenting us with the world, but by permitting *us* to view it unseen. This is not a wish for power over creation (as Pygmalion's was), but a wish not to need power, not to have to bear its burdens . . . In viewing films, the sense of invisibility is an expression of modern privacy or anonymity. It is as though the world's projection explains our forms of unknownness and of our inability to know. The explanation is not so much that the world is passing us by, as that we are displaced from our natural habitation within it, placed at a distance from it. The screen overcomes our fixed distance; it makes displacement appear as our natural condition.[12]

These conundrums of presence and absence, of temporal displacement, of the automated projection of screened views, emblematize the ontological position of modernity as skepticism, of being held at a distance from the world such that our terms of existence, our "reality" as such, is the modality of detached viewing. Filmic automatism thus reprises a metaphysical condition that Cavell implicitly relates to Leibniz's monadism. The situation of film viewing responds to what is, already, the situation or situating of the modern subject as closed within its self—consciousness:

> Our condition has become one in which our natural mode of perception is to view, feeling unseen. We do not so much look at the world as look *out* at it, from behind the self . . . Viewing a movie makes this condition automatic, takes the responsibility for it out of our hands, Hence movies seem more natural than reality. Not because they are escapes into fantasy, but because they are reliefs from private fantasy and its responsibilities; from the fact that the world is *already* drawn by fantasy. And not because they are dreams, but because they permit the self to be wakened, so that we may stop withdrawing our longings further inside ourselves. Movies convince us of the world's reality in the only way we have to be convinced . . . by taking views of it.[13]

The last phrase is important for understanding how the phenomenology of film projection expresses for Cavell both the metaphysical isolation of the modern subject and its possible overcoming. Film presents to us not only the visible world or the world as visible, but also our conditions of viewing in just this way. As such, it is not the perfect image of skepticism, nor is it a mechanism whose cultural pervasiveness holds us in a position of skepticism. Photography and film mechanically reproduce the subjective conditions and paradoxes of skepticism in the form of a possible philosophical solution, For Cavell, they pose both the condition of skepticism and a possible road of departure, the route back to our conviction in reality. In contrast to the psychoanalytic phenomenology of Christian Metz and Jean-Louis Baudry in the 1970s, which explored our unconscious submission to the projection of automated views, Cavell emphasizes how our epistemological situation of having "world-views" is held before us *as a perception*. This occurs for the very reason that these world projections are automated—they are not produced by us but for us by a cultural mechanism or instrumentality. That skepticism should reproduce itself in a technology for seeing might mean that it is no longer the ontological air we breathe, but a passing phase of our philosophical culture. If the reality that film holds before us is that of our own perceptual condition, then it opens the possibility of once again being present to self or acknowledging how we may again become present to ourselves. This is why Cavell emphasizes that "reproducing the world is the *only* thing film does automatically."[14] For these reasons, film may already be the emblem of skepticism in decline. The irony of this recognition now is that modernity may no longer characterize our modes of being or of looking. The possibility of recognizing photography's deep connectedness with a way of being in the world is becoming more and more evident as that mode of existence is passing into something else, and as photography itself is on the wane. The question now is what comes afterward. For skepticism in decline may be related to film in decline. Electronic and digital imaging may be responding to or provoking a new epistemological situation whose ontologies and ethical consequences remain as yet unexamined.

For Cavell, art becomes modern when, in the absence of a validating tradition, it is provoked to a state of continual self-questioning and self-invention. Similarly, the subject became modern when—its anchors being cast loose from moral and epistemological dogma—expressions of doubt and its overcoming became questions of the self in relation to its perceptions. No longer assured of its place in the world or in relation to the world, the subject is provoked to new strategies of self-actualization and self-invention. The modern ethical dilemma, then, is to how to regain contact with this world, to overcome our distance from it and restore its knownness to us.

We wish for the condition of viewing as such because this is our way of establishing and maintaining our connection to the world—by having views of it. Having views in just this way, one that requests conviction in the prior existence of this world even if it is present to us only in images, brings us out of our private reflections and encourages us to consider again the world as such. To say then that film presents a moving image of skepticism means neither that there is no reality to perceive, nor that we have renounced having anything to say about that reality because we are irretrievably detached from it. Nor does it imply that this condition of viewing is a fiction, an illusion of reality that we could overcome with another kind of filmmaking or another more critical philosophy. To assert any of the above would be a parody of skepticism. Cavell is after something else:

> Film is a moving image of skepticism: not only is there a reasonable possibility, it is a fact that here our normal senses are satisfied of reality while reality does not exist—even, alarmingly, *because* it does not exist, because viewing it is all it takes. Our vision is doubtless otherwise satisfiable than by the viewing of reality. But to deny, on skeptical grounds, just *this* satisfaction—to deny that it is ever reality which film projects and screens—is a farce of skepticism. It seems to remember that skepticism concludes against our conviction in the existence of the external world, but it seems to forget that skepticism begins in an effort to justify that conviction. The basis of film's drama, or the latent anxiety in viewing its drama, lies in its persistent demonstration that we do not know what our conviction in reality turns upon.[15]

At least perceptually.

Cinema provokes in us a divided, ambiguous, or ambivalent perception, not unlike Metz's "I know very well, but all the same . . ."[16] *Yet* the philosophical consequences of Cavell's arguments go much deeper. Metz's psychoanalytical observation is basically a sociological one that, contrary to his earlier phenomenology, demands we test cinema's projections as illusory. Cavell is responding to a moral or ethical dilemma that requires us to reflect upon the epistemological grounds or groundlessness of these convictions. One reason that "we do not know what our conviction in reality turns upon" is that we continue to demand (and often distrust) visual evidence when what maintains our conviction is in fact a *temporal* perception. But this unknownness of the grounds of our conviction in these ephemeral images—a world suspended in variable patterns of light—is itself a hopeful quality. For while cinema's automatism relieves us from the burdens of perception, it also holds open before us our own agency in acts of perception, and sustains our epistemological inquisitiveness regarding those acts and their consequences. Cavell concludes:

> The moral of film's image of skepticism is not that reality is a dream and not that reality confines our dreams. In screening reality, film screens its givenness from us; it holds reality from us, it holds reality before us, i.e., withholds reality before us. We are tantalized at once by our subjection to it and by its subjection to our views of it. But while reality is the bearer of our intentions it is possible . . . to refuse to allow it to dictate what shall be said about it . . . Flanked by its claims to speak for us, it is still open to us in moments to withhold it before ourselves and may gladly grant that we are somewhat spoken for. To know how far reality is open to our dreams would be to know how far reality is confined by our dreams of it.[17]

Perhaps the long dream or fantasy from which the self begins to be awakened through filmic perception is that of the division of humanity from nature, or of a Being speaking with a different voice from that of nature. In this respect, there is one last feature of Cavell's filmic ontology that has received little commentary, and it suggests another important dimension of our uneasy conviction in these images in which our subjectivity is at once sustained and displaced. In this automated perception, humans and things share the same qualitative state of being. As Cavell puts it, "human beings are not onto logically favored over the rest of nature."[18] In their automatic manufacture of an image of the world, film and photography displace us from yet reconnect us to this world, not by disfavoring or alienating humanity, but by casting humanity and nature in a common frame and reintegrating them in a common duration. In our views of the world, we are presented a situation wherein humanity is returned to (visible) nature sharing the same duration with it. And, according to Cavell, there are moral consequences in failing to grasp this fact: "Then if in relation to objects capable of such self-manifestation human beings are reduced in significance, or crushed by the fact of beauty left vacant, perhaps this is because in trying to take dominion over the world, or in aestheticizing it (temptations inherent in the making of film, or of any art), they are refusing their participation with it."[19] In response to the skeptical attitude, which sets the perceiving subject at a distance from nature, in film humanity and nature are of one substance and held in a common duration—they are expressed as having a common Being. They partake of the same ontological substance, and in addition have the same epistemological nature. For "reality" here is not what is, or the accuracy or not of what is pictured, but our condition of being in the world.

Cavell's uses of the terms *ontology* and *reality* in relation to film have nothing to do with the correspondence of an image and its referent. Our sense of the "reality" of film comes not through representation or even the representativeness of its projected images, but rather through the way in which this projecting world confronts us with our own metaphysical condition. And so Cavell concludes:

> Film's easy power over the world *will* be accounted for, one way or another, consciously or not. By my account, film's presenting of the world by absenting us from it appears as confirmation of something already true of our stage of existence. Its displacement of the world confirms, even explains, our prior estrangement from it. The "sense of reality" provided on film is the sense of *that* reality, one from which we already sense a distance. Otherwise, the thing it provides a sense of would not, for us, count as reality.[20]

What is important here is that the "automatic world projections" of filmic perception already promote a partial response to the skeptical attitude. We may not know in what our conviction in reality consists, or how it persists. Nevertheless, the wish to view the world (that is to say, everything) by viewing it unseen recapitulates the phases of skepticism: To assert that the external world is divided from us in perception is a way of beginning to justify our conviction in the existence of that world.

NOTES

* This chapter was earlier published in D. N. Rodowick, *The Virtual Life of Film* (Cambridge, MA: Harvard University Press, 2007), 61–73.
1. Stanley Cavell, *The World Viewed: Reflections on the Ontology of Film*, enlarged edition (Cambridge, MA: Harvard University Press, 1979), 73.
2. Cavell, "What Photography Calls Thinking" in *Cavell on Film*, ed. William Rothman (Albany: State University of New York, 1985), 116.
3. Cavell, *The World Viewed*, 73.
4. Ibid., 17.
5. Ibid.,18.
6. Ibid., 20.
7. Ibid., 21.
8. Ibid., 101–102.
9. Ibid., 22–23.
10. Roland Barthes, *Camera Lucida*, trans. Richard Howard (New York: Hill and Wang, 1981), 4.
11. Cavell, "What Photography Calls Thinking," 116–117.
12. Cavell, *The World Viewed*, 40–41.
13. Ibid., 102.
14. Ibid., 103.
15. Ibid., 188–189.
16. Christian Metz, "The Imaginary Signifier," in *The Imaginary Signifier: Psychoanalysis and the Cinema*, trans. Celia Britton, Annwyl Williams, Ben Brewster, and Alfred Guzzetti (Bloomington: Indiana University Press, 1982), 76.
17. Cavell, *The World Viewed*, 189.
18. Ibid., 37.
19. Ibid., xvi.
20. Ibid., 226.

2   Cinema's Compassionate Gaze
Empathy, Affect, and Aesthetics in *The Diving Bell and the Butterfly*

Jane Stadler

This study of Julian Schnabel's 2007 film *The Diving Bell and the Butterfly* (hereafter referred to as *Diving Bell*) seeks to understand the cinematic articulation of compassion by examining how screen aesthetics and narrative content affect audiences and inform the construction of meaning. Drawing in part on philosopher Martha Nussbaum's account of the ethical and social dimensions of compassion and on the semiotic approach to phenomenology pioneered by Vivian Sobchack, this analysis aims to further understandings of the ethics of affect, and to explore how film can express and invoke empathy and compassion.

This chapter begins with an interdisciplinary literature review critically engaging with phenomenological and cognitive film theory, moral philosophy, and work in the sciences and social sciences on the neurological and psychological underpinnings of empathy. It concludes with an ethical and aesthetic analysis of the film that is thematized in relation to compassion and empathy. Compassion and empathy take both corporeal and cognitive forms that, I argue, can be traced in film style and content. What I have called the film's "compassionate gaze" can be understood as an aesthetic mode that functions to bridge the distance between self and other, establishing a foundation for ethical understanding.

Diving Bell is based on the memoir of the editor of *Elle*, a French fashion magazine, Jean-Dominique Bauby (played by actor Mathieu Amalric). Chronicling the effects of a devastating stroke that left Bauby mentally alert but almost completely paralyzed, the film's compelling visual style and subjective soundscape locate the audience inside the experience of "locked in syndrome," an affliction characterized by quadriplegia, lower cranial nerve paralysis, and muteness.[1] In *Breaking Down: A Phenomenology of Disability,* Lisa Diedrich describes *Diving Bell* as a "neurological and phenomenological" case study representing the breakdown of the body as a crisis that raises "anew the question of the meaning of being."[2]

Bauby's silence and immobility, captured by the metaphor of the diving bell in the film's title, shift the emphasis from action and dialogue to affect and aesthetics as the film's immersive cinematography and internalized sound lock the audience inside his world. Excluding flashes of subjective imagery, the first act of the film is shot strictly in first-person point of view from Bauby's bed or chair. The second act documents the slow process of establishing communication with the help of speech therapist Henriette Durand (Marie-Josée Croze). Bauby worked with his transcriber Claude Mendibil (Anne Consigny) to write the book on which the film is based, painstakingly spelling out words by blinking to select letters as she recited the alphabet.[3] The affectionate relationships Bauby develops with these two women exemplify the reciprocity of compassionate engagement. As his communicative abilities develop and he comes to terms with his condition and with the ways others perceive his inert body, the audiovisual style of the film becomes freer and introduces flashbacks and poetic montage sequences revealing Bauby's inner world. In the film's closing scenes the camera careens through space, exploring Bauby's memories and imagination and rolling through hospital corridors unrestricted to his physical point of view.

Because the representation of locked-in syndrome in *Diving Bell* brings into focus the roles of affect and embodiment in the constitution of selfhood, in ethics, and in film spectatorship, I will start by reviewing published research and prevailing assumptions, first regarding spectatorship, then regarding affect and moral emotions in relation to film.

SPECTATORSHIP AND THE AFFECTIVE TURN

In an overview of theories of spectatorship, Carl Plantinga contends that both cognitive theory and what he terms "screen theory" (an amalgamation of psychoanalytic, semiotic, and ideological approaches to cinema) conceive of film spectators as hypothetical entities.[4] While screen theory also conceived of the spectator as a desiring subject, the psychoanalytic formulation of the concept of desire meant that spectator behavior was understood in a universalized, psychologically driven manner. According to Plantinga, even cultural and historical reception studies adopt aspects of the hypothetical spectator model in that they rely on assumptions and generalizations about audiences and their responses to film in particular periods, viewing contexts, and demographic categories.[5] As Plantinga suggests, the film spectator has traditionally been theorized in terms of a rather abstract social or ideological subject position, or a conscious or unconscious mind with little consideration for the role of the physical, sensory body beyond the eyes and occasionally the ears. The representation of Bauby's experience in *Diving Bell* illustrates that even if the eye and the mind are the only active parts of the body, subjectivity and spectatorship both involve a great deal more. Contrary to the conception of the subject implied by screen theory's construct of the hypothetical spectator, phenomenologist Maurice Merleau-Ponty argues, "The perceiving subject is not this absolute thinker; rather, it functions according to a natal pact between our body and the world, between ourselves and our body. The perceiving mind is an incarnated mind."[6] Following

Merleau-Ponty, phenomenological film theory has reframed cinema as a perceptual, affective experience and reconceptualized audience members as embodied spectators.

Sobchack, whose research is informed by Merleau-Ponty's thought, understands the body as an instrument of perceptual understanding: It is our "point of view" on the world and it enables us "to sense and respond to the world and others."[7] This perspective exemplifies the "bodily turn" or "the affective turn" in film theory, which marks a shift in critical attention to the sensory and emotive experience of spectatorship. In her 2011 review article "The Turn to Affect: A Critique," Ruth Leys demonstrates that this focus on the body, senses, and emotions "has been occurring in a broad range of fields, including history, political theory, human geography, urban and environmental studies, architecture, literary studies, art history and criticism, media theory, and cultural studies."[8]

As film scholar Tarja Laine observes, "the 'affective turn' seems to have deliberately moved away from the cinema as an objectively readable text and toward the cinematic as an emotionally experiential event, which *The Diving Bell*, as a case study, illustrates particularly well."[9] Here Laine points to the change from approaches that privilege the role of the text in creating meaning and constructing a subject position for the spectator to occupy, toward a holistic understanding of the audience's experience. Similarly, following Gilles Deluze, scholars such as Brian Massumi,[10] Martine Beugnet,[11] Elena del Río,[12] and Laura U. Marks[13] are interested in how film is able to foreground materiality and invite a sensorial response from audiences. More recently, Christiane Voss has argued persuasively that "a certain degree of affective entanglement is necessarily part and parcel" of the cinematic experience, contending that the film spectator's body cannot be excluded from consideration of how cinema forms the immersive illusion of narrative worlds peopled by engaging protagonists.[14] Voss goes on to advocate an expanded concept of cinema that includes the spectator's body and "emphasizes the relevance of intertwined sensations, and the interpretation of these sensations, for the aesthetic experience of the medium."[15]

According to Voss, because audience members share a mental and sensory "resonance" with characters in the two-dimensional narrative world of the cinema screen, the spectator "loans" a three-dimensional sensing body to the film: "The spectator thus becomes a temporary 'surrogate body' for the screen, and this body is, for its part, a constituent feature of the film architecture."[16] Voss's concept of resonance is pivotal to understanding how the audio-visual medium of film affects its audience because it signals the synchronous physiological and emotive experience that can connect audience members to screen characters. As Veit Erlmann points out in *Reason and Resonance: A History of Modern Aurality,* hearing has historically been understood in terms of the resonance occurring between vibrations in the air and the inner ear.[17] Erlmann goes on to argue that because the physical properties of airborne vibrations establish a tactile, aural connectivity with the ear, resonance itself entails *proximity* (in that sound waves physically touch the ear drum). Proximal senses such as touch and, in Erlmann's terms, hearing, are conducive to a kind of sympathetic attunement that renders boundaries between the perceiver and the perceived somewhat indistinct. While Voss uses the concept of resonance more figuratively, Erlmann's work points to the central role of sound and music both in sympathetic and empathetic relationships between persons, and within the interpersonal connections felt by audiences for screen characters. Indeed, in *Diving Bell,* the moment when Bauby learns to sing marks a profound reconnection with others and a deeply felt turning point in the narrative. The concepts of resonance and attunement are significant to this study in that they introduce a metaphor taken up by a number of scholars seeking to capture the felt quality of empathy. Maria Angel expresses it eloquently when she writes, "empathy is produced at the level of a sensation or a sensory echo,"[18] whereas Anna Gibbs speaks of "affective attunement."[19] Similarly, Nussbaum foregrounds perceptual and imaginative attunement in her philosophy of compassion, and other authors refer to synchrony, simulation, mimicry and mirroring, as discussed in the next section.

MORAL EMOTIONS

Moral emotions including compassion, sympathy, and empathy are members of a family of feelings or emotional processes that are both other-oriented and self-conscious in that they are evoked by self-evaluation and, in turn, they can evoke altruistic impulses.[20] Feelings such as anger, disgust, and guilt can also be considered moral emotions that are rooted in moral judgment and are preceded by appraisal, however automatic such appraisal may be. Here I focus on empathy, which has been studied in a number of disciplines including film studies, philosophy, neuroscience, psychology, and cognitive science. Models of empathy are converging across these disparate fields; indeed, empirical research in neuroscience and psychology has been used to support studies of emotion in cognitive film theory and in phenomenological interpretations of how empathy and somatic mimicry function in film.[21]

Empathy can be broadly defined as an other-oriented emotional process that involves a form of emotional imagination, understood as "feeling with" a person or a protagonist in a way that "depends on our imagining what [that person's] beliefs, desires, and so on might be."[22] This perspective is widely accepted, particularly by cognitivists who have developed theories of emotion that favor the role of imagination in accessing the intellectual component of emotional states like empathy. Cinematic techniques such as the use of subjective imagery and voice-over narration in *Diving Bell* certainly prompt and facilitate the imaginative component of empathy, as cognitive film theorists suggest. The phenomenological approach does not discount this understanding of empathic responses to film. Rather, phenomenologists typically place a stronger emphasis on the role of sensation and affect, which they understand to be related to value systems and to the cognitive content of emotional life through intentionality.[23] While acknowledging differences in emphasis and approach across these fields of research, I argue that moral emotions such as empathy and compassion include both cognitive and affective components and that insights from cognitivist and phenomenological approaches to film can complement one another.

Murray Smith adds nuance to the cognitivist model as he builds on the premise that empathy is fundamental to social interaction. According to Smith, film and other narrative arts play an important cultural role by extending the range of people, experiences, and cultures that an individual may have occasion to empathize with; furthermore, the aesthetic design of cinema texts can intensify empathy[24] or even obstruct it. A film such as *Diving Bell* exemplifies cinema's capacity to extend the scope of empathic engagement by introducing audiences to the experience of locked in syndrome. However, while the film's subjective audio-visual style might indeed augment empathy, it could also cause audience members such discomfort that they reflexively and self-protectively draw away from the narrative and its protagonist: "Empathy may also induce aversive distress responses that can lead to withdrawal behavior motivated by the desire to protect oneself from negative emotions."[25]

Considering how empathy functions in relation to technology, perception, imagination, and emotion in the cinema, Smith astutely argues that the devices of filmmaking can be understood as "cognitive prostheses, in much the same way that we think of other devices, like the telescope or microscope, as perceptual prostheses—devices which potentiate our native perceptual capacities."[26] However, as Smith acknowledges, empathy is not just a cognitive process; it includes social, emotional, and physiological components.[27]

In his investigation of subjectivity, Joel Kreuger adopts a phenomenologically informed approach in which he sees empathy as an integral part of interpersonal sensitivity and social understanding, claiming that "empathy is a kind of extended bodily-perceptual process."[28] Krueger goes on to state:

> As they are externalized via the expressive dynamics of the social body, certain aspects of the mind (such as emotions and affect) are present within the second-personal spaces of our social encounters. This phenomenological model moves intersubjectivity out of the head and into the interactive encounters of embodied social agents.[29]

Krueger underscores the fact that emotion is not simply a mental state: externalizing gestures and expressions are constitutive components of emotional experience as well as being conduits of meaning for those who perceive and interpret another person's emotions.

The idea that empathy has a physiological basis is gaining traction in cognitive theories of spectatorship, and also in phenomenological accounts of cinema where it has been taken up by researchers such as Jennifer Barker and Julian Hanich. According to Smith's cognitivist account, empathy includes affective mimicry—the perception and reflexive mirroring of a person or character's emotion or expression—and emotional simulation, which involves simulating feelings by forming hypotheses about how a person might respond to a certain situation.[30] The way emotional simulation works in the cinema is that spectators imaginatively project themselves into a character's situation to the extent that they empathically share the character's affective responses.

In cognitive psychology, empirical research has shown that those who mimic the expressions of another person or a character on screen are more likely to experience empathy for that person; furthermore, when compassion for a member of a stigmatized group is induced in this way, it leads to the development of enduring favorable attitudes toward members of that group and a reduction in prejudiced thinking.[31] Such research suggests that the role of the body, and particularly the face,[32] in displaying and mimicking the affective component of emotion is important in activating the ethical and altruistic dimensions associated with compassion and empathy. As Krueger claims:

> Because certain aspects of another's mental life are externally realized, played out across the topography of the body, [. . .] it follows that we can become more interpersonally sensitive, and thus more morally skillful and improvisational, by paying careful attention to and responding to the bodily dynamics that underwrite our lived encounters with other people. Heightened perceptual attunement breeds deeper forms of responsive empathy.[33]

The concept of attunement also figures in Nussbaum's work on moral emotions, particularly in *Love's Knowledge* (1990) and *Upheavals of Thought* (2001). Nussbaum argues that perceptual, imaginative, and emotional attunement to others is facilitated by narrative art forms that foster social sensitivity and inclusivity. She views attunement as an intentional movement of perception and attention that involves an "alternation between empathic and sympathetic perspectives."[34] This heightened attunement to the sensory body and the messages it conveys about subjectivity, I argue, is *Diving Bell*'s greatest aesthetic and affective accomplishment. It is indicative of the role cinema can play in engendering empathy and potentially breaking down the fear, prejudice, or misunderstanding that may surround marginalized groups such as the ill or disabled.

Diving Bell is an exemplar of the way empathy can be expressed and communicated through narrative and aesthetic techniques. The term empathy implies that we come to understand someone's experience by sharing in their emotional life and *Diving Bell* immerses audiences in the protagonist's subjectivity by means of voice-over narration and subjective imagery rendered through flashbacks and point of view. Such psychological access to and perspectival alignment with the protagonist invites a degree of emotional affinity with Bauby.

Laine, however, argues that empathy and compassion are not the right engagement strategies for *Diving Bell*, claiming that feelings of compassion connote pity and superiority.[35] Laine asserts that the audience does *not* share in Bauby's experience because the film "denies experiential access to his misfortune," stating:

> The emotional response in *The Diving Bell* does not come in the form of empathetic 'putting-oneself-in-the-shoes-of-another,' but with a respect to the otherness of Bauby's experience. In other words, this is an emotion that is grounded in the incitement of emotional proximity combined with experiential distance that emerges from a direct engagement with emotion as it is registered in the affective intentionality of the film.[36]

Laine's claims in this passage seem counterintuitive, yet her work does point to two important issues regarding theories of empathy and their application to *Diving Bell* in particular and to cinema in general. First, the affective mimicry that underpins empathy cannot be activated by mirroring Bauby's expressions because experiential access to his emotions is initially deferred by shooting from his optical vantage point and is later masked by his paralysis; second, Laine draws attention to the "affective intentionality" of film itself and the capacity for aesthetic cinematic techniques to facilitate perceptual attunement and emotional simulation. This point about the intentional quality of stylistic techniques and the capacity of the film itself to invoke a form of attunement or empathy has been developed in a novel way by Jennifer Barker.

In her phenomenological account of affect and the cinematic experience, Barker conceives of empathy as a mimetic relationship between the viewer and the film (rather than between the viewer and film characters).[37] She understands empathic responses to cinema in terms of "mimicry," "muscular reciprocity," and "resonance" with gestural and structural qualities shared by films and their audiences.[38] For example, the soaring camera movement in the penultimate scenes of *Diving Bell* may produce an elevated, elated sensation in the audience and the slow motion avalanche seen when Bauby imagines his cardio-vascular accident conveys a collapsing feeling or a sinking, crushing sense of inevitability. Empathy, for Barker, thus goes beyond the affective mimicry that prompts viewers to mirror a protagonist's emotions. She suggests the audience's responses to techniques such as camera movement and the rhythm or pace of editing constitute muscular empathy or kinaesthetic empathy wherein "the meaning and impact of the film makes itself felt in our muscles and tendons."[39] Barker's interest in empathy relates to how audiences are affected by the gestural, bodily motion of "the film itself"[40] as expressed through techniques such as mobile framing, yet her argument is relevant to films in which aesthetic and narrative structures facilitate empathy with screen characters by overtly replicating a protagonist's understanding of, comportment within, or engagement with the world. Certainly, the *lack* of camera movement or clarity of focus in the first act of *Diving Bell* invites spectators to share the experience of paralysis and impaired vision in a manner that corresponds to Barker's ideas about muscular empathy, but unlike Barker, I would argue that it does so in order to communicate the protagonist's somatic state—not necessarily to induce empathy with the film itself.

While Barker's work on muscular empathy is suggestive, Hanich's phenomenology of cinematic emotion offers more clearly defined terms for understanding the different facets of empathy. Hanich's distinction between two forms of empathy separates it into cognitive and affective components: imaginative empathy and somatic empathy.[41] Imaginative empathy involves what Smith has termed emotional simulation, whereas somatic empathy entails the congruence or "*partial* parallelism between a character's and my own body's sensations, affects or motions."[42] Somatic empathy is an involuntary, short-term response that does not necessitate "strong character allegiance."[43] However, emotional responses to film can definitely be amplified in instances when character allegiance occurs.

Somatic empathy comes in three forms: sensation, motor, and affective mimicry. Hanich defines sensation mimicry as the experience of "involuntarily and without reflection replicat[ing] a similar sensation as the character onscreen."[44] By contrast, motor mimicry is similar to what Barker describes when she speaks of audiences responding to the "muscular" movement of the camera, though most researchers apply the term to mimicking figure movement or a person's gestures. For Hanich, motor mimicry is "a weak or partial simulation of someone else's physical motion."[45] Affective mimicry is "the phenomenon whereby we—precognitively—mimic an emotion or affect expressed by someone else."[46] Drawing on theories of neural mirroring, Hanich discusses emotional contagion in terms of the propensity to replicate another person's expression as part of a facial feedback loop in which the respondent mimics and hence comes to feel a degree of the emotion that another person expresses.[47] Even though the mirroring processes involved in somatic empathy are precognitive, when they induce the audience to mirror a screen character's affective state the physiological effects can help to stimulate cognitive insight into another person's experience. The terms by which Hanich and the other researchers whose work is reviewed here understand the mental and emotional dimensions of empathy and compassion provide an analytic vocabulary that allows a rigorous and fine-grained interpretation of how affect relates to ethics and screen aesthetics.

DIVING BELL: TRAPPED IN THE BODY AND REFLECTED IN THE GLASS

To grasp how *Diving Bell* communicates Bauby's condition and cues compassion we must consider how the film directs the attention and perception of its spectators and represents the attention and perception of its characters. The intentional, selective quality of the film image and the direction of the spectator's attention are guided by two aesthetic modes: the conventions of optical visuality and high-fidelity sound, and a form of sound and vision known as haptics. Marks defines optical visuality as a familiar mode of perception that relies on seeing with adequate clarity and distance to label and classify the object of vision.[48] Similarly, the aural mode by which audiences ordinarily perceive film relies on identifying conceptual links between sounds and their physical sources, requiring cognition and narrative comprehension.[49] As distinct from optic images, haptic images have little sense of depth, and texture overrides form. Although the use of haptic imagery need not necessarily represent a screen character's way of perceiving, in *Diving Bell* it does offer a close approximation of the visual impairment that Bauby experiences when he loses perception of depth and clarity of focus as a result of his stroke.

Marks's work on haptic imagery suggests that it has the capacity to facilitate affective resonance and perceptual attunement with screen characters. Haptic imagery denaturalizes the object of vision or the source of sound, avoiding conditioned assumptions and judgments in a manner that is immersive, experiential, and sensory, yet it still requires cognitive processing. As Marks states, this mode of cinematic vision "pulls the viewer in close," privileges "material presence," and requires the "resources of memory and imagination" to complete the image.[50] Detailing the relationship between haptics and embodiment, Marks argues that haptic imagery in films requires a synaesthetic, "involved gaze" as the indistinct image invites viewers to invest all their senses in the act of seeing.[51]

To convey the damage to Bauby's vision and to his communicative capacity, the film uses haptics when representing his viewing position. The soundscape is dominated by Bauby's muted bodily sounds and subjective narration as the audience hears the voice of his mind reflecting on his life and responding when people address him—though these sounds are not heard by other characters in the diegesis. The film's music works powerfully to locate the audience in Bauby's subjectivity, giving access to his emotions and providing a soundtrack for his memories and flights of fancy. The internalized sound and the haptic, soft-focus close-ups lend the film an intimate quality that augments feelings of closeness and draws the audience toward the screen and into Bauby's physical and psychological domain.[52]

A swing-tilt lens is used to represent tiny variations in Bauby's attention, focusing only on the most compelling point in the visual field, such as a person's eyes or lips. The differential focus afforded by the swing-tilt lens represents the physiological effects of Bauby's condition by showing how his vision is impaired by the stroke. It also reveals the qualitative, attentive nature of perception. This provides a vivid illustration that consciousness is enacted by the physical body and its corporeal engagements with the material and social world. Perception is not a one-way process, however: That which is perceived affects the perceiver and we come to understand others and ourselves partly through knowledge of how we are seen by those around us. As the second act of the film reveals how Bauby is perceived by other people, the film illuminates the intersubjective processes at work in the moral emotions and in the constitution of selfhood.

In the film's exposition the audience is tied to Bauby's bedridden perspective. Access to his experience is restricted to minute camera movements and shifts in focus that imitate Bauby's faulty vision and temporal editing techniques such as fades that suggest lapses of consciousness and indicate the passage of time. After Bauby's damaged eye is sewn closed, the film literally sutures the audience into his viewing position as latex is sewn over the camera lens. As research on somatic mirroring suggests, and as Jens Eder points out in his work on ways of being close to film characters, it can be difficult to share the emotional experiences of a protagonist if the camera position is consistently restricted to their optical point of view and does not reveal their facial expressions.[53] In its opening scenes *Diving Bell* compensates for this with the use of voice over narration and an evocative musical score that gains prominence when Bauby's eye is stitched shut and the camera begins to roam through his imagination and memory as his sight and senses turn inward.

When Bauby establishes a way to communicate, the camera becomes more mobile and its perspectival range increases. The audience is then able to see Bauby himself in the frame, blinking his slow messages to visitors and glimpsing himself in mirrored surfaces. With Bauby's newfound agency and social reciprocity, the camera tracks his wheelchair, traveling along hospital corridors and roaming through his dreamscapes. The camera rotates on its axis and soars through the possibilities alive in Bauby's mind, embodying imagination and freedom of spirit like the butterfly referenced in the film's title. By the end of the film, the camera is unmoored from realist conventions, but the liberating final sequence of mobile framing takes us back to the beginning of the cardiovascular accident. When he finally remembers the stroke, Bauby has reached the end of the book he is writing and the end of his own story. The closing sequence conveys his disconnection from the physical and the phenomenal world as his health fails. Sound and image become disjointed and layered when his perception (and with it, the audience's) flickers and falters, as manifest in stuttering, superimposed images achieved by hand cranking the film stock forward and backward through the camera.

Disallowing the audience access to an external frame of reference or clear vision throughout the first act of *Diving Bell* defamiliarizes the usual mode of seeing and invites the spectator to reevaluate what he or she perceives. This technique positions the audience to bypass cultural hierarchies and judgments of value, and to bypass conditioned responses to illness such as fear or disgust.[54] In this way, the film enacts its own version of phenomenological bracketing, setting aside for quite some time the matter of how Bauby's damaged body is perceived by others.

When spectators are finally released from the tightly confined perspective enforced at the beginning of the film and shown Bauby himself, the freedom of the camerawork contrasts sharply with the stasis of the protagonist. Amalric's performance style powerfully underscores the sense that Bauby is a corporeal prisoner: physical tension is evident in his rigid face, giving the sense that he is locked into his paralyzed body, trapped in his own immobile corporeality as though strapped into a straight jacket. By contrast, the mobile framing in the film's final scenes signify the extent to which Bauby's subjectivity is liberated from his body, freewheeling along the pathways of his memory and imagination.

In an essay titled "Is Any Body Home?" Sobchack uses the metaphor of the body as a home, house, and prison to explore the ways in which we "experience our bodies as the existential ground of our being," and how this sense of self can be ruptured by illness.[55] *Diving Bell* illuminates the way vision mediates the relationship between consciousness and embodiment when Bauby catches sight of himself in a mirror or sees how people look at him and realizes how monstrous his condition is to others. Bauby claims:

> Reflected in the glass I saw the head of a man who seemed to have emerged from a vat of formaldehyde. His mouth was twisted, his nose damaged, his hair tousled, his gaze full of fear. One eye was sewn shut, the other goggled like the doomed eye of Cain. For a moment I stared at that dilated pupil, before I realized it was only mine.

At this moment in the film Bauby's self-consciousness is most profoundly anchored in his body, yet also most radically separate from it. Bauby's experience of glimpsing himself in a mirrored surface and realizing how other people must perceive his stricken, paralyzed face can be interpreted in terms of what Sobchack calls "interobjectivity": It is a moment in which he understands himself as a "subjective object whose intentionality and alterity can be sensed from without."[56]

In the words of film-philosopher Havi Carel, "The biological body and the lived body are normally experienced as identical, when they function flawlessly. The gap between the two becomes explicit in cases of bodily disorder, where the biological body behaves unpredictably, fails to perform previously effortless tasks and becomes a source of suffering."[57] The relationships between internality and externality, between mind and body, and between subjective first-person viewpoints and omniscient, third-person perspectives are central to the film. How, then, do these elements relate to the concept of compassion that this chapter set out to explore? What roles might compassion and intersubjectivity play in understanding the film, and how does the film cue or evoke this emotional response?

THE COMPASSIONATE GAZE

According to moral philosopher Martha Nussbaum, compassion is a "bridge from self-interest to just conduct."[58] Compassion connects individuals to the community and it is based on thoughts and evaluations regarding the well-being of others.[59] In other words, compassion necessitates a shift from subjective experience to understanding the experiences and situations of others. Aristotle's model of compassion, which Nussbaum adopts, rests on the belief that the suffering of another person is serious, the person is not the principal agent of their own suffering, and the misfortune they suffer could happen to oneself or to anyone, as is the case with Bauby's stroke.[60] This model involves making value judgments about the relative severity of suffering and attributing responsibility or causation for misfortune. It also suggests that perspective sharing—the ability to place oneself in another person's position—is central to feeling compassion. Following Aristotle, Nussbaum frequently uses the terms compassion and pity interchangeably, stating, "A crucial part of the ethical value of pity is its ability to cross boundaries of class, nationality, race, and gender as the pitier assumes these different positions in imagination, and comes to see the obstacles to flourishing faced by human beings in these many concrete situations."[61] While Nussbaum departs from Aristotle in her emphasis on perception,[62] her discussion of the imaginative exploration of ethical scenarios indicates she conceptualizes compassion primarily as a rational, cognitive process in which "value laden thoughts and perceptions" take precedence over empathic fellow feeling or a "twinge, pang, or feeling of any particular sort."[63] However, the analysis of film style offered in this chapter suggests another aspect of compassion: The way compassion functions in *Diving Bell* is not only through the insight facilitated by perspective sharing, but also through shared perceptual and affective experience that produces a form of understanding not necessarily limited to rational thought, nor mired in pity.

If we allow that compassion may take both affective and cognitive forms that can be traced in screen aesthetics and narrative content, and that bridging the distance between self and other is a central element of compassion, then it follows that intersubjectivity must be a key ingredient of the compassionate gaze that manifests in film and film spectatorship. Here I understand intersubjectivity to mean an overlapping or sharing of subjectivity such that a person gains knowledge of another subject's mental, experiential, or emotional state. Indeed, as previously detailed, the audience is granted access to Bauby's thoughts, imagination, and memories via subjective imagery and sound while being locked into his aural and optical point of view for much of the film. Additionally, qualitative understanding of Bauby's condition is also informed by viewpoints that enable audience members to see *how* he sees when the camera shifts its focus, and how his vision is blurred when the camera lens appears to be smeared with tears. The intersubjective experience the film offers is multiple and complex because the audience also experiences how others perceive Bauby as the narrative progresses. The film transcends the subject–object distinction, linking the spectator, the protagonists, and the film through stylistic techniques that represent perceptual and mental subjectivity. As Laine puts it, "The constant movement between subjectivity and objectivity, inside and outside, in *The Diving Bell* addresses our 'reversibility' (to use Maurice Merleau-Ponty's term), our interaction with the world registered in and through our body."[64] This suggests that the intersubjective knowledge of others that cinema affords is in no small part an embodied, affective, and experiential knowledge that exceeds cognition alone. Gibbs makes a similar point in her work on sympathy and mimetic communication, stating that "Visuality appears not only as a biophysical phenomenon but also as a social process, a way of relating to what is seen. Mimesis can then be understood as the primary mode of apprehension utilized by the body, by social technologies such as cinema"; furthermore, "it also forms the affective basis for ethical dealings with others."[65]

* * *

I have demonstrated that the subjective soundscape and haptic imagery enhance the intimate quality of *Diving Bell,* bringing the characters and the story world palpably closer to the spectator. The poetic montage sequences, slow motion imagery, and soaring, freewheeling cinematography that characterize Bauby's inner world do more than just provoke motor mimicry or insight into his mental state. The varied aesthetic techniques used in the film achieve a somatic mirroring of and an empathic attunement to the protagonist's subjectivity and his bodily experience. This reach of understanding, which is at once an act of embodied imagination, a movement toward others, and a means of understanding ourselves in relation to other people and situations, is central to the mechanisms of cinematic identification at play in the film.

Diving Bell engages the film audience ethically, perceptually, affectively, and cognitively in perspective sharing, thereby communicating a compassionate vision of how Bauby sees the world and how he is seen by others. The range of aesthetic techniques allows subjective, experiential immersion as well as more reflective distance. By engendering perceptual attunement to the sensory body and using voice-over narration, performance, and subjective imagery to cue the audience to imaginatively enter into the protagonist's perspective, the film invokes the cognitive and corporeal dimensions of compassion. In doing so it creates a link between self and other, offering the intersubjective experience of perspective taking that compassion requires. The cinematic articulation of Bauby's embodiment and his subjectivity in *Diving Bell* furnishes a compelling model for both observing and participating in the empathic sharing of perspectives that is so fundamental to the capacity for compassion and to understanding and bridging differences.

NOTES

1. Denise Dudzinski, "The Diving Bell Meets the Butterfly: Identity Lost and Re-membered," *Theoretical Medicine* 22 (2001): 34.
2. Lisa Diedrich, "Breaking Down: A Phenomenology of Disability," *Literature and Medicine* 20.2 (2001): 209.
3. Had Bauby's stroke happened more recently, medical science would have afforded him a swifter, more independent mode of communication by harnessing his neural activity directly to a computer. Research into the brain-computer interface has developed technologies that enable motor-impaired people to control a computer cursor using brain signals rather than their muscles. See, for example, Janis J. Daly and Jonathan R. Wolpaw, "Brain–Computer Interfaces in Neurological Rehabilitation," *Lancet Neurology* 7 (2008): 1032–1043.
4. Carl Plantinga, "Spectatorship," in *The Routledge Companion to Philosophy and Film,* ed. Paisley Livingston and Carl Plantinga (London: Routledge, 2009), 250.
5. Ibid., 252.
6. Maurice Merleau-Ponty, *The Primacy of Perception* (Evanston, IL: Northwestern University Press, 1964), 6.
7. Vivian Sobchack, *Carnal Thoughts: Embodiment and Moving Image Culture* (Berkeley: University of California Press, 2004), 3.
8. Ruth Leys, "The Turn to Affect: A Critique," *Critical Inquiry* 37.3 (2011): 434.
9. Tarja Laine, "*The Diving Bell and the Butterfly* as an Emotional Event," *Midwest Studies in Philosophy* 34 (2010): 304. See also Tarja Laine, *Feeling Cinema: Emotional Dynamics in Film Studies* (London: Continuum, 2011).
10. Brian Massumi, *Parables for the Virtual: Movement, Affect, Sensation* (Durham, NC: Duke University Press, 2002).
11. Martine Beugnet, "Cinema and Sensation: Contemporary French Film and Cinematic Corporeality," *Paragraph* 31.2 (2008): 173–188.
12. Elena del Río, *Deleuze and the Cinemas of Performance: Powers of Affection* (Edinburgh: Edinburgh University Press, 2008).
13. Laura U. Marks, *The Skin of the Film: Intercultural Cinema, Embodiment and the Senses* (Durham NC: Duke University Press, 2000). See also Laura U. Marks, *Touch: Sensuous Theory and Multisensory Media* (Minneapolis: University of Minnesota Press, 2002).
14. Christiane Voss, "Film Experience and the Formation of Illusion: The Spectator as 'Surrogate Body' for the Cinema," *Cinema Journal* 50.4 (2011): 139.
15. Ibid.
16. Ibid., 145.
17. Veit Erlmann, *Reason and Resonance: A History of Modern Aurality* (Massachusetts: MIT Press, 2010).
18. Maria Angel, "Seeing Things: Image and Affect," *Cultural Studies Review* 15.2 (2009): 141.
19. Gibbs, Anna. "After Affect: Sympathy, Synchrony and Mimetic Communication," in *The Affect Theory Reader,* ed. Melissa Gregg, Gregory Seigworth, and Sara Ahmed (Durham NC: Duke University Press, 2010), 197.
20. June Price Tangney, Jeff Stuewig, and Debra J. Mashek, "Moral Emotion and Moral Behaviour," *Annual Review of Psychology* 58 (2007): 345–372; Nancy Eisenberg, "Emotion, Regulation, and Moral Development," *Annual Review of Psychology* 51 (2000): 665–697.
21. Julian Hanich, *Cinematic Emotion in Horror Films and Thrillers: The Aesthetic Paradox of Pleasurable Fear* (New York: Routledge, 2010), 183;

Laine, *"Diving Bell,"* 297; Murray Smith, "Empathy and the Extended Mind" (paper presented at History and Philosophy of Art Seminar, University of Kent, 2007); Carl Plantinga, *Moving Viewers: American Film and the Spectator's Experience* (Berkeley: University of California Press, 2009), 124; Amy Coplan, "Will the Real Empathy Please Stand Up? A Case For A Narrow Conceptualization," *The Southern Journal of Philosophy* 49 (2011): 40–65.

22. Alex Neill, "Empathy and (Film) Fiction." In *Philosophy of Film and Motion Pictures: An Anthology,* ed. Noël Carroll and Jinhee Choi (Malden, MA and Oxford: Blackwell Publishing, 2006), 252.

23. A more extreme phenomenological approach, such as that taken by Jennifer Barker, frames empathy almost exclusively in affective terms as a "muscular," kinaesthetic sense of fellow feeling that is prompted by techniques such as camera movement. Jennifer Barker, *The Tactile Eye: Touch and the Cinematic Experience* (Berkeley: University of California Press, 2009), 73–82.

24. Smith, "Empathy," 10.

25. Boris Bernhardt and Tania Singer, "The Neural Basis of Empathy," *Annual Review of Neuroscience* 35 (2012): 3. Psychologists refer to the avoidance of painful feelings of empathy as aversive vicarious arousal or "personal distress regulation." See Eisenberg, "Emotion," 674.

26. Smith, "Empathy," 7.

27. Ibid., 3.

28. Joel Krueger, "Empathy and the Extended Mind," *Zygon* 44.3 (2009): 676.

29. Ibid., 683.

30. Murray Smith, *Engaging Characters: Fiction, Emotion and the Cinema* (Oxford: Clarendon Press, 1995), 99. Note that affective mimicry is typically involuntary and does not necessarily involve mental processing, but emotional simulation does require cognitive processing.

31. Tanya Chartrand and Jessica Lakin, "The Antecedents and Consequences of Human Behavioral Mimicry," *Annual Review of Psychology* 64.18 (2013): 11; Eisenberg, "Emotion," 673.

32. See psychologist Paul Ekman's influential study, *Emotions Revealed: Understanding Faces and Feelings,* second edition (London: Weidenfeld and Nicholson, 2007).

33. Krueger, "Empathy," 691.

34. Martha Nussbaum, *Upheavals of Thought: The Intelligence of Emotions* (Cambridge: Cambridge University Press, 2001), 253.

35. Laine, "Emotional Event," 301.

36. Ibid.

37. Barker, *The Tactile Eye,* 75.

38. Ibid., 73–74.

39. Ibid., 119.

40. In my view, empathy requires both cognition and affect, so it seems inaccurate to use the term *empathy* to refer to a purely physiological reaction to cinematic motility that is largely divorced from character engagement and from empathy's ethical and cognitive aspects. I have reservations about whether it is possible to empathize with the film itself because films themselves have no inner life and cannot feel emotion or even pain. However, there is great value in Barker's work, particularly where she illuminates how audiences might share in the feeling of something like camera movement and respond with a form of somatic mirroring or motor mimicry.

41. Hanich, *Cinematic Emotion,* 181.

42. Ibid., 103.

43. Ibid., 104.

44. Ibid., 182.
45. Ibid.
46. Ibid., 183.
47. Ibid.
48. Marks, *Skin,* 162.
49. Ibid.
50. Ibid., 163.
51. Ibid., 191, 189.
52. For an important discussion of different ways in which film can establish a sense of closeness to screen protagonists including perceptions of proximity, affective closeness, parasocial relations, familiarity, understanding, and perspective taking, see Jens Eder, "Ways of Being Close to Characters," *Film Studies: An International Review* 8 (2006): 68–80.
53. Eder, "Close to Characters," 75.
54. Sara Ahmed theorizes disgust as a self-protective recoil response to something perceived to be contagious or impure. When disgust is directed at the human body it has ethical ramifications associated with social stigma. See Sara Ahmed, "The Performativity of Disgust," *The Cultural Politics of Emotion* (Edinburgh: Edinburgh University Press, 2004), 82–100. In a phenomenological analysis of David Cronenberg's 1986 film *The Fly,* Havi Carel explores how disgust and fear are elicited by physical frailty and disfiguring maladies when the body is afflicted by illness. Havi Carel, "A Phenomenology of Tragedy: Illness and Body Betrayal in *The Fly,*" *Scan* 4.2 (2007): n.p.
55. Vivian Sobchack, "Is Any Body Home? Embodied Imagination and Visible Evictions," in *Home, Exile, Homeland: Film, Media, and the Politics of Place,* ed. Hamid Naficy (New York: Routledge, 1999), 46.
56. Sobchack, *Carnal,* 290. Sobchack discusses the "co-constitutive experience we have of ourselves and others as material objects" (296). She argues that the origin of ethical responsibility "lies in the subjective realization of our own objectivity" (310), which occurs when we grasp what it feels like to be perceived or treated as an object, momentarily displaced from our own subjectivity.
57. Carel, "Illness," n.p.
58. Martha Nussbaum, "Compassion: The Basic Social Emotion," *Social Philosophy and Policy Foundation* 13.1 (1996): 57.
59. Ibid., 28.
60. Ibid., 31.
61. Ibid., 51.
62. In Nussbaum's account of the relationship between perception and cognition in moral emotions, emotions figure as "intelligent responses to the perception of value" that "embody ways of seeing an object" (*Upheavals,* 1, 29). Because emotions entail complex beliefs regarding the impediment or attainment of goals and well-being, they play an important role in ethical judgment. Nussbaum argues the cognitive component of emotion is not necessarily based on reasons or thoughts that can be put into words: "Emotions always involve thought of an object combined with thought of the object's salience or importance; in that sense, they always involve appraisal or evaluation"; however, the form cognition takes does not necessarily require linguistic formulation, calculation, "or even reflexive self-awareness" (23).
63. Ibid., 55.
64. Laine, "Emotional Event," 298.
65. Gibbs, "Affect," 202.

3 Moral Change
Fiction, Film, and Family

Noël Carroll

Movies—meaning mass-market motion pictures (including television and other popular visual media)—are primarily aimed at arousing the emotions. Indeed, many movie genres are named after the predominant emotion that it is their function to engender. For example, horror, suspense, mystery, thrillers, and weepies or tear jerkers are labeled in terms of the affect they are predicated upon raising in viewers. Comedy does not name an emotion, but the emotion comedies are designed to provoke can be readily identified as comic amusement. Of course, no movie, in the typical run of things, is intended to evoke one and only one emotion. Rather, movies are structured to evoke an ensemble of emotions. You approve of the hero, you hate the villain, you feel suspense as the two lock in battle, and you feel relief and then joy when the protagonist prevails.

The emotions are evolved mechanisms for protecting and facilitating vital human interests. Fear alerts us to danger; anger to injustice; jealousy to loss of affection; and so on. Moreover, these emotions are not only engaged on behalf of our own interests; they can be extended to others whom we regard as belonging to our circle. The emotions are mechanisms for protecting and facilitating the vital interests and concerns of me and mine—although the *mine* here can be quite extensive; it can encompass the whole human race when we are attacked by intergalactic zombies.

Given their connection with interests, the emotions are obviously value laden. They may prompt us to act in such a way as to protect or to enhance what we value. Frightened, we prepare to flee, fight, or freeze. However, the emotions are not only goads to action. They also shape judgments. One might think of them as embodied value judgments or appraisals. This aspect of the emotions is especially pertinent to movie viewing which involves audiences in a virtually continuous process of issuing moral judgments.

Moreover, inasmuch as emotions are involved in value judgments, it should come as no surprise that the emotions are connected to morality in a number of ways. Some emotions have moral values as their formal object, such as indignation. Other emotions can be put in the service of morality, for example, fear and disgust. Because of the intimate connection that emotions as embodied value judgments have with morality, we find that the emotions that movies elicit are, as a matter of empirical fact, generally bound up with morality. Our affection for the hero is typically based on our moral approval of what he stands for; our indignation with respect to the villain is rooted in our moral disapproval of him. Indeed, this is reflected by our ordinary language tendency to call the protagonist the good guy and the antagonist the bad guy.

Movies do not create our emotions *de novo*. Rather, movie makers typically play on the already formed emotions that we bring with us into the screening auditorium. Likewise, inasmuch as those emotions are bound up with our morals, the movie maker will have to depend on igniting the emotions she desires by activating our antecedent moral convictions. If that is so, however, a question arises about how it is possible for fictions in general and movies in particular to participate in bringing about moral change in the audience. How can the creators of fiction, including movie makers, induce audiences to feel positive emotions toward objects about which they previously felt either nothing at all or even, in some cases, where they felt negative emotions, such as fear and disgust? How can audiences be led to feel indignant about the treatment of persons who they were previously disposed to regard with antipathy? That is, how is moral change possible in response to fictions in general and movies in particular? That is the question I would like to address in this chapter.

To repeat: I wish to begin to answer the question of how it is possible for movies to promote moral change in audiences, where the moral change in question occurs at the level of the audience's emotional response to the fiction and its characters. In order to answer this question, I will discuss the emotions, their inter-relation with morality, and the way in which moral change appears to occur outside of fiction. I will then turn to two cases where fictions have been designed, arguably successfully, so as to abet moral change by redirecting the emotions toward different objects. This will involve a close look at *Uncle Tom's Cabin* and the movie *Philadelphia*. In both cases, persons regarded previously as objects of disgust within a culture, are transformed into objects of moral respect. I will attempt to isolate the affective strategies that make this possible. In the last section of this chapter, I will discuss the way in which these devices can be mobilized for immoral effects as well as moral ones.

THE EMOTIONS, MORALITY, AND MORAL CHANGE

Emotions are embodied value judgments or appraisals regarding the vital interests or concerns of me and mine. With respect to fictions in general and the movies in particular, the relevant "mine" includes all those toward whom we are inclined to bear a pro-attitude. Arguably, these are, for the most part, characters who win our moral approval or who, at least, do not encourage a strong degree of moral disapproval. One thing to note about the judgments that we lavish upon such characters is that we usually size them up pretty quickly. Our approval of the character typically comes in the form of feelings of moral admiration, affection, and/or alliance. Our disapproval usually comes in the form of emotions of dislike, hatred, or even loathing. The disapproval is almost visceral sometimes. This is especially true of mass-market movies. We make snap judgments emotively that are typically pretty reliable, although we can be tricked, as we were in the last installment of the *Dark Knight* franchise.[1]

Of course, it is no accident that we reach these snap, emotive judgments almost upon contact with these fictional characters. Fictional creations, including the movies, are designed to bring that about. However, we also tend to arrive at a great number of our value judgments in the ordinary course of affairs with comparable rapidity and emotional urgency. This is not to say that all of our value judgments, including our moral judgments, are on such an emotional hair-trigger, only that a great many of them are—more than most of us would probably suspect.

Emotions are mainly automatic. They were once called *passions* to acknowledge the phenomenological impression they impart as something happening to us. This, perhaps needless to say, is not always the case. We can elicit an emotional response through deliberation. Nevertheless, it is generally the case that the emotions seem to be on a hair-trigger, frequently bypassing the frontal cortex and radiating directly from the amygdala. Moreover, this is what one would expect of biological mechanisms evolved to discharge the functions of the emotions. Emotions evolved to protect vital interests faster than the speed of deliberation. This is the case of the emotions in general and, by extension, the emotions in the service of the morality as well as the straightforwardly moral emotions.

Each of the emotions is concerned with a certain theme, which is of vital interest to me and mine. Fear is concerned with danger. Sadness is concerned with loss. Moral indignation is concerned with injustice. The emotions may be construed as bodily alarms that go off when these themes are detected—when we are threatened, for example, or wronged. The detection of these themes may or may not involve the subsumption of the stimulus under a concept. These alarms may be set off by matching the stimulus to certain perceptual eliciting conditions or event patterns of the sort that Ronald DeSousa calls paradigm scenarios.[2] That is, whether with regard to the non-moral or the moral emotions, an emotional episode may be provoked by the detection of a certain pattern in the stimulus as well as by the application of concept. Indeed, it seems that there is mounting empirical evidence to suggest that this fast-track reaction to affective relevant stimuli is the norm.

According to Jesse Prinz, our emotional responses are keyed to what he calls calibration files—roughly, records (including perceptual records) of the sorts of saliencies that caused the relevant emotional alarms to go off in the past.[3] Presumably, these calibration files also contain paradigm scenarios and even concepts. However, for our purposes, the perceptual records and the paradigm scenarios are of greater interest, because it is likely that they are the major agencies in play that account for our rapid emotional response to fictions in general and movies in particular.

For an example of the kind of ingredients to be found in a calibration, consider the perceptual memory of a rattlesnake. Detection of a rattlesnake in the wild will immediately elicit a reaction of fear, for most of us accompanied by a tendency to freeze and then withdraw. Likewise, in movies there are countless close shots of rattlesnakes, which send a chill down the spines of most viewers. We don't typically categorize the rattlesnake as dangerous before the emotion ignites. Matching it to an item in our calibration file for fear is enough to cause a bodily response. (I hasten to add that I do not believe Prinz's account of the emotions covers every case, but I think it likely covers a very large number of cases, especially with respect to many popular fictions, and notably movies.)

This account, supplemented by the notion of paradigm scenarios, arguably accounts for the largest number of instances, although not all, of emotion-elicitation in popular fictions, particularly movies. Fiction writers and movie makers rely on our possession of certain calibration files—including perceptual memory types and paradigm scenarios—that are already in place and which can be triggered by the imagery that they present to us. The giant spider enfolds the maiden in its hairy arachnid legs, its fangs slavering, and we flinch as reliably as we do when a smoke detector starts ringing as the fire below mounts. The success of popular movies and fictions typically depends on being able, by means of a sufficiently similar stimulus, to activate some perceptual memory type and/or paradigm scenario that antecedently exists in the calibration file of the typical viewer. Indeed, in some cases, the pertinent items in the calibration files of the audience may be image-types derived from prior popular entertainments, including movies.

This then prompts us to ask how movie makers can engineer a change in the emotional response patterns of their audiences. There is no question that it can be done. We know that it has been done in the past. Yet, how is it possible? The most plausible way to begin to answer this question is to look to how emotive change—and especially emotive moral change—is possible in everyday life.

Suppose we disapprove of the behavior of a colleague whom we regard as snobbish. Other colleagues find our judgment too harsh. They argue that she is not a snob, but instead that she is shy. In effect, they are attempting to recalibrate our perception of our colleague by connecting or associating her to the perceptual memories and/or paradigm scenarios that comprise our calibration file for our sympathy toward shy persons. Perhaps we connect our colleague's behavior with our own previous response to episodes in which we felt immensely intimidated. Of course, this gestalt-change does not come from nowhere. Rather it involves a calibration-file-switch. However, for this to succeed there must already be another calibration file, which can be accessed for the recalibration to obtain.

To speak less jargonistically, the object of our emotions needs to be linked with another already existing set of emotion elicitors. DeSousa employs the useful metaphor of cantilevering. To add a balcony to a structure, we need to support it from a wall that already exists.[4] To change an emotion requires building upon emotions and emotion elicitors (calibration files) that are already in place. We can be induced to have new feelings by redeploying sentiments antecedently in our emotive repertoire. In effect, we are modifying our preexisting emotional economy. Emotive change occurs by reorienting our emotional responses, by associating a previously indifferent or aversive stimulus with a different, preexisting paradigm scenario. A simple example of this process might be the way in which we coax a child to come downstairs and join the party. We try to allay her fears by enticing her with an alternative scenario—one that describes the fun she will have and the old friends who will be there to play with. We replace her fear with expectations based on memories of good times. In technical terms, we nudge her downstairs by recalibrating her party-file.

Moral change in movies follows a comparable pattern. Fiction writers and movie makers expressly work on our calibration files by supplying us with the sorts of perceptual images and/or paradigm scenarios that dispose us to relocate various persons, situations, and events from one calibration file to another. This strategy can be very clearly illustrated by the novel *Uncle Tom's Cabin* and the film *Philadelphia*. In both cases, a denigrated group is recalibrated as an object of moral concern. In each case, this ethico-moral realignment is cantileveraged by accessing the audience's paradigm scenarios regarding family relations.

UNCLE TOM'S CABIN

With respect to moral change, Harriet Beecher Stowe's *Uncle Tom's Cabin* is probably one of the most successful popular fictions of all time. As is widely quoted, but probably apocryphal, Abraham Lincoln supposedly asked, upon meeting Harriet Beecher Stowe, "Is this the little woman who started this great war?" The novel, along with its various dramatizations, brought about a reversal in the moral sentiments in many audiences. Whereas black slaves were previously often the objects of disgust, they became objects of sympathy. For example, the Bowery Boys—the name for street toughs including butchers, firemen, newsboys, and other working class types, distinguished by their red shirts, boots, and rowdiness—who had a reputation for anti-abolitionism and violence against blacks—were observed applauding fugitive slaves and booing slave-owners at theatrical presentations of *Uncle Tom's Cabin*. William Lloyd Garrison, the abolitionist, was impressed by this veritable reversal in working-class values. He wrote, in *The Liberator*, "If the shrewdest abolitionist among us had prepared a drama to make the strongest anti-slavery impression, he could scarcely have done better.

O, it was a sight worth seeing, those ragged, coatless men and boys in the pit (the very *material* of which mobs are made) cheering the strongest and sublimest anti-slavery sentiments."[5]

In many cases, Stowe was preaching to the choir. However, there can be little doubt that she also was able to influence the moral sentiments of a great many of her readers. The question is: How did she do it? She appears to have relied upon two major strategies, both of which involve altering the calibration file the historical reader deployed in response to black slaves. That is, Stow recalibrated the reader's emotional repertoire. Rather than figuring the black slave as a mongrel subhuman, she fielded a very different sort of imagery, which was primarily of two sorts. The first, and perhaps less interesting from our perspective, was the emphasis on the Christianity of the slaves, especially the Christianity of Uncle Tom, whose New Testament commitments are not only saintly, but pretty clearly verge on the Christlike. His whipping at the hands of Simon Legree is unmistakably reminiscent of Christ's flogging at the pillar by Pilate's legionnaires.

The idea here is that if black slaves are exemplary Christians—and, therefore, children of God—then there is something evil in the brutal treatment they suffer. Christians are neither animals nor should they be treated as worse than animals. This way of recalibrating the black slave probably drew forth an indignant response from Stowe's Christian readers—of course, virtually all of her contemporary American readers would have been Christian. Nevertheless, one thing that is striking about *Uncle Tom's Cabin* is that it has not only stoked the moral emotions of its American readers, but it was and has been for most of the time since its publication, a book that has stirred the moral emotions of peoples around the world. Moreover, I think that this is due to Stowe's second major strategy in the book, emphasizing the fact that black slaves are members of loving families and that slavery is a system, which Stowe observes, "whirls families and scatters their members as the wind whirls and scatters the leaves of autumn.[6] Again and again, Stowe describes black families only to record the heartless ways they are torn apart to be bartered on the market.

This relentlessly recurring motif begins in the first chapter of the book, "The Reader is Introduced to A Man of Humanity." The title is ironic. The "man of humanity" is a slave merchant named Haley. He is negotiating with Mr. Shelby who apparently, given his financial woes, has little option but to agree to Haley's demands. Haley is, in effect, calling for the dismemberment of two slave families. That of Eliza, her son Harry, and her husband George, on the one hand, and that of Uncle Tom, Aunt Chloe, and their children, on the other hand.

Stowe is very careful to emphasize the deep affectionate ties between black family members in order to undercut callous remarks by slavers like Haley that allege "T'ant, you know, if it was white folks that's brought up in the ways of 'spectin to keep their children, and all that."[7] Stowe takes every opportunity to stress how genuine the family love is among the slaves.

By invoking the image of loving families, Stowe is able to marshal the pro-family sentiment of the reader in such a way that the sundering of families, which Stow represents as one of the primary features of slavery, erupts into not only sympathy for the slaves but indignation about their treatment.

Although I have not done a statistical analysis of the book, I would speculate that Stowe spends more ink on detailing the ways in which slavery tears families apart than she does on the literal physical brutality to which slaves are subjected. Of course, the book starts off addressing this aspect of slavery. Upon hearing Haley's plans, Eliza takes her young son Harry and flees from the Selby's plantation. Her husband, George, likewise breaks away from his master. He says, "I saw my mother put up at a sheriff's sale, with her seven children. They were sold before her eyes, one by one, all to different masters; and I was the youngest."[8]

The family—Eliza, George, and Harry—is a sort of Holy Family, portrayed as an exemplary, loving Christian family in contrast to the heartless, mercenary slavers who pursue them. As Eliza leaps her way across the ice flows in one of the most famous scenes in popular literature, any reader who has either had a loving family or wished for one is on her side and likewise in the scene where her husband George stands off his pursuers. The reader is on the side of the fugitive family's flight to Canada because the slaves have been calibrated as an ideal family whose unity is sacrosanct. All threats to its integrity are thus regarded as wrong. The slaves are recalibrated under the image of the good family, or, to use DeSousa's metaphor of cantilveraging, approval and alignment with the slave family is supported by the audience's preexisting moral commitments to the value of the family unit.

As previously mentioned, Eliza's story is not the only one that sounds the theme of the dismemberment of the slave family. Uncle Tom's family is being sundered as well. Moreover, as his story unravels, not only is he never reunited with his kin folks, but a stunning number of the slaves he meets in the course of his adventures also have been victimized in the same way. At an auction, a mother begs Haley to buy her after he has purchased her son, but Haley refuses.[9] Before the auction, when Haley tells Tom about men he intends to buy, Tom wonders "how many of these doomed men had wives and children and whether they would feel as he did about leaving them."[10]

Later, Tom talks to another one of Haley's prisoners, John, only to learn that John has been separated from his wife.[11] Shortly afterward, while being transported on a riverboat, we learn of the slavers kidnapping the child of a woman named Lucy, who, upon discovering the abduction of her child, commits suicide. Tom is sold along with Emmeline and Susan, a mother and daughter, but the mother and daughter go to different owners. Cassy, Simon Legree's mistress, who eventually revolts against him, has a backstory in which she has been cruelly separated from her children. It begins to seem as though most of the slaves Tom meets have been torn from their loved ones.

Although for the most part, Stowe makes her case by showing rather than telling, there are moments when she makes the point of the recurring motif of family dismemberment explicit—namely, that the dissolution of these black families is no different than the sundering of white families would be and that whites should regard it with comparable horror. Little Eva, worrying about what will happen to his slaves should St. Clare die, says, "Papa, these poor creatures love their children as much as you do me." Indeed, the death of the saintly Little Eva and its wrenching effects on St. Clare are seemingly meant to portray the impact that the loss of a white child can have on a white father in a way that we are supposed to metaphorically transfer to black parents who lose their children through the vagaries of slavery.

In Stowe's argument, the patent evil in separating loving families is a leading premise. The argument as a whole is rehearsed by two ladies on the riverboat, where Haley's slaves are imprisoned. One of the ladies says:

> "The most dreadful thing about slavery, to my mind, is its outrages on the feelings and affections—the separating of families for example."
>
> "That is a bad thing, certainly," said the other lady, holding up a baby's dress she had just completed and looking intently on its trimmings; "but, then, I fancy, it don't occur often."
>
> "O, it does," said the first lady eagerly; "I've lived many years in Kentucky and Virginia both, and I've seen enough to make anyone's heart sick. Suppose ma'am, your two children there, should be taken and sold?"[12]

Occasionally, Stowe will call upon readers, especially mothers, to consider the case the slaves and their families encounter analogously to their own. Implicitly, Stowe is invoking the Golden Rule, but of course, for that line of argument to take hold, it is necessary that the white reader accepts that slaves are embedded in the same sorts of loving families that they value. That is, they must recalibrate the slaves in terms of the paradigm scenario of the loving family to call forth the indignation that goes with the paradigm scenario of the loving family being torn apart.

I began noting that Stowe utilized at least two major strategies for recalibrating the response to black slaves. There is the Christian imagery and the family dismemberment imagery. Of course, sometimes these converge, as when the integrity of the black family is explicitly connected to their being good Christians. However, in many countries outside of Christendom and in our own times, it is likely the family paradigm scenarios are more effective. For one of the touchstones across cultures is what has been called the "ethics of community," which pertains to norms of communal order; and to these communal norms will be some value bestowed on the integrity of the family, however that is construed. Thus, by emphasizing the violence done to the family, Stowe manages to touch a nearly universal ethical chord, whereas the Christian motif lacks comparable reach.

This, of course, is not to say that the Christian strategy wasn't immensely effective in its own time and place, but only that the more extensive ethico-emotional response across continents and centuries is probably due to the use of the ideal family paradigm scenario in recalibrating the audience's affective response to the black slaves.

PHILADELPHIA

One conceit that Stowe occasionally employs in *Uncle Tom's Cabin* is for the reader to imagine seeing the unfolding action. For example, we are told that Tom is studying his Bible and that "there we see him now."[13] Or, we encounter sentences such as "Miss Ophelia, as you now befold her, stands before you. . . ."[14] It is as if Stowe thinks that if the reader can be made to visualize the story, it will function as a more vivid image in our calibration files. When we shift from novels to movies, that advantage accrues automatically.

Philadelphia, Jonathan Demme's 2000 film about AIDS, takes on a moral project analogous to *Uncle Tom's Cabin*. It proposes to state the case for the homosexual male suffering from AIDS. Like the black slave in the nineteenth century, the gay AIDS victim of the twentieth century was widely regarded as an object of disgust. *Philadelphia* sets out to recalibrate him as an object of sympathy whose unjust treatment merits our indignation. *Philadelphia* is the story of a gay man, Andrew Beckett, played by Tom Hanks, who has been illegally terminated by his law firm because he has AIDS. He is defended by Joe Miller (played by Denzel Washington), the kind of lawyer we call in the United States "an ambulance chaser." Although initially leery of the case, due to his self-professed prejudice against gays, Miller takes it on and against all odds, wins a decision of unlawful termination for Beckett. A great deal of the drama depends on the trial and the suspense that comes with that format, including the duel of wits between the lawyers, especially the brilliant tactical victories that Miller, the underdog lawyer, is able to score against the substantial stellar team of lawyers fielded by Beckett's former employers.

However, even before the trial and Miller's impressive maneuvers in demonstrating his client's case, we are already on Beckett's side morally. Interestingly, the audience—and here I have in mind primarily heterosexuals—are drawn to him, not only because of his personal qualities (he seems quite decent and considerate), but more importantly because of the way in which he is inserted into what we can refer to as the paradigm scenario of the ideal family. The third scene of the film introduces the viewer to Andrew's relationship with his family. He is on the phone speaking to his mother, reassuring her that his blood work is fine—something we quickly realize is a lie intended to keep her from worrying about his condition, which we learn about in a subsequent scene flagged as "9 Days Later."

The family theme is not only developed with respect to Beckett. As he is watching an ad for Miller's law firm during which the camera moves in for a point-of-view shot of a lesion on his neck, the film cross-cuts to a scene of Miller's wife Lisa giving birth to their daughter Clarice. An analogy is set up between Miller's family and Beckett's. Often, when Miller is making some decision with respect to Beckett, the editing associates his deliberation with images of his family. The strong suggestion is that on those occasions, Miller's decisions on Beckett's behalf are made because he, Miller, sees Beckett as embedded in a family and its network of affections that is not different in kind than his own family.

When Beckett visits Miller's office to ask him to represent him in his wrongful termination case, the first thing Beckett mentions is the picture of Miller's family on Miller's desk, noting that he has a new girl and adding that "kids are great." Miller, who appears to be willing to chase any ambulance, surprisingly declines Beckett's case. Later, at home, referring to homosexuality, he confides to his wife that he "can't stand that shit."

Miller is intended to be a stand-in for certain members of the heterosexual audience, especially males. He, and presumably many of the people he represents, are swayed, or at least, are intended to be swayed, by what we can label the rhetoric of the family. This rhetoric appears in its strongest form in the sequence that begins with home movies of the Beckett family celebrating the fortieth anniversary of Andrew's parents, but which then merges into a present-day family conference about Andrew's decision to bring his case to trial. He is asking for his family's approval, warning them about the unpleasant publicity that is likely to erupt. The family, with almost no reservation, voices unconditional support, admiration, and love for Andrew.

As we can see, the scene represents the family as almost completely behind Andrew. His brothers affirm their support and love. The only brief hesitation comes from his sister who worries about whether her parents will be able to withstand the trial, but this allows the mother and father to weigh in with their support. Andrew's father says he is proud of his son; his mother says that she did not raise her kids to sit in the back of the bus and that he should fight. The scene ends with Andrew saying, in 1950s-TV style: "Gee, I love you guys." The whole scene has been articulated with tearful point-of-view shots between his assembled family and Andrew.

Next, there is a cut to the statue of William Penn atop city hall in Philadelphia. The trial is on and the thrust-and-parry, parry-and-thrust of Hollywood courtroom forensics moves ahead full throttle. However, there is an interesting feature in the way that Jonathan Demme and his director of photography, Tak Fujimoto, shoot the scene. They are very careful to include frequently not only Andrew's lover Miguel in the background of the shots of Andrew sitting at the plaintiff's desk, but also his family members, thus giving the feeling that part of the purpose of the extended family conference scene was to familiarize us enough with what his family members looked like so that we would constantly recognize them sitting behind Andrew and giving him support. Sometimes the camera will pick one of them out for special emphasis; often it is the mother. Andrew will turn to them and communicate by hand gestures; sometimes they will respond by silently but forcefully urging him on. In any event, the filmmakers go out of their way to weave the presence of the family into the trial even though from a strictly narrative point of view, it is unnecessary. For example, there is no narrative reason that we need to be lead into a scene by following Andrew's father re-entering the courtroom from the men's room, but the filmmakers want to remind us that the family is there for Andrew. That is, it is the key to the rhetorical strategy of the film to keep Andrew's identity as a beloved member of an ideal family in the foreground. When Andrew is being cross-examined, he begins to waver physically and we see his family's concern etched in close-up shots. When he collapses, they rush forward. In an overhead shot, we see his sister bent over him.

Just before Andrew takes the stand in court, he holds a costume party. His friends arrive attired as everything imaginable—as if to suggest symbolically the inclusiveness of the gay population. Joe Miller and his wife arrive. There is dancing. It is very communal. Afterward, Miller and Beckett meet to go over the trial. Instead Andrew plays him an aria, sung by Callas, about the death of a mother, and the family theme registers in a new key. Miller returns home and hugs his daughter. Then he goes to bed with his wife and embraces her. We are led to surmise by the cutting that whatever Miller is thinking about Beckett is being processed along with thinking about his own family. This is important because Miller as the heterosexual "every" man has more than once expressed his disgust with regard to homosexuality. Nonetheless, that disgust appears to be dislodged by his thinking about families.

Andrew wins his case, but is in the hospital on his deathbed. After the fireworks of the trial are over, the film returns to its primary emphasis on the family. Miller walks into the hospital. One of Andrew's brothers nods and Miller winks in a return close-up. Another brother embraces Miller. Miller enters Andrew's room where the Beckett family is encamped en masse with his sister Jill on the bed. After Miller and Andrew Beckett exchange last sentiments, there is a parade of Andrew's family offering last words. His father blesses him and repeats his love for Andrew. The brothers and sister say their farewells and finally the mother leans over and whispers, "Good night my angel, my sweet boy." There is a short scene with Andrew's lover Miguel. Andrew dies off-screen.

Then follows a coda. There is a party in Andrew's loft, presumably after the funeral. What is so very striking about this scene is that it is dominated by family imagery. Andrew's parents are visible as are his siblings, most of whom appear to have acquired children. Miller and his wife arrive with their daughter in tow. An older Latino couple enters whom, given their behavior, we infer are Miguel's parents. Gradually the camera homes in on some children who are watching a video on a monitor. There are unmistakably home movies of children, including undoubtedly Andrew, playing. The very notion of "home movies" reminds us of families and their cherished history. Finally the video settles on a young toddler holding a picnic basket. We assume it is Andrew. The image freezes.

If there is any doubt that the family is a major, if somewhat subliminal theme, of *Philadelphia* from the onset of Andrew's disease through the trial, by the end of the film there can be no denying that the family was always there as a persistent, latent image. Its function, moreover, seems to be to portray the gay victim of AIDS in a new light—not as the object of disgust, but as a beloved member of a family. In this regard, *Philadelphia*, like *Uncle Tom's Cabin*, employs the imagery of the family to recalibrate the audience's ethico-emotional appraisal of objects previously loathed.

Note that *Philadelphia* does not mobilize the paradigm scenario of the ideal family in exactly the same way that *Uncle Tom's Cabin* does; the former does not invoke indignation at the wrongness of destroying families. Rather, it appeals to Andrew's right to be treated justly not in virtue of abstract human rights but in virtue of his concrete instantiation of the paradigm scenario of the loving family. Thus, in their different ways, *Uncle Tom's Cabin* and *Philadelphia* appear to succeed in recalibrating moral attitudes toward certain abominated groups by recalibrating representatives of those groups in terms of paradigm scenarios regarding the family. In this, they show how moral change is possible in popular fictions by building on moral sentiments that are already firmly in place—by claiming, for example, justice for black slaves on the one hand and diseased homosexuals on the other hand, and by cantileveraging those claims on the paradigm scenarios in our calibration file for the loving family—either the one we have been lucky enough to have or the one we wish we had.

CONCLUSION

In this chapter, I have proposed that one way in which moral change can be engineered in movies and other popular fictions is to emotively recalibrate the targets of the desired moral sentiments in terms of antecedently positive paradigm scenarios—ones already in the audience's ethico-emotive repertoire. In such cases, where the audience comes to an issue with a bias (such as racism or homophobia), the fiction writers and movie makers will attempt to outweigh that bias with an even more entrenched one (such as the family).

I have tried to motivate this conjecture by looking at the way in which the paradigm scenario of the ideal family is mobilized in *Uncle Tom's Cabin* and *Philadelphia*—although the deployment of this paradigm scenario is somewhat subtle in *Philadelphia*, the examples that I have chosen are of the "grab you by the collar" variety. I would, nevertheless, want to defend my choice of samples on the grounds that it is more productive to begin theorizing with simple cases before going on to more complex ones. Moreover, I should add that I think that there are more available paradigm scenarios than only that of the ideal loving family.

I also acknowledge that this process of recalibration is no guarantee that the results will always be morally desirable. There are no such guarantees with any process of moral change. Recalibration can be employed by angels or demons. Leni Riefensthal's invocation of community in *Triumph of the Will* is perhaps the most notorious instance of the latter. However, that does not entail that audiences are at the mercy of just any invocation of a positive paradigm scenario. For, once the emotion process is set in motion by the invocation of a paradigm scenario, it is still open to deliberative monitoring in light of whether or not the scenario fits with or is coherent with our preexisting cognitive-emotive stock. Paradigm scenarios can be resisted. For example, the use of the family paradigm scenario invoked by Socrates in the Noble Lie section of Plato's *Republic* is (unfortunately) unlikely to dispose many toward moral acceptance of the reign of philosopher kings.

Lastly, I do not claim that fictions, including movies, are able to bring off moral change on their own. One does not typically see a film such as *Philadelphia* and suddenly undergo a conversion experience. Rather, such films and popular fictions are usually part and parcel of a multichanneled cultural transformation. In a similar vein, the cause of the abolition of slavery was issuing from many different sources already when *Uncle Tom's Cabin* was published. That novel did not single-handedly bring about the change in sentiment that resulted in the emancipation of the slaves. Stowe's book was one factor in a larger multichanneled cultural movement that it reinforced while simultaneously being reciprocally advantaged by finding support from the very same movement it reinforced.

This observation is not made to disparage the potential contribution of popular fictions to moral change, but only to acknowledge that, in the main, they are only one force among many converging forces in the process of moral transformation. Generally, overcoming strong moral biases, such as racism and homophobia, requires recruiting more powerful countervailing biases—more than once and along multiple, redundant channels of communication and feeling.[15]

NOTES

1. See Noël Carroll, "The Movies and the Moral Emotions" in his *Minerva's Night Out: Philosophy, Motion Pictures, and Popular Culture* (Malden, MA: Wiley-Blackwell, forthcoming).
2. Ronald De Sousa, *Emotional Truth* (Oxford: Oxford University Press, 2011), 34.
3. See Jesse Prinz, *The Emotional Construction of Morals* (Oxford: Oxford University Press, 2007).
4. DeSousa, *Emotional Truth*, 34.
5. Quoted in David S. Reynolds, *Mightier than the Sword: Uncle Tom's Cabin and the Battle for America* (London: W. W. Norton and Company, 2011), 145–146.
6. Harriet Beecher Stowe, *Uncle Tom's Cabin,* ed. Jean Fagan Yellin (Oxford: Oxford University Press, 1998), 438. This book was originally published in 1852.

7. Ibid., 13.
8. Ibid., 117.
9. Ibid., 126.
10. Ibid., 123.
11. Ibid., 127.
12. Ibid., 128.
13. Ibid., 149.
14. Ibid., 164.
15. The author wishes to express his gratitude to the audience at the conference on *Fiction and Morality*, held in Trondheim, Norway in September, 2012. Their comments have improved this chapter, but the remaining errors are all mine.

4 Fault Lines
Deleuze, Cinema, and the Ethical Landscape

Alasdair King

> The link between man and the world has been broken. Henceforth, this link must become an object of belief: it is the impossible which can only be restored within a faith. Belief is no longer addressed to a different or transformed world [. . . .] Only belief in the world can reconnect man to what he sees and hears. The cinema must film, not the world, but belief in this world, our only link.[1]

Recent critical engagements with Gilles Deleuze's two volumes on cinema, *Cinema 1: The Movement-Image* and *Cinema 2: The Time-Image*, first published in France in 1983 and 1985 respectively, have begun to explore the possibility that one of the most significant arguments forwarded by Deleuze in his complex film-philosophical taxonomy of Western cinema concerns the delineation of a 'cinematic ethics.'[2] While D. N. Rodowick argues that Deleuze's 'most provocative comments on ethics[3] appear in his two *Cinema* books, Ronald Bogue suggests that it is in Deleuze's exploration of ethics on screen that the relationship between philosophy and cinema in his writings becomes most intimate.[4] Both argue that Deleuze's specifically immanent understanding of ethics awards a central role to the aesthetic innovations of modern cinema, whose task is to return to us images of belief in this world so that, with the demise of faith in a better future, we believe that we can create new possibilities in the world of the present that we inhabit. While Rodowick and Bogue take care to outline the philosophical implications of the Deleuzian idea of 'belief' in this regard, neither examines closely how belief *in this world* might be traced across modern cinema. It is here that Deleuze's reading of the movement and immobility of bodies in the distinctive screen worlds created in modern cinema allows us to recognize acts of belief and, by extension, the workings of a cinematic ethics. In Deleuze's engagement with this corpus of primarily European films of the post-World War II period, he outlines the complex ways in which the body registers and remodels space and how, as a result, it can restore a link to this world. Here, Deleuze's cinematic ethics is coextensive with the wider sense of ethics as ethology, as the way that bodies register affects and assume modes of existence within a particular landscape or habitat.[5] The idea of the ethical landscape that is depicted in Deleuze's work on the films of the time-image is crucial to a fuller understanding of Deleuze's cinematic ethics, and is a concept that is productive for addressing the ethics of recent cinema. This chapter explores the implications of Deleuze's cinematic ethics through a reading of the ethical landscape encountered in Christian Petzold's recent film, *Wolfsburg* (2003).

1.

While Rodowick and Bogue focus primarily on the ethical implications of the cinema of the time-image, the subject of Deleuze's second *Cinema* book, to set their arguments in context, it is useful to recap the broader, and very different, ethical implications of the cinema of the movement-image. As outlined in *Cinema 1*, for Deleuze, the cinema that emerged in the West in its "classical" period up to the Second World War was composed of "movement-images" of various kinds. The cinema of the movement-image as a whole is characterized by a belief in the efficacy of action, purposeful movement, and human agency. These images of action and reaction—and of problem resolution—suggest, for Deleuze, a belief in the organic unity of the world, in causality, and in the potentially complete representation of the world in the form of images. Particularly in the "large form of the action-image," the cinema of classical Hollywood realism from Griffith to Ford and Kazan—the films of the movement-image form a specifically ethical cinema—concerned with moral judgment, distinguishing good from evil, and acting within the given situation to support the founding of American civilization:

> The ancient or recent past must submit to trial, go to court, in order to disclose what it is that produces decadence and what it is that produces new life [. . . .] A strong ethical judgement must condemn the injustice of 'things,' bring compassion, herald the new civilization on the march, in short, constantly rediscover America.[. . .] The American cinema [. . .] has succeeded in putting forward a strong and coherent conception of universal history, monumental, antiquarian and ethical.[6]

If classical Hollywood cinema utilizes the action-image to propose a teleological vision of history unfolding toward the emergence of a new society, its sense of propulsion is shared by Soviet cinema, despite the latter's ideological hostility to American capitalist democracy. Eisenstein's cinema of dialectical montage adapts Griffith's principles of organic montage to foreground an entire system of social injustice and an alternative endpoint—the emergence of the proletariat. In *Cinema 1*, Deleuze shows how these grand narratives of action and movement toward a world to come in both classical

Hollywood filmmaking and Soviet cinema are different versions of a linked formal enterprise. Both rely on confidence in the efficacy of movement, on a conviction of the achievability of social progress toward a universal end-point, and on the ability of cinema to produce images commensurate with this faith in movement.[7]

However, already present in the cinema of the movement-image are moments of vacillation. These are registered in the "affection-images" that Deleuze distinguishes in the cinema of Dreyer and Bresson, for example, in which protagonists are presented with a series of situations that require them to act in moral ways, conscious or not of the range of choice that confronts them. Whereas other categories of the movement-image are fully identifiable within a situation of causality, of actions and subsequent reactions, these affection-images register "virtual expression of choices yet to be accomplished," taking place in disconnected spaces or in an "any-space-whatever."[8]

These affection-images anticipate the full crisis of the movement-image that Deleuze sees in post-war European cinema. Although adamant that his books outline a taxonomy rather than a history of cinematic images, he locates an immense rupture in human thought around the emergence of European fascism and the horrors of the Second World War that destroyed this confidence in human agency: As Paola Marrati notes, after this point, "we no longer believe in a human becoming of the world."[9] Our confidence in movement and in the meaningfulness of history itself is shattered and the dominant cinema of the movement-image, undermined not least by the aestheticisation of politics under fascism and the exploitation of the action-image under filmmakers such as Leni Riefenstahl, loses its hold as we witness the emergence of a new series of signs and images on screen, the cinema of the time-image. Time emerges on screen in direct forms just as our purposeful movement toward the construction of a new world and our confidence in a universal unfolding of history are shattered: "Time presents itself as such where history fades away."[10] For Deleuze, these time-images constitute a post-traumatic cinema in which belief in the possibility of coherent action and in the complete representability of the world in images is placed into crisis. Deleuze argues that the destruction and geno-cide wrought by the war are marked obliquely in cinema by films that register the inability of their characters to understand situations fully and to react to them purposefully, paralyzed by an accompanying loss of belief in their links to the world itself. The protagonists of the cinema of the time-image find themselves, famously, in environments in which they no longer know how to act or, on occasion, even to move. Deleuze describes this as the breakdown of the sensory-motor regime: The protagonist becomes less an agent and more an observer confronted by pure optical and acoustical images. The act of seeing does not lead directly to action, as it does in the cinema of the movement-image, but to an exploration of the protagonist's location in time and space: seeing as a means of orientation, of finding a link back to the world. In Deleuze's depiction, we experience a new condition on screen, where the protagonist is:

> a seer who finds himself struck by something intolerable in the world, and confronted by something unthinkable in thought. [. . .] For it is not in the name of a better or truer world that thought captures the intolerable in this world but, on the contrary, it is because this world is intolerable that it can no longer think a world or think itself. The intolerable is no longer a serious injustice, but the permanent state of a daily banality. Man *is not himself* a world other than the one in which he experiences the intolerable and feels himself trapped.[11]

The ethical dimension of films that employ (or predominantly rely on) the movement-image, grounded as it was on the establishment of the better world to come, no longer guides human action. Characters are no longer able to perceive their actions as consequential or themselves as fully part of a community. Their links to each other, events, and the world itself are no longer apparent. The aim of an ethical modern cinema, for Deleuze, is to produce images that allow us to rediscover belief in immanence. This is its revolutionary task, to find new ways to register our link to this world, not to imagine a utopian world to come. The key difference between the ethical mode in films of the movement-image and those of the time-image concerns our belief in this world: Cinema no longer participates in the "revolutionary dream of peoples"[12] and we no longer believe in a universal history progressing toward an endpoint. Instead, cinema now opens up numerous possibilities of how we may relate to the world in time—of how we may create new ways of living, outside the chronological linearity and teleology that the historical model implies.

Deleuze's typology of movement-, time-, and affection-images provides the starting point for both Rodowick's and Bogue's analysis. Both locate in the *Cinema* books an ethics of cinema that is identifiable through the registration of an expression of belief in the world and in the potentiality of creation and transformation of the world. Deleuze's cinematic ethics, according to Rodowick, is based on the capacity of film images to restore a belief in the world, defined as a world of potentiality, change, movement and becoming, or in Rodowick's apt Nietzschean phrasing, "the eternal recurrence of difference."[13] Belief in this world is a belief in the myriad possibilities of the immanent, and not in a transcendent or universal redemption: a belief in the possibility of choosing again and again. The cinematic powers of the time-image, in Rodowick's reading, are such that the time-image's capacity to show the powers of the false—the range of possibilities existing beyond the already given—supports a belief in the world itself.

It is crucial for Rodowick's take on Deleuze that the latter's argument departs from a major route in Western philosophy that derives from Descartes and is grounded in skepticism about the knowability of the external world. Instead, Rodowick argues, Deleuze's philosophy takes the road less traveled, building on the work of Spinoza, Nietzsche, and Bergson, and declares, "the fundamental ethical choice is to believe in this world and its powers of transformation."[14] Deleuze's immanent philosophy, derived largely through his reading of Spinoza's doctrine of univocity, denies the existence of any transcendental substance, thought, or world: The fundamental first principle of ethics is to choose to believe in *this* world. Deleuze goes beyond this, however. Deleuze's Spinozan ciné-ethics, an "ethics without morality," downplays traditional ideas in moral philosophy, pertaining to the judgment of actions according to the criteria of transcendent values of good and evil. Instead, Spinoza insists on the ethics of affect, the intensive relations between bodies that result in positive or negative encounters, in joy or in sadness.[15]

Yet in Deleuze's Spinozan ethics, movement, time, and differentiation are still crucial—this world is one that is always in flux, always becoming. Deleuze's second ethical principle, according to Rodowick, derives from Bergson's idea of the continuing metamorphosis of the universe, and also from Nietzsche's emphasis on time as a force of returning, or the eternal recurrence. For Rodowick, Nietzsche's ethical understanding of time and recurrence is central to Deleuze's cinematic ethics, an ethics beyond universal moral rules and transcendent values:

> The ethical choice for Deleuze, then, is whether the powers of change are affirmed and harnessed in ways that value life and its openness to change, or whether we disparage life in *this* world in fealty to moral absolutes. Do we affirm life and remain open to powers of continuous, qualitative self-transformation, or do we maintain an image of thought whose movements are stopped or frozen?[16]

For Bogue, Deleuze's *Cinema* books provide us with philosophy as immanent ethics connected to our ways of seeing. The modern cinema allows us to see differently in order to think differently. Bogue's exploration of Deleuze's cinematic ethics isolates the key ideas of faith and of "choosing to choose" with their antecedents in the transcendent terms of Pascal's wager of God's existence and Kierkegaard's leap of faith. Deleuze focuses on the mode of existence of the one who chooses, finding most noteworthy the mode of one who 'affirm[s] a life of continuous choosing,' thus opening out their being toward an indeterminate number of future possibilities.[17]

What is essential for modern filmmakers in Bogue's reading, is to find new forms of registering belief in this world. For Bogue, following Deleuze, we perceive the world in discrete sets of linked images. The task that modern filmmakers set themselves is to find ways of breaking the conventional sequences of images that underpin our ways of thinking. Through relinking images in new chains, films may disrupt our habitual and clichéd ways of seeing and allow us to open ourselves to possibilities and differences. Bogue focuses on Deleuze's example of Bresson as a director who works with an explicit theme of grace or chance that typically emerges within an ascetic and pared down sensual material world of isolated objects and bodies. Deleuze focuses on Bresson's formal fragmentations, on his counterpointing of sound and image, and on his restructuring of space. It is in Bresson's "cinema of hyperalert sleepwalkers," as Deleuze describes it, that arises, above all, from the filmmaker's handling of nonprofessional actors, where they are subjected to repeated mechanistic rehearsal, that Deleuze sees elements of a new way of thinking in film.[18] These lived bodies on screen, in Bogue's reading of Deleuze, manifest the 'thinker within modern cinematic thought'—the *spiritual automaton*. Bogue reiterates that the cinema is hugely significant to Deleuze's conception of ethics in that it allows new ways of thinking, precisely because it can juxtapose new image-chains and provide us with the capacity to "think [. . .] differently by seeing differently."[19] As Bogue concludes,

> Thinking differently entails choosing to choose, adopting a way of living that allows a belief in the world's "possibilities in movements and intensities to give birth once again to new modes of existence."[20]

Bogue's contextualization of Deleuze's reading of Bresson emphasizes the centrality of the mode of existence of choosing to choose to the reforging of links to the world. Bresson's use of bodies and fractured spaces helps to outline how Deleuze's ciné-ethics is grounded on seeing differently as a precursor to thinking differently, and with this comes the possibility of a reconstituted belief in this world. However, this issue is explored more fully in the examples of post-Bressonian cinema outlined in *Cinema 2* and not covered by either Bogue or Rodowick. If, as Marrati suggests, Bresson's films offer "fragmented spaces" that construct a cinema that "films time as open and as a dimension of spirit,"[21] then it is in the emergence of films of the time-image that Deleuze explores further the ethical landscapes constructed by directors working in Bresson's wake.

It is through the body, Deleuze argues more fully in *Cinema 2*, that we may come to learn what it means to live in this world. Borrowing from Spinoza the dictum, "we do not even know what a body can do,"[22] Deleuze claims that the presentation of the body is the means through which modern cinema may rethink the world and isolate the "unthought in thought." For Deleuze, the body is essential to formulating the operations of the time-image. The body registers time and the layerings of time:

> "Give me a body then" is first to mount the camera on an everyday body. The body is never in the present, it contains the before and after, tiredness and waiting. Tiredness and waiting, even despair are the attitudes of the body.[23]

For Deleuze, the registration of temporal effects on the body, and indeed of the body in time, can have political implications. In the images on screen and in the links between images, Deleuze infers vanished bodies in some cases and in others exhaustion and atomization; above all, the "people are missing."[24] Yet the body is not just within time: Deleuze's cinematic ethics initiates an understanding of how the body registers affects within a particular landscape and how it can restore a link to this world through its ethological encounter with the spaces of the screen world.

It is important to note that the world that the Deleuzian cinematic ethics conceives is spatially complex. In the *Cinema* books, Deleuze borrows the mathematical term *topology* to explore the complex ways that cinema creates space and constitutes different layerings of time within that onscreen space.[25] In contrast to geometry, which categorizes spatial properties in quantitative dimensional terms, topology explores the qualitative consistencies and continuities in spaces under differing conditions of manipulation and deformation. As Arkady Plotnitsky has argued, Deleuze's work can "be seen as a kind of topo-philosophy."[26] In the *Cinema* books, Deleuze's concepts of screen topology owe a substantial debt to his encounters with Leibniz and Bergson, as well as to the mathematical concepts of space developed by Riemann. The ethical landscape of modern cinema, as conceived by Deleuze, should be understood along the lines proposed by Riemann as specifically non-Euclidean and shaped by the emergence of layers of time and duration in the image. For Deleuze, in the cinema of the time-image, "the image no longer has space and movement as its primary characteristics but topology and time."[27] The Deleuzian screen topology that appears at the heart of the ciné-ethics of the modern cinema is constituted by the mode of existence of the body within a landscape that is no longer meaningful in terms of either its abstract geometric properties or in terms of the mental mapping, physical actions, or reactions of the protagonists, whose movements within its parameters are now curtailed. These landscapes might be composed of disconnected spaces, disturbingly empty, unrecognizable, or even hallucinatory. In all these cases, the sensory-motor schema has broken down and space assumes non-Euclidean forms.[28] Deleuze argues that modern cinema, from Antonioni, Godard, and Cassavetes through to the post-*nouvelle vague* directors in France, has produced a mapping of postures and attitudes of the body in such fractured landscapes. As Deleuze notes, modern cinema often foregrounds the use of maps and diagrams as specific objects that function to draw attention to the habitat to which the protagonist has to adapt. Yet these cartographies are often limited if read purely as representations of geometric space. On the one hand, for Deleuze, these artifacts register additionally a being in time as well as in space:

> Each map is in this sense a mental continuum, that is, a sheet of past which makes a distribution of functions correspond to a distribution of objects.[29]

On the other, the precise mapping of space in terms of location and distance underplays the complexities of modern cinema's constitution of screen worlds. Belief in this world requires the reforging of a link to the landscape constructed on screen, as even in its most fragmented forms it points to the constitution of a wider world around it: "The cinema does not just present images, it surrounds them with a world."[30]

Drawing directly on the work of the second-generation French *nouvelle vague* directors, a corpus that he proposes shares "the unity of a category" across a number of directors and narratives, Deleuze picks out elements of a shared "cinema of the body."[31] Deleuze proposes that Philippe Garrel, particularly, acutely constructs space as it is attached to the bodies of his key characters. For Deleuze, Garrel offers:

> . . . the first case of a cinema of constitution, one which is truly consti-tutive: constituting bodies, and in this way restoring our belief in the world, restoring our reason. . . . It is doubtful if cinema is sufficient for this: but, if the world has become a bad cinema, in which we no longer believe, surely a true cinema can contribute to giving us back reasons to believe in the world and in vanished bodies?[32]

Garrel's value lies in his ability to construct a topology of the screen world through precise camera positions and movements that offer "formal link-ages" to the postures of bodies. In Garrel's films, there is a "construction of space as this is attached to bodies."[33] Deleuze argues,

> the problem is *not* that of a presence of bodies, but that of a belief which is capable of restoring the world and the body to us on the basis of what signifies their absence.[34]

Deleuze specifically contrasts this cinema of the body, with the action-image produced in films dominated by the movement-image. He draws on the work of German-American psychologist, Kurt Lewin, whose concept of "hodological" space refers to the mental representation of space encoun-tered by goal-driven persons and forms a dynamic way of mapping the film world, coextensive with the distances and parameters mapped out by Euclidean geometries of space. Using Lewin's terminology, Deleuze argues that the functioning sensory-motor schema, and by extension the overall mode of the movement-image, is situated within hodological space.[35] If Euclidean space is characterized by its linearity and measurability, and by its susceptibility to geometric ordering, then hodological space is this abstract mapping made concrete by a psychological conception of such space bor-dered, framed, and inflected by the mental states and dispositions of the protagonist. Hodological space underpins movement across the frame in films of the action-image. For Deleuze, however, the cinema of the time-image focuses on the operations of a character unable to determine space in hodological terms. From the perspective of the seer, the person for whom the sensory-motor schema has been disrupted,

[s]ensory-motor situations have given way to pure optical and sound situations to which characters, who have become seers, cannot or will not react, so great is their need to 'see' properly what there is in their situation. [. . .] Thus movement can tend to zero, the character, or the shot itself, remain immobile [. . .] But this is not what is important, because movement may also be exaggerated, be incessant, become a world movement, a Brownian movement, a trampling, a to-and-fro, a multiplicity of movements on different scales. What is important is that the anomalies of movement become the essential point instead of being accidental or contingent. This is the era of false continuity shots as [. . .] crystalline narration will fracture the complementarity of a lived hodological space and a represented Euclidean space. [. . .] It is here that a crystalline narration will extend crystalline descriptions, their repetitions and variations, through a crisis of action. But, at the same time as concrete space ceases to be hodological, abstract space ceases to be Euclidean.[36]

Given that Lewin's hodological space can be equated with conscious and planned movement across measurable Euclidean space, it is also linked with the ability to judge action in moral terms deemed by Deleuze to be central to the ethics of movement-image cinema. In the cinema of the time-image, which seeks to create new links to this world, the space before action, or "pre-hodological space," takes on significance. This pre-hodological space becomes central to the cinema of the body, and for Deleuze, a basis for thinking through his ciné-ethics. The body's inability to move decisively within this non-Euclidean space is not down to a kind of hesitation before forking paths but to "a mobile covering-up of sets which are incompatible, almost alike and yet disparate."[37] In the presentation of the body in this pre-hodological space, Deleuze implies that modern cinema reaches a point at which it can reconstitute a belief in this world.

In his analysis of the films of Jacques Doillon, whose corpus extends the work of other post-new wave directors, Deleuze identifies the way that time-image cinema registers the movement of bodies caught in this pre-hodological space. He argues that Doillon places his characters in a specific milieu in which their bodies are traversed in terms of affects and intensities by "two groupings, two modes of life, two sets demanding different attitudes."[38] In this, Deleuze argues, Doillon explores an ambiguous 'space of the non-choice," distinct from the moral choice typically faced by the Bressonian character, in which bodies no longer move purposefully, not because of psychological indecisiveness but because of an inability to discern exactly how to move. The character in Doillon "inhabits his body like a zone of indiscernibility."[39] In relation to Doillon, Deleuze argues,

the obstacle does not, as in the action-image, allow itself to be determined in relation to goals and means which would unify the set, but is dispersed in 'a plurality of ways of being present in the world,' of belonging to sets, all incompatible and yet coexistent.[40]

Doillon's strength, according to Deleuze, is "to have made this pre-hodological space, this space of overlappings, the special object of a cinema of bodies" that can be contrasted with the action-image seen in earlier cinema, with its goal-setting and dynamic movement within a hodological space:

> But the body is initially caught in a quite different space, where dispa-
> rate sets overlap and rival each other, without being able to organize
> themselves according to sensory-motor schemata. They fit over each
> other, in an overlapping of perspectives which means that there is no
> way to distinguish them even though they are distinct and also incom-
> patible. This is space before action, always haunted by a child, or by a
> clown, or by both at once. It is a pre-hodological space, like a *fluctuatio*
> *animi* which does not point to an indecision of the spirit, but to an
> undecidability of the body.[41]

In films such as *Les doigts dans la tête* (1974) and *La Drôlesse* (1978) Doil-lon creates isolated spaces, closely linked to but out of step with the everyday world, where the protagonists adapt to new modes of existence through sta-sis and disrupted movement within these newly constructed milieus. In their changed modes of existence, they suggest a belief in reforging a link with this world, which provides the basis for an ethics of cinema.

2.

Although Deleuze doesn't offer further examples of how the body can reconstitute the link to this world, his cinematic ethics can be useful in considering the ethical import of recent films. The films of the Berlin School that emerged in Germany from the late 1990s as a counterweight to the mainstream success of German comedies and heritage films, arguably, rely typically on an intense and destabilizing focus on marginalized characters in contemporary provincial landscapes. One of the leading directors asso-ciated with the Berlin School, Christian Petzold, produces an ethology of protagonists forced to adapt to specific and carefully chosen environments primarily situated in the German provinces. In contrast to the traditional backdrops for German films, such as Munich, Hamburg, and Berlin, Pet-zold prefers to constitute his ethical landscapes in the politically decentered and previously unfilmed location, rendered not in a wholly naturalistic fashion. His films are particularly constructionist, in that he utilizes the echoes of scenes from a range of Hollywood and European cinema as well as from paintings, and constitutes but not directly represents, contempo-rary Germany.[42]

Petzold's films screen a series of ethical landscapes that allow the audience to reflect on modes of behavior and living appropriate to changing economic and social conditions. Like his Berlin School associates, Petzold offers a cinema that registers the ways in which characters reforge links to this world, primarily through the stasis and movement of their bodies in and across particular spaces. Petzold's is a cinema of ghosts and of the living. As with that of Doillon and of the other post-*nouvelle vague* directors who constitute a key influence, it is a cinema of vanished and reawakened bodies. The lived experience of the "hyperalert sleepwalkers," to use Bogue's depiction of Bresson's cinema, constitutes the world of Petzold's central characters. Their mode of movement and labor under contemporary capitalism is suddenly halted by a traumatic event—a rupture or the emergence of the "unthought in thought," where they are confronted with an alternative set, a virtual or not yet fully formed, mode of existence. The early catastrophic event shows up a series of lines or fracture in the mode of existence that had previously characterized the protagonist. It is in the aftermath of the event, in the post-traumatic duration that follows, that the bodies of Petzold's characters register these fault lines as affects, and attempt to find new links to the world via working through two sets of alternatives. From a position of comparative safety and security in the contemporary world, Petzold's protagonists become quasi-foreign bodies in their landscape.[43] In films from *The State I'm In* (2000), with its focus on the opaque legacy of the Federal Republic's generation of violent political activists, to *Yella* (2007), the study of the impact of the rules of engagement underpinning contemporary venture capitalism, Petzold creates recognizable screen worlds that challenge the detached and near-spectral modes of existence of his key characters.

For Deleuze, the complexity of the landscape in the cinema of the time-image is found in that the space constituted correlates to the construction of a specific world in thought and in time:

> Landscapes are mental states, just as mental states are cartographies, both crystallized in each other, geometrized, mineralized.[44]

In Deleuze's example, for Resnais, it is always Auschwitz and Hiroshima that frame his screen worlds. In contrast, for Petzold it is always the economic settlement in the Federal Republic of Germany. Petzold uses landscape to engage with a dissection of the present moment and also with its stratified underpinning from Germany's traumatic history. His films present the disalignment of his characters with contemporary force fields and their subsequent attempts to regain a place in the social world. These conflicts are Petzold's pathway into making films that do not attempt to moralize the dilemmas faced by his protagonists, but which are ethical in Deleuze's sense in that they disclose the need to regain belief in this world.

In *Wolfsburg,* screened in the Panorama section at the 2003 Berlinale, the car sales executive Phillip is initially shown in a serene long shot, driving along a muted, flat rural landscape in a rare NSU sports car. Phillip's calm existence is disturbed by a phone call from his angry partner, Katja. A row ensues and, as Phillip attempts to pick up his fallen mobile phone, he is momentarily distracted from the empty road ahead. At a curve his car hits a young cyclist. Shocked, Phillip immediately stops the car and, without leaving the car, looks back at the scene. He hesitates at first, but decides to drive on without helping the child lying at the side of the road. Struggling to make sense of his actions, he traces the child to a local hospital and initiates contact with Laura, the child's distraught mother. Unable to articulate his guilt to either Katja or Laura, he broods on the accident. Relieved by the fact that the child is making a good recovery, he goes on holiday to Cuba with Katja in an effort to restore their relationship and to recover his equilibrium. On returning to Wolfsburg after what appears to have been a successful trip, he realizes with horror that in his absence the child has died. In the meantime, Laura has set out to hunt down the hit-and-run driver, using a map of the area and searching for accident-damaged vehicles. Philipp's world begins to unravel: he drives around aimlessly at night, on one occasion encountering Laura, who attempts suicide by jumping off a bridge into the canal. Phillip rescues her and begins to care for her. His relationship with Katja founders again. He is thrown out of their shared bungalow, and subsequently sacked from the car dealership run by her brother. As Phillip gets closer to Laura, she begins to piece together the events surrounding the fatal accident.

In an echo of the cinema of Doillon, a child haunts Petzold's film. The death or suffering of a child has occupied a significant strategic place in European art cinema from Italian neorealism onward.[45] The "missing child," as Emma Wilson notes, assumes many contemporary cinematic forms and marks something beyond the end of innocence or nostalgia for lost childhood. The fractured cinematic explorations of loss, mourning, and survival triggered by such an event drive numerous contemporary narratives, wherein this structuring absence or vanished body is "increasingly the lost object of desire, origin and vanishing point."[46] For Wilson, the central concern of filmmakers has been often to use the missing child as a signifier of "a limit or absolute in ethical thinking."[47] Petzold's film uses the death of the child, about whom we learn very little, to set up a revenge narrative steered by way of Laura's eliminative cartography of the distinct work and residential zones of Wolfsburg, like Eindhoven in the Netherlands and Zlin in the Czech Republic, a planned company town. Yet the film concerns itself ultimately less with action and movement through space, or with the overcoming of obstacles necessary to achieve the goal of retribution, but more with the undecidability of the body of Phillip as he considers modes of reparation. At stake in using the missing child as the catalytic event here is the lack of care for the vulnerable other generally, but specifically also a sense of responsibility to temporal others, future generations, and our legacies on Phillip's part. In this sense, the missing child is not just an event *in* time; it is also, and significantly, an event *of* time.

This haunting by a child, which has antecedents directly in Chabrol's *Que la bête meure* (1969) and obliquely in Almodovar's *All About My Mother* (1999) and Cassavetes's *Opening Night* (1978), opens up a space where the two competing sets or modes of existence within which Phillip is caught, start to operate. The accident stops movement, literally. Phillip is unable to perform the chain of actions typical of movement-image films: to perceive, to register affect, and then to act. The accident lays bare the deficiencies of the mode of existence adopted by Phillip to make his way in German society, causing quite explicitly a momentary paralysis and an attempt at taking stock through looking.

How to think differently by seeing differently? Phillip fails to be equal to the event that has just occurred. The argument with Katja, made explicit in a beautifully constructed dialogue, concerns quite specifically Phillip's incapacity to see properly, even to the point of remaining unaware of the presence of another in the room. Here he is able only to look at the boy before driving away, unable to fully believe in the world before him either as an image in his car mirror or as an event directly in front of him. Perception is at the heart of this dilemma of a lack of belief. As Deleuze argues, we experience ourselves in the world as if we are displaced and watching, in detached fashion, movements on a screen:

> We no longer even believe in the events that happen to us, love or death, as if they only half concerned us. We do not make cinema; rather, the world looks to us like a bad film.[48]

Phillip's development in *Wolfsburg* will be to see the world anew and to reforge a link to it, to believe in it again. Phillip's route to becoming human and to believing in this world necessitates him leaving the constraining and isolating regime constituted by the spaces and places of his bourgeois mode of existence in Wolfsburg: designer bungalow, luxurious showroom, and car interiors. Deleuze's description of the "mystery of this begun-again present" in Bresson's films is apt here.[49] For Phillip, the accident is a chance to learn, literally, to see people again, with the act of seeing related to the spatial constitution of the landscape.

At the beginning of the film, the long-take of Philip's car framed in long shot holds the viewer at a distance and prevents him or her from seeing the world fully from Phillip's perspective. This objective mode is interrupted momentarily at the point of the accident, where a subjective POV shot is used from Phillip's position inside the car, first as he struggles to pick up the mobile phone, and then again after the collision when he looks through the rear car window at the child's prone figure. Phillip's car is framed from a low angle, aligned with the child's perspective. These shots apart, there is limited use of situated subjective framings; they occur principally at key narrative moments, such as Laura's discovery of the FO-RD number plate that reveals Phillip's identity. Petzold uses abrupt cuts that blur subjective and objective modes, typical of the free indirect discourse central to the cinema of the time-image.[50] As Phillip's car drives away after the accident, from the long shot of the road with the chimneys of the VW works on the horizon the camera cuts directly to CCTV images of Laura at work in the supermarket, seemingly captured in the act of stealing frozen lobsters. Laura glances at the camera, indicating her awareness of the CCTV surveillance.[51] Yet Petzold refuses to cut to someone monitoring these CCTV images. This is not the subjective shot it could have been, but an unmotivated shot without any specific character's perspective that allows us an insight into Laura's regimented mode of existence. This refusal to utilize subjective shots or conventional shot-reverse shot for much of the film, reduces the likelihood of character alignment on our part. Such style emphasizes the fact that the film neither makes a moral proposition about the goodness of a specific character nor invites us to offer parallel judgment accordingly. Instead, the blurring of the subjective and the objective allows us to be aware of the complexity of human behavior in this landscape and to see how certain forms of behavior cause comfort and pain to others.[52]

As I shall discuss below, Phillip's erratic movements after the accident and his slow awakening to the ethical demands of the world around him are modes of behavior that can be placed in a longer tradition of filmmaking in Germany. For Deleuze, German cinema in the wake of National Socialism has produced a specific inflection of the time-image—one he characterizes as the narrative of the "false movement." This occurs,

> as a result of the war, in the constantly variable link between these elements: spaces reduced to their own descriptions (city-deserts or places which are constantly being destroyed), direct presentations of an oppressive, useless and unsummonable time which haunt the characters; and from one pole to the other, the powers of the false which weave a narration, in so far as they take effect in "false movements."[53]

Like his rehearsed confession that is never delivered, Phillip's distracted meanderings around the peripheral roads of Wolfsburg at night, his repeated visits to the site of the accident, and even his unsuccessful trip to Cuba, constitute a series of false movements of this kind, as he attempts to move on, literally, from the accident yet cannot. His body is traversed by two disparate and irreconcilable sets—two possible modes of behavior corresponding to the before-state to which he attempts to return and an aftermath, a mode of existence in which Phillip will become human and recognize his links to the world. At ease initially only in his car and in the bland, affluent glass and chrome spaces of his bungalow and car dealership, his movement is severely limited, with his body frequently immobile or frozen. His upward mobility in his career, starting as a mechanic before reaching his current position as a sales executive, is registered in his postures: His attitude as perceptive salesman and unseeing husband, as well as his increasing tiredness and stupefied state at home and work, follow the line established, for Deleuze, by Cassavetes, who reduces the character to "his own bodily attitudes."[54] After the accident, his body is characterized by a slight trembling while driving, and by moments of stasis in the spaces familiar to him.[55] When Phillip returns to his bungalow, he is filmed entering the hallway but placed behind a frosted glass screen, rendering his body opaque, as if he becomes a ghost in his own home. The undecidability of the body encountered by Phillip, caught between the two modes of existence, appears set for resolution: In his acts of care toward Laura he is able to physically move again, evidence for his reforged link with the world based on responsibility *for* another.[56] Yet with the open declaration of his role in the child's death never forthcoming, ultimately he is never responsible for the child's death *before* Laura, and it is through an act against his body that reparation is finally made and Laura's retribution is actioned.

Phillip further embodies a metonymic status, representative of Germany's economic renaissance, thriving on the material foundations constructed by National Socialism. Petzold's film refuses to thematize the legacy of German history explicitly. Instead, the weight of the past on the present is filmed through the use of the offscreen space implied adjacent to the frame. The screen world that Petzold constructs extends offscreen in a spatial dimension—the city landscape just over the frame's horizon—and also a temporal one. Deleuze sees the decaying time-image constructed in Visconti's films as "history growls at the door." That is, the historical context that layers the constitution of time and space in the screen world is never represented directly in the frame but present as the out-of-field, its affects registered on the modes of existence enacted by the protagonists.[57] Petzold's deliberate choice of setting and the precisely framed landscapes in *Wolfsburg* allude to more than the narrative of a singular case of becoming human. The eponymous city of Wolfsburg fits Petzold's cinematic provincialism yet it is also at the heart of the contemporary Federal Republic. Its centrality to the German economy and to current employment practices must be stressed. Likewise, it holds a distinctive place in German economic history: a new industrial town developed under National Socialism around the enormous Volkswagen industrial works.[58] *Wolfsburg* remains outside the frame—the dominant VW complex and any mention of the city's specific history. These concerns are registered only obliquely, as the film deliberately frames movement and encounters on the edge of the city, the familiar industrial chimneys of the VW works just visible in some shots on the horizon. Phillip's rescue of Laura from the water is an apt linking of film aesthetics with wider forces of political history. On one level, such a rescue pays clear homage to the celebrated scene in the San Francisco Bay from Hitchcock's *Vertigo;* on another, the suicidal jump is made here into the Mittelland Canal, the transport route that specifically divides the city into its distinct zones, and which was the key landscape feature that encouraged the Nazis to plan urban expansion there. Phillip's active intervention at this point constitutes the belief in this world that was so lacking after the initial accident. Phillip is even asked later if his kind acts toward Laura constitute his own *"Vergangenheitsbewältigung."* (coming to terms with the past). The trauma of Germany's emergence into modernity is registered as the film's out-of-field, the legacy of which is carried on in part in Phillip's inability to respond appropriately to the accident that he causes. In this way, the ethical reckoning in *Wolfsburg* also carries with it subtle echoes of Germany's reflective discourse on its relationship to its brutal national past. Although the film makes no direct connections to German history, the location and the themes of penance and atonement, and of coming to terms with the past, are inescapably linked to long-standing debates on the moral history of Germany. If the film is treated in part as an analogy for Germany's postwar history and its processes of reparation, Phillip's attempts at becoming human allude to a possible belief in *this* world for Germany itself.

While Phillip's attempt at reparation proves ultimately misguided without his confession, he finds in his care for Laura the possibility of reforging a link to the world and creating new forms of life. His ability to look out for and to *see* Laura and his ability to break through his paralysis in his acts of care, demonstrate an awakening belief in this world. This is brought about by the traumatic event at the film's beginning that shows the intolerability of the mode of existence that he had adopted. The film climaxes with Phillip's punishment, he lies prone and gravely wounded at the roadside in the position of the child at the start of the film. The ending returns to the conventions of the revenge narrative with its basis in processes of movement: eliminating clues, pursuing the culprit, and exacting retribution. It opens up the possibility of an assessment of the moral value of such an act of revenge; yet the film is hardly concerned with the need for the restitution of a transcendent moral order. Phillip's transgression in driving away from the scene of the original accident does not diminish the centrality of his subsequent ethical awakening and his reforged links to the world. In his late volume, *Negotiations,* Deleuze writes:

> What we most lack is a belief in the world, we've quite lost the world, it's been taken from us. If you believe in the world you precipitate events, however inconspicuous, that elude control, you engender new space-times, however small their surface or volume.[59]

In Phillip's turning toward an immanent ethics of responsibility for (if not before) the other and a process of reparation or *"Wiedergutmachung,"* *Wolfsburg* explores the birth of an immanent ethics in contrast to the prevailing universal morality established under German capitalism in the postwar period. Petzold's film constructs a recognizable German landscape and shows the possibility of a reforged link to the world despite the prevailing social forces generated by Germany's troubled history and its adoption of potentially dehumanizing economic practices. In its constitution of Phillip's screen world, it shows the fault lines and moments of stasis generated by the incompatibility of alternate sets picked out by Deleuze as a basis for recognizing modern cinema as potentially ethical. For Deleuze, the task for an ethical modern cinema is to film a restored belief in the world. In Phillip's awakening within this contemporary German landscape there is the possibility of thinking differently by seeing differently; of acting differently and of reforging links to this world.

NOTES

1. Gilles Deleuze, *Cinema 2: The Time-Image,* trans. Hugh Tomlinson and Robert Galeta (London and New York: Continuum, 2005), 166.
2. D. N. Rodowick, "The World, Time" and Ronald Bogue, "To Choose to Choose—to Believe in This World," in *Afterimages of Gilles Deleuze's Film Philosophy*, ed. D.N. Rodowick (Minneapolis and London: University of Minnesota Press, 2010), 97–114 and 115–132, respectively.
3. Rodowick, "The World, Time," 98.
4. Bogue, "To Choose to Choose," 115.
5. For an outline of Deleuze's linking of ethics to ethology, see Anthony Uhlman, "Deleuze, Ethics, Ethology, and Art," in *Deleuze and Ethics,* ed. Nathan Jun and Daniel W. Smith (Edinburgh: Edinburgh University Press, 2011), 154–170.
6. Gilles Deleuze, *Cinema 1: The Movement-Image,* trans. Hugh Tomlinson and Barbara Habberjam (London and New York: Continuum, 2005), 155. See also Richard Rushton, *Cinema After Deleuze* (London and New York: Continuum, 2012), 32–40.
7. See Paola Marrati, *Gilles Deleuze: Cinema and Philosophy,* trans. Alisa Hartz (Baltimore: Johns Hopkins University Press, 2008), 99–102.
8. Rodowick, "The World, Time," 104.
9. Marrati, *Gilles Deleuze*, 63.
10. Ibid., 65.
11. Deleuze, *Cinema 2,* 164.
12. Marrati, *Gilles Deleuze,* 79.
13. Rodowick, "The World, Time," 112.
14. Ibid., 99.
15. See Patricia Pisters, *The Matrix of Visual Culture* (Stanford: Stanford University Press, 2003), 85–86.
16. Rodowick, "The World, Time," 101.
17. Bogue, "To Choose to Choose," 121.
18. Ibid., 125.
19. Ibid.,127.
20. Ibid., 129. Here Bogue is quoting from Deleuze and Guattari, *What is Philosophy?*, trans. Hugh Tomlinson and Graham Burchill (London and New York: Verso, 1994), 74.
21. Marrati, *Gilles Deleuze,* 123, fn. 23.
22. Deleuze, *Cinema 2,* 182.
23. Ibid.
24. See Pisters, *The Matrix of Visual Culture,* 90–91.

25. For an extended discussion of the use of 'topology' in Deleuze's *Cinema* books, see Felicity Colman, "Topology," in *Deleuze and Cinema: The Film Concepts* (Oxford and New York: Berg, 2011), 163–178.

26. Arkady Plotnitsky, "Manifolds: on the concept of space in Riemann and Deleuze," in *Virtual Mathematics: The Logic of Difference,* ed. Simon Duffy (Bolton: Clinamen Press, 2006), 187–208, here 190.

27. Deleuze, *Cinema 2,* 121.

28. Ibid., 125.

29. Ibid., 117.

30. Ibid., 66.

31. Ibid., 190–191.

32. Ibid., 193.

33. Ibid., 194–195.

34. Ibid., 194.

35. Ibid., 124.

36. Ibid., 124–125.

37. Ibid., 125 and 196. Deleuze footnotes this notion of 'pre-hodological' space as a concept taken from Gilbert Simondon's *L'individu et sa genese physico-biologique* (Paris: PUF, 1964), 233–234.

38. Deleuze, *Cinema 2,* 195.

39. Ibid.

40. Ibid., 196.

41. Ibid., 195–196.

42. See also Marco Abel, "Imaging Germany: The (Political) Cinema of Christian Petzold," in *The Collapse of the Conventional: German Film and Its Politics at the Turn of the Twenty-First Century,* ed. Jaimey Fisher and Brad Prager (Detroit: Wayne State University Press, 2010), 277.

43. See Petzold's comment, "Das Leben beginnt schon, ihn auszuscheiden," in Stefan Reinecke "Das Kino als Versuchsanordnung. Ein Werkstattgespräch mit dem Regisseur Christian Petzold." *epd-film,* October 2, 2003), accessed July 13, 2011, http://www.filmportal.de/node/263489/material/1020977.

44. Deleuze, *Cinema 2,* 199.

45. See Vicky Lebeau, *Childhood and Cinema* (London: Reaktion, 2008), especially 146–149.

46. Emma Wilson, *Cinema's Missing Children* (London: Wallflower Press, 2003), 15.

47. Ibid., 157.

48. Ibid., 166.

49. Deleuze, *Cinema 1,* 111.

50. Deleuze, *Cinema 2,* 181. See also Rushton, *Cinema After Deleuze,* 111–113.

51. Harun Farocki, who worked as a consultant on Petzold's film, has used this technique similarly in his essay films. See Georges Didi-Huberman, "How to Open Your Eyes," and Thomas Elsaesser, "Holocaust Memory as the Epistemology of Forgetting? Re-wind and Postponement in *Respite,*" in *Harun Farocki: Against What? Against Whom?,* ed. Antje Ehmann and Kodwo Eshun (Cologne: Walter König, 2009), 39–50 and 58–68, respectively.

52. Pisters, *The Matrix of Visual Culture,* 86–87.

53. Ibid., 131–132.

54. Deleuze, *Cinema 2,* 185.

55. Petzold frequently notes the attention paid in rehearsals to the movement and postures of his cast as they learn their roles. See, for example, the interview with Claudia Lennsen, "'Diese typische BRD-Generation' Interview mit

Christian Petzold," *Taz*, February 13, 2003), accessed July 13, 2011, http://www.taz.de/1/archiv/archiv/?dig=2003/02/13/a0182.

56. On responsibility for, and responsibility before, see Erinn Cunniff Gilson, "Responsive Becoming: Ethics between Deleuze and Feminism," in *Deleuze and Ethics,* ed. Nathan Jun and Daniel W. Smith (Edinburgh: Edinburgh University Press, 2011), 63–88, here especially 79.

57. Deleuze, *Cinema 2,* 92.

58. The city and its specific history is very familiar to Petzold, who worked there as an assistant director on Hartmut Bitomsky's acclaimed essay film, *Der VW-Komplex* (1989).

59. Gilles Deleuze, "Control and Becoming," in *Negotiations 1972–1990*, trans. Martin Joughin (New York: Columbia University Press, 1995), 176.

Part II

Documentary and the Ethical

5 The Ethics of Contemplation
Kim Ki-duk's *Arirang*

Jinhee Choi

An ethical turn in contemporary film studies and theory has redirected attention from the rational and universal to the emotional and particular as grounds for assessing the ethical value of the film medium. Through its affective and sensorial engagement with the spectator, film can become a site to forge an ethical relationship between the self and the world, as well as the self and others. Kim Ki-duk, the provocateur from South Korea, has never failed to entice the spectator with his "corporeal exclamation point,"[1] startling the world film scene with his films of extreme cruelty, often set against scenic, serene beauty. For three years (2008–2011), however, Kim withdrew himself from the film industry and his overall community. It is claimed that one of his principal reasons for doing so comes from his inability to trust—his feelings of betrayal toward—his film crew, some of whom have turned to more "commercial" filmmaking rather than continuing the hard-edged cinematic style for which Kim has been known.

Arirang (2011) is a documentary directed and performed by Kim himself, recording his hiatus as he leads a solitary life, meeting his everyday needs at only a minimum, basic level. More importantly, the film is a contemplation on the ethical consequences of his previous filmmaking, exploring such issues as the physical risk involved in filmmaking and the moral implications of acting and performance. In this chapter, I focus on Kim's representation of his solitary life as well as his philosophical contemplations of his filmmaking. Drawing on Aristotle's philosophy, Martha Nussbaum once noted that contemplation is an ethical goal.[2] However, for Nussbaum, ethical contemplation is not just to achieve "individual clarification and self-understanding" but to "move toward communal attunement."[3] Kim's *Arirang*, I argue, fails to achieve such attunement. The making of *Arirang* may have helped Kim to resuscitate his desire toward filmmaking, but it remains as a means of self-fashioning and evinces an inability to embrace the vulnerability inherent in both the self and one's relationship with the other.

1. SOLITUDE

A solitary life led by Kim in *Arirang* is selectively modern. His hut is not too far from a small village. Inside his tent, which is set up within the hut, we see a computer monitor, through which his imaginary others conduct interviews with Kim. When Kim chops wood, he does so with an electric saw. Kim even operates a crane himself when he digs into the ground, the reason of which remains unclear. When he makes rice, he lets an electric cooker do the job for him—and of course, there is an elaborate espresso machine that he builds. Yet inside his hut, he has a bare minimum of furniture and household items. On a couple of shelves mounted to the walls, ripe bell-shaped persimmons are orderly placed. He has an old-style stove, on which he occasionally boils water, and with which he sometimes broils fish or chestnuts.

Kim's solitude is a form of waiting as well as a self-imposed exile. It is waiting for self-reconciliation and social acceptance. After we witness the daily routines that preoccupy Kim, we see him enter his tent to sleep. He hears knocks on the door. Kim unzips the tent, walks toward the door, and finds no one outside the hut. Another set of knocks is heard. Again, no one is there. Instead of returning to the inside of the tent, Kim sits by the stove and waits for knocks on the door to be heard possibly for the third time. The knocks are repeated. Kim looks off screen to the direction of the door. Unlike in the two earlier instances, where the camera awaits Kim's opening the door, the camera cuts to show the cracked heels of Kim in close-up, who is outside the hut and starts just another day. This invisible visit marks the end of Kim's "first day" that we have just observed.

Throughout the film, we see not only the repetition of Kim's daily routines, such as eating, drinking, and defecating but also temporal progression. The weather seems to become severe and harsher, as the yard outside the hut is covered with snow. Kim's hide-and-seek with himself is repeated three-quarters into the film, signaling the end of his lamentation and solitude. Unlike the previous invisible visit, where the knocks at the door awaken Kim, the visit takes place during the daytime, shortly after his morning routines. However, it does not fail to lure Kim. Kim exits his tent with no luck of spotting any visitor outside. Left on the snow are some animal footprints and the traces of Kim's short walk to the yard in the morning. The "day" ends with Kim's uncontrollable weeping, while watching the winter sequence from his own film *Spring, Summer, Fall, Winter . . . and Spring* (2003, *Spring Summer* hereafter)—his international breakthrough.

Eric Kohn views the strange knocks as a metaphor for Kim's "lingering need for confession."[4] Could Kim's tent be considered a confession room, where he talks to a religious figure? Possibly. Regardless, imagery of islands, both literal and figurative, is prevalent in Kim's films, from the fishing huts in *The Isle* (2000), to the floating temple in the middle of a lake in *Spring Summer*, to the boat in *The Bow* (2005) and the prison in *Breath* (2007) to list a few. *Arirang* adds another form of island/isolation to this list—the tent inside the house. Kim resembles his protagonists, who withdraw themselves from, yet want to reach out to, the world, however unsuccessful their attempts may be. Protagonists often receive an unexpected visit, which disturbs their lives through developing an intense, often sexual, relationship (*The Isle, Spring Summer,* and *Breath*) with a visitor. Kim in *Arirang* appears to wait for such a mysterious visitor, who may lift from his chest the weight of moral conscience and reignite his passion for filmmaking.

A parallel between *Spring Summer* and *Arirang* is striking, not only due to occasional aesthetic affinities in terms of the setting, motifs, and framing, but also due to their respective circumstances. In *Arirang*, Kim watches his own performance of playing an elder monk—the protagonist in the winter sequence of *Spring Summer.* As a form of penance, the monk has a large stone attached to his waist and ascends the snowy mountain, while carrying in his arms a small sitting Buddha statue. The monk's penance in *Spring Summer* is triggered by the death of a woman, for which he feels responsible. A mysterious woman, whose face is covered with purple scarf, brings a baby boy to the temple and abandons him, hoping that the monk will raise the boy. As she flees in the middle of the night, she accidentally falls into a hole dug by the monk in the frozen lake and dies.

The monk's solitary life in the film resembles Kim's current status: a guilt-ridden hiatus, which is in part attributed to the near death of actress Lee Na-yeong during the shooting of a suicide scene in *Dream.* While the scene from *Spring Summer* foregrounds an eternal cyclicality and loose causality between the self-inflicted versus other-inflicted suffering, in *Arirang* a comparable relationship is reconfigured to show how the two are inseparable. In the former, when the camera cuts to the shot of a frog from an earlier sequence in the film, we see the frog unable to swim forward because of the stone that the mischievous boy monk has attached to its leg. This insert underscores the shift of the suffering subject from the other to the self, as if the latter pays the consequences of the harms he has once inflicted in others, including the animals that he tortured as a child, and the woman, for whose death he may be partially responsible. In contrast, the reasons for Kim's hiatus, as Kim states in *Arirang,* are as much internal as external—not only Kim's increasing awareness of moral responsibility as the director, but more importantly, his inability to shake off the feeling of being betrayed, and a subsequent resistance to reconcile his position within the transient working relationship that he has experienced with his crews.

The object of Kim's contemplation is his life, not so much his surroundings. Commenting on the winter sequence of Kim's *Spring Summer,* Hye Seung Chung notes how the distinction between character, actor, and the director is all blurred and the sequence revolves around Kim's "centralizing gaze."[5] This is further amplified in *Arirang* when Kim watches his own performance from another film, or footage that has been shot, adding another role—that of the spectator—to his existing role of character/actor/director. *Arirang* is severely controlled by the gaze of and at Kim, who is constantly on-screen. It is interesting to contrast Kim's solitude with Jake in *Two Years At Sea* (Ben Rivers, 2011), both of which premiered at major film festivals in the same year—Cannes and Venice, respectively. Jake is as much off-screen as on-screen, observed both from inside and outside his house. Ben Rivers presents Jake as one of the most content human beings on earth, with his secluded bucolic life filled with his objects and past memories. Jake, who is reading by his desk or falling asleep by the fire, resembles the look of content philosopher. The slow rhythm of the film expands the subject of contemplation to include *the spectator*; one not only observes and con-templates Jake's "simple" life, but also reflects on his or her own life and perhaps desire to escape from it. Kristin Thompson notes, "As with any film about someone who has fled to a simpler life, we are lured to contemplate our own occasional fantasies of giving up society's complex challenges and joys and living somewhere isolated and peaceful."[6]

In contrast to Jake, Kim is tormented, and, like many protagonists in his films, is waiting for a mysterious visit that would disrupt his life. If the camera in *Two Years at Sea* appreciates changes within the overall stasis of bucolic landscape and scenery (such as slight movements of tree branches within an extended long take), the camera in *Arirang* is uncomfortably close to Kim's face while he is eating or when he seems truly intoxicated. In his analysis of Kim's *Address Unknown* (2001), Steve Choe elaborates on Kim's use of close-up as a possible site for ethical encounter, drawing on the phi-losophy of Emmanuel Levinas, for whom a face-to-face encounter with the other can both challenge and invite one's moral sense as well as respon-sibility.[7] In *Address Unknown*, Dog Eyes is a character who breeds and sells dog meat for dog stews, while Chang-guk, who works for Dog Eyes, could not come to terms with the inhumane act of slaughtering dogs. Choe pays a particular attention to a dialogue sequence between Dog Eyes and Chang-guk, where the former commands the latter to stare at him like dogs do. According to Choe, the shot-reverse shots employed between the two posit the ultimate alterity of the other person, yet are unable to yield any meaningful ethical relation between the two. When Chang-guk finally stares back at and confronts Dog Eyes, unlike the two-shots of these characters up until that moment, they are never framed in the same shot. Dog Eyes asks Chang-guk to look away, as he can't bear the intensity of Chang-guk's stare. Choe interprets this rather conventional editing pattern as a sign that Dog Eyes's vulnerability momentarily emerges, which then is quickly fed into the master-slave dialectic that dominates the film, annihilating, rather than acknowledging, the alterity of the other.[8]

In *Arirang,* however, close-ups play out differently due to the absence of the other, which indeed spares Kim from face-to-face encounters except the imaginary murder of his nemesis. Kim occasionally looks at the camera, but there are two salient moments when Kim stares at the camera: One, while he is watching his own footage played on the computer screen and informs us that his solitude has been the main source of his artistic endeavor

(Figure 5.1). The other occurs when he is addressing anonymous actors, who he claims exploit films as a means to satisfy their own maliciousness. Who is it that Kim confronts through his stare? Who is Kim's addressee? In the first instance, I would argue, it is the spectator, who is invited to view Kim as the agent who sets up and controls the entire scene, including the weepy Kim appearing on the computer screen. It is one of the many forms of self-inscription prevalent in the film, as I will demonstrate later.

Kim's address toward actors is more complex. Unlike the earlier moment when Kim repeats the same line, charged yet poised as if he is performing for a screen test, here Kim seems to be pushed off the edge, cursing and slurring, with more signs of his intoxication. Furthermore, this is the only instance we see Kim operating the camera, although the camera still remains off-screen. He reaches out his hand to zoom the camera lens in and out to frame his face more tightly. Kim claims that his performance at the moment is identical to that of "villainous" actors. Kim does not present or posit himself as the other to absent others, but instead holds up the mirror to the absent others, urging them to recognize the symmetry between themselves and himself.

Kim executes his alleged nemeses, who remain off-screen, possibly his former assistant directors and some of the industry personnel. Kim's imaginary revenge is followed by his own fictive suicide. The camera cuts to show his artworks mounted on the walls, which were made and supposedly exhibited on the streets of France, followed by the snapshots of himself, including him garnering international film festival awards. It appears that the imaginary revenge fantasy has provided Kim a closure that he desperately needed. In contrast to an earlier scene, where his art is shown in the basement as if it is incapacitated, his art is now "freed" from the dungeon,

Figure 5.1   Kim stares at the camera. (*Arirang*, 2011)

signaling his resuscitated desire to resume filmmaking. The film ends with Kim's off-screen performance of *Arirang,* a Korean folk song after which film is titled. It has been sung in various tones throughout the film, subject to Kim's mood, but this time it is heard against the black screen, followed by the final credit—Kim Ki-duk.

Like the girl in *Spring Summer,* who awakens the innate desire of the adolescent monk and lures him into the world outside the temple, Kim waits for someone who could convince him to leave the hut to return to filmmaking. However, no one could interrupt his hiatus but Kim himself. Kim's awareness of his own desire to seek his happiness and to continue his artistic legacy can only be the sole cause to terminate the self-imposed exile.

2. CONTEMPLATION

Kim investigates the relationship between performance and moral value, and to be more precise, how the latter tends to be downplayed or bracketed for the former to stand out. Kim himself performs the same line with a different tone of voice, changing facial expressions, either subtly or overtly. Kim simplifies the matter by claiming that the superb performance of playing a villain is often predicated on the moral propensity of an actor—a means to express the malicious nature of the actor. As Mette Hjort points out, a risk is involved in screening acting—there is always a possibility of conflation between the role and the person, by both an actor and the spectator.[9] But Kim's unsophisticated view on the relationship between performance and morality is perhaps meant to underscore his switching roles from director to actor and to challenge the authenticity of his own performance in *Arirang.* If, as Kim claims, a vicious character is the manifestation of the moral character of a performer, then by the same token, Kim's films of extreme sensibility may fall under the same kind of critique—i.e., that his films are a means to express his cruel nature. If filmmaking, as Kim states in the film, is to amplify everyday events and encounters to yield dramatic effects, the correlation between film and reality, and between acting and morality, would also become tenuous.

Two subsequent conversations with himself—one with what Kim calls *jayeonin* (his "natural self") and another with his shadow—further underscores the risks involved in filmmaking. Kim confesses that he feels at ease in the secluded environment, although it would compromise his dream of living and making films outside his home country. In her discussion of Jean-Jacques Rousseau's autobiographical writings such as *Confessions* (1770), Linda Anderson claims, "If Rousseau derives most happiness from his own company, when he places himself at a distance or excludes himself from society, it is also, in part, because he already feels himself to be excluded."[10] Kim's background prior to the launching of his filmmaking career—his lowly social status and lack of higher education—has always placed Kim outside and against the mainstream in the industry.[11] In *Arirang*, Kim thanks his natural self for giving him an opportunity to grumble, complain, or make excuses. Anderson further notes that Rousseau "claim[s] his right to be heard despite his social inferiority, to assert another 'natural' order which gives priority to inner qualities of mind and feeling, and according to which his own distinction will be recognized."[12] In a similar vein, Kim's filmmaking and performance are a forum for his feelings to be understood and shared, without any moral judgment passed on him.

The near death of actress Lee Na-yeong during the filming of *Dream*, awakens in Kim the "moral" responsibility of filmmaking—that is, his artistic decisions on the set may subject actors and actresses (his crews by the same token) to physical risk and even possibly death. Kim confesses that the Lee's incident has affected his view on death—he no longer views death as a new beginning of, or gateway to, the transcendental or the mythical, but merely the termination of life. Kim acknowledges that his pursuit of "realism" in his filmmaking had occasionally brought about hazards of varying degrees. However, it is not the veracity of Lee's accident that matters, but how it is employed.

Hjort characterizes as "flamboyant risk-taking" a contemporary documentary trend that boasts the filmmaker's own risk.[13] Such filmmaking displays and foregrounds risks that were avoidable and excessive, with *Supersize Me* (2004) being a typical example. Morgan Spurlock, producer and director of the film, tries to demonstrate the correlation between obesity and consuming fast food by eating three McDonald's meals per day for a month. Hjort finds in Werner Herzog a precedent of such flamboyant risk-taking and shares his usual anecdote—that is, when Herzog was directing an opera, he jumped from thirty-five feet above the stage to test out the feasibility of a jump, which resulted in a serious neck injury.[14] In a similar vein, Kim Ki-duk occasionally boasts about his spontaneous filmmaking and the physical hardship it entailed. It is reported that during the shooting of the winter sequence in *Spring Summer,* on the spur of the moment Kim decided to climb up to the summit of a 3,600-feet-high mountain under severe weather conditions (-22 degrees Fahrenheit).[15] He was also carrying a stone, while his crews transported the camera and other equipment. Such an episode is presented as evidence of Kim's merged roles, which turns into a "subject-in-process" seeking transcendence and atonement in *Spring Summer*.[16]

There is no doubt that Lee's accident marked a turning point in Kim's filmmaking career due to its severity. However, the question should be redirected to the extent to which the physical harm incurred on the set is *directly* correlated to Kim's artistic risk-taking. To what extent has such an anecdote been employed to boost or ameliorate his "reputation as a risk-taker"?[17] Kim's auteur status on the international film festival circuit is closely tied to the extreme sensibility and cruelty manifest in his films.[18] Lee's near-death experience has been reported and mentioned repeatedly at the premiere and the press conference prior to the release of *Arirang*, as if his film were atonement for the accident.[19] In contrast to the risk to which he is willing to subject himself (as in the case of *Spring Summer*), Kim foregrounds his sensitivity to others at risk, the death being the ultimate risk/consequence that one hopes to avoid. Kim's "natural self" on the computer screen informs the viewer that after having rescued actress Lee, Kim ran to the next room and cried.

Kim's philosophical musings on death, however, do not last long and quickly turn into another reason why he has completely stopped making films, as if the former is a pretext for the latter. Kim's distrust of people is triggered by Kim's former assistant director, Jang Hun, who accepts an invitation from the majors to direct a big-budget film, after the critical and commercial success of his directorial debut *Rough Cut* (2008), which Kim scripted. In Korea, *sadan* (incorporated body, society, association) is used to refer to a sustaining working relationship in the entertainment industry, based on both apprenticeship offered for crews and (often) bankable stars—for instance, female television drama writer Kim Su-hyeon *sadan,* or entertainment agent SM *sadan.* Although not always legally bound, "unofficial" *sadan* promotes trustworthy relationships among film producers, crews, and stars, as well as with the spectator.[20] That is, they can deliver work of a certain level of quality. However, *sadan* also connotes a form of exclusivity, which often relies on the context-dependent interpersonal relationships that have prevailed in Korean society—communities and clubs often constellate around sites of family origin, province, and alumni. Within the film industry, the producer or director becomes the principal figure around which *sadan* revolves. Juhn Jai-hong (also spelled Jeon Jae-hong), the director of *Poongsan* (2011), is identified as a member of "Kim Ki-duk *sadan.*" So is Moon Si-hyun, who worked with Kim for his films *Time* (2006) and *Breath* and was introduced as "the first *female* director coming out of the Kim Ki-duk *sadan*" for her directorial debut *Home Sweet Home* (a.k.a. *Sins of Fathers*, 2011).[21] The rhetoric of *sadan* is rather paternalistic (or maternalistic depending on the gender of the principal figure), the members of which should be looked after.

The vulnerability of the working relationship with his *sadan,* and consequently that of his happiness in filmmaking, has produced in Kim self-doubt regarding the value of filmmaking. Filmmaking, Kim confesses, has provided an outlet to cure his loneliness and to earn him a respect that he never had. Kim's confession is intercut with, or dubbed over, various footage of a cat, him building an espresso machine, and him digging into the ground with a crane, all three of which mirror or are tied into his filmmaking career.

Kim expresses his desire to garner more prestigious awards; this is told against the image of him experimenting with different types of coffee machines—the mentioned goal was indeed achieved with his *Pieta* (2012) winning the golden lion award at the 69th Venice International Film Festival.

We have glimpses of Kim building from a simple drip device that is hung by the shelf, to a complex espresso machine with steam press. A juxtaposition between the simple and complex, or pre-modern and modern, is prevalent throughout the film: from a small garden shovel to the crane, or breaking the wood with his foot versus cutting it with an electric saw. However, the process of building the coffee machine is not only visually more salient in terms of frequency and duration, but also appears to parallel his film career. Like the machines that Kim manufactures, his films have also transformed from the raw to the subdued, with his success at European film festivals and breakthrough in the North American market.

Kim constantly drinks espresso throughout the film, and occasionally uses the same mug for drinking Korean cheap liquor, *soju*. Drinking espresso is a culture recently imported to Korea through various chains of coffee shops that have replaced the traditional Korean *dabang* (tearooms). Dabang used to serve instant rather than brewed coffee, and in the outskirts of a city or small village, it occasionally liaises local prostitutions with customers. By the mid-1990s, there were 42,000 tearooms in Korea but it is hard to spot any dabang in the urban areas as the number of "modern" coffee shops reached 15,000 in 2012.[22] Starbucks Korea, for instance, opened its first store in Seoul in 1999, and there are over 480 stores nationwide as of 2013.[23] Yet espresso is still associated with its "European" origin and taste and remains foreign to many Koreans. Visually juxtaposed with Kim's building of the machine and drinking of espresso are Kim's humble meals made of simple ingredients such as boiled rice mixed with Korean condiments, grilled fish, and ramen noodles.

The juxtaposition of two different food cultures—European and Korean—that may seem at odds further underlines the irony often embedded in cultural export. As Kim notes, his films expose some of the deplorable aspects of Korean society that have resulted from undergoing rapid modernization. Despite such a negative portrayal and criticism of the nation, Kim adds, the Korean government views his films as a "national" achievement. While Kim further speculates that if a state pension is offered to Korean directors for their artistic achievement at international film festivals, no one would refuse to accept, a cat is shown through the window and eats its food. The relationship between Kim and his cat is a metaphor for the endless cycles of feeding and being fed (instead of *nurturing*) to survive or just stay within the loop of competition—a line of thought that Kim develops as his philosophy of life. A similar cut to the cat is made earlier, when Kim reminisces about his former assistant director Jang, who at first refused to accept the offers from major directors in honor of his loyalty to Kim.

Kim is repeatedly seen (though not in full view) as he empties his bowels in the field. Tsai Ming-liang's films have similar recurring tropes, as Tiago de Luca notes. De Luca observes that Tsai's work not only "expose[s] irreducible bodily dimension of human being," it also "magnifies bodily function in the context of a private realm."[24] According to de Luca, the recurrence of narratively insignificant moments of such "physiological situations" in fact underscores the corporeality of the body. Similar tropes of "bodily function" are found in Kim's work—characters are shown urinating in such films as *Address Unknown* and *The Isle*. Yet, in Kim's films, they embody more narrative significance. When American solider James was accused of suspicious behavior, he claims that he ran away to take a leak. James is told that such behavior is only for dogs. Such logic, Choe notes, connotes the master-slave relationship between America and Korea, equating Koreans with dogs: Both have been seen urinating in public in the film.[25]

In *Arirang*, Kim's defecation might be to supply everyday realism and underscore his chosen lifestyle—one without toilet facilities. Yet the actions associated with it (both burying his bodily waste, and later digging up the site with a crane) can be seen as a form of catharsis. Catharsis, argues Aristotle, is the spectatorial effect of consuming tragedy, and often interpreted by philosophers as release or clarification. Through the act of making *Arirang*, for which Kim is both the maker as well as the spectator, Kim releases his emotions—including remorse, anger, or desire—and comes to an understanding of his own filmmaking. Kim interprets the word *arirang* as "self ("*a*" 我) understanding of organizing principles or philosophy ("*ri*" 理)," instead as "one's leaving sweetheart," which is derived from one of the multiple origins of the word. Making the film *Arirang* provides Kim with self-understanding and knowledge of the value of his filmmaking. However, it remains merely as a tool to gain self-knowledge. Kim laments the frailty of the working relationship with his film crews and the majors' domination of the industry, which deprived him of his insatiate will to filmmaking.

Kim identifies his happiness in terms of excellence in activity (i.e., filmmaking), which echoes Aristotle's notion of *eudaimonia* (living well, good living). For Aristotle, virtue (*arete*) encompasses both moral virtues and excellence in activities that require skills—that is, "the proper function" of a given individual, whether he or she be a flute player, a sculptor, a shoemaker, or any kind of expert. Aristotle takes an example of harpist:

> The proper function of a harpist, for example, is the same as the function of a harpist who has set high standards for himself. The same applies to any and every group of individuals; the full attainment of excellence must be added to the mere function. In other words, the function of the harpist is to play the harp; the function of the harpist who has high standards is to play it *well*.[26] (italics added)

Kim has not only excelled in his filmmaking, but has also enjoyed his working relationship with his former apprentices, who he claims approached him and respected his filmmaking style. What devastates Kim more is the depravation of the communal relationship—his working relationship with others, because filmmaking can be, as seen in *Arirang* and many other personal or diary films shows, a product of solitary activities.

In her interpretation of Aristotle's ethics, Nussbaum underscores the importance of vulnerability in *eudaimonia*; it can be partially predicated on luck and external goods in carrying out virtuous actions. Aristotle states:

> Still happiness, as we have said, needs external goods as well. For it is impossible or at least not easy to perform noble actions if one lacks the wherewithal. For many things can only be performed with the help of instruments, as it were: friends, wealth and political power. And there are some external goods the absence of which spoils supreme happiness, e.g., good birth, good children, and beauty; for a man who is very ugly in appearance or ill-born, or who lives all by himself and has no children cannot be classified as altogether happy; even less happy perhaps is a man whose children and friends are worthless, or who has lost good children and friends through death.[27]

Nussbaum interprets the passage above to mean that that Aristotle entertains two conditions by which external circumstances may diminish *eudaimon*. They can deprive one of the means or resources to perform excellent activity (e.g. wealth and political power), but also the object/recipient of that activity (in the case of the death of friend or children).[28] This means that good living is subject to, and contingent on, the absence of chance and risk that would impair one's excellence in activity. Kim's desperate torment depicted in *Arirang* results from his acute awareness of the frailty of his happiness and self-worth, as Kim's desire and capability to continue filmmaking are hampered by something external to the self, such as the control of the majors and the leaving of his former staff to accept better offers. It is beyond the scope of this chapter to examine in detail the rich scholarship on the intricate relationship between *makariotēs* (being happy) and *eudaimonia* (living well) in Aristotle's ethics—whether the two are used interchangeably or not. Nevertheless, as Anthony Kenny notes, "happiness, for Aristotle, in both the *Nichomachean Ethics* and *Eudemian Ethics*, retains an essential vulnerability."[29]

Aristotle advances and strongly proposes that the human being is social and political in nature, and similarly that happiness cannot be self-sufficient (or that solitary man cannot be happy). The making of *Arirang* may be the first step for Kim to regain his "proper function" as a filmmaker in the Aristotelian sense, yet it falls short of fully embracing the vulnerability of the self and the contingency of happiness. Kim's "natural self" in the film once berates Kim and comments on how the ruthless protagonists in Kim's other films would take pity on the drunken Kim for his vulnerability and naiveté. Instead of acknowledging and accepting vulnerability as a constituent part of good living (and thus his happiness), Kim symbolically eradicates the vulnerable self through the fictive killing of his nemesis and himself.

The world map that is symbolically hung on the wall inside Kim's hut could then be interpreted to signal both Kim's expansion of the self and his denial of the other, neither of which allows him to properly grant the alterity of the other. Kim falls into a similar kind of pitfall, which Anderson attributes to the stance manifest in Rousseau's autobiographical writing: "Either totally absorb others into his own self-image or reject them. As his fictional self-image expands to fill the world, he retreats inside it; others, now re-created in the form of phantasmal presences, becomes, paradoxically, even more threatening, since they can easily pass through the flimsy walls of his self, monitoring and judging him from the inside."[30] Kim's contemplations on the other is, as seen in his address to the anonymous actors, deeply embedded in and manifest through, his self-image.

3. SELF-PORTRAIT

> Further evidence, as if it were needed, that digital is both the liberation of low-budget filmmaking and the enabler of self-indulgence, the pic was made entirely by Kim, according to credits culled from the production notes. (Indeed, the only word onscreen, apart from subtitles on the version shown in Cannes, was the title.)[31]

While distinguishing the essay cinema "proper" from so-called self-portrait films, Laura Rascaroli characterizes the latter as "narcissistic genre, as well as the epitome of self-analysis and intimate dissection."[32] In delineating the genealogy of self-portrait films back to the painting tradition and convention, she notes Rideal's observation that self-portrait carries the function of self-promotion—"to ensure one's artistic survival and recognition; and to indicate one's perception of his or her position in society."[33]

Self-portrait, by definition, involves self-representation as a means to self-expression, which, for both Rascaroli and Tim Corrigan, is a quintessential aspect of the essay film.[34] The means of as well as requirement for self-representation in cinema, however, is ambiguous. The camera in Jonas Mekas's *Self Portrait* (1990), for instance, is in the hands of another, whose voice we hear intermittently; Mekas is standing in front of the camera, as he describes the weather in St. Paul, his family background, and his views on cinema. One of the self-portrait moments in Agnes Varda's *Gleaners and I* (2000) is visually conveyed through her filming of her own hands—"old and whimsical." The camera in *Arirang* is what Kim glances and sometimes stares at, not that we as the spectator have a chance to see this. Kim, unlike Varda, does not show himself shooting. Even when Kim walks down the hill (he must have held the camera as the shot seems to be a handheld shot that travels with him), the camera is indiscernible, as his body is shown only in cast shadows. Kim mentions the benefits of digital technology—the Mark II digital camera that he uses to film himself—but we never get to see the apparatus. The only time that we see him operate the camera is, as discussed earlier, when he addresses the actors, but the camera is placed still off-screen.

In addition to Kim's daily routines, including eating, excreting, drinking, and building various machines including the espresso machine and a gun, we see Kim grooming constantly. Kim's various hairstyles—from a well-coiffed ponytail to messy hair—not only differentiate his multifaceted selves between his super-ego (as well as his shadow) and his tormented self, but constitute a form of self-fashioning or "performance." Kim not only executes various types of everyday actions, but he also performs the filming of those actions. Rather than using uninterrupted long takes throughout the film, Kim often edits his daily routines, with the camera position and/ or shot scale slightly altered. When Kim answers the door for the invisible visitor, there are a couple of cuts, which piece Kim's action(s) together from different camera positions—the camera inside and outside the tent, and in front of and behind the door. Even when we see Kim sitting by the stove and broiling and eating nuts, and then biting off persimmons, we see his actions in different shot scales: from medium-long to medium close-up and extreme close up. When Kim shovels snow, which he melts and boils to use as a substitute for water, we see Kim shoveling in an establishing shot, followed by him performing the continuous action in the medium long shot. Kim's actions are "filmed" then "edited" in camera, rather than merely "recorded" or "chronicled," underscoring the constructive nature of his own filmmaking process. Kim defines his film *Arirang* as "drama," in which he plays the protagonist.

Kim's self-inscription takes various forms, from literally inscribing his own name on a wooden pedal of espresso machine that he has built, to his own name appearing on the desktop wallpaper (Figure 5.2), to the sole end-credit. Kim incorporates some devices to distance himself from his emotionally charged self, such as his viewing of the conversation between the two "selves" on the computer monitor—a rush of *Arirang* perhaps— which renders his own self-portrait as ironic.

Orientalism is not the way Kim articulates how film festivals sometimes operate, but he is acutely aware of the inevitability of the disparity existing between the domestic and international reception of his films. Film festivals have developed and become the institutional force that propels a mode of distribution alternative to that of "mainstream" filmmaking. However, as Kenneth Turan notes, "yet when a film hits here, when it wins a major award and touches a nerve in the audience, it really hits.[35] At one point, Kim thanks international film festivals for their "discovery" of his films, which otherwise would have been dismissed as box office failures. In the scene in question, Kim refers to himself as *jeo* instead of *na*, the former being a

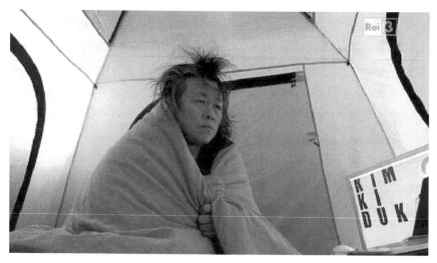

Figure 5.2 Kim's self-inscription.

Figure 5.3 Kim uses dried fish as a lampshade.

more polite mode of address between the two Korean expressions for "I." His gratitude expressed toward the festival personnel is intercut with shots of the head of big dried fish, which Kim uses as a lampshade. Not only is it visually striking (Figure 5.3), but its various framings yield jarring perceptual experiences of the same object. The dried fish shot from below obscures

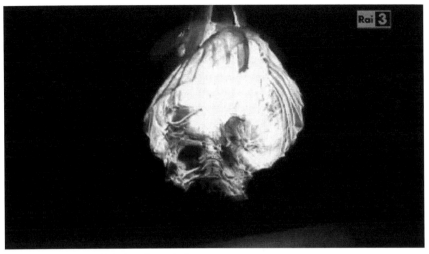

Figure 5.4   Dried fish shot from below.

its identity, as if it were a butterfly or a bat or pelvic bones or even a human skull (Figure 5.4). Such perceptual experiences of the fish could be linked to the status of his own films, whose reception changes drastically inside and outside of the country of origin. Kim's films are often commercial failures in the South Korean domestic market, with many audiences finding his intense aesthetics hard to swallow, but ironically, Kim is one of the most renowned South Korean directors at international film festivals, and, despite many controversies, continues to garner awards.

* * *

Kim's *Arirang* is multifaceted: It is Kim's personal statement on the value of filmmaking, and a contemplation on—and self-fashioning of—the self. One may find tangential my examination of Kim Ki-duk's *Arirang* in light of ancient philosophy, and Aristotle's virtue ethics, in particular. Certainly it is not my intention to argue that Kim is influenced by Aristotle or familiar with virtue ethics, yet Kim's concerns regarding the self, the other, risk, vulnerability, and happiness resonate with the philosophy of Aristotle. With the ethical turn in film studies and other disciplines, discussion of the self and the other constantly seeks to escape and avoid ego-centered ethics. Kim Ki-duk's filmmaking presents here another strong case study, which tests out and fiercely inquires whether a move toward other-oriented ethics is even feasible when sustaining the self is possible only through annihilating the other.[36]

NOTES

1. Hye Seung Chung, *Kim Ki-duk* (Urbana, Chicago and Springfield: University of Illinois Press, 2012), 22.
2. Martha C. Nussbaum, *Love's Knowledge: Essays on Philosophy and Literature* (New York and Oxford: Oxford University Press, 1990), 384.
3. Ibid., 173.
4. Eric Kohn, "Cannes Review: In 'Arirang' Kim Ki-duk Turns the Camera on Himself," *Idiewire*, May 14, 2011, accessed January 15, 2013, http://www.indiewire.com/article/cannes_review_in_arirang_kim_ki-duk_turns_the_camera_on_himself.
5. Chung, *Kim Ki-duk*, 113–114.
6. Kristin Thompson, "Ponds and Performers: Two Experimental Documentaries," October 7, 2011, accessed January 19, 2013, http://www.davidbordwell.net/blog/2011/10/07/ponds-and-performers-two-experimental-documentaries/.
7. Steve Choe, "Kim Ki-duk's Cinema of Cruelty: Ethics and Spectatorship in the Global Economy," *Positions* 15.1 (2007): 71–72.
8. Ibid., 75, 82.
9. Mette Hjort, *Film and Risk* (Detroit: Wayne State University Press, 2012), 8.
10. Linda Anderson, *Autobiography* (London and New York: Routledge, 2001), 44.
11. Chung, *Kim Ki-duk*, 8.
12. Ibid.
13. Hjort, "Flamboyant Risk Taking: Why Some Filmmakers Embrace Avoidable and Excessive Risks," in *Film and Risk*, 41.
14. Paul Cronin, *Herzog on Herzog* (London: Faber & Faber, 2002), 20, recited in Hjort, 40.
15. Chung, *Kim Ki-duk*, 114.
16. Ibid., 115.
17. Hjort, "Flamboyant Risk Taking," 39.
18. Choe, "Kim Ki-duk's Cinema of Cruelty," 65–66.
19. Leslie Felperin, "Arirang" *Variety*, May 13, 2011, accessed January 15, 2013, http://www.variety.com/review/VE1117945216/?refcatid=2531.
20. Eunjin Min, Jinsook Ju and Hanju Kwak, *Korean Film: History, Resistance and Democratic Imagination* (Westport: Greenwood, 2003), 94.
21. Cheol-hyeon Kim, accessed January 22, 2013, http://koreafilm.co.kr/news/news2011_7–7.htm.
22. Go Eun-kyeong, *Hanguk Ilbo*, July 23, 2013.
23. Jeon Hui-jin, *Economic Review*, January 17, 2013.
24. Tiago de Luca, "Sensory everyday: Space, Materiality, and the Body in the Films of Tsai Ming-liang," *Journal of Chinese Cinemas* 5.2 (2011): 170.
25. Choe, "Kim Ki-duk's Cinema of Cruelty," 76.
26. Aristotle, *Nichomachean Ethics,* translated by Martin Ostwald (New York: Macmillan, 1962), 1097^{b}25–1098^{a}15.
27. Ibid, 1099^{a}31–^{b}9.
28. Nussbaum, *The Frailty of Goodness*, 327.
29. Anthony Kenny, *Aristotle on the Perfect Life* (New York and Oxford: Oxford University Press, 1992), 55.
30. Anderson, *Autobiography*, 45.
31. Leslie Felperin, "Arirang" *Variety*, May 13, 2011.
32. Laura Rascaroli, *The Personal Camera: Subjective Cinema and The Essay Film* (London and New York: Wallflower Press, 2009), 176.
33. Ibid.

34. Timothy Corrigan, *The Essay Film: From Montaigne, After Maker* (Oxford: Oxford University Press, 2011), 72.
35. Kenneth Turan, *Sundance to Sarajevo: Film Festivals and The World they Made* (Berkeley: University of California Press, 2002), 29.
36. I would like to thank the audience members at the research seminar hosted by Cambridge University and by the University of Aberystwyth, where I presented an earlier version of this chapter, and Chris Berry, who read a draft of this chapter and provided insightful comments.

6 Uncomfortable Viewing
Deauthorized Performances, Ethics, and Spectatorship in Sacha Baron Cohen's *Borat*

Robert A. Clift

The highly publicized 2006 release of *Borat: Cultural Learnings of America for Make Benefit Glorious Nation of Kazakhstan* thrust questions over the ethics of documentary filmmaking into the center of public discourse. The film's value to society, the methods used to make it, and the people who appeared in it were met with praise, condemnation, lengthy exposés, countless editorials, and comments from at least two heads of state. Lawsuits were filed against the film's producers by, first, a group South Carolina University students who were expelled from a fraternity on the basis of their behavior while appearing in the film. The students' lawyers claimed *Borat*'s producers, including lead actor Sacha Baron Cohen, encouraged their clients to drink heavily, act in a way they would not normally act, and sign consent forms while under the impression that the film would never be shown in the United States. Other participants in the film quickly followed, leaving more than half-a-dozen lawsuits filed to date in relation to *Borat*.

As lawyers raced to court to argue the merit of these claims, audiences and the press scrutinized the film's interactions to debate the ethical dynamics at play. Cohen's deception of social actors—people playing themselves—was of particular concern. In contrast to the imaginary realm occupied by the characters of fictional film actors, social actors are "agents in history, not narrative."[1] Their presence in a film adds "a level of ethical consideration" to documentary and a "burden of responsibility" for documentarians that is less prominent in fictional filmmaking.[2] Documentarians, to offset concerns over the hazards presented by representing social actors, have long justified their "practices by claiming social amelioration" as "the objective."[3] The spectatorial contract most often invoked by documentary—what theorists call "epistephilia," or a desire to know—is deeply rooted in the tradition's association with appeals to the public good.[4] Documentaries promise information and knowledge to spectators, who, in turn, take pleasure in feeling informed and knowledgeable. The public benefits as a whole. Within the parameters of such a contract, the ethical costs inherent to nonfictional representation take a backseat to epistemological aims while ethics, as a matter of consideration for viewers, is left untreated or written off as an unavoidable casualty in the march toward greater public knowledge.[5]

Borat, by contrast, makes ethics the most prominent element of its viewing experience. First, Cohen explicitly violates ethical protocol by deceiving social actors into believing the character Borat is real and thwarting their ability to understand the situation in which they find themselves. Second, because *Borat* maintains a fictional, mockumentary narrative throughout, spectators are left without any explicit appeal to social purpose, the bedrock of documentary's justification for incorporating social actors.[6] As a result, *Borat* inhibits the comfortable distance that typically characterizes documentary viewing and asks spectators, instead, to take pleasure in a narrative that doubles as the very fabrication used to deceive the film's social actor participants. Whereas most documentaries downplay ethical considerations—carving out a space in which viewers can unemotionally engage in an epistemological realm—*Borat* digs into the experiential domain of its viewers, leaving epistemological matters in the shadows and forcing speculations over the ethics permeating the film's performances: Is it permissible for Cohen to deceive social actors? Do the social actors who appear in his film deserve their right to privacy, or is there a countervailing public good? Should I laugh? Should others laugh? How should I, if I were confronted with Borat, respond?

This chapter seeks to address these ethical reactions, starting with the ways in which fabrication and deception are used to solicit and manage performances that deliberately undermine the authority of the people giving them, performances I call "deauthorized performances." Cohen intentionally throws the film's participants off-balance, deploying tactics designed to confuse their sense of the filming situation in which they find themselves. At times, these tactics open a space to represent prejudices and offer insights that would have been otherwise difficult to ascertain. Invariably, they are also tactics that invite scrutiny of their ethical integrity. *Borat* uses the absence of a social purpose narrative to heighten this scrutiny, and to open a space for spectators to consider their own positions in relation to a film asking them to take pleasure in the ethical violations of others.

1.

The opening sequence of *Borat* introduces the character Borat Sagdiyev, played by Cohen, standing in front of his home in the fictional town of Kuzcek, Kazakhstan. Addressing the camera directly, Borat describes himself as a reporter commissioned by the Kazakhstan Ministry of Information to make a documentary about the "US and A." The documentary, he explains, will follow him as he travels to the United States and documents, "for make benefit Kazakhstan," what makes America the "greatest country in the world." Before beginning his journey, Borat suggests the camera accompany him on a tour of Kuzcek. During this tour, he introduces members of his family, including his sister ("the number four prostitute in whole of Kazakhstan"), his mother (at forty-three years old, "the oldest woman" in Kuzcek), and his brother (a boy kept in a cage because of "his mental retarded"). He then displays one of his most prized technological possessions: a "VHS Videocassette Recorder." Borat also shares some "facts" about his "countryland": it is "locate between Tajikistan, Kyrgyzstan, and assholes Uzbekistan"; its national drink is made of horse urine; and women rank below horses and dogs in the social hierarchy.

Borat's opening sequence exhibits many characteristics typically associated with mockumentaries, fictional films presented in the style of documentaries. According to Alexandra Juhasz and Jesse Lerner, mockumentaries ape documentary conventions but use "disingenuousness, humor, and other formal devices to create critical or comic distance" between themselves and actual documentaries.[7] *Borat*'s distance from documentary proper is achieved primarily through parodic exaggeration. Conventions such as documentary's association with civic-minded aims or the neutral position of the documentarian are invoked only to be parodied and pushed beyond the point of believability. In the opening moments of the film, for example, Borat describes the film's purpose as one of cross-cultural learning, but he quickly distances the film from that purpose by framing it in prejudicial terms: "The Ministry of Information send me to U.S. and A. to learn a lessons for Kazakhstan's problems of economic, social, and Jew."[8]

If *Borat*'s opening sequence indicates it will be a mockumentary, the film abruptly shifts once Borat arrives in the United States. Beginning in New York City and ending in Los Angeles, Borat's journey includes a series of unscripted encounters with social actors who are unaware Borat is fictional. These encounters, which consist mostly of interviews, are framed by the fictional, mockumentary purpose crafted by the film (i.e., to learn about American culture "for make benefit Kazakhstan"), but they depart radically for their documentary depiction of social actors in the process of being deceived. These social actor participants do not join Cohen in the manufacture of a fictional persona; rather, they treat his fictional persona as if it were real. For them, Borat is part of social historical reality, not a character in a fictional scene. When the fictional Borat is introduced into the social historical world, he ceases being purely fictional and becomes part of a fabrication, making the film less of a mockumentary than a documentary of that fabrication. This is not to say Borat becomes real but rather to point out that he is a character played by a real-world person to deceive other real-world people.

Noting the distinction between Borat as a fictional character and Borat as a tool of deception is critical: In the former, the film functions as a fiction, orienting viewers toward *a* world; in the latter, the film functions as a documentary, orienting viewers toward *the* world.[9] Borat remains fictional in both orientations, but his presence in encounters with social actors steers spectators toward what Vivian Sobchack calls a "documentary consciousness." The term "documentary," notes Sobchack, designates "an experience" and "a mode of consciousness and identification with the cinematic image" as much as it does a specific cinematic object.[10] Even straightforward fictional films, she explains, can be viewed with a documentary consciousness. Citing the example of *Cleopatra*, a 1958 fictional film starring Elizabeth Taylor and Richard Burton, Sobchack points out how "cultural knowledge of the Burton/Taylor off-screen romance" can foster a mode of viewing in which spectators find themselves "watching not Cleopatra but Elizabeth Taylor kiss not Antony but Richard Burton."[11]

When *Borat* incorporates nonfictional elements into its otherwise fictional setup, it promotes a documentary consciousness in viewers. In the context of fiction, viewers are encouraged to suspend disbelief to facilitate greater involvement in an imaginary realm. Documentary aspects persist in fiction, as Sobchack illustrates in the previous example, but the pertinence of those aspects is secondary to the fiction they sustain. Cohen's relationship to Borat can be described in terms of a real person producing a fictional character. Cohen is an actor playing the character Borat, just as Elizabeth Taylor is an actor playing Cleopatra. To watch *Borat* as fiction means disregarding that relationship; to watch *Borat* as documentary means highlighting it. In the context of documentary, therefore, the relationship between Cohen and Borat takes on an ethical charge altogether different from that present in the context of fiction. Whereas the role of actor, as Erving Goffman observes, generally implies the person in that role is "little held responsible for the part he plays,"[12] Cohen's responsibility in generating Borat is heightened when the film begins to incorporate nonactors into its frame. This is because Borat is no longer produced as part of an open attempt at facilitating involvement in a fictional realm but is instead used as a tool of Cohen's fabrications. To overlook this shift is to miss how the film's fictional elements function differently once they become part of the shared historical world.

Borat's fabrications are perpetrated by the filmmaker himself, raising a set of ethical concerns related to Cohen's use of deception. Cohen deliberately misleads his subjects about his identity and, as a result, the film's intent. "My name a Borat," he often says as he greets them, adding several kisses too many to their cheeks to accentuate his outsider status. The terms of the fabrication are most explicit in the responses he solicits. When a New York City subway rider tells Borat to "get the fuck outta here before I break your jaw" or a rodeo manager in Salem, Virginia, tells him to "shave his mustache" so he doesn't look like "a goddamn Muslim," these participants indicate they are not operating under the assumption that Borat is fictional. When Cohen appears on a primetime newscast in Jackson, Mississippi, his success in deceiving others is given institutional authentication in the form of a lower-third title that reads, "Borat Sagdiyev—Traveling Across the USA," coupled with an anchor who announces without a hint of irony, "We have a very special guest in the studio. This is Borat Sagdiyev. He is traveling across America to get a taste of life here in the United States, and he spent the last few days in our area."

By fabricating situations and making those fabrications explicit for spectators, *Borat* cultivates an aesthetic that puts Cohen's authority as the film's maker and primary fabricator on display. Does Cohen have the authority to deceive the people appearing in his film? How we address the question of Cohen's authority depends on the role we assign to him: Is he a documentarian or a fictional filmmaker? What standard of authority do we use to evaluate him?

Measured against the ethical criteria set forth by fiction, Cohen's deceptions find little ground for justification. Ethical license in fictional film forms around a distance between the real world and the imaginary world the film presents. People play characters, not themselves. These characters function in an imaginary realm and, consequently, the actors producing them are not generally held accountable for their behavior in that realm. To look at *Borat* as fiction, however, is to overlook the deliberate efforts made by the film to communicate its fictions as fabrications perpetrated on the film's participants. In contrast to the film's spectators, who are encouraged to see Borat as fictional, Cohen intentionally leads the film's participants to an incorrect view of the filming situation. They do not see Borat as a fictional character played by an actor, nor do they produce fictional characters who function in the same realm of existence as Cohen's Borat. They play themselves.

The situation of people playing themselves invokes a different ethical standard than that present when people play fictional characters. Social actors, Nichols explains, are not invited to "act in a film" but "to be" in a film:

> Most of us think of the invitation to act in a film as a desirable, even enviable, opportunity. But what if the invitation is not to act in a film but to be in a film, to be yourself in a film? What will others think of you; how will they judge you? What aspect of your life may stand revealed that you had not anticipated? What pressures, subtly implied or bluntly asserted, come into play to modify your conduct, and with what consequences? These questions have various answers, according to the situation, but they are of a different order than those posed by most fictions. They place a different burden of responsibility on filmmakers who set out to represent others rather than portray characters of their own invention.[13]

The "burden of responsibility" associated with the representation of social actors often leads documentary filmmakers to justify their representational authority in the film's narrative.[14] These justifications rely on documentary's affiliation with matters of public interest and knowledge. Described by Brian Winston as the "public's right to know," appeals to public interest and knowledge offer documentarians a counterclaim to potential hazards faced by social actors; they also affirm the prominence of epistemological concerns in the documentary tradition.[15] As Michael Renov writes, "When we talk about the prospects for documentary representation, we are most likely asking about knowledge: What can we know from this film, what can we learn about this person or that event, how persuaded can we be by this filmmaker's rhetorical ploys?"[16]

Configured primarily as an epistemological discourse, documentary approaches ethical concerns in a manner similar to any research field dealing with human subjects. Although a number of differences certainly exist between the work of social or physical scientists sanctioned by academic institutions and that of the documentarian, both, according to filmmaker/ theorist Calvin Pryluck, rely on the claim of "advancing knowledge" for their continued existence.[17] In the more positivist modes of documentary representation, discussions over the ethical treatment of documentary subjects are often silenced altogether in favor of an aesthetic of detached objectivity. As Nichols describes it, such an aesthetic foregoes "emotional, biased, or subjective response(s)" to preserve the documentarian's "professional standing" as detached and impartial.[18]

Even documentaries that do not rigorously toe the line of objectivity often put ethical considerations in the back seat.[19] Ethics in such cases becomes a vehicle of repression itself, a trusty handmaiden vouching for the filmmaker's responsibility, honesty, and reliability—a perspective aptly characterized by filmmaker/theorist David MacDougall in the following exchange about reflexive modes of documentary representation:

> Question: How has your orientation to reflexivity changed over the course of your work?
>
> MacDougall: Reflexivity at one time was at the center of our enterprise. . . . It was important to remind audiences that films come about through the agency of filmmakers, not the gods. There was always the danger, though, that the self-reflexive stance would be taken as a stamp of authenticity—that because we acknowledged the constraints upon our view, that view would be more completely believed. There was the parallel danger that anthropologists would assert one had only to declare one's bias in order for the truth to be revealed. . . . This nurtured the naive positivist view that science really could describe external reality accurately if all the filters of subjectivity were identified and done away with.[20]

Whether silent subordinate or vocal partner, ethics in documentary is most often formulated according to what Nichols describes as an "ethic of responsibility."[21] A documentary's ethical register, Nichols argues, is discerned in its aesthetics or style, which testifies to the "different relations . . . between camera and subject and between camera and viewer".[22] Although every documentary must construct these relations in its own way, Nichols suggests all documentaries count on an "ethic of responsibility" to legitimate their continued filming of the historical world and those who occupy it.[23]

Unlike the scholars cited above, Linda Williams warns against the idea that documentary is fated to justify its practices through an aesthetic that champions its own responsibility. Rather, Williams proposes that the sense of a filmmaker's irresponsibility may, paradoxically, open "a level of ethical questioning" more productive than that found in documentaries flaunting their responsibility. In this, Williams not only cautions against thinking the ethical implications of representation are clear-cut but also offers a rationale for amplifying attention to the more questionable, disreputable aspects of the documentary enterprise.[24]

Williams opens a critical avenue to approach the complicated ethical dynamics put forth by a film like Borat. If awareness of a filmmaker's irresponsibility offers the potential for greater ethical reflexivity on the part of spectators, it follows that a film might amplify the sense of its irresponsibility to generate that reflexivity. Cohen's deceptions mark him as an "irresponsible" filmmaker; his authority to represent social actors is called into question by his flaunted ethical violations and the absence of claims to the greater good to justify those violations. Such an aesthetic makes clear the ties between a documentary's ethical register and the ways in which it manages its authority to represent reality. The question of ethics in documentary, in other words, might fruitfully start with questions about a film's authority to represent reality: Does a film's aesthetic function is support of its authority, or does it throw that authority into question?

2.

Borat deploys an aesthetic designed to put its own authority to represent the historical world and those who occupy it into question. Instead of suppressing ethics in the name of epistemological aims or diminishing the sense of ethical magnitude by discussing it in epistemological terms, *Borat* turns ethics into an experiential mode of engagement for spectators by actively undermining the comfortable distance that typically characterizes documentary spectatorship. "Distance," asserts Nichols, "is the prerequisite for sight, realism, desire, and power" in documentary and holds the effect of allowing the spectator to fulfill the desire to know "vicariously, without openly acknowledging complicity."[25]

Borat undermines the safety of epistemological distance in two respects. First, Cohen gives a deauthorized performance that puts his own authority as the film's maker into question. Drawing on Erving Goffman's observation that the sense of authenticity granted to a performance often turns more on evaluations of whether a performer is authorized to play a role than the truthfulness of the performance itself, I consider the relationship between a performance and the authority of its performer paramount.[26]

Cohen's performance dashes the behavioral conventions of the documentarian, inviting suspicion over the appropriateness of Cohen's behavior in that role. He misleads the film's social actors and offers spectators little justification for doing so. As a result, the distance between Cohen's performance in the film and the expectations for the filmmaker who works with social actors is unmistakably marked, leaving the film vacant of the authority figure typically deployed to transmit information and knowledge. Instead, spectators are only offered the empty authority of a fictional character working toward fictional ends, aptly summarized by the film's grammatically incorrect subtitle. Because Cohen never steps out of character and the film never ceases to maintain its fictional narrative, there is a sense of truancy to its authority. Cohen is not simply absent, he is absent in the name of Borat, a character used to deceive the social actors appearing in the film. Spectators, in turn, are put in the position of "being in the know" about fabrications without the comfort of having any justification for being there.

Second, the fabrications presented by the film are used to solicit deauthorized performances from its participants. Cohen, as Borat, deliberately pushes buttons, testing the limits of what his subjects deem appropriate and turning them into the objects of a joke. In some cases, the joke seems innocent, similar in effect to the type of fabrications perpetrated on participants in the television show *Candid Camera*. When Borat appears at the local television news station in Jackson, Mississippi, for example, an anchorman sits him down to discuss "his views on America." Borat, however, feigns ignorance of the parameters guiding participation in a live primetime newscast, leaning over to kiss his interviewer and making sexual and scatological references that undoubtedly cross the boundaries of "decent language" for television. When the producer quickly cuts the segment short, Borat walks over to the weatherman (who is in the middle of a live broadcast), introduces himself, and asks where he can "take a urine." The weatherman, faced with the task of trying to maintain a straight face in an absurd situation, doubles over in laughter. Although the fabrication is the same as that experienced by other subjects in the film, the news sequence demonstrates no clear harm to its subjects. By contrast, when the rodeo manager tells Borat hanging homosexuals is what "we're trying to get done here" or when the USC fraternity members join Borat in expressing hyperbolically racist and sexist views, discrediting behavior is brought to the fore.

Regardless of the results coming at the hand of the film's fabrications, the terms of each encounter are set by an ethic of irresponsibility that carries the potential for humiliation. Encouraged to think Borat is real, the film's social actors are led into interactions designed to make them lose composure. As a result, they often find themselves in the midst of what Goffman describes as a "negative experience": The subject "loses command over the formulation of viable response. He flounders. . . . He has a 'negative experience'—negative in the sense that it takes from its character from what it is not, and what it is not is an organized and organizationally affirmed response."[27] Although the social actors appearing in *Borat* vary in the degree to which they seem aware of not having a secure footing in the situation, each undergoes negative experiences from the spectators' perspective. Aware that some participants are taken in by fabrications, spectators not only see the terms of those fabrications and thus the mistaken reality that subjects are attempting to engage with but also see them with the knowledge that the subjects themselves will come to realize they were duped. Watching the film in the context of a highly publicized and extensive US release gives rise to the insight that the film's social actors will inevitably come to realize they were taken in and their performances were not given for a Kazakh audience as they believed but for an audience of fellow citizens, neighbors, colleagues, friends, and family.

Spectators, in on the joke, bear witness to the negative experiences induced by Cohen's fabrications. Each encounter is shot through with the intrigue of watching subjects attempt to formulate viable responses to situations that are manifestly absurd. How far can Cohen push his subjects before the conceit falls apart? Will they come to the realization that Borat is not real? Will they go along with his inappropriate views and behavior, or will they attempt to correct him? At what point will they opt out and end the interview? These questions permeate the film's encounters, positioning spectators as witnesses to potentially humiliating situations and calling forth a response Goffman describes as typical for spectators confronted with the negative experiences of others: "some sort of blend of affective sympathy" for those subjects.[28] When Borat tells the husband of a woman at a dinner party, for example, that his wife is ugly, one feels sympathy for the couple. They are undoubtedly in the midst of a negative experience, their behavior giving testimony to a profound sense of discomfort and a desire to bring the occasion back into control. *Borat*'s spectators vary in their responses to such scenes, but the fact that it elicits a response at all testifies to the spectatorial involvement called forth. As Goffman explains, "When he who is observed becomes upset, those watching are likely to become a little concerned, too."[29]

Although it is difficult to discuss *Borat* without addressing the ethical problems presented by the film, it would be wrong to presume that ethical considerations are the inherent result of deauthorized performances in documentary. A film such as *The Yes Men* (2003), for example, also features filmmakers who intentionally fabricate situations and deceive participants with the purpose of soliciting deauthorized performances. The makers of *The Yes Men*, however, maintain their representational authority because the social actors they deceive are marked by the film's narrative as participants in a broader injustice perpetrated against the greater good. Ethical matters, in this case, are not forced into consideration because the film's deceptions are committed for the spectator, in the name of the public good. By contrast, *Borat* submits a variety of social actors to its deceptions (politicians are sometimes included, but "everyday people" figure more prominently), abdicates any explicit social purpose to justify those deceptions, and actively calls Cohen's authority (as the one behind the fabrications) into question. As a result, the sense of social purpose typically maintained by documentary is suspended, and spectators are left to address the difficult question of whether the film's ethical violations are justified.

Contrary to the tradition of justifying ethical violations through appeals to public knowledge, *Borat* amplifies its ethical violations by forgoing such claims. The film achieves this by maintaining a fictional, mockumentary narrative unable to account for the fabrications perpetrated against the film's participants. Cohen never breaks character to position himself as a responsible documentarian. The film does not offer an explanatory frame to ground its encounters with people playing themselves. Instead, *Borat*'s original premise—that Borat is a reporter dispatched to the United States to learn about American culture for "make benefit Kazakhstan"—only becomes more absurd as the film progresses. Upon arrival in New York City, Borat watches an episode of *Baywatch* in his hotel room, falls in love with Pamela Anderson's character, CJ ("so different than any Kazakh woman"), and devotes the rest of his journey to locating her. The film ends with Borat kidnapping Pamela Anderson, who agreed to play herself for the film's fictional narrative, at a book signing in Los Angeles.

The mapping of an overtly fictional, mockumentary narrative onto a series of documentary encounters further highlights Cohen's irresponsibility. Following classic mockumentary plot lines, the story of Borat's hunt for CJ is presented as a "behind-the-scenes" look into the actual motives underlying the film's overtly stated, yet nonetheless fictional, purpose of cross-cultural learning and civic betterment. The encounters are real and the topics sometimes serious, but the film never gives them the seriousness they seem to deserve. When Borat sits down to interview three women representing the Veteran Feminists of America, for example, he maintains the fictional guise of a Kazakh reporter seeking information on feminism in the United States, but in voiceover narration, Borat tells us he is unable to concentrate because all he can think about is CJ, the "lovely woman in her red water panties."

In an essay examining the interplay between mockumentary and documentary elements in *Borat*, Leshu Torchin argues that the scene with the Veteran Feminists of America demonstrates how the film's narrative "rejects the women's political autonomy and cognitive capacity."[30] The women respond to Borat's questioning as if he were sincerely seeking answers, unable to participate in the same fictional realm of existence forwarded by the film's narrative. The narrative, in effect, dismisses the avowed content of their responses, forcing their perspectives on feminism to function in service of a fictional storytelling of a man's obsessive search for a *Baywatch* character.

In spite of Cohen's culpability in deceiving subjects and the questionable status it brings to his authority as a result, spectators are left with a number of participants who do not seem to be simple victims of his fabrications. Rather, the conceit of Borat's cultural difference draws many of them into complicit alignment with the character's misogynistic, racist, and homophobic views. Sometimes participants do correct Borat's overt bigotry, but more often, they wholeheartedly endorse or at least tolerate it. When Borat, for example, tells the rodeo manager that "homosexuals are hanged" in his country, the manager responds, "That's what we're trying to get done here." After Borat joins a small group of fraternity students in their RV, one tells him the United States would be better off if "we still had slavery." At other times, Borat's interviewees do not so much express their own bigoted views as tolerate those put forth by Borat. When Borat asks a Texas gun shop owner for the "best gun to defend against a Jew," the owner responds unhesitatingly, "A 9 mm or a .45."

It is Borat's status as an incompetent cultural performer, as an outsider without authority in Western ways of thinking and being that allows the character to bring prejudices to light. As the film's interviewees struggle to communicate across what they perceive to be real cultural differences, they are forced to take positions in relation to those differences. Their responses vary, but all are tested for how far they are willing to go in tolerating Borat's hyperbolically bigoted behavior. At the dinner party, for example, he consistently breaches the lines of acceptable behavior, at one point even bringing what appears to be his excrement back to the dinner table after using the bathroom and asking the guests at the table what to do with it. It is only when a hired escort shows up that the dinner party host decides Borat has gone too far and asks him to leave.

In the process of formulating a stance toward *Borat*'s ethical problematics, spectators are drawn into debates over the status of its images. Do the performances given by the film's subjects represent their views, or are they solely determined by the fabricated situations imposed on them? Are subjects such as the gun shop owner merely "going along" with Cohen, or are they revealing their own prejudiced views? The film never offers conclusive evidence to answer these questions, leaving the status of its epistemological value in doubt and refusing to give spectators the sense of having reliable referents to hang onto. Spectators, in turn, are put in the position of having to negotiate an ethical stance toward a film with decidedly ambiguous referents.

Although it is certainly possible for a spectator to remain unmoved by the film's ethical provocations, discussions following the release of the film indicate this was not the case. From scholarly journals to popular blogs, introspective critical reflections to observations of casual moviegoers, the overwhelming consensus is that *Borat* provokes ethical discomfort for viewers: "*Borat* is not guilt-free pleasure. We can laugh at Cohen's unwitting marks, because they're not us. But really, we're just lucky that we weren't in his line of fire";[31] "The ambiguities of laughter are explored and the connections between mockery and sadism revealed. If you examine your response to *Borat*, you'll have to face some dicey truths about the joy of bigotry";[32] "Humor often works [when] we find ourselves laughing at things which we really shouldn't be laughing at. *Borat* taps brilliantly into this discomfort, which is why *Borat*'s political satire can be so devastatingly funny. Without the social discomfort, *Borat* would not be interesting at all, nor would he be funny";[33] "Each scene . . . unveils either embarrassment or humiliation, unredeemed by laughter, inviting us to savor, and then to applaud, our own discomfort";[34] "I, along with the rest of the audience, laughed about once every half minute to three minutes at a degree ranging from mild to hysterical. . . . There were moments, though, where the laughter seemed to be reserved and mixed with discomfort";[35] "My uptight discomfort took a back seat to dozens of genuine, uncommonly loud guilt-free belly laughs";[36] "By saying the unsayable, Borat encourages others to do the same, with depressing—but very funny—results";[37] "There was a feeling of uneasiness, and doubly so, as I consequently became most uneasy about my own uneasiness";[38] "Watching Borat skewer these people somehow caused me a bit of discomfort. Sure, it was an uneasiness punctuated by laughter—but still the whole process left me a little queasy."[39]

These excerpts are neither the isolated knee-jerk reactions of a few critics nor the byproduct of an autonomous realm of reception. They are, rather, a consequence of the very experience offered by the film. Discomfort results because *Borat* asks spectators to take pleasure at the expense of others, employing a narrative constructed out of deception and designed to make fun of the film's subjects. In the process, spectators are encouraged to consider their own acquiescence to the film's ethical problematics and to reflect on the nature of their own ethical framework in relation to what they watch. The question "Should I be laughing at this?" repeatedly surfaces because the film offers no adequate justification to insulate spectators from its ethical violations. Instead, *Borat* stokes the unease caused by the absence of any clear justification further by offering laughter in the face of social actors being deceived and sometimes humiliated as its only explicit justification. Spectators, in turn, are left to come to their own conclusion as to whether the film's ethical violations are justified.

3.

Borat calls forth a consideration of documentary ethics that seeks less to determine which films are ethical and which films are not than to determine which films open avenues for ethical reflection and which films close them off. It offers what film theorist Michelle Aaron calls an "ethics of spectatorship." "An ethics of spectatorship," explains Aaron, "requires us to think about how we are positioned, and interpolated, with regard to the morality, immorality or amorality of film."[40] *Borat* performs this task by refusing to offer any satisfactory justification to license the ethical violations it depicts and by putting spectators in the uncomfortable position of taking pleasure in a film constructed on the displeasure of others.

Borat makes the ethical costs involved in documentary representation the basis of the film's viewing experience. Whereas most documentaries seek to downplay the ethical problematics of representation, in part to secure the sense of an undiluted representation of the reality presented, *Borat* plays up those problematics, making the always tenuous reliability of documentary truth claims a matter open to question. Rather than shifting concerns away from matters of epistemological import, *Borat*'s ethical transgressions put discussions over the nature of that import in an ethical light. *Borat* offers itself more as a force to incite epistemological discussion than as an object of epistemology itself. The film feeds epistephilia, making audiences hungry to debate and determine the truth-value of its performances instead of simply satisfying that hunger. Spectators must decide on their own what the film means, what lessons it teaches, what claims can be reliably drawn from it, what it tells them about the people participating in it, and what it reveals about American culture more broadly. The epistemological work performed by *Borat*, in other words, is not performed *in* the film but *after* the film; it is played out in the conversations, arguments, and inquiries incited by the experience of viewing *Borat*.

Public discussion and debate about *Borat* revolved around the central ethical dilemma of documentary: the rights of the individual documentary performer versus the value of documentary to the public at large. Although *Borat* is rare in treating that dilemma as a matter of primary concern at all, it is even rarer for throwing spectators into the thick of it. The ethical dilemma of documentary representation is not only a question of how a film treats its subjects and whether that treatment can be justified by epistemological claims, but it is also a question of how a film treats spectators and whether they find themselves implicated in the documentary enterprise or merely looking on from an innocent, detached position.

If raising questions over ethics in documentary representation means addressing the rights of the people involved in making those representations, those benefiting must recognize their own role in the equation. Traditionally, documentary has precluded the possibility of such recognition, in part because it has long clung to a perspective of the documentary spectator as someone in need of instruction. *Borat* offers a different model, asking spectators to recognize the conflicted ethical dilemmas at stake and to draw their own conclusions about the lessons the film affords. For many critics, the model is an unsettling one—leaving spectators to draw their own conclusions raises the possibility that they will draw the wrong ones. As the Jewish Anti-Defamation League asserts in a "Statement on the Comedy of Sacha Baron Cohen, aka 'Borat'": "The audience may not always be sophisticated enough to get the joke." In this, *Borat* not only asks that spectators reflect on their own responsibility toward the film but that they consider others as well—not necessarily the most encouraging proposition.

NOTES

1. Bill Nichols, *Representing Reality: Issues and Concepts in Documentary* (Bloomington: Indiana University Press, 1991), 230.
2. Bill Nichols, *Introduction to Documentary* (Bloomington: Indiana University Press, 2001), 6.
3. Brian Winston, *Claiming the Real II, Documentary: Grierson and Beyond* (London: Palgrave Macmillan, 2008), 260.
4. Bill Nichols describes the conventional evaluative criteria applied to documentary as "one that draws attention to an issue and not itself follows from the documentary's epistephilic foundations." See his *Representing Reality,* 178–179. Also see Winston, *Claiming the Real II, Documentary*, 260.
5. Michael Renov, "The Address to the Other," *The Subject of Documentary,* ed. Michael Renov (Minneapolis: University of Minnesota Press, 2004), 161.
6. Winston, *Claiming the Real II, Documentary*, 260.
7. Alexandra Juhasz and Jesse Lerner, "Introduction: Phony Definitions and Troubling Taxonomies of the Fake Documentary," in *F Is for Phony: Fake Documentary and Truth's Undoing*, ed. Alexandra Juhasz and Jesse Lerner (Minneapolis: University of Minnesota Press, 2006), 1–2.
8. *Borat's* subtitle, "Cultural Learnings for Make Benefit of Glorious Nation Kazakhstan," further references the appeals to social purpose that characterize documentary rhetoric.
9. Bill Nichols, *Blurred Boundaries: Questions of Meaning in Contemporary Culture* (Bloomington: Indiana University Press, 1994), 112.
10. Vivian Sobchack, "Toward a Phenomenology of Nonfictional Film Experience," in *Collecting Visible Evidence,* ed. Jane Gaines and Michael Renov (Minneapolis: University of Minnesota Press, 1999), 241.
11. Ibid., 252.
12. Erving Goffman, *Frame Analysis: An Essay on the Organization of Experience* (New York: Harper & Row, 1974), 277.
13. Nichols, *Introduction to Documentary*, 6.
14. Nichols, *Representing Reality*, 230.
15. Brian Winston, *Claiming the Real II, Documentary*, 228.
16. Michael Renov, "The Address to the Other," in *The Subject of Documentary*, ed. Michael Renov (Minneapolis: University of Minnesota Press, 2004), 161.
17. Calvin Pryluck, "Ultimately We Are All Outsiders: The Ethics of Documentary Filming," in *New Challenges for Documentary*, ed. Alan Rosenthal and John Corner (Manchester: Manchester University Press, 2005), 199.
18. Bill Nichols, *Representing Reality*, 87.
19. David MacDougal, *Transcultural Cinema* (Princeton, NJ: Princeton University Press, 1998), 88; Nichols, *Representing Reality,* 59; Winston, *Claiming the Real II, Documentary*, 203.
20. Lucien Taylor and Ilisa Barbash, "Reframing Ethnographic Film: A 'Conversation' with David MacDougall and Judith MacDougall," in *American Anthropologist* 98.2 (1996): 371–387.
21. Nichols, *Representing Reality,* 85–87.
22. Ibid., 82.
23. Ibid., 88–89.
24. Linda Williams, "The Ethics of Intervention: Dennis O'Rourke's *The Good Woman of Bangkok*," in *Collecting Visible Evidence,* ed. Jane Gaines and Michael Renov (Minneapolis: University of Minnesota Press, 1999), 176–189.

25. Nichols, *Representing Reality*, 223.
26. Erving Goffman, *The Presentation of Self in Everyday Life* (Woodstock, New York: Overlook Press, 1973), 59.
27. Goffman, *Frame Analysis*, 379.
28. Ibid., 380.
29. Ibid., 380–381.
30. Leshu Torchin, "Cultural Learning of *Borat* Make for Benefit Glorious Study of Documentary," *Film & History* 38.1 (2008): 55.
31. Stephanie Zacharek, "Borat: Cultural Learnings of America for Make Benefit Glorious Nation," *Salon*, November 3, 2006, accessed October 5, 2008, http://www.salon.com/2006/11/03/borat_2/.
32. Richard Goldstein, "The Tao of Borat," *The Nation*, November 2, 2006, accessed October 5, 2008, http://www.thenation.com/article/tao-borat.
33. Bruce, response to "Borat Is No Ali G," *3 Quarks Daily*, March 28, 2007, accessed August 6, 2008, http://www.3quarksdaily.com/3quarksdaily/2007/03/borat_is_no_ali.html.
34. Melik Kaylan, "Spoiled Borat," *Wall Street Journal*, November 9, 2006, A14.
35. "Anthony's Film Review, *Borat: Cultural Learnings of America for Make Benefit Glorious Nation of Kazakhstan*," *Anthony's Film Review*, accessed October 5, 2008, http://www.anthonysfilmreview.com/Film/B/Borat.htm.
36. Eugene Novikov, "*Borat: Cultural Learnings of America for Make Benefit Glorious Nation of Kazakhstan*," *Film Blather*, March 11, 2006, accessed October 5, 2008, http://filmblather.com/films/borat/.
37. Tom Charity, "'*Borat*' is most excellent comedy," *CNN*, November 6, 2006, accessed October 3, 2008, http://www.cnn.com/2006/SHOWBIZ/Movies/11/02/review.borat/.
38. Wojciech Malecki, "Borat, or Pessimism: On the Paradoxes of Multiculturalism and the Ethics of Laughter," *PostScript: Essays in Film and the Humanities* 28.3 (2009): 123–133.
39. Harv Spangle, "*Borat*—Destined to Have a Short Shelf Life," *IMDB*, November 14, 2006, accessed August 6, 2008, http://www.imdb.com/title/tt0443453/.
40. Michele Aaron, *Spectatorship: The Power of Looking On* (London: Wallflower Press, 2007), 119.

7 Heddy Honigmann's Contemplations on *Ars Vitae* and the Metamodern Turn

Annelies van Noortwijk

"If the city of Lima was covered in dust, nobody would see it. It is not really, but all the same hardly anybody sees it or thinks about it, about its people cheated century after century and neglected by its rulers. In order to come out of oblivion, there needs to be an earthquake grade 8 on the Richter scale or . . . a discovery, in the most desolate mountains in Peru, of one of the largest mass graves in the history of the dirty war between the Peruvian army and the guerrilla movement Shining Path."[1]

These are telling remarks from filmmaker Heddy Honigmann, introducing her last documentary film to date *El Olvido* (Oblivion, 2008), which is her homage to her native city, Lima. In spite of this sad but realistic observation, the way her documentary presents this city and its people violates one's expectations. Instead of presenting the facts and the situations and letting the characters[2] describe how they have suffered from social, political, and economic injustice, the characters in *El Olvido* are surprisingly optimistic and prove themselves extremely inventive in finding ways to survive.

Honigmann was born and raised in Peru (1951) as a child of Eastern European Jewish Holocaust survivors. She went to a French school and studied literature for a few years in Lima. She left Peru in her early twenties to travel through Latin America, Israel, and Europe, and moved to Rome, where she studied filmmaking at the Centro Sperimentale di Cinematografia. In 1979, she directed her first documentary, *The Israel of the Bedouins* (1979), and since then has directed over twenty features, most of which are documentaries. Some of these include documentaries made for Dutch television, as she left Rome for Amsterdam in her early thirties, where she has resided ever since. This shows that Honigmann, who is normally identified as 'Peruvian-Dutch,' has, in fact, a more complex identity than her dual citizenship may indicate. Her breakthrough came with the documentary *Metal y Melancholia* (1993), which like *El Olvido* was about the people of her native city, Lima, and for which she earned at least ten different important international film awards. All of her feature-length documentaries garnered international awards. Two of her most recent documentaries, *Forever* (2006) and *El Olvido*, received more than a dozen film awards, two of which were conferred for her life achievement: the Hot Docs Outstanding Achievement Award (2008) and the Golden Gate Persistence of Vision Award (2007).[3]

Honigmann's films reflect on themes as diverse as poverty, loneliness, loss, trauma, war and remembrance as well as the power and vitality of love, art and music. The characters in Honigmann's filmic portraits range from taxi-drivers in Lima (*Metal y Melancolía*) to elderly people in Rio de Janeiro (*O Amor Natural*, 1996) and musicians exiled from their homelands (*The Underground Orchestra*, 1997). Her films also include portraits of war widows living in Bosnia (*Good Husband, Dear Son*, 2001), Cuban exiles in New York (*Dame la Mano*, 2003) and the visitors of various artists' graves in Paris' 'Pere-Lachaise' cemetery (*Forever*, 2006). In her most recent documentary (*El Olvido*, 2008) she returns to the poor of Lima. It is not difficult to see the relationship between Honigmann's engagement with the victims of war, or social, political, or economic injustice across the world, and her multifaceted identity and past as one of the second generation of Holocaust survivors. However, her innovative ethical and aesthetic approach to these subjects further explains the powerful impact of her documentary films.

This chapter will show how Honigmann presents her characters as active and autonomous subjects, who are, almost without exception, real 'artists of life.' This approach, I argue, provides an ethical alternative to the conventions of documentaries that portray the subjects as victims. I characterize Honigmann's oeuvre as a series of ethical contemplations on 'Life as a work of Art' (*Ars Vitae*), an ancient philosophical concept that was reformulated by Michel Foucault during the last phase of his scholarship in the early eighties.[4] After studying the archeology of discourse and constructing a genealogy of power in the first phases of his work, where he prioritized the power of politics and knowledge, Foucault shifted his focus to questions of ethics, prioritizing the power of the individual self as laid out in in *The Hermeneutics of the Subject*,[5] *The Use of Pleasure*,[6] and *The Care of the Self*.[7]

After a brief reflection on Foucault's ethics of the self, I will provide a 'close reading' of Honigmann's documentaries, employing *Metal y Melancolía* and *El Olvido* as prime examples of the most distinguishing aspects of her filmmaking. I will delineate how her films evoke emotions, not only of empathy and comfort, but also of inspiration and hope, and examine how they embody the concept of *Ars Vitae*. My discussion of her films cannot, however, be limited by the theoretical framework of Foucault, for such an interpretation would reduce the filmic expression and experience to its philosophical content and fail to pay sufficient attention to the cinematic (aesthetic) dimensions of her work. Drawing upon the ideas of Barend van Heusden, I will briefly situate Honigmann's work in the broader context of the evolution of human culture and argue that her work is emblematic of the paradigm shift from postmodernism to what should be referred to as 'metamodernism.' The reevaluation of the subject as an active, embodied, and emotional individual is fundamental to such a shift, something that

Foucault's ideas allow us to better understand. The ethical transition we currently witness in film studies is intimately related to this paradigm shift and marks a general renewed interest in ethical questions in the Humanities.

SITUATING FOUCAULT'S ETHICS OF THE SELF

In the last phase of his life, Foucault elaborated a philosophical approach that was already manifest in ancient Greek philosophy. This approach revolves around a way of life rather than a search for truth, and develops 'ethics of the self,' the *epimelesthai sautou* or 'care of the self,' to be achieved through the practice of technologies of the self. Foucault's emphasis on the 'ethics of the self' is especially noticeable in his last two volumes on the history of sexuality, *The Use of Pleasure* and *The Care of the Self*, as well as in the seminars he taught at the Collège de France in 1981–82 (collected in *The Hermeneutics of the Subject*), where he argued, "experience is located in individual persons, who are themselves, however, situated in the fields of knowledge and systems of normativity (. . .)."[8] He observed that since Descartes, the practical question of how to live had remained outside the realm of philosophy, resulting in the increasing estrangement of modern philosophy from everydayness. To remedy this problem, an alternative ethics of the self should be formulated. Greek ethics, Foucault states, were centered on the problem of personal choices, and the ethical question for the Greeks was the *techne tou biou*, or the technique of how to live one's life, rather than the technique of the self.[9] Furthermore, the so-called Delphic principle of 'self-knowledge' (*gnothi seauton*) that would eventually become dominant in ancient philosophy was initially conceived as only one part of a more general 'care of the self,' a set of principles that concerned both elements of the mind (reason) and the body.

   According to Foucault, this 'care of the self' was originally conceived as "a real activity, not just an attitude."[10] However, the concept is inclusive, encompassing both. As he further explains in the *Hermeneutics of the Subject,* care of the self implies "a certain way of attending to what we think and what takes place in our thought. The word *epimeleia* is related to *meletē*, which means both exercise and meditation."[11] Moreover, "[care of the self] not merely designates this general attitude or this form of attention turned on the self," but "always designates a series of actions exercised on the self by the self, actions by which one takes responsibility for oneself and by which one changes, purifies, transforms, and transfigures oneself."[12] As Foucault puts it in *The Care of the Self,* the "technologies of the self" are devices that "permit individuals to effect by their own means or with the help of others, a certain number of operations on their own bodies and souls, thoughts, conduct, and way of being, so as to transform themselves to attain a certain state of happiness, purity, wisdom, perfection, or immortality."[13] Foucault's encounter with the ancient Greek philosophy led to a rather surprising turning point in his thinking, a shift in his theoretical focus from systems of power to the active subject as an embodied and emotional being. Foucault prioritizes the power of the individual self over political power and knowledge, moving away from the techniques of dominance he studied in his earlier work toward the techniques or technologies of the self. It should be noted, however, that these two terms are used interchangeably in Foucault's explanation, while post-Foucauldian literature almost exclusively uses the term *technology* and rarely, if ever, *techniques*.

As McNay suggests, the notion of technologies of the self "enables Foucault to elaborate a theory of resistance—an ethics of the self—which is situated in the interstices of power relations, at the level of individuals' daily practices."[14] In doing so, Foucault indirectly aligns his work with the tradition of the Enlightenment, (of which he, as an anti-essentialist, was otherwise sharply critical), incorporating a number of other Enlightenment ideas, such as dignity, autonomy, self-determination, reflexivity, critique, and autonomy.[15] As Foucault puts it, "the thread that may connect us with the Enlightenment is not faithfulness to doctrinal elements, but rather the permanent reactivation of an attitude—that is of a philosophical ethos that could be described as a permanent critique of our historical era."[16]

Foucault's early death, in 1984, prevented him from further advancing his project. Nonetheless, his reassessment of ancient Greek philosophy provides a fruitful basis of inspiration for philosophers, scientists, critics, and artists, who, each in their own way, contribute to the advancement of a humanistic world-view, based on a rejection of the reductive Cartesian model of the rational subject in favor of the more complex Foucauldian model of the subject in transition. One of them is, I argue, Heddy Honigmann, whose filmic contemplations on *Ars Vitae* I will now discuss in more detail.

TAXI-DRIVERS AS THE SEAFARERS OF THE TWENTIETH CENTURY

Metal y Melancolía was shot in Lima during the escalation of the economic crisis in Peru in the early nineties when almost half of the country's population was below the poverty line. By interviewing taxi-drivers in Lima, Honigmann shows the means to which the middle classes had to resort in order to make ends meet. Almost all of the taxi-drivers interviewed also hold day jobs such as actor, professor, medical salesman, and policeman. However, instead of foregrounding their difficult financial circumstances, Honigmann inquires about their lives, families, dreams for the future, and their actual professions. In the opening credits, Honigmann presents a taxi driver whose car is close to completely falling apart. The advantage, he explains, is that he does not need to worry about whether his car may be stolen; to start with, the door may fall out when a thief tries to open it; second, the thief won't be able to start the engine, and third, even if they succeeded in doing so, he would not make it very far, since water should be added to the car every five blocks or so. There are quite a few such ironic scenes, which contrast with the scenes in which the viewer is confronted with the misery and the hopelessness of the political and economic situation. Humor and irony thus serve as a tool to make the whole film more bearable for the viewer, but also, more importantly, to make life more bearable for those who suffer, because it allows them to maintain control over their situation instead of succumbing to it. By portraying a number of taxi-drivers in a similar way, Honigmann adroitly restores humanity to those who otherwise would be mere statistics for us.

The title of the film is explained by a poem that another taxi-driver presents. In the first shot in which he appears, he sings a nostalgic bolero about a lost love. When he finishes, the driver remarks that he gets nostalgic whenever he thinks of Lima. "As a famous Spanish poet wrote, Peru is made of metal and melancholy (. . .) and this poet was right." "Why metal and melancholy?" asks Honigmann. "I think because pain and poverty made us hard as metal and melancholy because we are tender too and wish for the good old days. When I think of Peru I get melancholic, it's a pity the state the city is in." Honigmann carefully constructs her social and political comments using only interviews, and in fact all of her documentaries consist solely of interviews without any mediation of voice over.

The aesthetics of the film is reminiscent of road movies from the 1960s and 1970s, due to the 16-mm format. Most of the film is shot from inside the taxicabs with Honigmann as an invisible passenger, interviewing the cabdrivers while they drive through the city. The traffic noise comes through the open windows, and a handheld camera renders unsteady images of the city, contributing to the feeling that the viewer is placed inside of the taxi as a customer. The micro-histories of taxi drivers not only allude to the political and economic situation of Peru (by denouncing the immorality of the political class and bankers); they also provide a window to the history and reality of Peru. As the taxi driver who sings bolero puts it, "we, the taxi-drivers are the seafarers of the twentieth century; we know the city like the sea; we take the stories from one place to another; we spread the news like the old seafarers."[17] The attitude of the different taxi-drivers toward life can be viewed in terms of Foucault's care of the self. Although perfectly aware of the political, social, and economic circumstances, they shift their focus to the part of their lives over which they can exercise control. This attitude allows them to take responsibility for their own lives so as to transform themselves to attain a certain state of happiness or wisdom.

"SURROUNDED BY HORROR, I ALLOW MYSELF JUST THIS SILENT POEM."

A similar approach can be found in *El Olvido,* which Honigmann directed fifteen years later, when she returned to the subject of the poor population of Lima. The film is to some extent inspired by the poem *The Scream* (1994), written by her friend, the poet and screenwriter, José Watanabe. Honigmann takes the last phrase of Watanabe's poem, an ekphrasis of Edvard Munch's famous painting transferred to a Peruvian context: "Surrounded by horror, I allow myself just this silent poem."[18] When Honigmann returned to her native country in 2008, she saw that 15 percent of the population were still extremely poor in spite of significant economic development and a growing middle-class; this fact becomes the focus of *El Olvido*. Its main characters are bartenders, small retailers, and street artists, the latter of whom belong to the extreme poor in Lima. Some try to make a living by performing acrobatic tricks, like the little girl and her sister who do cartwheels on the crosswalk hoping for a tip from waiting drivers. Their mother insists that she is not forcing them to show their skills and that they are only on the streets for a few hours a day. It is quite shocking therefore to hear her say, almost in the same breath, how her eldest daughter died on the same streets, doing the same 'work,' after having been hit by a car only a few months ago. At the end of the film we see how the girls still continue their activities on the now dark streets of Lima. Honigmann does not seem to pass on to the viewer any judgment on the mother, who has already been condemned by poverty and maybe depression. Instead Honigmann asks the girls about their dreams for the future. "I want to compete in the Olympics," one of them answers. The mother tells how every night the youngest girl brings up her memories of the sister who passed away, identifying a star as the sister and saying hello. Memories and dreams are, in this way, part of these people's practices of the self that not only permit them to survive and cope with their harsh reality, but to even achieve a certain degree of happiness and immortality.

A young man, who teaches his circus tricks to the other boys in his neighborhood during the day, attends evening classes to become a service worker in the catering industry. Their teacher, a man in his late sixties, tells him and his classmates that service is about making the client feel comfortable. Providing their service to customers does not need to be done at the expense of their dignity, lectures the teacher, as long as they are aware of the fact that they are like actors who *perform* the role of servants. This wise master works as a bartender himself in one of the most luxurious bars in the city, where the upper class drink champagne and cocktails in front of a glass tank containing dolphins that, mirroring the children on the streets, do tricks to amuse the public. The wise master, who elaborates his ethics of the self at the level of individuals' daily practices, is well aware of the power relations within which he operates. This has been made clear in the opening-shots of the film: The bartender is shown in close up, preparing his specialty, the national cocktail of Peru—'Pisco Sour.' While preparing the cocktail he gives a perfect, cynical analysis of Peru's political history with an almost poetic delivery:

> In my fifty years as a bartender I mixed this cocktail for many presidents. When I think of the presidents I see history as a badly mixed

cocktail, made of semi democratic elections, coups, terrorism and corruption. And it is always the same old story, like in a cartoon. [. . .] We
have done everything to be a perfect South American country: scandals,
a dirty war between the army and various guerrilla movements, tower-
ing inflation [. . .]. We had elections lately, and if you would ask me,
'What would you prefer?' Hepatitis B or Aids, we choose the man called
Hepatitis B, the man called Alan García, the very man who ruined the
country between 1985 and 1990. Now he is in power again and I may
have to prepare him a Pisco Sour one day. Because that's for sure, the
man knows his drinks.[19]

Then he invites us to try the Pisco Sour he has just finished preparing, offering the cocktail toward the camera. On the glass appears the title of the
film, which clearly refers to Buñuel's neorealist film, *Los Olvidados* (1953),
about the street children of Mexico city. The viewer is already well informed
about the wider political context here at this early stage of the film, in which
personal histories are situated and against which they will unfold.

The political commentary becomes more salient here than in *Metal y Melancolía*, not only because of the opening credit sequence, but also because of
the editing; scenes are often juxtaposed with the archival footage of various
presidents of Peru. There is a moving scene where the images of Alan García
(1985–1990) being inaugurated are crosscut with shots of a businessman
who had a flourishing leather company but lost 80 percent of his capital during the hyperinflation that Peru suffered under Garcia's regime. His former
leather business is now reduced to a little shop. When Honigmann asks him
if he preserves any nice memories of those difficult times, he starts to cry,
but claims that he weeps tears out of happiness and not of sorrow—through
the memory of his thriving business achieved with the help of his children.

El Olvido is shot in high-definition digital, which helps Honigmann to
capture even the night scenes in spectral detail. A steady camera shows the
scenes on the streets and inside the shops and bars, with very little movement. Slow tracking shots and zooms imitate the speed of our own scanning
eyes when we are walking or standing still. The point of view is mostly that
of the camera, as if the characters directly address the viewer, and results
from the omission of Honigmann's sparse remarks and interview questions.
In both films we are always close, either very close or almost uncomfortably close to the subjects. Furthermore the camera maintains extremely
prolonged concentration on the characters faces shot in extreme, normal as
well as medium close-ups, with occasional, very slow, zoom-ins.

As I have analyzed more elaborately elsewhere, Honigmann's documentaries contain extremely long takes of the characters' faces (or portions of
their faces) in close-ups and extreme close-ups, directing the audience's
attention to their emotions.[20] Considering the human face as a sensorial
means of communication, Carl Plantinga defines these kinds of takes as
the *scene of empathy*, which he characterizes as that which is intended to

elicit empathetic emotions in the viewer. The universal recognition of facial expression implies an underlying innate ability to perceive a number of basic emotions such as fear, sadness, or joy. Seeing the human face can thus move beyond linguistic communication and provoke an emotional response in the spectator. The sight of another human face elicits emotion in the spectator, as neuroscience has proved, by various means including the processes of emotional contagion induced by 'affective mimicry' and 'facial feedback.' It is further noted that emotional contagion is a natural reaction, and that from the perspective of an evolutionary psychology, it is a very important reaction for survival.[21] To empathize with others is the capacity to know, to feel, and to respond congruently to what the others are feeling. According to Plantinga, this does not mean that emotions shown on characters' faces would automatically elicit empathy in the viewer, but through the credibility of the context in which the human facial expressions are shown would be judged in terms of their effectiveness.[22] If the spectator of *Metal and Melancholy* and *El Olvido* experiences Honigmann's use of the scene of empathy as credible and respectful, this is because the film carefully balances the emotional intimacy and distance between the viewer and the characters whose life experiences are not only firmly grounded in the wider political and social context of Peru, but also are represented as people who hold onto their dignity and autonomy, which is reinforced through the lack of any domineering voiceover by the director.

TECHNE TOU BIOU THROUGH LOVE, ART, AND HUMOR

In these two cine-poems, Honigmann depicts the protagonists' strength, virtue, lust for life, humor and, above all, their humanity; she invites us to reconsider not only their positions, but also our own. In this way, she proposes a more personal as well as pragmatic ethics based on the viewer's engagement with others, who are represented as autonomous and responsible subjects despite their social, political, and economic circumstances, and who not only try to cope with the injustice but also try to lead a meaningful life. This does not mean that the political and social circumstances are downplayed. Through the interviews conducted, (and, in the case of *El Olvido*, via the footage of the presidential inaugurations), the political context is certainly foregrounded. However, this is done in a very basic and sometimes ironic way that diverges from the dominant form of social-political documentary, i.e., "observational" or "direct cinema." In these more conventional types, a great deal more effort tends to be invested in the accurate representation of facts and political backgrounds. With the aim of representing reality as objectively as possible, it is shown from multiple points of view, precluding, as far as possible, the subjective point of view of the filmmaker.

Honigmann approaches similar subject matter, but through the viewer's empathic engagement with the subject(s). Empathy plays an important role in establishing such an engagement; Honigmann's films provoke feelings of empathy with the characters we as viewers feel very close. By employing film-specific techniques, she shows people, magnifying their emotions as 'larger than life.' We are invited to empathize with the people's 'suffering'— their difficult situations or even traumatic experiences—respect them, and feel *with* them. Although Honigmann's films encourage us to reflect upon their (and our) circumstances and act upon them, if we wish, they never impose specific solutions upon the viewer. All this means that we do not feel pity if the camera makes us watch, for example, three minutes of the face of the silently weeping man from the leather shop in *El Olvido*; we not only empathize with him but also admire him for his integrity. Feelings of intersubjectivity and senses of sameness, or being alike, are thus constructed in Honigmann's documentaries.

Love, creativity, and art are fundamental aspects of the characters, whose lives unfold in Honigmann's films. They are creative and share deep feelings of love, esteem, and loyalty with others. These characters develop or have developed, to put it in Foucauldian terms, techniques of the self, which permit them to, by their own means and with the help of others, transform themselves to attain a certain state of happiness, wisdom, perfection, or even immortality. As Foucault points out in *The History of Sexuality*, taking care of oneself as understood by the early Greek is not a rest cure:

> There is the care of the body to consider [. . .] the carefully measured satisfaction of needs. There are the meditations, on the readings [. . .] or on the conversations one has heard [. . .] the recollection of truths that one knows already but that need to be more fully adapted to one's own life. [. . .] There are also the talks that one has with a confidant, with friends, with a guide or director. Add to this the correspondence in which one reveals the state of one's soul, solicits advice, gives advice to anyone who needs it—which for that matter constitutes a beneficial exercise for the giver, who is called the preceptor, because he thereby reactualizes it for himself.[23]

It is clear from my analysis of *Metal y Melancholia* and especially of *El Olvido* that Honigmann's characters put into practice practically all of these devices. They meditate and reflect upon life through conversations and dialogue with others; they guide and are being guided; and they know that being a guide is potentially just as beneficial as being guided. For Honigmann as well as in Foucault's reassessment of ancient philosophy, taking care of the body through loving and being loved includes sex as a major constituent of the self's creation of a meaningful and enjoyable existence. Honigmann elaborates this theme very explicitly in her documentary

O Amor Natural (1996). Shot in Rio de Janeiro, Honigmann provides her elderly subjects (often very old) with the erotic poetry of the Brazilian poet Carlos Drummond de Andrade and lets them discuss their love life in relation to the poems. Through this invitation Honigmann makes a group of elderly, who are normally invisible and marginalized, visible. Not only that, we are invited to learn of their memories and reflections on love and sex, to respect them as our own older and wiser self, and as people who embody the same kind of fears and desires as the young. As an 81-year-old woman after reading a poem of "a water ballet on a deep-pile carpet" remarks: "We are old, but not dead."

The power and vitality of art (in its broadest sense) is not only a central theme in *O Amor Natural* but also in her other documentaries. This is also the case in *The Underground Orchestra* (1997), a journey through a community of international musicians who perform in the Paris Metro while in exile from their own countries. In *Forever* (2006) we get a sense of the melancholic beauty of the famous resting-place of many artists and authors, the Père-Lachaise cemetery in Paris, through the eyes of visitors. Some come for their own family members or friends that have passed away but most of the visitors, many of whom are artists themselves, come to honor artists such as Proust, Chopin, Ingres, Maria Callas, Sadegh Hedayet, Georges Meliès, or Modigliani, in the hope of finding inspiration or consolation at the grave of the beloved author or musician, whose art keeps on living forever, becoming a part of the memory of the lives of those visitors. The film's contemplation of art is self-reflexive; it uses the filmic medium to explore the essence of art. In their reflections on and practice of art, which is intermingled with life, love, and death, the subjects develop and practice the art of life itself.[24]

In the cycle of documentaries directed between 1993 and 2008, Honigmann, I conclude, elaborates the themes that bear similarities to what McNay described as Foucault's formulation of "an 'ethics of the self,' which is situated in the interstices of power relations, at the level of individuals' daily practices around reflections on technologies of the self."[25] Just like Foucault, Honigmann's study of the technologies of the self is conducted with an eye on the systems of power and knowledge, which impinge on the self. Honigmann's formulations of *Ars Vitae* and elaborations of technologies of the self breathe the same metaphysical optimism as Foucault's theoretical and philosophical writings on the same theme, but both articulate in their different fields an aesthetic and ethic of the self from the conviction that, as Foucault asserts in an interview, "knowledge can do nothing for transforming the world if it is not employed by the individual." He continues, "[. . .] political power may destroy us. All the knowledge in the world can't do anything against that [. . .] I am not interested in the academic status of what I am doing because my problem is my own transformation [. . . and] this transformation of one's self by one's own knowledge."[26] These interview comments show us that Foucault did not merely advocate, but also personally put into practice the 'real activity' of taking care of oneself. The phrase from Watanabe's poem *The Scream* chosen by Honigmann as the motto for *El Olvido* expresses the same idea: "Surrounded by horror, I allow myself just this silent poem." Honigmann's interest in filmmaking can therefore be interpreted as a Foucauldian desire to accomplish a transformation of the self by one's own knowledge. In dialogue with others, Honigmann meditates and reflects upon, as she puts it herself, 'how to survive' and 'the importance of music and the arts in life,'[27] which are the questions that I have reformulated in terms of Foucauldian ethics of the self. She is being guided by her filmed subjects but also guides them in their mutual search for the meaning of live, and for the *techne tou biou*; it is the technique of how to live one's life and how to achieve a certain state of happiness, in spite of the circumstances. The survivor memories of the Holocaust inherited from her mother and father are likely influences in how she exhibits facing these kinds of terrible truths of human existence.

By orientating her characters (through interviews and, probably, off-screen conversations) toward this search for self-care, or how to make of one's life a 'work of art' even in the most difficult circumstances, she places herself in the tradition of *cinema verité* as practiced and theorized by the French anthropologist Jean Rouch, who started filming in the late fifties. Rouch always acknowledges the camera as an active force in documentary filmmaking and states that inevitably a different reality, a *film-truth* ("cinema verité") would be created. Furthermore, Rouch explicitly acknowledges the camera as a catalyst that, he believed, could provoke dialogues and actions that otherwise would be hard to reveal.[28] Honigmann's process of conducting interviews is reminiscent of *Chronique d'une Eté* (*Chronicle of a Summer* 1961), Rouch's revolutionary documentary, which was shot in Paris. Marceline Loridan (a young Holocaust survivor) and her friend pose a question to people on their ways to work or school; they inquire "Est-vous hereux?" ("Are you happy?"). This is a question suggested and guided by Rouch and his co-director Morin, both of whom reveal themselves in the film. Unlike Rouch, Honigmann is not explicit at all about the off-screen and pre-filmic process of her documentaries within the film-text. As a filmmaker, she has a limited presence as shown in her two films set in Lima. As we have seen she is, apart from her voice, (almost) always physically absent. Nonetheless, an attentive viewer and listener would detect that the nature of her leading question is similar to that of Rouch and Morin—and that could be formulated as: how to live, and even be happy, while surrounded by horror.

TOWARD A METAMODERN ETHICS?

Foucault's shift from a weak, peripheral subject, that was the victim of institutional force to a centered and active subject reassessed as an embodied and emotional being should be understood in the light of a broader cultural paradigm shift that moves beyond postmodernism. Some speak of this shift as transmodernism[29] others of hypermodernism,[30] or post-postmodernism.[31] More terms sprawl in the last decade such as digimodernism,[32] the age of per-formatism,[33] or the consensual age.[34] Although scholarship on the changes we are currently experiencing is still in its infancy (and the debates surround-ing them are still quite confusing) the turn toward the real and the active embodied subject seem to be at the heart of the discussion in the various attempts to come to terms with it. As has been shown, Foucault's delineation of an ethics of the self provides important new insights on the different intel-lectual and artistic attempts to construct an alternative ethics that prioritizes the power of the individual self above the power of politics and knowledge.

   Although it is not so much about the name we give to this paradigm shift as about how we define it, I propose to use the term *metamodernism*, trans-lating *meta-* not in its strict original sense of 'after' or 'beyond' but more so in its epistemological sense of 'about.' Metamodernism, thus, implies a return to a modern attitude from a postmodern awareness.[35] As Barend van Heus-den, who theorizes and historicizes culture and art from a cognitive-semiotic perspective,[36] explains, after a continuous search for cruxes of truth during the period of modernity, within which postmodernity was the final phase (consequently putting the premises of modernity into question), contempo-rary culture displays a renewed interest in the multiple dimensions of the representation of reality. Under the dictum of postmodernity, we were fully aware of the fact that 'truth' is to a certain degree relative, in the sense that it is always value-based, embedded in a discourse of power. The technological changes of the last few decades, and especially the rise of digital technology, have contributed to the dissemination of the idea of reality as a multidimen-sional construct, of which truth is one dimension only. Consequently, the focus in culture, and in the arts as well, has shifted from an essentialist search for truth to the construction of an interesting, provocative and/or beautiful representation of 'reality' from the perspective of the subject, that is now reconsidered as an embodied and emotional individual.[37] Honigmann's films, considered as representations of contemporary artistic consciousness, have been discussed as exemplary of this transformation in contemporary culture, where the question of 'how to live, and even be happy, while surrounded by horror' occurs to us with increasing urgency due to changing perceptions of time and place provoked by (digital) technology.

   Antonio Damasio, a leading neuroscientist who specializes in the rela-tions between the working of the human brain and creativity, suggests that we are currently living an emotional revolution as a result of spectacular new insights into the working of the human brain and the terrain of human consciousness.[38] The study of emotions and the related question on how we produce moral behavior (or the question of whether we are able to produce any moral behavior at all) have once more become central topics of research and reflection. This renewed awareness that we are not only rational, but above all emotional beings, may explain the turn to ethics in film and screen studies. The power of these media, which exploit both our innate as well as learned aural, visual, and linguistic competences, lies precisely in their emotional impact. It is from this perspective that I have studied Honigmann's filmic contemplations on *Ars Vitae*, through which a metamodern ethics of resistance is beautifully conveyed.

NOTES

1. Heddy Honigmann, "Homepage," on Heddy Honigmann's official website, last modified 2011, accessed January 17, 2013, http://www.heddy-honigmann.nl/hhonigmann/films/elolvido/index.php.
2. Although the films discussed in this essay are all documentaries, it is more and more preferred within the contemporary debate on documentary film studies to use the term *character* rather than *filmed subject* or *interviewee* to emphasize that all films are representations, from which it follows that even the subjects of documentary films are to some extent fictional.
3. A complete list of the awards Honigmann obtained for her work is published on her homepage, last modified 2011, accessed January 17, 2013, http://www.heddy-honigmann.nl/Honigmannonigmann/doc/awards/awards.php.
4. In particular, Foucault used this term in some interviews on his late work, the most systematic reflections of which are to be found in "On the Genealogy of Ethics: An Overview of Work in Progress," in *The Foucault Reader*, ed. Paul Rabinow (London: Penguin), 340–372.
5. Michel Foucault, *The Hermeneutics of the Subject: Lectures at the Collège de France, 1981–1982*, trans. Graham Burchell, ed. Frédéric Gros (New York: Picador, 2004).
6. Michel Foucault, *The History of Sexuality, Volume II: The Use of Pleasure*, trans. Robert Hurley (New York: Random House, 1985).
7. Michel Foucault, *The History of Sexuality, Volume III: The Care of the Self*, trans. Robert Hurley (New York: Pantheon, 1986).
8. Garry Gutting, "Introduction: Michel Foucault: A User's Manual," in *The Cambridge Companion to Foucault*, second edition, ed. Garry Gutting (Cambridge: Cambridge University Press, 2005): 13.
9. Foucault, "On the Genealogy of Ethics," 347–348.
10. Michel Foucault, "Technologies of the Self," in *Technologies of the Self: A Seminar with Michel Foucault*, ed. Luther H. Martin et al. (Amherst: University of Massachusetts Press, 1988), 51.
11. Foucault, *The Hermeneutics of the Subject*, 11.
12. Ibid., 11.
13. Foucault, "Technologies of the Self," 8.
14. Lois McNay, *Foucault: A Critical Introduction* (Cambridge: Polity Press, 1994), 7.
15. Ibid., 7–8.
16. Foucault quoted in ibid., 7.
17. Heddy Honigmann, "Forever," in *Heddy Honigmann in Focus* (Hilversum: Beeld en Geluid, 2012).
18. For a reading of Watanabe's poem as an ekphrasis of Munch's painting, see Alberto Valdivia Basfuselli, "Ekphrasis como traducción visual y correspondencias literarias en el lenguage pictórico desde 'museo interior' de José Watanabe," *Revista de Literatura Ajos & Zafiros* 7 (2005): 239–255.
19. Heddy Honigmann, "El Olvido," in *Heddy Honigmann in Focus* (Hilversum: Beeld en Geluid, 2012).

20. Annelies van Noortwijk, "Ars Longa, Vita Brevis: The Importance of Art in Human Life, a Proustian Interpretation of Honigmann's *Forever*," *Widescreen* 4.1 (2012), accessed January 17, 2013, http://widescreenjournal.org/index.php/journal/article/viewArticle/139.
21. Carl Plantinga, "The Scene of Empathy and the Human Face on Film," in *Passionate Views, Film, Cognition and Emotion*, ed. Carl Plantinga and Greg M. Smith (Baltimore: Johns Hopkins University Press, 1999), 239–255.
22. Ibid.
23. Foucault, *The Care of the Self*, 51.
24. An elaborated analysis of *Forever* is given in Noortwijk, "*Ars Longa, Vita Brevis*."
25. McNay, *A Critical Introduction*, 7.
26. Michel Foucault, "Ethics: Subjectivity and Truth," in *The Essential Works of Michel Foucault, Volume I: 1954–1984*, trans. Robert Hurley, ed. Paul Rabinow (New York: The New Press, 1994), 130–131.
27. Honigmann, *Vijf Documentaires*, 30–31 and 80.
28. See Jean Rouch, *Ciné-Ethnography*, trans. and ed. Steven Feld (Minneapolis: University of Minnesota Press, 2010), 10–17.
29. Michael Epstein, "Manifestos of Russian Postmodernism, Literary Manifestos," in *Russian Postmodernism, New Perspectives on Post-Soviet Culture*, ed. Mikhail N. Epstein et al. (New York and Oxford: Berghahn Books, 1999), 457–460.
30. John Armitage, ed., *Paul Virilio: From Modernism to Hypermodernism and Beyond* (London: Sage, 2000).
31. A systematic attempt to define post-postmodernism in contemporary American fiction has been undertaken by Nicole Timmer in *Do You Feel It Too? The Post-Postmodern Syndrome in American Fiction at the Turn of the Millennium* (Amsterdam: Rodopi, 2010).
32. Alan Kirby, *Digimodernism: How New Technologies Dismantle the Postmodern and Reconfigure our Culture* (New York: Continuum, 2009).
33. Raoul Eshelman, "Performatism, or the End of Postmodernism," *Anthropoetics* 6.2 (2000 /2001), accessed April 16, 2012, http://www.anthropoetics.ucla.edu/ap0602/perform.htm; and Raoul Eshelman, *Performatism, or the End of Postmodernism* (Washington: Library of Congress, 2008).
34. Jacques Rancière, *Dissensus*, trans. Steven Carcoran (London: Continuum, 2010).
35. The term metamodernism was already used by Donald N. McCloskey, who proposed it as a term alternative to postmodernism in his critical work on political scientist Jeffrey Friedman. Since then it has been taken over and modified in political theory. To my knowledge, Timotheus Velmeulen and Robin van den Akker were the first who proposed to use it as an alternative term for post-postmodernism, defining it as "a discourse oscillating between a modern enthusiasm and a postmodern irony," in Timotheus Velmeulen and Robin van den Akker, "Notes on Metamodernism," *Journal of Aesthetics and Culture* 2 (2010), accessed January 17, 2013, doi:10.3402/jac.v1i0.5677. In my view, however, the new discourse should not be understood as one *oscillating* between a modern and a postmodern one, but precisely as a synthesis of both.
36. Barend van Heusden, "Semiotic Cognition and the Logic of Culture," *Pragmatics and Cognition* 17.3 (2009): 611–627; Heusden, "Theorizing and Historicising Art," (lecture series taught at the University of Groningen, Groningen, 2010–2011).
37. Heusden, "Theorizing and Historicising Art."
38. Antonio Damasio, *Self Comes to Mind: Constructing the Conscious Brain* (London: William Heinemann, 2010).

8 Self-Reflexivity and Historical Revision in *A Moment of Innocence* and *The Apple*

Vincent Bohlinger

Since the late 1980s, Iranian cinema has found wide-scale attention and acclaim on the international art-house scene. While there have been some notable detractors—including Roger Ebert, David Denby, and Andrew Sarris—many critics have found one group of these films to be notable for their presentation of otherwise simple and straightforward stories that, as Godfrey Cheshire describes, "are unusual in seeming to mean far more than their face-value, literal contents at first reveal."[1] For example, with each subsequent film in Abbas Kiarostami's 'Koker Trilogy,' we engage with a concentrically expanding diegesis in which the fictional space and action of an earlier film is depicted as contained within the supposedly real space and action of the latter. The second film of the trilogy, *Life and Nothing More* (1992), concerns a filmmaker searching for two of the young actors who performed in the first film, *Where Is the Friend's Home?* (1987). The second film is set a few days after the devastating earthquake of June 1990, and takes place around the town of Koker, where the first film was shot. The filmmaker never actually finds the boys, but throughout the film he speaks with survivors of the quake—including a young newlywed couple—as they all attempt to continue the routines of daily life in the face of great personal and material loss. This newlywed couple is then prominently featured in the third film, *Through the Olive Trees* (1994), which is ostensibly about the filming of their scene from the second film. The newlyweds are revealed to be a fictional couple, but the man is smitten and continually proposes as the woman struggles over whether she will take on the role of the very wife that she is supposed to be performing. In Jafar Panahi's *The Mirror* (1997), a headstrong little girl named Mina attempts to find her way home from school through the city of Tehran without knowing her full address or even basic directions. Partway through the movie, the actress playing Mina—Mina Mohammad Khani—quits the film we have been watching and decides to go home, with Panahi surreptitiously continuing to film her documentary-style as she herself now attempts to navigate through Tehran with neither her home address nor directions.

Critics have been quick to characterize, label, and ascribe potentially competing aesthetic agendas to such a clear interest in self-reflexive filmmaking.

Godfrey Cheshire argues that these films explore "far more profound matters . . . not simply a matter of metaphor and careful ambiguity."[2] Richard
Peña asserts that "Many of the questions modernism had posed . . . were
taken up with fresh energy by the Iranians."[3] For Peña, the "modernist film
practice" found in Iranian festival cinema openly explores such issues as
"the process of film production, the question of spectatorship, [and] the line
between fiction and documentary."[4]

Film scholar Hamid Naficy, on the other hand, describes this filmmaking as 'postal cinema,' as in the prefix 'post-,' which he situates historically
as those films having "been produced since the late 1980s, surfacing after
cinema's reinstitutionalization, after [Iran's] Iraq war, and after Ayatol-
lah Khomeini's death."[5] Naficy argues that this cinema is "not a complete
political and aesthetic break" with earlier Iranian filmmaking, but rather a
"reject[ion of] the exclusionary high culture, authoritarian certainties, and
politicized aesthetics of modernism for the more nuanced, open, ambiguous,
self-reflexive, self-inscriptional, intertextual, pluralist, playful, and humanist
ethics and aesthetics of postmodernism."[6] Regardless of whether the label
for such artistry should be deemed 'modernist' (à la Peña) or 'postmodern-
ist' (Naficy)—though postmodern seems more appropriate—these films are
widely recognized and discussed by critics and scholars and are compelling,
in large part, because their tendency toward self-reflexivity and intertextuality brings to the fore broader questions about filmmaking, specifically the
ethics of documentary filmmaking.

In this chapter, I am focusing on Mohsen Makhmalbaf's *A Moment of
Innocence* (1996) and Samira Makhmalbaf's *The Apple* (1998), two key films
from Iran during the late 1990s, internationally renowned on the art cinema festival circuit for their deceptively simple stories, yet self-reflexive and
intertextual filmmaking. In *A Moment of Innocence*, Mohsen Makhmalbaf
recounts the autobiographical story that led to his five-year imprisonment
in the last half of the 1970s: as a seventeen-year-old antigovernment protes-
tor, he stabbed a policeman while attempting to steal his gun. In *The Apple*,
Makhmalbaf's daughter Samira tells the tale of two girls who have been
locked inside their home for over a decade by their father and mother. It is
worth noting that Samira Makhmalbaf, at seventeen, purportedly became
the youngest person to have directed a feature-length film in Iran with
The Apple—her father having worked on the editing and screenplay. (This
record has since been eclipsed by her younger sister Hana Makhmalbaf,
who at fourteen directed *Joy of Madness* (2003), a documentary on the
making of Samira Makhmalbaf's *At Five in the Afternoon* (2003), a fiction
film about a woman who seeks political and social empowerment in conservative post-Taliban Afghanistan.) Both *A Moment of Innocence* and *The
Apple* seemingly meld documentary with fiction, and both are striking in
that the real-life personages of these true stories actually portray themselves
in these films. In *A Moment of Innocence,* the policeman whom Makhmalbaf stabbed two decades ago contacts him with the expectation of being

made an actor in his next film project, thereby inspiring the turn to auto-biography. In *The Apple,* all principal actors in the real-life account play themselves: The father, the blind mother, the social worker called to inter-vene by alarmed neighbors, and the two girls themselves, both now suffering mental and physical developmental disabilities likely in part caused by their long confinement.

Both films involve recreations of crime. The stabbing that inspires *A Moment of Innocence* is an immediate, singular act, while the child abuse and neglect of *The Apple* is more likely to be considered a long-term accu-mulation of offences. These crimes are historical events that—without question—actually took place in reality, yet the manner of their retelling complicates our understanding of the events themselves because we are made to realize and contemplate the varied motivations surrounding them. One of Abbas Kiarostami's most well-known films, *Close-Up* (1990), is a similar recounting of real-life criminal activity. A man impersonates director Mohsen Makhmalbaf, cons money from a family by offering to cast them and their house in his next film, and is confirmed to be a fraud by a journal-ist brought in by a suspicious family member. The imposter, the semi-duped family, the journalist, and Mohsen Makhmalbaf himself all play themselves in their reenactments in the film. I bring up this example from Kiarostami to emphasize that *A Moment of Innocence* and *The Apple* are not unique, but rather representative. In the interest of limited space and because of the symmetries drawn out in the father-daughter film pairing, I have chosen to focus only on the two Makhmalbaf films.

This chapter analyzes *A Moment of Innocence* and *The Apple* to explore the ethical ramifications of self-reflexive filmmaking. The techniques of self-reflexivity and intertextuality encourage contemplation in the viewer and, I argue, carry a political edge. The very nature of the self-reflexivity in these films forces the audience to recognize and consider—up front—the extent and limits of control that the film's subjects have over the content of their own films; thereby, we are made more aware of and question the extent and limits of control that any film subject has over his or her own depic-tion. In having the real-life personages of true stories portray themselves, the films potentially posit multiple subjectivities. Not only does this overt self-reflexivity allow for the suggestion that real-life personages are getting a chance to tell 'their side of the story,' but such a filmmaking strategy also underscores to the viewer the mutability of both history and the historical record—optimistically, that historical wrongs can be righted, but skeptically, that historical wrongs can be rewritten as right. Although both films are technically fiction, they address and inform criticisms that circulate in the field of documentary film theory. In this chapter, I will first rehearse a few of the principal concerns in documentary theory pertaining to questions of power, exploitation, and truth claims in the relationship between filmmakers and their subjects. Then I will consider how *A Moment of Innocence* and *The Apple* call attention to and perhaps complicate these questions. These two films certainly do not resolve any debate in documentary, but they help to expose the nuances, contradictions, and maybe even dangers to be found in what might be posited as a more self-aware and ethical documentary film practice.

"The question of ethics," documentary theorist Brian Winston insists, "has been repressed in documentary studies and practice."[7] Winston offers a number of substantial critiques of documentary for what he considers to be its long troubling history, from its tendency to impose or force simplified narratives on far more complex real-world situations to its predilection for merely describing social inequalities rather than actually effecting change. The criticisms most salient to a discussion of *A Moment of Innocence* and *The Apple* pertain to questions of the seemingly inherent unequal power relationship existing between the subjects being filmed and the individuals doing the filming. If documentaries are to be a part of a historical record, by virtue of their appeal to realism and their purported rhetorical stance, then the very subject matter being filmed—or not—carries weighted importance. It is a commonplace assumption that the person behind the camera wields enormous power and carries incredible responsibility in not only choosing the subject matter but also selecting how it is to be presented and, therefore, preserved. As historian Edward Carr famously declares, "History means interpretation."[8] But the documentary filmmaker is a critical gatekeeper at the moment of historical inscription, and the recording of history as it is happening is always subject to the selection and mediation of the filmmaker.

Anthropologist Michel-Rolph Trouillot identifies what he considers to be four 'silences' that should always be considered in relationship to history and the creation of a historical record in and of itself. He writes, "Silences enter the process of historical production at four crucial moments: the moment of fact creation (the making of *sources*); the moment of fact assembly (the making of *archives*); the moment of fact retrieval (the making of *narratives*); and the moment of retrospective significance (the making of *history* in the final instance)."[9] All four of these silences that Trouillot describes—'fact creation,' 'fact assembly,' 'fact retrieval,' and 'retrospective significance'—seem to be taken up by the Makhmalbafs in *A Moment of Innocence* and *The Apple*. Both films present accounts of crimes for which there is something of an external official story, at least in the form of legal or bureaucratic proceedings. However, do such governmental records, no matter how thorough, suffice as complete histories of these crimes? Trouillot explains, "Inequalities experienced by the actors [in real-life events] lead to uneven historical power in the inscription of traces. Sources built upon these traces in turn privilege some events over others, not always the ones privileged by the actors. Sources are thus instances of inclusion, the other face of which is, of course, what is excluded."[10] Applying Trouillot's argument to the cases presented in these two films would suggest that there is inherently something missing—that, plainly speaking, not all sides of the story have been told. Two otherwise straightforward documentaries on these two crimes would still somehow be lacking. For Trouillot, "Silences are inherent in history because any single event enters history with some of its constituting parts missing. Something is always left out while something else is recorded."[11]

By having the characters of these films reenact their original deeds, as opposed to having had these crimes filmed at their very moment of initial trespass, the Makhmalbafs seem to address the issue of silence raised by Trouillot. Simply put, the individuals depicted in *A Moment of Innocence* and *The Apple* seemingly are given more of a voice. Documentary film theorist Bill Nichols offers terminology that might prove helpful. He contends that the argument of a documentary—its purported rhetorical stance and its stake in the truth—involves what he distinguishes as the film's 'perspective' and its 'commentary.' For Nichols, "perspective is the view of the world implied by the selection and arrangement of evidence."[12] Nichols acknowledges that where the camera has been pointed and how the film has been edited must always be recognized as mediation—a winnowing of reality and, thereby, the historical record. To add Trouillot, perspective leads to the production of silences, particularly in terms of fact creation, fact assembly, and possibly even fact retrieval. "Commentary," for Nichols, "is the view of the world stated by the filmmaker or social actors recruited to the film."[13] Commentary more plainly demonstrates overt subjectivity, and it is here where we can see Trouillot's silences produced in terms of fact retrieval and retrospective significance. Nichols continues, "commentary serves to provoke a sense of distance for the purposes of orientation, evaluation, judgment, reflection, reconsideration, persuasion, or qualification between the text as a whole and the evidence it presents."[14] Such measures of evaluation, judgment, and the like are demonstrated by an audience being convinced by what it sees. Presumably for a documentary to be deemed successful, the subjective position of the filmmaker and/or the film subjects must be taken up by the viewers of the film.

Insofar as we might recognize Nichols's distinction between the concepts of perspective and commentary, we have multiple sites of mediation, and this seems to be a good thing. When the subjects featured in a film reenact the very actions they have already committed, they have greater access to direct mediation alongside the filmmaker. In other words, individual subjects are contributing to the selection of the raw material for the film by virtue of how they are reenacting that raw material. To apply Trouillot's concepts, they are, with the advantage of retrospection, selecting their own 'silences.' How these individuals choose to perform in front of the camera and all the other ways in which they might be involved with representing themselves on film increase the likelihood that their subjectivities are not entirely subordinated to that of the filmmaker. It is a question of degree on the part of any collaboration between the filmmaker and the subjects of a film. My point is not that original actions (not reenactments) carried out in front of the camera are entirely free of mediation by the individuals performing them; rather, I believe that with reenactments the mediation on the part of the subjects being filmed seems more deliberately self-conscious, the individuals themselves more self-aware even if not necessarily in greater control.

With *The Apple*, instead of a talking-head style documentary in which real-life participants narrate their experiences pertaining to the event or encounter at hand in the past tense—something like *The Thin Blue Line* (Errol Morris, 1988), with or without the third-party reenactments—Samira Makhmalbaf seems to have all the family members simply relive their experiences, however harsh and uncomfortable, by re-performing them. On the Makhmalbaf Film House website, where the entire screenplay for *The Apple* is downloadable in English, Mohsen Makhmalbaf, as the film's credited screenwriter, offers a statement that he is responsible only for having planned the screenplay for *The Apple,* as the actual dialogue spoken in the film belongs to the actors themselves.[15] The film's screenplay, therefore, is simply an after-the-fact transcription of all the film's dialogue. Samira Makhmalbaf claims that she restrained herself from interfering with the performances, asserting that even when she "wanted certain things to happen, she would hold back."[16] She interestingly takes a rather direct cinema approach to her film's reenactments, musing "You wait and wait and listen and do not judge, and then something happens to make you think, yes, I never dreamed it would be as good as this."[17] She reveals, for example, that the idea to give the girls hand mirrors came from the social worker Azizeh Mohamadi.

In *A Moment of Innocence,* on the other hand, the multiple mediations seem on the surface to be far more overt. Mohsen Makhmalbaf and Mirhadi Tayebi, the man who was serving as a policeman when he was stabbed by Makhmalbaf, take responsibility for their respective young counterparts and then direct their junior selves in how to behave and feel as they once did back then for their reenactments of those fateful actions from twenty years ago. Each seems to be in control and is shown manipulating their respective junior, yet the limited control they ultimately exercise over their juniors demonstrates another level of mediation. The question here, however, is whether Tayebi and, by default, the other performers in the film actually have any of the control they are depicted as maintaining, or is everyone just written by Makhmalbaf to seem that way? In interviews, Makhmalbaf is coy, which suggests that Makhmalbaf deftly manages to have it both ways, ethically speaking: He exercises control over the reenactment to underscore his theme on the very limits of control in both the original production of the historical record and reenactments of them.

Active participation by the individual subjects of a film project—even in reenactments—is therefore no guarantee of their fair treatment in the resulting film. There is certainly the danger of exploitation. Brian Winston fears "a filmmaker wittingly or unwittingly exploiting the subject to one degree or another."[18] He warns, "Being filmed can have consequences and they might be profound."[19] Indeed, Iranian film actress and scholar Shahla Mirbakhtyar levels such criticism against Abbas Kiarostami's *Close-Up* for what she sees as Kiarostami taking advantage of both the real-life imposter and the family that he has deceived. Mirbakhtyar asks the "question of whether an artist has the right, even for the sake of art, to cross certain lines concerning the humiliation of people."[20] At issue, then, is the extent to which individual subjects may be exploited in their own films, even when they seem to be granted positions of power and authority. The degree to which individuals are directly embarrassed onscreen seems to be an appropriate means by which to measure for potential exploitation.

Humiliation is very much front and center in *The Apple*—and perhaps for good cause due to the nature of the crime—but this humiliation does not appear wholly contrived by Samira Makhmalbaf. Many of the father's speeches throughout the film present both his shame and his anger at being accused of maltreating his daughters. These speeches grant him the opportunity to defend his actions and rebut those reports that he considers to be false—all for the historical record. When one of the neighbors who filed the report with the Welfare Department pays the family a visit, the father complains that she has lied and slandered him and that neither he nor God will forgive her. He disputes the claims that he never let his daughters out and that he had them chained. The neighbor agrees that the people who accused him of such did commit slander, but then argues that he has kept his children malnourished and unschooled for eleven years. When he harps on the accusation that he has chained up his children, she argues that keeping them locked up is the equivalent of chaining them up. He expresses his frustration that the media and his neighbors have all singled him out and he again keeps focusing on the charge that he chained up his daughters. This reenacted verbal altercation, presumably similar to many that he has had with his neighbors, conveys a much stronger sense of his subjectivity by virtue of his repetition and the intensity of his speech. His argument as such seems much more effective and induces more sympathy than it likely would were he presented as simply a talking head defending himself while recounting his actions.

Throughout the film the father offers his various reasons for having kept his daughters locked up. With the neighbor who visits, he breaks down and cries, explaining that he had to lock the doors because his wife is blind and they did not want the girls to get out. Later, with the social worker Azizeh Mohamadi he expresses his worry about the boys playing in the street outside. Their ball often flies into the courtyard and they climb over his wall to retrieve it. He claims that if his girls were not locked up, they could be touched by these boys and he, the father, would be dishonored. In terms of filmmaker perspective and commentary, as if on cue a ball is shown flying into the yard and we soon see three very young boys peering over the outer metal door and asking for it back. These chaps seem anything but malicious or sinister, and the father's claims therefore are undercut as paranoid and misogynist. Yet the father has still been granted extended opportunities to say his peace, and across the film he details the extraordinary difficulty of his impoverished circumstances: his advanced age, his lack of a job and reliable income, and his limited amenities—no refrigerator, no cold water, no air-conditioning, and not even a fan.

The blind mother comes across as far less sympathetic, but this seems entirely due to her own behavior more than anything else. After the social worker locks up the father and mother and forces the girls to play outside in the street, the mother scolds the social worker, even using profanity. Such language might be expected from someone locked inside and forced to destroy her own front door in order not to have her children taken away from her. Indeed, she curses at her husband as he attempts to saw through the metal bars. Still, the mother does not seem exploited by the filmmaker. Even though she is blind, she surely is aware of the presence of the camera. Her apparent desire to have her face entirely covered throughout the film goes fulfilled, as we only see her face when it appears in a photograph accompanying the newspaper article that a neighbor shows to the father. It is perhaps in deference to the mother and father that the first shot that we see of them in the film shows them from behind, their backs to us as she whispers and speaks to herself.

In contrast, Mirhadi Tayebi in *A Moment of Innocence* sometimes comes quite close to being depicted as a stooge, and throughout the film there is quite a bit of wry humor at Tayebi's expense. At the beginning of the film, when he tells Makhmalbaf's daughter Hana that her father stabbed him, she does not measure any response—seemingly ignoring what he is saying—and continues to ask him why he wants to be an actor. When he leaves, she throws out the socks he has gifted to her father along with a wrapped present that he claims is for her. Hana does not even open the gift, perhaps because she, like us, is already convinced of its bumpkin or shoddy quality and is not even curious for confirmation. Is he in on the joke? Later, when Tayebi is trying to cast his role in the reenactment of the stabbing, he focuses on a good-looking boy and claims that he has the same eyes. Makhmalbaf's assistant Zinalzadeh asserts that the boy does not look like the Tayebi, even if he were to wear a policeman's cap as Tayebi insists. The boy acts a bit too-cool-for-school, even insolent, answering Tayebi's request to say something ordinary with 'I don't like you,' which he then even repeats when Tayebi does not seem to notice. Again, is he in on the joke? Tayebi says the boy is photogenic and has a nice face and announces that he should play the young Tayebi. When the assistant leaves the room to chat with Makhmalbaf about the decision, Tayebi attempts to chat with the boy, who seems bored with Tayebi, if not the whole venture. Tayebi is clearly annoyed when the assistant then sends the boy away and replaces him with a less comely, more awkward and nervous boy, who just happens to be dressed very similarly to Tayebi. This dorkier, garrulous boy continually attempts to make small talk with Tayebi, who suddenly and uncharacteristically does not seem so gabby. Tayebi's reversed behavior between the two boys serves to confirm Makhmalbaf's opinion that the second boy is clearly a much more fitting, even if less idealized, younger version of Tayebi. These scenes emphasize the limited role that Tayebi has over his own performance at the same time that we are exposed to Tayebi's seeming lack of commitment to a truly authentic reenactment. The issue of Tayebi's control over his own depiction is over-ridden by the very content of these scenes showcasing that such control is always contested and undermined.

One concern we might have is that Tayebi is so emotionally invested in being in a film—any film—that he will do or say just about anything to achieve that. The extended scene at the tailor's shop offers us 'dead time' in the spirit of Italian neorealism, but the conversation between Tayebi and the tailor does demonstrate Tayebi's longstanding, even if superficial, interest in film. He listens in wonder as the tailor babbles on about the likes of Anthony Quinn, Sophia Loren, Kirk Douglas, *Spartacus,* and John Ford. With the tailor we see a genuine love of cinema, particularly Western cinema. Even though he has worked on costumes for actors in the Iranian film industry, he does not offer any details or anecdotes about his experiences and instead rambles on about 1950s- and 1960s-era cinema, presumably the films he grew up with. What Tayebi lacks in knowledge about film, he makes up for with his ambitious posturing as a player in the industry, offering to speak to Makhmalbaf about giving the tailor a role in the film if the tailor makes a good costume for Tayebi junior.

The hint of exploitation becomes much more pronounced when Tayebi suddenly realizes that the girl of his memories, who has for so long car-ried his infatuations, is actually Makhmalbaf's cousin and, even worse, was an accomplice in Makhmalbaf's attack. Tayebi tells his junior that he was stabbed because he was in love with a girl who always asked for directions. On that fateful day, he was going to give her a flower but allowed himself to be distracted and ultimately got stabbed. He is devastated to learn that this girl of his dreams had no genuine interest in him all along. More poignantly, he must face the fact that the future he always thought he lost because of the stabbing was worse than a mere illusion: a deliberate deception. The biggest surprise—shock, even—is that Makhmalbaf admits in an interview with scholar Hamid Dabashi that the character of the young female cousin is entirely made up.[21] There never was a female cousin recruited to help distract Tayebi in the days leading up to the stabbing. So what, then, do we make of this deliberate untruth inserted into the reenactment and therefore revising the historical record with wild inaccuracy? Film scholar Eric Egan argues that "the self-reflexive form of *A Moment of Innocence* reveals the hermetic conceit of narrative film, casting the reality it seeks to portray as a site of active intervention. . . . This dissection of the means of representation accommodates the heterogenous voices—Makhmalbaf's and the police-man's—of personal memory, love and loss."[22] It is perhaps as pernicious as it is an ingenious move on the part of Makhmalbaf, for it calls all the supposed facts of the reenactment into question. Moreover, the film itself never directly reveals this falsehood to its viewer. The young girl hired to play the role of Makhmalbaf's cousin is said to be the cousin of Makhmalbaf junior, but beyond that everything is in doubt. The earlier parallels that had been drawn between two generations of a young boy's love for his female cousin—wanting to change the world, sharing books that get returned full of dried flowers—are exposed as utterly fabricated. The scene in which the daughter of Makhmalbaf's real cousin reveals herself to be plotting the same reenactment of the stabbing with Makhmalbaf junior therefore makes sense; it is all whimsically fake.

Hamid Dabashi describes Makhmalbaf's jest here as 'factasy,' which he characterizes as a "cross-breeding of fact and fantasy, seriousness and frivolity."[23] Elsewhere, Dabashi has described this kind of filmmaking as "a kind of virtual realism."[24] The addition of such overt fakery serves to remind us of the susceptibility of history to subjectivity. Indeed, the reenactment begins to spiral ever further away from the historical record after Tayebi's revelation. After he is persuaded yet again not to quit the film project, Tayebi attempts to subvert the reenactment by having his junior shoot the girl and/ or Makhmalbaf's junior before he is to get stabbed. As for Makhmalbaf's role, his junior has already broken down in tears, crying that he does not want to stab anyone, and that one need not do that to save mankind. Of course, both the gun and the knife are recognized as fakes by all parties, but that point seems moot in the face of a largely fake reenactment. But why the turn to such blatant character and audience deception in the first place? I suspect that it allows Makhmalbaf to grant Tayebi his long sought-after 'good guy' role, one infused with bittersweet romance. Tayebi after all is the victim of Makhmalbaf's initial crime, yet Makhmalbaf has far more power as an established filmmaker. Less generously perhaps, the role of the female cousin also shifts some of the burden of guilt off of Makhmalbaf himself, because Tayebi talks far more about what might have been had he married

Figure 8.1   The reenacted letter to the Welfare Department in *The Apple*.

that girl than what might have been had he not been stabbed by Makhmal-baf and then resigned from the police force.

It does not seem that Samira Makhmalbaf engages in the same level of trickery. From early on, *The Apple* establishes a fairly recognizable distinc-tion between the events supposedly recorded on the fly immediately as they were taking place and the events that are reenacted, with the former far grainier and washed out. The less-polished 'original' footage is made to serve as an index of sorts, confirming that the actual individuals involved have returned to play themselves in the reenactment. The issue of reenact-ment is addressed directly early on. During the film's opening, we see the text of the original letter to the director of the Welfare Department as it is being written. We get a few jump cuts as the signatories all put their names on the letter. Soon after, however, we see this same letter referenced by the social worker as she discusses the case with the father. The letter is briefly shown in the grainy footage coded as authentic, and it looks quite different from the letter we had first been shown. The action of the film begins after the Welfare Department has already been informed about the two girls, so we immediately recognize the process of reenactment as it is happening.

With the issue of reenactment, Samira Makhmalbaf seems to explore the limits of subjectivity. The film seems to draw our attention to Trouil-lot's silences. Shortly after the girls are taken home, we get a brief scene in which they stare from behind the metal bars of the closed door as we hear the sound of a baby crying. There is a cut to a window with similar metal grating, as well as a blanket and curtain blocking our view of what is inside, followed by a cut back to the girls as the baby's cries continue. Makhmalbaf here relies upon a point-of-view editing structure to suggest subjectivity. In the first shot, Zahra (left) and Massoumeh (right)—are shown to be looking up and off-screen to the left at something—that something strongly sug-gested by the persistent off-screen sound of the baby crying. In the second shot, of the window with the drawn curtain, the low-angle camera setup approximates the spatial positioning of the two girls, thereby suggesting that the shot is from their point-of-view. This shot interestingly denies us visual confirmation of an actual baby crying, so that we are forced to think that what we are hearing is a baby behind the curtain we see. With the third shot, a return to the two girls looking up off-screen, we then ponder what the two girls must be thinking about this baby as they both hunch down and hang upon the door (see Figure 8.2). Makhmalbaf here relies on the Kuleshov effect with the addition of sound: We believe we have access to the interior states of these two on-screen personae by virtue of an assumed spatial prox-imity made by editing. At this point, there has been no establishing shot that clarifies the location of this window, yet we imagine contiguous space because of eye-lines, camera position, and continuous sound.

It is highly doubtful that Makhmalbaf has any command of what these two girls are genuinely thinking. They have difficulty just stating how old they are, so any moment-by-moment reflection or personal revelation is

Figure 8.2   Zahra and Massoumeh seem to respond to off-screen sounds in *The Apple*.

simply impossible. But are we really ever shown what they think? The scene continues by returning to a shot of the window and we hear the baby stop crying, and then the camera returns to the two girls. Even as the film seemingly pushes to offer details of the girls' subjective experiences, what we are actually given is far from a definitive idea of what they are thinking. We hear a rooster and other farm animals, and the point-of-view structure then presumably has the girls looking up at the sun through a chain-link fence. The editing pattern is repeated and the girls are then shown running inside to get ink. One says, 'flowers,' and the girls are shown slapping their handprints on the wall. As they are slapping their hands on the wall, they look back at the sun and repeat the word, 'flowers.' They are particularly adept at overlapping their handprints, palm on palm with fingers fanning out in opposite directions. Then Massoumeh is shown sipping water from a cup and, in an echo of the film's opening shot, pouring water from the cup into a clay pot almost out of reach on the ground. In the pot is a measly plant with two modest stalks of small, unassuming yellow flowers. The film here presents a chronology of shots that suggests causality via inferred motivations, but these motivations are recognizably rather flimsy. Do the girls stop looking up at the window because the baby stops crying? Do they look at the sun because they hear a rooster crowing and draw the same commonplace association between the two as we do? Does the radiating sun remind them of a flower and thereby initiate their fun with ink? Or is it the sun's yellowness that reminds them of the flowers in their pot? Are the handprints an attempt to make flowers (which perhaps better resemble crabs)? Do these handprints remind Massoumeh to water the plant? Or were the girls considering the flowers in the pot all along and just happened to look up at the sun as well? This episode leaves us wondering what they might be thinking as we question why they might be behaving in the manner we witness. While the linking of the anecdotes themselves—of the girls hearing a baby's cry to their handprints on the wall to the watering of the plant— may well be contrived, their very presentation emphasizes the barriers that prevent us from understanding or even accessing their mental and emotional states. Obviously any account of these girls is necessarily incomplete. But what are we to make of the father when we see him reflected in the hand mirror given to him by Zahra after he is locked behind the metal door? His expression is blank and certainly seems sad. He is indeed ready and willing to speak his mind throughout the film, but here we get no access. We are reminded of the greater point that, in fact, any account of any individual is necessarily incomplete.

Both films interestingly end with a turn toward the very objects of their titles. The original title of *A Moment of Innocence* is *Nun va Goldoon*, or *The Bread and the Vessel*. Hamid Dabashi reports that the film's French distribution company, MK2 (Marin Karmitz 2), changed the title to a more recognizably alliterative French title *Un instant d'innocence.*[25] Michel-Rolph Trouillot argues, "There is no perfect closure of any event, however one chooses to define the boundaries of that event."[26] These films conclude with sudden rhetorical shifts that aim to bring closure through the ambiguity to be found in the symbolism of objects instead of through the depiction of concrete physical words or actions spoken or performed by one or more participants in these events. Such a shift is not at all surprising for international art-house cinema. Across *The Apple*, these fruits are shared between multiple individuals, and in the family we only have yet to see the mother with one until the final moments of the film, when the impish boy dangles it before her (see Figure 8.3). Film critic Hamid Reza Sadr explains that the symbolism of the apple should not be read according to the Judeo-Christian story of the fall of Adam and Eve, but rather through traditional Iranian poetry, in which the apple serves as a symbol of life and knowledge.[27] Sadr offers us an optimistic reading, in which the poor, fearful, and bitter mother now grasping the apple is somehow indicative of the positive changes she will be lured to experience alongside her seemingly much improved husband and daughters.

The symbolism at the end of *A Moment of Innocence* resonates just as, if not even more, strongly. With both boys off-screen, the freeze-frame that closes the film has the flowerpot being thrust forward by Tayebi junior and the bread being thrust forward by Makhmalbaf junior. Before the confused female cousin, the younger generation has defied the wishes of the older generation by replacing the gun with the potted flower and the knife with the bread (see Figure 8.4). Hamid Sadr explains that the bread and vessel are symbolic of life and friendship and interprets that "reality meets fantasy in a work that shows that life and art can triumph over theory and politics."[28]

Figure 8.3   The final shot of *The Apple*.

There is no accuracy remaining in the reenactment, as the very crime itself has been erased. In his interview with Mohsen Makhmalbaf, Hamid Dabashi describes the ending as "a mutual questioning of violence as a means of achieving ends, any ends, no matter how just and noble," a "focus on the theme of love and forgiveness."[29] Makhmalbaf himself characterizes the ending as "bring(ing) my cinema to a poetic conclusion, something that perhaps I have always been after, even if I didn't quite know it."[30] The rewriting of the events that actually happened out of the reenactment does not erase the historical past here. In fact, the historical revision offered by the younger generation is all about the stabbing precisely because the stabbing is absent. Within the context of the film, and due to its self-reflexive aesthetic, we know that something different and far better has happened. Like *The Apple*, the film ends on a positive note that promises a brighter future. Both films are about forgiveness; that these individuals all joined and worked together to make their respective films confirms the personal progress that has been made from a negative past to a positive present and future.

Filmmaker and scholar Mehrnaz Saeed-Vafa reports that international Iranian audiences were disappointed with *The Apple* along with other internationally popular Iranian films because of their depiction of poverty and neglect,[31] while Hamid Sadr argues that Samira Makhmalbaf's international fame "encapsulated the irony of Iranian life," in which twelve-year-old girls might be locked away, but an eighteen-year-old girl can make a film about them.[32] Sadr also reveals that the success of *A Moment of Innocence* in a series spotlight on Mohsen Makhmalbaf at the Jerusalem Film Festival in 1997 led to an Iranian condemnation of a purported Israeli plot.[33] Because of the West's longstanding difficulties with the Iranian state, many critics read the cinematic self-reflexivity found in these films through various political

Figure 8.4   The final shot of *A Moment of Innocence.*

lenses. As Eric Egan argues, "By presenting a variety of conflicting voices Makhmalbaf attempts to open a space for public discourse, one that introduces certain problematic Iranian cultural traits, like individualism and the belief in absolute truths."[34] Scholar Zohreh T. Sullivan sees self-reflexivity in Iranian filmmaking as serving as a 'critique of absolutism,' and writes "Makhmalbaf's *A Moment of Innocence* screens his own life to question the pastness of his past and that of the nation."[35] Sullivan quotes Makhmalbaf himself, "There is no center of truth," and argues, "Art and truth are negotiated, communal, ongoing processes."[36] She argues that because the film "resists appeal to traditional pieties like prayer, nation, and poetry" and "is fragmentary and resists resolution, therefore provoking thought," it serves as a "critique against mass culture's power to evoke conformity, to manipulate the audience with false promises of gratification that would lead them [sic] toward blind faith in past, present, and future."[37] With an appeal to Raymond Williams's notion of 'a structure of feeling,' Sullivan explains the characteristics of the film and its effects as follows: "Against the effort to forge monolithic moralities and censorial evaluations, all these films may be seen as subversive and liberating . . . because their values embrace playfulness, subversion, deflation, evasion, expansiveness, inclusiveness, and embrace of process, and above all, of humility."[38] Even critics who do not read these films politically find it necessary to assert such a claim in terms of the seeming ethical stance of these films. Bill Nichols, for example, argues that these films "serve neither as the focus for covert political criticism nor for expressions of moral condemnation."[39]

Citing *The Apple* as a key example, Shahla Mirbakhtyar argues that self-reflexive filmmaking "has put the sense of national identity of Iranian cinema in danger."[40] Mirbakhtyar's concern seems to be that self-reflexivity as an aesthetic choice is not tied to any particular national cinema. I disagree in that there clearly does sccm to be a well-developed group style utilizing this technique to such a high degree that these films distinguish themselves from other contemporaneous national cinemas. However, I concede her point that this filmmaking is more international in scope and ambition, but therein lies its strength. Eric Egan argues that "here is a political art that operates on the level of the personal and that seeks to de-familiarize history by drawing its meaning from the inclusive differences between two worldviews and multiple art forms, but does so in such a way that appeals to the viewer's connections to these worlds."[41] The questions raised by these films extend, as Egan suggests, not only across the arts but also to much broader cultural and intellectual issues. These films raise awareness of the contingencies and consequences of various artistic practices, and that perhaps justifies Hamid Naficy's labeling of them as "spiritual and ethical cinema."[42] Whereas Mohsen Makhmalbaf directs our attention to the ethics of allowing film subjects to be in control of their own representations in *A Moment of Innocence*, Samira Makhmalbaf actually practices it in *The Apple*.

NOTES

1. Godfrey Cheshire, "How to Read Kiarostami," *Cineaste* 25.4 (2000): 8–12.
2. Ibid., 12.
3. Richard Peña, "Iranian Cinema at the Festivals," *Cineaste* 31.3 (2006): 41.
4. Ibid.
5. Hamid Naficy, *A Social History of Iranian Cinema, Volume 4: The Globalizing Era, 1984–2010* (Durham, NC: Duke University Press, 2012), 176.
6. Ibid.
7. Brian Winston, *Claiming the Real: The Documentary Film Revisited* (London: British Film Institute, 1995), 241.
8. Edward Hallett Carr, *What Is History?* (New York: Vintage, 1961), 26.
9. Michel-Rolph Trouillot, *Silencing the Past: Power and the Production of History* (Boston: Beacon Press, 1995), 26.
10. Ibid., 48.
11. Ibid., 49.
12. Bill Nichols, *Representing Reality: Issues and Concepts in Documentary* (Bloomington: University of Indiana Press, 1991), 126.
13. Ibid.
14. Ibid.
15. "*The Apple*," Makhmalbaf Film House, accessed April 26, 2013, http://www.makhmalbaf.com/books.php?b=26.
16. Sally Vincent, "Beyond Words: Samira Makhmalbaf," *The Guardian*, April 3, 2004, 40.
17. Ibid.
18. Brian Winston, *Claiming the Real*, 232.
19. Ibid.
20. Shahla Mirbakhtyar, *Iranian Cinema and the Islamic Revolution* (Jefferson, NC: McFarland, 2006), 135.

21. Hamid Dabashi, *Conversations with Mohsen Makhmalbaf* (London: Seagull Books, 2010), 33–37.
22. Eric Egan, *The Films of Makhmalbaf: Cinema, Politics & Culture in Iran* (Washington, DC: Mage, 2005), 153.
23. Hamid Dabashi, "Mohsen Makhmalbaf's *A Moment of Innocence*," in *Life and Art: The New Iranian Cinema*, ed. Rose Issa and Sheila Whitaker (London: British Film Institute, 1999), 118.
24. Hamid Dabashi, *Close Up: Iranian Cinema, Past, Present and Future* (London: Verso, 2001), 263.
25. Hamid Dabashi, "Mohsen Makhmalbaf's *A Moment of Innocence*," 115.
26. Michel-Rolph Trouillot, *Silencing the Past,* 49.
27. Hamid Reza Sadr, *Iranian Cinema: A Political History* (London: I. B. Tauris, 2006), 244.
28. Ibid., 248.
29. Hamid Dabashi, *Conversations with Mohsen Makhmalbaf,* 187.
30. Ibid.
31. Mehrnaz Saeed-Vafa, "Location (Physical Space) and Cultural Identity in Iranian Films," in *The New Iranian Cinema: Politics, Representation and Identity,* ed. Richard Tapper (London: I. B. Tauris, 2008), 201.
32. Hamid Reza Sadr, *Iranian Cinema,* 245–246.
33. Ibid., 215.
34. Eric Egan, *The Films of Makhmalbaf,* 152.
35. Zohreh T. Sullivan, "Iranian Cinema and the Critique of Absolutism," in *Media, Culture and Society in Iran: Living with Globalization and the Islamic State,* ed. Mehdi Semati (London: Routledge, 2008), 193.
36. Ibid., 200.
37. Ibid.
38. Ibid., 201.
39. Bill Nichols, "Discovering Form, Inferring Meaning: New Cinemas and the Film Festival Circuit," *Film Quarterly* 47.3 (1994): 24.
40. Shahla Mirbakhtyar, *Iranian Cinema and the Islamic Revolution,* 162.
41. Eric Egan, *The Films of Makhmalbaf,* 153.
42. Naficy, *A Social History of Iranian Cinema, Volume 4,* 176.

Part III

Exploitation and the Extreme

9 The Ethics of Extreme Cinema

Mattias Frey

Hardly a season passes without news about a controversial art-house film. At the 2010 Cannes film festival, *Ça commence par la fin* (*It Begins with the End*, dir. Michaël Cohen) caused a stir: It featured the actors (and real-life pair) Emmanuelle Béart and Michael Cohën having sex in extreme close-up. In spite of the furor—*The Observer* ran a notice entitled "Outrage as French couple's film judged too sexy for Cannes"[1]—this "shock" is perennial. The previous year it was over Lars von Trier's *Antichrist,* in which Willem Defoe's penis is made to ejaculate blood; in 2004 Michael Winterbottom's *9 Songs* "disgusted" for its depictions of live coitus; and two years earlier Gaspar Noé was the bête noire for the twelve-minute rape of Monica Bellucci's character in *Irréversible* (2002). Whether the next incarnation in the "Asia Extreme" DVD series or Michael Haneke's latest provocation, these films are ubiquitous on the festival circuit and in cinemas and appear reliably in the media cycle—often accompanied by a critic, politician, or lobby group's consternation at how these productions might deform our brains or our impressionable children.[2]

This is "extreme cinema:" a production trend of "quality" films that, because of violent, sexual, or other graphic content, create critical and popular controversy. Indeed, the trend is distinctive insofar as it is defined by a marketing strategy that anticipates a controversial response. Premiering at glamorous film festivals among cultural sophisticates, playing at upmarket cinemas, and featuring in the "world cinema," "independent," or "art-house" sections at video stores and online DVD and download services, this production trend depends on (offending) culturally inscribed boundaries between art and exploitation. This is the paradox of extreme cinema: These productions attain the status of "art" by using the very tools of the lowbrow—the gratuitous or disturbing sex and violence of pornography, snuff films, horror, and action movies.

Critics have developed a number of idioms to describe this trend and its genealogy, from "subversive cinema," "the auteur's sex movie," "post-porn," or the "sexually explicit art film," to the "new extremity" and the "cinema of excess," from "unwatchable" films to "feel-bad" movies. I will evaluate these claims focusing both on the filmmakers' own rhetoric and the rhetoric of the critical reception. As a point of departure and to distinguish my own approach to this subject, however, it is useful to turn to the perhaps most important recent scholarly study of the larger historical phenomenon of extreme representations in art cinema.

In her prescient monograph *Cutting Edge: Art Horror and the Horrific Avant-Garde,* Joan Hawkins shows that some fan communities elide boundaries between high art and low art in their reception of what she labels "art-horror."[3]

Hawkins's insights are extremely valuable. They help show how, for example, *Salò* (1975) or *Funny Games* (1997), which are usually considered by critics as "works" by the "artists" (or at least "great directors") Pier Paolo Pasolini and Michael Haneke, might be received in practice also by individuals who watch *Saw* (dir. James Wan, 2004) or *Hostel* (dir. Eli Roth, 2005) or any "popular" or cult horror film. In other words, these spectators do not discern between the categories of "high-culture" cinema and (lowbrow) trash/cult flicks. In common sites of reception—such as Times Square, art-house cinemas, and peep shows—these productions commingled; the marketing of "art-house" films in the United State frequently called attention to their liberal attitudes toward nudity and sex, rather than their aesthetic innovation. In the 1990s, fanzines and video-order catalogues, *Zontar, the Thing from Venus* (dir. Larry Buchanan, 1966) is listed alongside Jean-Luc Godard's *Alphaville* (1965) or Stan Brakhage's *The Act of Seeing with One's Eyes* (1972). Hawkins uncovers the often porous boundaries that have divided high art from low horror.

Written at the tail end of the debates over the modern and postmodern, Hawkins is concerned with blurring high culture and pop culture to show how arbitrary these categories are. My questions pursue the opposite avenue in the debate and extend the discussion to recent extreme cinema. If these "high-art" works are different from low horror or pornography often times only in artistic intention or pretension, we need to consider what kinds of strategies are employed to enact and police this distinction. Why and by which means are these productions considered by both filmmakers and opinion leaders to be artistic at all and thereby "different"? In other words, we need to examine why these films engage with violence, sex, and realism and why certain critics and audiences—who would usually criticize "excessive" violence and "exploitative" sexuality—often sanction these works. I argue that many of these films are distinguishable from "low" horror/pornography largely in the *ethical discourses* that surround their marketing and distribution; media performances by filmmakers and their agents and the interpretive work of critics and consumers delimit and define these productions as artistic works. This chapter proceeds, first, by examining theoretical concepts of cultural taste and distinction, which I argue are essential to the self-understanding of extreme filmmakers and of many consumers of extreme cinema. The insights in this section help us understand the focus of the following two sections: the rhetorical strategies of extreme filmmakers and the rhetoric of extreme's cinema reception—both of which revolve around ethical claims.

TASTE CULTURES AND THE SPECIAL ABILITY TO DISTINGUISH

Clearly, engaging with the questions I have outlined in the preceding paragraph must involve examining loops of filmmakers' and consumers' artistic positioning and critical discourses, supply and demand, production, and reception. These circuits feed into each other organically, and so these concerns must be treated as overlapping and interlocking. At the heart of this discussion are matters of taste and the need—both on the side of the filmmaker and his or her commercial apparatus, as well as on the side of the consumer of such films—to be perceived as part of an alternative culture and in possession of the capability to distinguish between art and exploitation. Examining notions of cultural taste and distinction allow us to understand how (and why) extreme cinema constructs itself as unique and as an ethical alternative to horror or erotic films.

Extreme cinema always defines itself "against" other genres or production trends with which it shares affinities. For example, contemporary extreme cinema positions itself in dialogue with (and above all in opposition to) what has been termed "torture porn," a cycle of lowbrow films that "construct scenes of torture as elaborate set pieces, or 'numbers,' intended to serve as focal points for the viewer's visual pleasure, and (in critics' view) for which the narrative is merely a flimsy pretext."[4] These include *Saw* and its sequels, *Hostel* and its 2007 follow-up, *The Devil's Rejects* (dir. Rob Zombie, 2005), *Turistas* (dir. John Stockwell, 2006), *Captivity* (dir. Roland Joffé, 2007), *The Human Centipede* (dir. Tom Six, 2009) and its sequels, and others. Unlike older horror films, which trade on the uncanny and the fantastic, the "torture porn" cycle depends on realistic situations and aesthetic: The scare is that this "could happen to you."[5]

Although extreme cinema indulges many of the same narrative and aesthetic devices as "torture porn," both the filmmakers and many critics (later referred to as the "highbrow" appraisers) differentiate the two as distinct projects. To distinguish itself from mainstream and "cult" versions of horror, "torture porn," and other quotidian genres, extreme cinema engages with discourses of exclusivity and connects itself to circumscribed cultural groups. In his essay, "Base and Superstructure in Marxist Cultural Theory," Raymond Williams theorizes the distinction of alternative and oppositional cultures toward the hegemonic mainstream. In Williams's idiom, alternative culture implies a subject "who simply finds a different way to live and wishes to be left alone with it," while oppositional culture suggests "someone who finds a different way to live and wants to change society in its light."[6]

The makers and many "highbrow" consumers of extreme cinema imagine themselves as an alternative culture, therefore preserving the consumer's positioning as different than others. "Cultural consumption," as we know from the sociologist Pierre Bourdieu, "fulfill[s] a social function of legitimating social differences."[7] He continues:

> Taste classifies, and it classifies the classifier. Social subjects, classified by their classifications, distinguish themselves by the distinctions they make, between the beautiful and the ugly, the distinguished and the vulgar, in which their position in the objective classifications is expressed or betrayed.[8]

In a series of articles and books, Bourdieu explored how the capacity for appreciating art—having taste—is intimately related to one's education and class. His studies of behavior toward cultural institutions such as museums evinced the middle classes' heightened confidence in contrast to the working class. Bourdieu concluded that the middle classes' attitude toward these institutions derived from their families and schools, rather than any innate or genetic talent to appreciate art. Taste is a social construction, rather than a "natural" quality.

Extreme cinema trades on appeals to alternative taste that are endemic to the phenomenon of "art-house cinema." As Barbara Wilinsky describes in her book on the birth of art-house cinema, commercial imperatives and artistic remits meant that postwar American art-house cinemas functioned on a seeming paradox: maximizing profits by selling the exclusivity of alternative culture to as wide an audience as possible. Art cinema, Wilinsky reminds us, has always "worked to create its image of difference for particular (and, oftentimes, financial) reasons."[9] Even with the consolidation of the art-house circuit, this phenomenon is a common marketing technique even today. Extreme cinema, which is a subset of art cinema that uses and exaggerates strategies of popular, cult, and exploitation movies, depends on this "image of difference" to distinguish itself from these lowbrow forms.

Specifically, extreme cinema depends on two hermeneutic transformations: (1) the creator's intention and/or pretension to be producing something more sophisticated than simple horror; and (2) the consumer's belief and/or desire to have the capability of rarefied taste to appreciate larger, deeper meanings beyond the obvious horror. Understanding these exaggerations as such—that is, recognizing irony, excess, allegory, and other tactics that these films employ to assert their status as extreme cinema—distinguishes the consumer or critic as being a member of this special group. This applies whether this understanding takes the form of a sympathetic or redemptive review or even the alternative positioning that one likes or enjoys watching the gory moving images on offer.

Bourdieu describes the highbrow aesthetic positioning as the "pure gaze," a "quasi-creative power which sets the aesthete apart from the common herd."[10] This rarefied form of taste operates in contrast to the "barbarous" popular taste and, indeed, embraces art that is anti-popular and thus divides society into "those who understand and those who do not."[11] If the popular taste desires beautiful and sensual representations and objects that will quench sensual needs, then the "pure taste" rejects "what is generic, i.e., *common*, 'easy' and immediately accessible, starting with everything that reduces the aesthetic animal to pure and simple animality, to palpable pleasure or sensual desire."[12] While the popular taste is intimately and primarily interested in the immediately and clearly beautiful and sensual, the pure taste indulges "indifference and distance" toward the very question of *content* (or, indeed, praises the "ugly") and favors intricate, challenging, or innovative *form*.[13] Bourdieu's categories gesture toward explaining the paradox of extreme cinema as a highbrow ethical sanctioning of the lowbrow. On the one hand, the highbrow recuperation of the ugly or disgusting, a key characteristic of extreme cinema, deemphasizes or overturns the idea of the aesthetic and adheres to Bourdieu's formulation of the "pure gaze." On the other hand, of course, the indulgence of the animalistic, the violent, and the sexual by itself constitutes an engagement of the lowbrow; in common parlance, extreme cinema is slumming.

The cultural sociologist Herbert J. Gans helps to understand this blurring of consumption across taste categories. Compared with Bourdieu's studies, Gans offers perhaps a less-rigid correlation between taste and social class in his study of the American context when he urges that "there is no simple correlation between the 'higher' and 'lower' taste cultures . . . and the higher and lower classes";[14] he notes, following others, that individuals often consume culture as "omnivores" and that much culture has a converging or cross-over appeal.[15] Noting the erosion of the difference between the "sacred high culture and its profane counterpart,"[16] Gans examines the trend for "cultural straddling," by which upward straddling is often for status-seeking, whereas "downward straddling is usually justified by the need for catharsis or relief from the cultural routine."[17] Gans also demonstrates how higher culture publics frequently take up popular culture only after it has been dropped by its original users.

Interrogating the larger phenomena of "slumming," or "cultural straddling," and especially intellectuals' engagement with popular culture and the debates over the cultural and legal shibboleths between pornography and erotic art in the United States, Andrew Ross has further shown how the distinction between "art" and "obscenity" is matter of distinction which responds "to the demand for new forms of discrimination made inevitable by the unfolding spectacle of a full-blown mass culture."[18] Ross demonstrates how, time and again, intellectuals have laid claim to the ability to separate their appreciation of sexually explicit art from a visceral, emotional response typical of Bourdieu's "popular taste."

Ross offers the example of Susan Sontag's recuperation of French erotic writing, "The Pornographic Imagination," in which she argues that Georges Bataille and others produced not pornography in its contemporary patriarchal, lowbrow understanding, but rather genuine literature.[19] Speaking of a sublime, intellectual genealogy of pornography, Sontag redeems a tradition of (French, avant-garde) sex literature as "the pornographic imagination." Later addressing an interviewer's question as to what distinguishes "the pornographic imagination" from other iterations of erotic culture, Sontag claims that the former "treats sexuality as an extreme situation," meaning that "what pornography depicts is in one obvious sense, quite unrealistic."[20] This rhetorical gesture retrieves Bourdieu's insistence on the "pure taste" as focusing on the stylized and defamiliarized. In Ross's analysis, Sontag's sub-genre of avant-garde eroticism seeks to "disrupt" the traditional "controlled hedonism of consumer capitalism" associated with quotidian pornography "by pursuing pain and pleasure in excess of its conventional limits; as Sontag puts it approvingly elsewhere, 'having one's sensorium challenged or stretched hurts.'"[21]

Sontag's recuperation of pornography clearly relies on a very important distinction between, simply stated, "good" intellectual eroticism and "bad" lowbrow exploitation. In Ross's terms, Sontag's "pornographic imagination" is "a realm of radical chic pleasure, far removed from the semen-stained squalor of the peep show, the strip joint, the video arcade, and other sites of popular pornotopian fantasy."[22] Sontag's case for pornography as serious *belles lettres* is an act of distinction that celebrates a literature of extremity which is transgressive in production and liberating in consumption—that is, for those privileged consumers, who because of "subtle and extensive psychic preparation,"[23] are able to understand its subversion.

Ross demonstrates that these assumptions about elite taste and the ability to discern are endemic in intellectuals' engagement with mass culture, and in particular, sexually explicit culture. These distinctions have become institutionalized insofar as obscenity laws and public and private television dictates make exceptions to censorship for works of medical or scientific value or artistic merit. Nevertheless, this moral–legal principle has been put under critique, not by the least of which is the US Supreme Court judge Jerome Frank, who in a decision on the federal obscenity statute queried the exemptions usually granted to sexual explicitness in books of "literary distinction." The judge found "no evidence that the elite has the moral fortitude (an immunity from moral corruption) superior to that of 'the masses.'"[24]

Nevertheless, as we shall see, this supposed cognitive capability to "distinguish" and "appreciate" on an aesthetic level is important for both the critics and the makers of extreme cinema; this "disinterestedness" enables an ethical stance toward the work. According to Andrew Ross, it is not the individual semantics of such categories that is important, but rather "the capacity to draw the line between and around categories of taste; it is the power to define where each relational category begins and ends, and the power to determine what it contains at any one time."[25] Distinction becomes the source of status for both the "artist" and the spectator. Just as consuming art and foreign-language films constitute one way to distinguish oneself from others in middlebrow, middle-class society, the ability to "appreciate" sex and violence on an aesthetic, rather than exploitative or physiological level becomes, paradoxically, a means to establishing oneself as part of a discerning, highbrow taste culture. Stated simply, it is the ability to handle a hot object without being burned, to be exposed to illness without becoming infected. Bourdieu calls this "moral agnosticism": the special ability that the highbrow profess to have to appreciate art for art's sake and apart from moral quandaries.[26]

THE RHETORIC OF EXTREME FILMMAKERS: MORAL AGNOSTICISM AND THE "ETHICAL" ALTERNATIVE

This special ability to separate or distinguish between exploitative representations of violence and sexuality and a higher critical appropriation is claimed, time and again, by extreme cinema's directors in statements and interviews. In theoretical declarations or sophisticated interpretations of their work, the filmmakers actively create a distance to their object of inquiry that makes them immune to its potential for titillation. Examining extreme filmmakers' public statements reveals another paradox: a "moral agnosticism" toward violence and violent sexuality, but one developed in the higher service of morality.

It is vital to understand the context of these ex post facto interventions. Whether disseminated as published production notes, DVD commentaries, public addresses in cinemas or museums, essays in (scholarly) publications, answers in newspaper or magazine interviews, or statements on websites, these pronouncements and performances seek to shape the reception of graphically violent or sexual film as a higher form of art. The sophistication—and, even, very *existence*—of these statements distinguish extreme cinema from *Saw* or *Hostel*, whose makers assert no claims to artistic intentions, nor deny their primary function as emotional—rather than intellectual—experiences.

The ethical imperative of extreme cinema, in other words, derives from the very articulation of a potentially moral objective. (It is the critic's task, as we shall see, to evaluate whether these stated objectives are achieved or even actually addressed in the works themselves.) The very expression of ethical intention distinguishes these films as "extreme" by gesturing toward a transcendent purpose. If conventional horror delivers a tactical disgust, that is, moments of repulsion arranged throughout the narrative with logic that ultimately serves a larger, strategic purpose of entertainment, the media performances of extreme filmmakers claim an altogether different animus: a commitment to disturb, a pedagogical instruction to self-reflection, and, even, an invitation to end the screening.[27] We see this alternative strategy plainly in the case of extreme filmmaker Gaspar Noé, whose films are regularly abandoned in festival screenings; he provokes his audiences with literal invitations to leave. His *Seul contre tous* (*I Stand Alone*, 1998) opens with the message: "ATTENTION / YOU HAVE 30 SECONDS TO LEAVE THE

SCREENING OF THIS FILM." Flashing on the screen, the 30 seconds count down in real time to 29, 28, 27, and so on. His later production *Irréversible* not only depicts graphic and gruesome violence and rape; it includes strobe lights engineered to induce epileptic seizures and sounds at frequencies designed to onset headaches in spectators. For his part, Michael Haneke has claimed in statements and interviews that the purpose of his filmmaking is to "rape" the viewer into a critical spectatorship.[28] When told by an interviewer that his theoretical comments on his films make the experience seem stressful rather than entertaining, Haneke replied, "I am merely trying to provoke you to independence. Furthermore, you can walk out of the film. I have nothing against that."[29] Commenting on an American focus group that walked out of a test screening for *Funny Games U.S.* (2007), Haneke said: "To that I say: the film worked, it spoiled the fun of the consumer of violence." In the interview Haneke revealed that he feels "confirmed" when the viewer leaves the theater.[30]

In this context it is useful to consider further examples, such as Michael Winterbottom and his *The Killer Inside Me* (2010), which, on account of its representations of sex and violence was deemed by *Times* critic Demetrios Matheou to be "the most disturbing film of the year."[31] Responding to this criticism in interview, Winterbottom asked: "Surely what would be immoral would be for the violence to be entertaining or acceptable?"[32] In Winterbottom's idiom, disturbing violence is moral violence.

Remarkable also are comments by another prominent director of the "new extremity," Catherine Breillat, whose films are notorious for their explicit treatment of sexuality. In interviews she has referred to herself as a sort of sex "entomologist," who examines the microdynamics of sexual relations and desire.[33] Typical of the public comments of several extreme filmmakers, Breillat positions herself using the language of science; her "experiments" are meant for the "benefit" of others. These attempts to establish a clinical, ethical distance from the subject itself reminds one of the statements of American politicians who "experimented" with drugs as young men—as if their pleasure-seeking was a somehow scholarly attempt to understand the appeal to "others," rather than self-serving or patently hedonistic. These directors imply that their extreme cinema, in contrast to mere horror or torture porn and related lowbrow genres, contains its own analysis. These filmmakers "know better."

Michael Haneke's public statements and interviews offer another set of examples of this phenomenon. Speaking about the difficulties of adapting *Die Klavierspielerin* (*The Piano Teacher*, 2000), which depicts public urination, voyeurism, genital self-harm, and sadomasochistic sex acts, the director revealed in interview that the main challenge was one of distinction: "to make an obscene film but not a pornographic one."[34] Much in the manner of the consumer or critic of extreme cinema, the extreme filmmaker distinguishes himself by claiming the ability to separate himself from the physiological effects of extreme representation; it is also a measure of differentiation from other directors. Whereas Oliver Stone (in *Natural Born Killers*,1994) or Stanley Kubrick (*A Clockwork Orange*, 1971) were unable to make this distinction (to depict the titillating without titillating the audience), according to Haneke—in response to an interviewer's question about *Funny Games*—*he* was.[35]

Indeed, Haneke has gone so far as to outline a sort of instruction manual for filmmakers to represent violence ethically: a public statement, originally delivered before a screening of *Benny's Video* (1992) at a Munich cinema in 1995, and later published under the title "Violence and Media."[36] Noting that violence has been part and parcel of narrative filmmaking since its beginnings, the essay makes a medium-specific argument for the special bearing of violence and cinema. Because of film's indexical connection to reality, according to Haneke, the filmic representation of violence is judged by other criteria than literature or painting. Furthermore, whereas painting and even photography show the results of violence, film shows violence in action. This—together with cinema's larger-than-life format and its simultaneous appeal to both eye and ear—produces a unique engagement with the viewer; if the still picture encourages identification between the spectator and *victim*, the motion picture creates an alignment between the spectator and the *perpetrator*.[37] Technological developments have made these connections ever stronger: Violence has increased in quality because of advances in special effects and the new media have enabled violence to proliferate. Indeed, the new media landscape has leveled verisimilitude between real (e.g., news reports of war) and fictional violence to such an extent that children growing up in this era may be unable to distinguish between the two.[38]

According to Haneke, an ethical representation of violence must avoid the typical problems of mainstream media violence, which "de-realizes, exaggerates, aestheticizes or ironizes" violence. These conventional tactics make violence palatable by three means: First, by locating violence in a setting or era far from spectator's normal life (e.g., Western, science fiction, or horror films); second, by providing exceptional, "morally justifiable" narrative situations in which violence is the only logical choice (war films, rape-revenge films, vigilante films); or, third, by contextualizing violence in comedy or satire (slapstick, spaghetti Western, postmodern cynicism).[39] The only ethical alternative, Haneke claims, is to deliver forms to represent violence in a way that respects victims, returns pain (rather than aesthetic pleasure) to the representation of violence, and allows viewers to identify with the victims rather than the perpetrators.[40]

How are we to deal with these statements, these programmatic ethical explanations? The interventions of Breillat, Winterbottom, Haneke, and Noé are surely authorial gestures, media stunts, and, in their idiom, "experiments" with the darker areas of society and the human mind. By positioning themselves as both artists and "scientists," they claim a certain immunity from the subjects that they examine. Their rhetoric serves the function of morally sanctioning the apparently exploitative representation of violence. In various shades of gray and to various extents (Haneke perhaps the most overtly didactic, Noé perhaps the most explicitly provocative), extreme film-makers assume a moral agnosticism to broach moral questions.

It is useful to understand these directors' statements with two theoretical concepts. The first, already raised, is the idea of cultural straddling, or slumming. Andrew Ross defines the latter as "secure opportunities for intellectuals to sample the emotional charge of popular culture while guaranteeing their immunity from its power to constitute social identities that are in some way marked as subordinate."[41]

The second is Bourdieu's concept of heterodoxy, the need of artists to differentiate themselves from mainstream values; this "subjective" perspective on the world becomes the key to the artist's self-construction and positioning. Although faced with a real material dependence on the economic field (whether commercial capital or public grants or subsidies), the artistic habitus projects the fantasy of disinterestedness: distance from economic and social necessity, art for art's sake, artistic creation as self-expression rather than commerce. This encompasses eccentric, abject, or other representations or forms opposed to bourgeois respectability or normality; as art historian John A. Walker has demonstrated, "provocation and outrage" have been a crucial constituent of visual art since the nineteenth century.[42] Indeed, the artistic habitus often invites behavior inimical to accepted social norms—or at least the performance of such a disposition. It is here that we recognize the carefully cultivated reputations—whether deserved or not—of Lars von Trier, Michael Haneke, and others, as eccentric, exotic, volatile, or as "particularly difficult" to work with. (Perhaps we also begin to understand the preprogrammed provocation and outrage over Lars von Trier's "I'm a Nazi" comment at the 2011 Cannes Film Festival.)[43] In Bourdieu's terminology, this "heterodoxical" artistic self-positioning bespeaks the identity of the artist as aesthetically and ethically opposed to the status quo and social norms.[44]

Compared with other film trends and genres, extreme cinema resounds particularly with the paradox of the artistic habitus—the disavowed clash between aesthetic disinterestedness and economic necessity. On the one hand it engages themes, forms, and representations associated with commercial genres, which encourages publicity and/or controversy; on the other hand, marketing materials and the statements by the filmmakers ascribe these "works" (not "movies") artistic motivation and purpose, and intellectual worth.[45] Differentiation and the artist's subjective expression—after all a basic feature of the artistic habitus and art cinema as an institution[46]—become the paradoxes of extreme cinema: To differentiate himself or herself, the art filmmaker must indulge in some extremity of sex or violence and thus conform to what every other art filmmaker does. In the words of Steve Neale, "Even where the marks of enunciation themselves are heterogeneous, they tend to be unified and stabilised within the space of an institution which reads and locates them in a homogenous way."[47] For each of these "radical" filmmakers, the answer is remarkably similar: To be moral one must indulge the immoral.

CRITICAL DISCOURSES: DISTINCTION AND "DUMBING-DOWN"

The contemporary journalistic and scholarly debate on extreme cinema can be divided along two rough lines. First, the "highbrow appraisal" applies complex academic theories to explain the productions' difference from lowbrow genres such as horror. This hermeneutic largely "rescues" extreme cinema from critiques of exploitation; its approach revolves around marking and reinforcing distinction.

For example, in Asbjørn Grønstad's reckoning with what he calls the "mischievous appetite for the unwatchable," he differentiates the extreme cinema trend from torture porn's "prosaic desire to shock."[48] "The unwatchability of the films by someone like Noé, Haneke, or Breillat lies not so much on an experiential level as on a philosophical one"; these filmmakers are "motivated by a need to introduce other ways of seeing and to transcend the threshold of the visible world."[49] Grønstad maintains that these films can be usefully regarded "as an antidote to the numbing complacencies and stock humanity of much mainstream cinema"; these productions "defy the processes of representational homogenization" and "are really preoccupied with deeply humanist issues even as they at time seem disturbingly misanthropic."[50]

The highbrow appraisal takes extreme cinema seriously at its word. It ascribes to these films' complex regimes of representation and spectatorship positioning, often deriving these insights from the interviews or public performances of the filmmakers. (The directors often analyze their own work in similar terms.[51]) In this form of criticism, a broad auteurism is implied and accepted as given, the films are decoded for their significance in their domestic cinema (rather than considering how these cultures translate in their international reception), and little attention is paid to the industrial and commercial determinants of this implied positioning: funding structures, marketing, locations of consumption.

In many ways, the highbrow line of inquiry responds to the second approach, what one might call the "middlebrow critique." The latter loathes art directors' recourse to the lowbrow as "dumbing-down," cynical, or nihilistic. Unlike the highbrow appraisal, which privileges authorship at the expense of materialist analysis, the middlebrow critique belittles the filmmakers' artistic intentions and focuses on underlying commercial interests. Occasionally, the middlebrow critique denies that there is any formal, stylistic, or thematic distinction between extreme cinema and the worst splatter or pornographic films. Even more often, it implies that extreme cinema is *even worse* than those films because of its pretensions to high artistic value.

In this vein, a set of contemporary commentators mourn extreme cinema's "infection" of (highbrow) art cinema. Writing on Park Chan-Wook's *Oldboy* (2003) and in particular, its award of the Grand Jury Prize at the Cannes Film Festival, *New York Times* critic Manohla Dargis bemoaned the jury's choice of an "arty exploitation flick"; it represented "a dubious development in recent cinema: the mainstreaming of exploitation."[52] Dargis's comments are a declaration of war against extreme cinema and respond to these hybrids as intrusions into highbrow taste cultures: She laments *Oldboy*'s "integration into the upper tier of the festival circuit." Later, Dargis writes about the company Tartan films, "which puts out works of undisputed artistic worth, genre classics, and pure schlock under the rubric Asia Extreme."[53]

In many ways Dargis's comments represent a form of the so-called "dumbing-down thesis." According to Gans, this form of critique "can suggest that the culture being supplied is less sophisticated or complicated, or tasteful, or thoughtful, or statusful than a past one," although sometimes it is also employed to describe the audience being addressed, "who are thought to have declined in taste, intelligence, and status."[54] The dumbing-down thesis is frequently employed to express disapproval of "blockbuster" exhibitions by venerable museums or when public television channels replace documentaries and foreign films with popular music programs. It is also a common feature of much middlebrow extreme cinema criticism. In one form of this argument, extreme cinema is simply cheap thrills for highbrows, who, it is argued, are not able to be morally agnostic. The other side of this critique is to suggest that although the films are coded and marketed in authored and foreign formats, the filmmakers are, as Ginette Vincendeau suspects about Breillat, "aimed at attracting the attention of festivals and critics with more nudity, more erections, more violence and more *outré* sexual practices."[55]

In many ways, the dumbing-down argument extends to the origin of the term *extreme cinema*, which derives from an article by James Quandt on the "New French Extremity." In this piece, which appeared in the February 2004 issue of *Artforum*, Quandt examines critical reactions to Bruno Dumont's *Twentynine Palms* (2003) after his quieter, more Bressonian efforts, *La vie de Jésus* (*The Life of Jesus*, 1997) and *L'Humanité* (1999). The anxiety, Quandt perceives, revolves around Dumont's "borrowing the codes of Hollywood horror films," but above all that the *auteur*, "once impervious to fashion, has succumbed to the growing vogue for shock tactics in French cinema over the past decade."[56]

Quandt outlines a series of filmmakers—among them François Ozon, Gaspar Noé, Catherine Breillat, and Phillippe Grandrieux—"suddenly determined to break every taboo, to wade in rivers of viscera and spumes of sperm, to fill each frame with flesh, nubile or gnarled, and subject it to all manner of penetration, mutilation and defilement," thereby appropriating the stuff "once the provenance of splatter films, exploitation flicks, and porn."[57]

Quandt's take on these films, which he describes at one point as "absurd, false, and self-important," is caustic.[58] Whereas French cinema previously provoked with innovative forms, politics, or philosophies, the New French Extremity is merely "a narcissistic response to the collapse of ideology in a society traditionally defined by political polarity and theoretical certitude."[59] His comments almost always imply the trend to be limited to France, although in closing he admits the possibility that the films might be "symptomatic of an international vogue for 'porno chic,' widely apparent in art-house films from Austria to Korea."[60] Most tellingly, Quandt speculates that:

> The drastic tactics of these directors could be an attempt to meet (and perchance defeat) Hollywood and Asian filmmaking on their own *Kill Bill* terms or to secure distributors and audiences in a market disinclined toward foreign films; and in fact many of these works have been bought in North America, while far worthier French films have gone wanting.[61]

Quandt's piece is both the prototype and, in many ways, the archetype of the "middlebrow" extreme cinema criticism. His dumbing-down argument is underpinned by a nostalgia, in this case for the "innovative" and "philosophical" French *nouvelle vague* and late 1960s political cinema. As Gans writes, "dumbing down requires a comparison, which is always made from the perspective of a more statusful past culture as well as a more intelligent public."[62]

This opposition between yesterday's smartly innovative art films and today's "dumb" provocations is present in much of the reportage on these films. In an article on the production trend, Peter Brunette describes new art films' "unflinching look" and in particular how directors "push the envelope with realistic-seeming violence."[63] Looking at productions by Noé and Haneke as well as Patrice Chéreau's *Son frère* (*His Brother*, 2003), Brunette conceives of the phenomenon as a highbrow attempt to anger conventional middle-class people and to create "unforgettable moments" in the form of explicit sex or violence; these leave the trace of the artist and his or her pretension to a unique interpretation of reality. The article comes with a sidebar, however, which opposes two groups of three films according to two rubrics: art and agony. Charting a supposed trajectory from innocent to in-your-face in art films, *L'année dernière à Marienbad* (*Last Year in Marienbad*, dir. Alain Resnais, 1961) contrasts with *Memento* (dir. Christopher Nolan, 2000), *À bout de souffle* (*Breathless*, dir. Jean-Luc Godard, 1960) with David Cronenberg's *Crash* (1996), *Un homme et une femme* (*A Man and a Woman*, dir. Claude Lelouch, 1966) with *Baise-moi* (dir. Virginie Despentes, 2000), and *The Piano* (dir. Jane Campion, 1993) with *Die Klavierspielerin*. The comparisons rest on incidental plot points (the car accident in *À bout de souffle*, for instance) or coincidental overlaps in titles (e.g., between the Campion and Haneke productions) to make sweeping generalizations about a supposed (downward) trajectory in all art cinema. The dumbing-down nostalgia is exemplary of much journalistic criticism on the new extremity of art cinema. It ultimately *preserves* distinction (the rigid binaries of commercial vs. art-house, lowbrow vs. middle/highbrow) by mourning extreme cinema's lack of difference to exploitation and by claiming that extreme cinema is a tainted or unpure form of art-house cinema.

Indeed, examining the reactions of the middlebrow critics reveals it is above all the hypocrisy of extreme cinema—its mixing of highbrow and lowbrow elements or the perceived emptiness of the films' gesture toward higher intentions—that provokes the most heated attacks. The often furious, ad hominem reactions against Michael Haneke, for example, bear this out. Lowbrow horror films receive easy dismissal or "camp" enjoyment by cultural elites. When Haneke's *Funny Games,* premiered at Cannes, according to a *Variety* reviewer, it "appealed to some Euro highbrows but turned off nearly everyone else"; critics and prominent filmmakers, such as Wim Wenders, demonstratively left the theater.[64] Wolfram Schütte has written that "no other director—with the possible exception of the Straubs—has been so persistently persecuted by German critics with more hate and spite than Michael Haneke."[65] We can understand these reactions if we look, not merely to the actual content of *Funny Games*, but to its pretensions. Rather than blithely producing horror films, Haneke has outlined a serious aesthetic program according to how he believes violence should or should not be represented in media. These aspirations and, in particular, these statements in public and in interviews, this very *attempt* to transcend the usual boundaries of representing violence blurs the lines between the popular and the pure and incenses a range of critics. The aesthete-critic, as Bourdieu writes, "prefers naivety *to 'pretentiousness.'*"[66] If popular horror poses no threat to those with cultural capital, the middlebrow and those forms that mix the popular and pure create immense anxiety. Because regimes of taste depend on clearly defined oppositions, aesthetic judgments are "often constituted in opposition to the choices of the groups closest in social space, with whom the competition is most direct and most immediate."[67]

CONCLUSIONS

A case could be made for extreme cinema as a genre. It might list, for example, self-reflexive narratives punctuated by graphic depictions of violence or sexuality, the indulgence of taboo, absurd, or abject themes or situations, and so on. Nevertheless, it would be a weak claim and might exclude as many presumed exemplars as it includes; this is because, as I have argued, extreme cinema as a critical category exists largely because of the pretensions of distinction made by the producers and consumers of these films. For this reason, I consider extreme cinema to be a production trend within global (art) cinema, rather than as a genre in a strict semantic or syntactic sense.[68] Following the work of Tino Balio in the context of Hollywood, the term "production trend"—unlike a "genre"—recognizes the "fashion" of certain subjects, themes, and semantics in patterns of commercial production and allows one to organize these films, in addition to their content, on the basis of the programmed media performances that accompany their marketing.[69] There is clearly a genealogy of extreme cinema to be explored, whether one begins with the dark works at the tail end of the golden age of cinephilia—*A Clockwork Orange, Salò,* and *Ai no korîda* (dir. Oshima Nagisa, *In the Realm of the Senses,* 1976)—or even traces a broader pre-history from Thomas Edison's *Electrocuting an Elephant* (1903). Indeed, major film historians and theorists, such as Siegfried Kracauer and Amos Vogel, have identified "phenomena overwhelming consciousness" and "subversive cinema" as special affinities of film, more so than other arts or media.[70]

Extreme cinema is an industrial product with important material contexts of production, distribution, and exhibition; but it also aspires to be an aesthetic and cultural form. It can be located between the fronts of popular and highbrow culture and between developments in technology and individualized viewing practices. This production trend is caught between the confessionalism of reality-TV and celebrity culture and the traditionally exhibitionistic and personal self-representations of contemporary art; it is a product of the regular cycles of art culture and film festivals and the vagaries of global commercial distribution.

Like the highbrow commentators, I feel it is essential to pay attention to these films' representational and stylistic tactics and their concomitant demands on spectators. Nevertheless, in the vein of the middlebrow critique, I take a skeptical stance to wholly "disinterested" aesthetic appraisals and certainly the calculated value of the "extreme" label for distributors and exhibitors—but without dismissing the productions out of hand, in the manner of the middlebrow critics. The key to these works is the statements and media performances of the filmmakers and their agents, the crisscrossed ethical pretensions that form the ontological backbone of the production trend. In sum, understanding extreme cinema means understanding the ethics of extreme cinema.

Further, this case study demonstrates how some perennial concerns in film studies traditionally treated under the rubric of "aesthetics" and so on can be productively studied from an ethical standpoint. Art cinema and its historical modes of production and reception, authorship and its presumption of signature style, the concept of genre and production trends, the classification and self-understanding of filmmaking, and the industrial and marketing histories that inform them: The example of extreme cinema shows all these issues to depend on ethical discourses.

In turn, this study gestures toward a further layer of moral questions at stake in film studies as a discipline: the ethics of criticism itself. Of course, judgment, distinction, and evaluation are always at the heart of the critical activity. Yet in this case—because of the friend-or-foe logic that has historically marked the production, reception, and very meaning of art-house cinema (as a supposed antidote to a monolithic conception of Hollywood)—critical discourse has been especially polarized around ethical imperatives. As evidenced by the highbrow and middlebrow appraisals of extreme cinema, traditionally, the film critic or scholar has often been forced to either be for art cinema or against it and thus, by extension, to advocate or castigate Hollywood and the ideological and economic systems that it has come to signify in much scholarly writing. (A clear through-line between the otherwise antagonistic critical movements of liberal-humanistic criticism of the 1940s and 1950s, e.g., André Bazin and the ideological subject-theory beginning in the late 1960s, for instance Peter Wollen, is an ethical "ought.")[71] Soberly investigating such tendencies in writing about film is perhaps the most urgent task of a new cine-ethics.[72]

NOTES

1. Vanessa Thorpe, "Outrage as French couple's film judged too sexy for Cannes," *The Observer,* May 16, 2010, 7.
2. David Rose, "Evidence Mounts That Violent Videos Desensitise Teenagers," *The Times*, October 19, 2010, 17.
3. Joan Hawkins, *Cutting Edge: Art Horror and the Horrific Avant-Garde* (Minneapolis: University of Minnesota Press, 2000).
4. See Jason Middleton, "The Subject of Torture: Regarding the Pain of Americans in *Hostel*," *Cinema Journal* 49.4 (2010): 1–24; here 1–2. See also David Edelstein, "Now Playing at Your Local Multiplex: Torture Porn," *New York Magazine*, February 6, 2006 as well as Peter Gormley, *The New-Brutality Film: Race and Affect in Contemporary Cinema* (Bristol: Intellect, 2005).
5. Middleton, "The Subject of Torture," 24.
6. Raymond Williams, "Base and Superstructure in Marxist Cultural Theory," *New Left Review* 82 (1973): 3–16; here 11.
7. Pierre Bourdieu, *Distinction: A Social Critique of the Judgement of Taste,* trans. Richard Nice (London: Routledge, 2010), xxx.
8. Ibid., xxix.
9. Barbara Wilinsky, *Sure Seaters: The Emergence of Art House Cinema* (Minneapolis: University of Minnesota Press, 2001), 3–4.
10. Bourdieu, *Distinction,* 23.
11. Ibid.
12. Ibid., 24.
13. Ibid.
14. Herbert J. Gans, *Popular Culture and High Culture: An Analysis and Evaluation of Taste,* second revised edition (New York: Basic Books, 1999), vii.
15. Ibid., 9.
16. Ibid., 148.
17. Ibid., 136.
18. Andrew Ross, *No Respect: Intellectuals and Popular Culture* (New York: Routledge, 1989), 180.
19. Susan Sontag, "The Pornographic Imagination," in *A Susan Sontag Reader* (New York: Vintage, 1983), 205–234.
20. Geoffrey Movius, "An Interview with Susan Sontag," in *Conversations with Susan Sontag,* ed. Leland Poague (Jackson: University Press of Mississippi, 1995), 71.

21. Ross, *No Respect,* 184. Sontag's quotation is from her essay "One Culture and the New Sensibility," in *Against Interpretation* (New York: Farrar, Straus & Giroux, 1966), 303.
22. Ross, *No Respect,* 184.
23. Sontag, "The Pornographic Imagination," 233.
24. Quoted in Ross, *No Respect,* 180–181.
25. Ibid., 61.
26. See Bourdieu, *Distinction,* xxviii. This position marks a categorical similarity between the popular and the highbrow: The former supposedly do not concern themselves with these moral dilemmas, the latter are supposedly too sophisticated to *need* to care about them.
27. For more on this subject, see Mattias Frey, "Tuning Out, Turning In, and Walking Off: The Film Spectator in Pain," in *Ethics and Images of Pain,* ed. Asbjørn Grønstad and Henrik Gustafsson (New York: Routledge, 2012), 93–111.
28. Philipp Oehmke and Lars-Olav Beier, "'Jeder Film vergewaltigt,'" *Der Spiegel,* October 19, 2009, 112–114.
29. Ibid., 113.
30. Ibid.
31. Demetrios Matheou, "He'll Hit Her—And Think It Feels Like a Kiss," *The Sunday Times,* May 30, 2010.
32. Quoted in Hannah McGill, "Inside Out," *Sight and Sound,* June 2010, 40–42; here 41.
33. "Interview with Catherine Breillat," Tartan Video DVD of *Anatomy of Hell* (2004).
34. Margret Köhler, "Fremd ist jeder," *Berliner Morgenpost,* February 1, 2001.
35. Julian Hanich, "Gehört die Gewalt ins Kino, Herr Haneke?," *Der Tagesspiegel,* September 10, 1997.
36. An English translation has recently been published as Michael Haneke, "Violence and the Media," trans. Evan Torner, in *A Companion to Michael Haneke,* ed. Roy Grundmann (Malden, MA: Wiley, 2010), 575–579; for an elaborated investigation of Haneke's film theory, see Mattias Frey, "The Message and the Medium: Haneke's Film Theory and Digital Praxis," in *On Michael Haneke,* ed. Brian Price and John David Rhodes (Detroit: Wayne State University Press, 2010), 153–165.
37. Haneke, "Violence and the Media," 575–576.
38. Ibid., 577.
39. Ibid., 576–577.
40. Ibid., 579.
41. Ross, *No Respect,* 5.
42. John A. Walker, *Art and Outrage: Provocation, Controversy and the Visual Arts* (London: Pluto Press, 1999), esp. 1ff.
43. See Nick James, "The Confessions of Lars von Trier," *Sight and Sound,* October 2011, 30–34, or Jack Malvern, "Film Director Vows to Remain Silent After Nazi Remarks," *The Times,* October 6, 2011, 4.
44. Pierre Bourdieu, *Free Exchange,* trans. Randal Johnson and Hans Haacke (Stanford, CA: Stanford University Press, 1995), 11–12.
45. On this, see, for example, Gans, *Popular Culture and High Culture,* 76: "High culture is creator-oriented and its aesthetics and its principles of criticism are based on this orientation. The belief that the creator's intentions are crucial and the values of the audience almost irrelevant functions to protect creators from the audience, making it easier for them to create."
46. Steve Neale, "Art Cinema as Institution," *Screen* 22.1 (1981): 11–19; here esp. 14.
47. Ibid., 15.

48. Asbjørn Grønstad, "Abject Desire: *Anatomie de l'enfer* and the Unwatch-able," *Studies in French Cinema* 6.3 (2006): 161–169.
49. Ibid., 163–164.
50. Ibid., 164.
51. Michael Haneke, for example, understands his cinema as "polemical state-ments against the American 'barrel down' cinema and its dis-empowerment of the spectator"; it is "an appeal for a cinema of insistent questions instead of false (because too quick) answers, for clarifying distance in place of vio-lating closeness, for provocation and dialogue instead of consumption and consensus." Quoted in Mattias Frey, "A Cinema of Disturbance: The Films of Michael Haneke in Context," second revised edition, *Senses of Cinema* 57 (2010), accessed July 5, 2013, http://sensesofcinema.com/2010/great-directors/michael-haneke/.
52. Manohla Dargis, "Sometimes Blood Really Isn't Indelible," *New York Times,* March 3, 2005, B7. Quoted in Joan Hawkins, "Culture Wars: Some New Trends in Art Horror," *Jump Cut* 51 (2009), accessed July 5, 2013, http://www.ejumpcut.org/archive/jc51.2009/artHorror/.
53. Dargis, "Sometimes Blood Really Isn't Indelible," B7.
54. Gans, *Popular Culture and High Culture,* 80.
55. Ginette Vincendeau, "Sisters, Sex and Sitcom," *Sight and Sound,* December 2001, 18–20; here 18.
56. James Quandt, "Flesh & Blood: Sex and Violence in Recent French Cin-ema," *Artforum* 42.6 (2004): 126–132; here 127.
57. Ibid., 127–128.
58. Ibid., 132.
59. Ibid., 128, 132.
60. Ibid., 132.
61. Ibid.
62. Gans, *Popular Culture and High Culture,* 80.
63. Peter Brunette, "Art Films Offer Unflinching Look," *Boston Globe,* March 9, 2003, N13, N16.
64. Todd McCarthy, "All That Glitters Not Always Gold," *Variety,* May 19–25, 1992, 7–8; here 8.
65. Wolfram Schütte, "Eine deutsche Psychose?," *perlentaucher.de,* accessed July 5, 2013, http://www.perlentaucher.de/artikel/5806.html.
66. Bourdieu, *Distinction,* 55.
67. Ibid., 53.
68. See Rick Altman, "A Semantic/Syntantic Approach to Genre," *Cinema Jour-nal* 23.3 (1984): 6–18; and Rick Altman, *Film/Genre* (London: British Film Institute, 1999).
69. See the work of Tino Balio: for instance, *The American Film Industry* (Madi-son: University of Wisconsin Press, 1976) or "Hollywood Production Trends in the Era of Globalisation," in *Genre and Contemporary Hollywood,* ed. Steve Neale (London: British Film Institute, 2002), 165–184.
70. See Siegfried Kracauer, *Theory of Film: The Redemption of Physical Reality* (Princeton, NJ: Princeton University Press, 1960), esp. 57f., and Amos Vogel, *Film as a Subversive Art* (London: Weidenfeld and Nicolson, 1974).
71. For a similar phenomenon in literary criticism, see Rónán McDonald, *The Death of the Critic* (London: Continuum, 2007), 120–121.
72. To be sure, this has already begun. See, for example, D.N. Rodowick, "An Elegy for Theory," *October* 122 (2007): 91–109.

10 Moral Agency, Artistic Immorality, and Critical Appreciation

Lars von Trier's *The Idiots*

Trevor Ponech

Artworks frequently incorporate morally troublesome thinking. Sometimes artists disregard—if not embrace—the risk of discomfiting audiences' moral sensibilities and reactions. Some works are indeed calculated to elicit just such an uptake. Here, the work *qua* generative process involves adapting an artistic design to the flouting of notions of moral goodness or the transgressing of prohibitions, norms, or proprieties.

I shall argue that, insofar as it is operative within the artist's compositional activities, morally troubling or reprehensible thinking meshes with the work's creative design and artistically evaluable features. I begin by describing what I take to be a fitting target of ethical interpretation, on a pragmatic, causalist understanding of artworks as a species of utterances. At the same time, I examine how sources of ethical disvalue intrinsic to such utterances might be relevant to critical appreciation of artworks. Moral demerits might make it harder for audiences to approve of works artistically. Some philosophers have difficulty imagining how moral failings could be artistically good-making; others reject this possibility outright.[1] In eventually defending it, I do not propose that the nature of art—or a genre thereof, like transgressive cinema—is such that moral defects are especially apt to enhance artistic value. Yet given the potential entanglement of morally defective thinking with the creative process, we should recognize that a work's artistic value cannot always be prized apart from, and sometimes emerges in virtue of, a morally unvaluable intrinsic feature. This feature can merit our artistic approval, even if we withhold it for moral reasons.

In the course of my argument, I draw upon cinematic examples of morally ambivalent, perhaps even transgressive works. Lars von Trier is well known for combining morally dangerous, ethically combustive thematic and conceptual elements with risky cinematic experimentation. It will help to take a look at the entanglement of moral provocation with artistic design characteristic of von Trier's cinema. I turn to one of von Trier's works in particular, *The Idiots*, as a heuristic device to clarify and respond to puzzles about how artworks intrinsically possess moral properties and about the prospects for explaining the bearing of moral upon artistic value.

MORAL AGENCY AND CRITICAL APPRECIATION

Moral inquiry is directed at persons and their actions. Thus philosophers are often at pains to accommodate artworks as proper objects of moral scrutiny and to establish moral concerns as integral to aesthetic judgment. Artworks supposedly are "inanimate" items not themselves endowed with mental lives.[2] Moreover, interpretation *per se* is assumed to be principally sustained by appeal to features of a text or display itself rather than to psychological facts about that artifact's makers. A popular remedy is to associate the ethical critic's target with a psychological perspective the work somehow manifests or projects.[3] The artistic structure's properties are such that suitably informed audiences conversant in the applicable artistic and semantic conventions and possessing relevant cultural knowledge are likely to get the impression that this structure evokes or indicates certain morally valenced attitudes toward the represented situations and entities. These attitudes might diverge from either the author's actual moral character or the perspective she intended to evoke or prescribe. Supposing it to be an essential, constitutive part of an artwork, W, this perspective, rather than the maker's mental states, is the correct target of our aesthetic regard and moral appraisal.

The formalist strategy of displacing a work's moral facets onto an ascribed perspective, manifested artist, or other such fictional construct is unsatisfactory. Briefly stated, my sympathies reside with an understanding of the interpretative object conforming to the tenets of the partial intentionalism championed by Paisley Livingston.[4] Livingston's arguments are cogent and comprehensive, yet it is worth reprising a few core premises. Makers' intentions determine some, but far from all, of the semantic and other artistically relevant characteristics of at least some artworks. It is thus sometimes true that W means *m* because W's actual maker or makers acted on the content of a functionally specialized type of reasoning- and action-guiding executive psychological attitude, namely, an expressive intention to indicate or manifest *m*. The maker's intention thereby fixes W's meaning *m*—but only if this intention effectively meshes with features of the artistic structure or display. "Meshing" refers to the congruence or coherence relations among the intention to indicate *m* and the display's various parts and properties, including its observable structural features, conventionally determined meanings, rhetorical patterns, and formal elements. Authors and artists often work meticulously—if with mixed results—to design displays that are apt to evoke the ideas they settle on expressing, some of these meanings being highly implicit or expressed by way of implication.

Partial intentionalism considers the work to be not so much a freestanding object as a process and achievement. It is an achievement in that the display manifests a sample of the maker's sometimes admirable capacities, skills, and dispositions. Upstream of the completed artifact is a course of creative actions directed toward shaping or adapting display features according to the artist's frequently vague, provisional, or shifting preferences. Spontaneous, unconscious, and nonreflective thought and action blend into the generative mixture, as do more deliberative and purposive actions, especially those comprising forward- and backward-feeding, reciprocally related episodes of practical reasoning and problem solving, imagination and reverie, planning, intention formation and revision, and efforts to implement the resultant artistic design ideas so as to realize them in a material structure or arrangement of some kind.

Consistent with this emphasis on the pragmatic dimensions of art-making, I conceive of the typical artistic display as type of complex utterance. An utterance is any publicly observable vehicle in any medium—it need not be a text—by means of which an agent tries to express or communicate ideas and attitudes. "Utterance" also designates the expressive action, or course of coordinated actions, of making such a vehicle. (Whenever I use this term, I have this dual sense in my mind.)

To treat artworks as utterances is to attend to the causal networking of mental items with display features. Sophisticated interpreters perplexed by a work are justified in seeking evidence of the actual artist's intended meanings and delving into the work's etiological psychohistory. No empirical source of biographical and historical evidence pertaining to W's creation is off-limits. Sometimes there are insurmountable practical obstacles to gathering this data; and we can never know everything that went on in the artist's mind while composing W. The familiar restrictions and epistemic predicaments accompanying intentionalism are not, however, sufficient reasons for interpreters in the humanities and social sciences to reject the modest garden-variety explanatory and descriptive advantages of understanding artists, their doings, and their creations in terms of agency and the meaning-determinative powers of mental attitudes. The kind of critical investigation I favor holds that insight into exercises of moral agency during W's creation can enhance work appreciation. Intentionalist, process-oriented interpreters could adopt a standard moral concern with the praiseworthiness or blameworthiness of an utterance, construed as action and product. This version of critical appreciation is predicated on correctly fathoming the agent's planning and intentions regarding semantic content and how to realize it by actively working within a medium. Such comprehension is sometimes deepened with reflection on whether it was morally good, bad, ambivalent, or neutral of a particular artist, or particular collaborating artists, to have made the utterance just as they did. In the arena of critical appreciation, as in life generally, a moral evaluation's warrant depends on it being true to facts about the responsibility a person bears toward something they have done or some attitude they evidently embrace. Such appraisals need not ascribe underlying, persistent character traits either to the actual artist or to a textually projected persona. Rather, ethical criticism can usefully concentrate on episodes of practical reasoning and action involved in an artistic performance.

THE TROLL'S MIRROR

Lars von Trier's *The Idiots* (*Dogme #2—Idioterne,* 1998) affords opportunities to consider the relevance to ethical criticism of artists' practical reasoning, precommitments, and emotionally laden motivations with respect to their works.

The Idiots was bred and born under the Dogme 95 Manifesto's "Vow of Chastity," which binds participating filmmakers to a set of precepts regarding how and why they are to renounce "bourgeois" formal and artistic conventions, aesthetic norms, and stylistic and commercial excesses endemic to contemporary mainstream narrative cinema.[5] Dogme's ten "indisputable rules" include commandments to shoot only on location, a prohibition of all but handheld cinematography, and a ban on special optical effects and filters. Although their manifesto's ironical tone is unmistakable, co-authors von Trier and fellow Danish filmmaker Thomas Vinterberg are serious about the artistic fruitfulness of submitting one's creative activities to explicitly formulated constraints.[6] Dogme's rules are presumed conducive to one payoff especially, the Vow ending with this oath: "My supreme goal is to force the truth out of my characters and settings. I swear to do so by all means available and at the cost of any good taste and any aesthetic considerations."[7]

The Idiots evinces von Trier's embrace of the potential costs of adhering to Dogme's supreme directive. The director encapsulates the movie's premise as the "distasteful idea of people who are not in fact retarded pretending to be."[8] The story follows a group of mostly young people who, with assorted and generally obscure motives, live as communards and collaboratively apply themselves, with individually varying degrees of earnestness, to the project of "spassing." To spass is to feign mental retardation, the band of spassers fancifully embellishing their fictive intellectual disabilities with palsy spasms and prodigious drooling. Despite the spontaneous, improvisational quality to their enactments of make-believe incontinence, the spassing game is not without rules and expectations. When, for example, the ensemble ventures out in public, it is with the objective of fooling people into believing they really are mentally retarded and prolonging this deception no matter— indeed, because of—how uncomfortable and humiliating the situation becomes for both the tricksters and their dupes.

The spassing game is not, however, a mere fiction. In an interview conducted just after completion of *The Idiots,* von Trier calls the Dogme technique the "idiot technique," stressing that the constraints under which he produced the movie make a virtue of drastically reducing the number of elements and choices over which it is allowable and possible to exert rational control, thereby handicapping the director accustomed to operating with a normal complement of filmmaking faculties.[9] This loss of control is not merely formal. Dogme's rules fold into a larger, actual course of game playing inseparable from the movie's generative process. Von Trier himself has often articulated a conception of his cinematic practice as the devising and orchestrating of a psychologically engrossing game, the playing of which comprises his and the other participants' artistic performances.[10] In the case of *The Idiots*, Dogme's regulations are inputs to von Trier's strategy to induce in key artistic collaborators a kind of "moral" vertigo or *ilinx*, to evoke Roger Caillois' notion of play linked to a desire for disorder and the thrill of rambunctious, disruptive behavior.[11]

Von Trier's "idiot technique" has marked affinities with a special strain of *cinéma-vérité*, the aim of which is not passive recording of reality but "active intervention to cut across appearances and extract from them their hidden or dormant truths."[12] His filmmaking plan, like that of certain documentary cinema's *vérité* practitioners, was to wring out psychodrama and emotional authenticity from the work's participants. During day-to-day games of make-believe spassing, both on and off camera, and in prolonged exercises of free-ranging improvisational acting, facilitated by the ban on lighting and camera set-ups and the use of handheld digital recording equipment, the director encouraged his cast to "live their characters rather than act them."[13] As evident from *The Humiliated* (*De ydmygede*, 1998), Jesper Jargil's documentary of the making of *The Idiots*, and from von Trier's published diaries of the shoot, the director sought to engineer intimacy and attachment between cast mates and crew while encouraging actors to experiment, in the interest of personal discovery as well as for the good of creating compelling fictive characters, with releasing their own "inner idiots."[14] Like any committed participant-observer, he joined into the topsy-turviness he instigated. On "naked days," he and other crewmembers disrobed, too. Sometimes he experimented with amateur psychotherapy, in one unsettling episode taking to "the verge of sadism," he admits, his aggressive efforts to motivate actor Anne Louise Hassing (Susanne) to excavate unhappy childhood memories.[15]

Dogme's policies, as interpreted by von Trier, result in a movie that fits the profile of avant-gardist cinematic transgression. The rules themselves trespass against technical and aesthetic norms dominating popular forms of cinema, including works within the traditions of ostensibly daring European art cinema to which von Trier himself is a major contributor. However, beyond this abstract sort of infraction, *The Idiots* has demonstrable powers to disconcert audiences. Many find the movie aesthetically jarring and bewildering. One theorist labeled it "traumatic," referring to its power, shared with other von Trier works, to leave spectators "feeling unsettled and exposed to unpleasant affect."[16]

Imagery is poorly lit and haphazardly composed; there is a preponderance of murky colors, ugly close-ups, and clumsy refocusings; boom microphones dangle inside the frame; unhinged camera work and jumpy editing occasionally render spatial-temporal orientation and shot-to-shot continuity unintelligible. These formal traits seem more coherent, if no prettier, once we realize that von Trier's directorial performance involves his playing at cinematic spassing, his "idiot technique" being a formally rigorous, strategic kind of as-if ineptitude that can only be executed by an expert cinematic practitioner able to break the rules to calculated effect.

A potentially vexing uncertainty attaches to the narrative's content and force. The movie makes it difficult to tell whether certain characters are cognizant of participating in a fiction about make-believe disabled people. The patient tour guide for a factory field trip (Claus Strandberg) could not seem more genuinely awkward, or more surprised when he sees who is driving the van as the visitors depart. Equally convincing are the very accommodating Hells Angels gang members who lend a gentle guiding hand to an anxious, child-like Jeppe (Nikolaj Lie Kaas) at the urinal of a rough bar.[17] In another twist, von Trier intersperses throughout the movie interviews with the fictive spassers. We hear, but do not see, that it is von Trier who asks the questions from outside the frame. In grappling with these twists, some critics favor the possibility that *The Idiots* somehow presents itself as a documentary about the spassers, with the further premise that it thereby subverts or problematizes the stability of its relations to fiction and nonfiction.[18]

The intrusive microphones, brief glimpses of crewmembers, and shaky camera might evoke a stereotype of nonfiction filmmaking, but they also cohere with von Trier's overarching policy to film haphazardly—and nowhere other than the interview segments is there an explicit indication that a documentary crew follows the troupe. The alternative, then, is to deny that *The Idiots* masquerades as nonfiction or effectively undermines the conceptual boundaries between fiction and documentary. The characters and their exploits are fictional because they are markedly the products of von Trier's imaginings, as refined by the director and actors in the course of the latter's pretending to be these characters. Although there is nothing fictive about actor Jens Albinus's erection in the women's locker room, it is the vehicle by which von Trier and his collaborators make it fictionally true that Albinus's character, Stoffer, becomes excited in the shower. Facts about how they imagine Karen's fragile emotional states manifest themselves are—judging from *The Humiliated* and von Trier's journal— sometimes on loan from manifestations of Bodil Jørgensen's emotional distress over her young son's serious illness. We can also affirm that there are fictive documentary sequences embedded in the work, namely those in which von Trier shares with viewers a fantasy of interviewing his characters and mingling with them in their fictional world. At the same time, we may recognize that the interviews, plus other narrative and thematic elements, integrate artistically relevant aims beyond fiction-making, such as the director's game of trying to extract psychosocial truth and personal authenticity by inducing an assimilation of performers and characters. For these exchanges challenge the actors to decide how to respond: as their imaginary characters, or as themselves commenting on their imaginary characters.

There are more sensational aspects to *The Idiots'* deviations. Mette Hjort observes that "the very idea of able-bodied individuals voluntarily mimicking the involuntary behaviours of the disabled is intentionally distasteful and provocative," becoming increasingly so with the accretion of further provocations.[19] These include an interlude in which a group of nonactors with Down's syndrome visit the spassers—a scene no less provocative when we contemplate the reality of the encounter between visitors and pretenders. In addition to nudity, there is graphic, unsimulated sexual activity, the most notorious instance depicting an orgy the group holds while pretending to be mentally retarded.

One might believe that exhibitions of nudity, sexuality, and people imitating the mentally retarded are inherently immoral, independent of authorial intentions or popular reception, perhaps because such contents are proscribed by taboos, religious doctrines, or political correctness. Most philosophers and critics would object that such a belief obscures the possibility that an artwork can portray reprehensible situations without itself being reprehensible. The general solution is to shift attention to the work's perspective, its cluster of expressed or indicated attitudes. As I argued, that perspective attaches to the agent(s) responsible for the work's creation, with the provisos that artists need not sincerely or unequivocally hold these attitudes and sentiments, expressive intentions are not always realized, and works contain plenty of unintended meanings. Adverting to the perspective of *The Idiots* might help exculpate von Trier, because the spassers' all too realistic hypocrisies and moral confusions rather than the mentally handicapped are clearly the targets of his satire. But the concept of "perspective" does not adequately map the work's richly pragmatic dimensions. Potential moral flaws belong to the work as complex utterance, that is, to the artist's moral thinking, insofar as it effectively informs and shapes his or her artistic performance and the resultant display.

One regard in which we might deem von Trier's artistic performance morally flawed concerns his aggressive stance toward his audience. *The Idiots* is contrived to violate rules not merely for the sake of formal experimentation or the generation of novel content but thereby to distress or outright offend. Indeed it seems that von Trier's satisfaction with his work partly turned on his thinking that it could elicit distress or offense both from his collaborators and from a heterogeneous swathe of not especially uptight, puritanical, or hypocritical bourgeois audiences. *The Idiots*, unlike, say, Geert Wilders's propagandistic anti-Islam film, *Fitna* (2008), is hardly a contemptuous attack on the worth of a certain person, population, or type of person, least of all the mentally handicapped. It is nonetheless plausible that von Trier sought to inflict moral discomfort on viewers, expecting that realistic cinematic representations of improprieties, the very thought of which he himself finds distasteful, would likewise provoke squirming and disapprobation from others. For example, he gauges that a penetration shot in the orgy sequence delivers a "sense of danger": "There are people there pretending to be retarded while really fucking. This provides exactly the kind of transgression of limits that the scene and the film as a whole need."[20]

Von Trier once characterized himself as having a "troll's shard" in his eye, alluding to the evil troll in H. C. Anderson's *The Snow Queen* who makes a mirror in which the good and the beautiful look worthless and ugly and the defects of already loathsome things appear magnified.[21] When shattered, a grain of its glass embedded in the eye makes everything look bad. The metaphor evokes the director's propensity, manifested from work to work, for stories of humiliation, misguided idealism, and the perversion of goodness. It also implies an artistic self-concept as one who values if not delights in occasioning genuinely unpleasant or painful audience experiences. The homely, graceless "troll's shard" visual poetics of *The Idiots* is accompanied by a troll-like interest in crafting the story so as to incite soured and aggravated emotional uptakes. Consider the movie's final scene, which one reviewer says, "descends to truly contemptible emotional brutality."[22] Von Trier delays until this scene the revelation that Karen's sojourn with the spassers is partially explained by her having cracked under the pressure of her unsympathetic petit bourgeois family's stultifying expectations following the death of her infant child. Having fled before the funeral, she has left them wondering whether she herself was dead. On her unexpected return home, she alone has the bravery and purity of heart to spass in the faces of those closest to her. When coffee and cake are served in agonized silence, Karen spits the cake back up like a baby, pitching her head and twitching as her mouth foams. Shocked by her indecorousness, Karen's husband slaps her on behalf of her mortified kin, an outburst captured in an atypically well-timed, deftly framed shot sequence. The film ends moments later under this unrelieved emotional pall.

If von Trier subjects his audience to artistically or otherwise unmitigated "emotional brutality," it is but a taste of the distress he sometimes wrought upon his collaborators while filming. Fictions do not require performers actually to experience the feelings and emotions expressed in the work. In pursuit of extraordinary authenticity, von Trier was preoccupied with the idea that, under the unorthodox filmmaking rules and creative procedures he had imposed, he might manage either to turn actors' real emotional turmoil into sources of the fictional affect or to make their actual emotions congruent with the fictional ones he imaginatively planned in the screenplay. This authenticity was extruded from performers in a morally problematic generative process. From *The Humiliated* we learn that von Trier, overtly anxious and intemperate throughout the shoot, abused cast members with insults and fits of pique, subjecting Hassing to particularly cruel treatment when her performances disappointed him. Another of the director's preoccupations centered on his wish to instigate an episode of sexual abandon. Von Trier had hoped that, in the spirit of social and artistic experimentation, the actors would "end up fucking," thus supplying him with the orgy sequence.[23] Spontaneously collective erotomania failing to erupt, von Trier had to stage this fictional event while working around the actors' refusals to engage in unsimulated sex acts. Wanting a penetration shot, he resolved the problem by hiring professional porn performers to join the *mise en scène*—in violation of the Dogme rules against such manipulations and to the consternation of some of the core cast.

Certain artistic performances in *The Idiots*, here focusing on those of Lars von Trier, are morally flawed. The issue is not so much that the cluster of attitudes the filmmaker expresses and commends to viewers is morally defective. Rather, there is something amiss with a proximal source and substance of the work's content, namely, the maker's imaginative thinking and artistic problem-solving. Ethical flaws also arise within those procedural dimensions of artistic creation involving interpersonal coordination. Artists' endeavors to realize a particular work, feature, aesthetic effect, or body of works sometimes involve unethical practices, techniques, or strategies. Fitting within this category are cases in which the maker acts in a selfish, malicious, insensitive, or cruel manner toward collaborators and other participants. *The Idiots* is one among a great many motion pictures belonging to this category of morally blemished works.

ARTISTICALLY ADMIRABLE IMMORALITY

Someone attending exclusively to the cinematic display of *The Idiots* might not apprehend the aforementioned procedural moral defects. Why would these and other indiscernible, or not readily discernible, aspects of a work be pertinent to ethical criticism of the artwork itself versus study of the production means or the biographical author's moral character?[24] And how might moral qualities of the agent's work-constitutive creative and practical actions vitiate, or give rise to, artistic value?

Von Trier's formation and execution of a plan integrating precepts resembling those of *cinéma-vérité* with Dogme's chastisements exemplify the artistic relevance of pragmatic factors. So do his propensities for troll's-shard poetics and his exceptional skills for imaginatively devising moral and affective rigors for his audience, designing displays accordingly, and motivating and guiding collaborators to help him elaborate and execute this mischief. The notion that pragmatic factors have artistic relevance entails that knowledge of compositional activities and psychological dispositions implicated in the creative process tends to help us understandingly and appropriately evaluate and respond to the work, globally or in part, *qua* both object and achievement. *The Idiots* is well described as an audacious and bold artwork precisely because of the morally risky choices von Trier made in the course both of determining its content and designing and leading its unorthodox production process. Had he not thought of himself as a transgressor and not anticipated, in Sadean fashion, the unique gratifications of transgression, the nature of his artistic performance would have been correspondingly different. Likewise, had von Trier only inadvertently risked discomfiting his audience, perhaps because he was oblivious to the reasons why his movie could upset them, we would have to reconsider the nature of his achievement *qua* artistic risk-taking and its relation to his inter-work artistic project of provocative experimentation.

Mention of a still more disquieting film sheds additional light. Terayama Shūji's crudely shot and edited *Emperor Tomato Ketchup* (*Tomato Kecchappu Kōtei*, 1970) resembles *The Idiots* in several ways, including its embrace of a messy, ill-composed visual style and a thematic preoccupation with taboo violation. More disconcertingly, though, it contains imagery that explicitly sexualizes children, including images of a naked prepubescent boy writhing and mimicking sex acts with a trio of naked women.[25] Any adequate account of Terayama's surrealist underground movie about fascistic children violently and shortsightedly revolting against adult society must answer the obvious question: What *was* he thinking? Terayama conceived of himself and his literary, theatrical, and cinematic output as in the vanguard of an anti-establishment arts movement. *Emperor Tomato Ketchup*'s fantastical if nihilistic intervention in serious postwar Japanese political and social matters travesties political power, family structure, and social order as inevitably dissembling their underlying infantile urges and wantonness. The work's *modus operandi* includes attempting to make viewers acutely and uncomfortably self-aware of their own portion of these putative impulses, right to the point of offering them a taste of an eroticized experience of children's bodies. Terayama's strategy for soliciting this response is itself disturbing to contemplate. It must have involved him and other adult collaborators coaxing children into physically intimate, confusing situations. It also would have involved Terayama's rationalizing, or being somehow unmindful of, the rapport between, on the one hand, salient possible harms to the children resulting from his instrumental treatment of them and, on the other, the felt exigencies of his artistic project. Considered as process and achievement, the work's identity is thus indiscernible from its meshing of creative with morally parlous reasoning and action.

Noël Carroll, defending his "moderate moralist" thesis that moral defects can be but need not be artistic flaws, cogently identifies a way in which artistic and moral thinking meld seamlessly. Carroll contends that an artist's immoral attitudes sometimes steer formal choices, that is, selection and adaptation of design features with a view to realizing the work's point or purpose. He goes on to argue that a wicked choice of design feature is both pertinent to aesthetic value and deleterious to the feature's possessing that kind of value if this choice of formal property fails in its purpose or function because of its wickedness.[26] Immoral artistic preferences are therefore akin to cognitively irrational or incompetent artistic choices, like when the monster in a serious horror movie is too ridiculous to scare anyone. The immoral formal choice might be similarly self-defeating. Carroll imagines a painting of Hitler, the cruciform structure and title of which, *Saviour*, allude to Christ. Rather than achieving its purpose of moving ordinary audiences to admire Hitler as a self-sacrificing redeemer, surely such a depiction would or should misfire by triggering profound offense.

Certain artistic transgressions pose a problem for Carroll's functionalist formalism. Terayama expresses and commends morally unmerited sentiments that many audiences would be loath to endorse or adopt as their own. The same can be said of von Trier: Morally sensitive people who believe on ethical grounds that burlesque imitations of the developmentally handicapped are never funny might resist or be unable to experience the type of emotional response congruent to the one von Trier recommends toward many of the spassers' fictional antics. Both filmmakers anticipate and desire that some audiences, unable to react congruently to certain proffered emotional experiences, will instead suffer discomfort and take umbrage at the invitation. Their wicked formal choices and wish to upset agents not sharing their delight in transgression perversely aim at and succeed in virtue of precisely this sort of alienated, ethically reproving uptake. One could sympathize with the thesis that moral defects can occasion artistic value yet be wary of an analysis that formulaically counts *Emperor Tomato Ketchup*'s prescription to sexualize children as meriting artistic approval, or not meriting artistic disapproval. Although Carroll denies that moderate moralism precludes moral defects counting as artistic virtues, he does not argue in support of that possibility and remarks that few or no examples come to mind.[27] Hence I doubt Carroll means to underwrite the implication that *Emperor Tomato Ketchup* is paradigmatic of how moderate moralism might accommodate admirable artistic immorality. Yet certain cases of twisted—in the dual sense of morally suspect plus scheming and motivationally intricate—artistic planning with respect to uptake apparently trick his formula into returning a (false?) positive detection of such admirableness.

A pragmatic approach to integrating ethical with other critical-interpretive concerns need not make the artistic relevance of immoral attitudes and actions contingent on their producing or constituting formal defects in the work. Needing authentic-looking extras to play Catalan peasants in *Tiefland* (1954), Leni Riefenstahl solved her artistic problem by using Sinti and Roma Gypsy prisoners from Nazi internment camps as unpaid performers.[28] Whatever the extent of this choice's pay-off in verisimilitude, it counts as an artistic defect in my reckoning because the aesthetic gain is much less pleasing to contemplate than the artistic choice is reprehensible. By the same token, I do not make an artwork's moral defectiveness dependent on its prescribing morally unworthy attitudes and emotional responses. My more latitudinarian approach employs a coarser admissibility filter. It admits instances of morally defective artistic reasoning and action, perceivable from the display or not. The right sorts of psycho-historical factors to consider encompass those which constitute, or are more rather than less directly and deeply causally networked with, artists' steps toward settling on, filling in, refining, revising, and implementing, usually in the face of artistic problems and mundane obstacles, designs for the completed work's system of semantic and formal features. We are particularly interested in morally flawed artistic thinking, knowledge of which *could* make it harder for any one of us—though not necessarily all of us together, to borrow Michael Tanner's prudent distinction—to grant our artistic approval to the work globally or in a given respect.[29]

As I understand it, artistic approval manifests as a pair of not necessarily coinciding responses.[30] You might esteem a work, or element of it, without enjoying it or your experience of it. Furthermore, the esteem one bestows on or enjoyment one gets from W or its facet can be ambivalent and in tension with one's artistic disapproval of other of W's facets. Knowledge of deficiencies in the artist's moral agency can appropriately compromise one's approval of the work. Nevertheless, it need not prevent one from responding somewhat approvingly. It might even appropriately enhance one's esteem for and enjoyment of W. Now let us revisit *The Idiots* and *Emperor Tomato Ketchup*—members of a class of artworks that promise to violate taboos, usually in expectation of gratifications to be had, if only by the makers themselves, from witnessing or partaking in these violations. Such works realize their artistic purpose only in virtue of achieving a particular kind of immorality. Kieran, employing Carroll's functionalist formalism argument, asserts that their artistic value arises because of, not despite, their immorality.[31] This conclusion strikes me as overreaching. Von Trier's and Terayama's movies afford opportunities to satisfy curiosity about and savor out-of-reach, forbidden, acts and events and to thrill in transgression itself. Aspects of their makers' artistry are estimable, including their successful adaptation of their displays to achieve their generically specified artistic purposes. Knowing them to have these merits, an appreciator might nonetheless withhold or withdraw artistic approval on most or many things considered better judgment of the works globally. One's esteem for the directors' means-end rationality in fulfilling their genre-specific objectives is, in principle, independent of one's enjoyment of their movies. Any one of us might find it subjectively impossible to enjoy either the depicted forbidden acts or the transgressions as such. More importantly, my knowledge of the nature of the artistically relevant breakdowns in moral agency underlying the filmmakers' transgressive cinematic experiments ought to have a bearing on how artistically valuable *The Idiots* and *Emperor Tomato Ketchup* are. Given this knowledge, it can be rational as well as appropriate, given my moral feelings and principles, for me to reduce my overall artistic approval of the filmmakers' immoral formal choices and what it is, exactly, that they have accomplished by making and acting on these choices. One might not want to approve of an artwork's formal success if doing so means approving of the artist's carelessness toward others' wellbeing.

I doubt that the artistic value of a work or facet thereof is compromised or improved just because it is morally defective (or good). It has been said that we cannot deal summarily with the relations between moral and artistic value in advance of considering the complex issue of the range of considerations that are relevant to assessing a work's value.[32] The intricate ways in which moral agency meshes with artistic creativity and with artistic appreciation figure prominently among those considerations and deserve greater attention.

NOTES

1. An example of the former is Noël Carroll, "Art and Ethical Criticism: An Overview of Recent Directions in Research," *Ethics* 10.2 (2000): 379–381. I discuss his views below. Berys Gaut, *Art, Emotion and Ethics* (Oxford: Oxford University Press, 2007), is a proponent of ethicism, which holds that any aesthetically relevant moral flaw is always also an aesthetic flaw of the artwork. Defenses of immoralism, the position that a moral flaw can be an aesthetic merit, include Daniel Jacobson, "In Praise of Immoral Art," *Philosophical Topics* 25.1 (1997): 155–199; Matthew Kieran, "Forbidden Knowledge: The Challenge of Immoralism," in *Art and Morality*, ed. José Bermúdez and Sebastian Gardner (New York: Routledge, 2003), 56–73; Kieran, "Art and Morality," in *The Oxford Handbook of Aesthetics*, ed. Jerrold Levinson (Oxford: Oxford University Press, 2005), 451–470; A. W. Eaton, "Robust Immoralism," *Journal of Aesthetics and Art Criticism* 70.3 (2012): 281–292.
2. A. W. Eaton, "Robust Immoralism," 282.
3. Wayne Booth, *The Company We Keep: An Ethics of Fiction* (Berkeley: University of California Press, 1988); Noël Carroll, "Art and the Moral Realm," in *The Blackwell Guide to Aesthetics,* ed. Peter Kivy (Malden, MA: Blackwell, 2004), 141; Mary Devereaux, "Moral Judgments and Works of Art: The Case of Narrative Literature," *The Journal of Aesthetics and Art Criticism* 62.1 (2004): 3–11; Gaut, *Art, Emotion and Ethics,* especially chapter 6; Eaton, "Robust Immoralism," 282.
4. Paisley Livingston, *Art and Intention: A Philosophical Study* (Oxford: Oxford University Press, 2005); *Cinema, Philosophy, Bergman: On Film as Philosophy* (Oxford: Oxford University Press, 2009), especially chapter 4.
5. For invaluable background on the Dogme 95 movement, along with insightful studies of key Dogme-certified movies, see Mette Hjort and Scott MacKenzie, eds., *Purity and Provocation: Dogma 95* (London: British Film Institute, 2003). A portion of the "Dogme 95 Manifesto" along with the "Vow of Chastity" are reprinted in that volume, 199–200.
6. Peter Schepelhern, "'Kill Your Darlings': Lars von Trier and the Origin of Dogma 95," in *Purity and Provocation: Dogma 95,* ed. Mette Hjort and Scott MacKenzie (London: British Film Institute, 2003), 58–69, examines von Trier's extensive use of self-imposed rules as a technique of stimulating innovation and creativity. Vinterberg discusses the artistically enabling role of rules in his own filmmaking practices during an interview with Mette Hjort; see Mette Hjort and Ib Bjondebjerg, *The Danish Directors: Dialogues on a Contemporary National Cinema,* trans. Mette Hjort (Bristol: Intellect Press, 2001), 275–276.
7. Lars von Trier and Thomas Vinterberg, "Vow of Chastity," in *Purity and Provocation: Dogma 95,* ed. Mette Hjort and Scott MacKenzie (London: British Film Institute, 2003), 200.
8. Lars von Trier, *Dogme 2: Idioterne, manuskript og dagbog* (Copenhagen: Gyldendal, 1998), 173, quoted in Mette Hjort, "Lars von Trier," in *Fifty Contemporary Filmmakers,* ed. Yvonne Tasker (London: Routledge, 2002), 363.

9. Peter Øvig Knudson, "The Man Who Would Give Up Control," in *Lars von Trier Interviews,* ed. Jan Lumhold (Jackson: University Press of Mississippi, 2003), 123–124.

10. See, for instance, von Trier's remarks to Stig Björkman in "The Idiots," in *Trier on von Trier,* ed. Stig Björkman, trans. Neil Smith (London: Faber and Faber, 2003), 207. Peter Schepelern's "'Kill Your Darlings': Lars von Trier and the Origins of Dogma 95," in *Purity and Provocation: Dogma 95,* ed. Mette Hjort and Scott MacKenzie (London: British Film Institute, 2003), 58–69, offers useful background on the relevance of games and play to von Trier's cinematic practice. Jan Simons's *Playing the Waves: Lars von Trier's Game Cinema* (Amsterdam: Amsterdam University Press, 2007) applies game studies and game theory to von Trier's work. Ponech, "Work and Play: The 5-O Game," in *Dekalog 1: On The Five Obstructions,* ed. Mette Hjort (London: Wallflower Press, 2008) examines the connection between the artistic process and game play in *The Five Obstructions* (*De fem benspænd,* 2003), a movie co-authored by von Trier and Jørgen Leth.

11. Roger Caillois, *Man, Play, and Games,* trans. Meyer Barash (New York: Free Press, 1961), 24.

12. Edgar Morin, "Chronicle of a Film," in *Ciné-Ethnography: Jean Rouch,* ed. Steven Feld (Minneapolis: University of Minnesota Press, 2003), 252–253. My "Work and Play: The 5-O Game," in *Dekalog 1: On The Five Obstructions,* ed. Mette Hjort (London: Wallflower Press, 2008), 76–94, looks at von Trier and Leth's *The Five Obstructions* in relation to a seminal work of *vérité* cinema, Edgar Morin and Jean Rouch's *Chronicle of a Summer* (*Chronique d'un été,* 1960).

13. Stig Björkman, "The Idiots," in *Trier on von Trier,* ed. Stig Björkman, trans. Neil Smith (London: Faber and Faber, 2003), 208.

14. Von Trier's screenplay of *The Idiots* and diary record of its filming are published in *Dogme 2: Idioterne, manuskript og dagbog* (Copenhagen: Gyldendal, 1998). Although unavailable in English, this book exists in a French translation: *Les Idiots: Journal intime et scénario,* trans. Inès Jorgensen (Paris: Atelier Alpha Bleue, 1998).

15. Stig Björkman, "The Idiots," in *Trier on von Trier,* ed. Stig Björkman, trans. Neil Smith (London: Faber and Faber, 2003), 210.

16. Caroline Bainbridge, "The Trauma Debate: Just Looking? Traumatic Affect, Film Form and Spectatorship in the Work of Lars von Trier," *Screen* 45.4 (2004): 392.

17. In their DVD commentary, von Trier and actor Jens Albinus explain that the bikers were played by bouncers and that scene was already planned in the screenplay. Von Trier and Jens Albinus, "Commentary," *Idioterne. Dogme Kollektion 1–4,* Disc 2, Electric Parc, 2005, DVD.

18. Ove Christensen, "Spastic Aesthetics: *The Idiots,*" *P.O.V. A Danish Journal of Film Studies* 10 (2000): 35–60; Emma van der Vliet, "Naked Film: Stripping with *The Idiots,*" *Post Script* 28.3 (2009): 14–30; Tim Walters, "Reconsidering *The Idiots:* Dogme 95, Lars von Trier, and the Cinema of Subversion?," *The Velvet Light Trap* 53 (2004): 40–54.

19. Mette Hjort, "The Globalization of Dogma: The Dynamics of Metaculture and Counter-Publicity," in *Purity and Provocation: Dogma 95,* ed. Mette Hjort and Scott MacKenzie (London: British Film Institute, 2003), 149.

20. Von Trier, *Dogme 2: Idioterne, manuskript og dagbog,* 249–250, quoted in Hjort, "The Globalization of Dogma: The Dynamics of Metaculture and Counter-Publicity," 150.

21. Quoted in Stig Björkman's documentary film, *Tranceformer: A Portrait of Lars von Trier* (1997).
22. A. O. Scott, "Colloquies on the Finer Points of Drooling," *New York Times*, April 28, 2000, accessed October 20, 2012, http://www.nytimes.com/2000/04/28/movies/film-review-colloquies-on-the-finer-points-of-drooling.html?scp=1&sq=The=Idiots&st=nyt.
23. Björkman, "The Idiots," 217.
24. Robert Stecker articulates reservations along these lines in *Aesthetics and the Philosophy of Art: An Introduction* (Lanham, MD: Rowman and Littlefield, 2005), 208.
25. Carol Fisher Sorgenfrei's *Unspeakable Acts: The Avant-Garde Theatre of Terayama Shūji And Postwar Japan* (Honolulu: University of Hawai'i Press, 2005) covers Terayama's theatrical poetics, touching on some of his cinematic works, including *Emperor Tomato Ketchup*. Steven Ridgely's *Japanese Counterculture: The Antiestablishment Art of Terayama Shūji* (Minneapolis: University of Minnesota Press, 2010), studies in depth Terayama's relation to the Japanese underground art of the postwar period.
26. Carroll, "Ethics and Aesthetics: Replies to Dickie, Stecker, and Livingston," *British Journal of Aesthetics* 46.1 (2006): 85–86. See also his "Art and Ethical Criticism: An Overview of Recent Directions in Research," 377–381; and "Recent Approaches to Aesthetic Experience," *Journal of Aesthetics and Art Criticism* 70.2 (2012): 173–177.
27. Carroll, "Art and Ethical Criticism: An Overview of Recent Directions in Research," 380.
28. The melodrama *Tiefland*, which she worked on sporadically throughout the war years, is Riefenstahl's last directorial outing in fiction (her first outing was *The Blue Light* [*Das blaue Licht*, 1932]). Jürgen Trimborn, *Leni Riefenstahl: A Life*, trans. Edna McCown (New York: Faber & Faber, 2007), 181–208, discusses *Tiefland*'s production history and the circumstances of Riefenstahl's use of Gypsy prisoners of the Nazi regime and the subsequent controversies.
29. Michael Tanner, "Morals in Fiction and Fictional Morality," *Proceedings of the Aristotelian Society*, Supplementary Volumes, 68 (1994): 65.
30. Denis Dutton, "Artistic Crimes: The Problem of Forgery in the Arts," *The British Journal of Aesthetics* 19.4 (1979): 305–306.
31. Kieran, "Art and Morality," 467.
32. Tanner, "Morals in Fiction and Fictional Morality," 65.

11 Something to Hide
The Ethics of Spectatorship in *Saw*

Jason Middleton

The *Saw* series (James Wan, 2004; various directors, 2005–2010) has proved the most durable and popular of the films that emerged during the "torture porn" cycle of the mid-2000s. With a focus on the first *Saw,* but with reference to subsequent installments in the franchise, this essay argues that the films construct a form of spectatorship I characterize as "intimate distance." Spectators of *Saw* are linked to the experiences of characters at a visceral, affective level: Scenes in the films are staged to make viewers cringe or recoil in horror at spectacles of bodily suffering and abjection. At the same time, the films attenuate the possibilities for viewer identification with characters and ethical reflection upon the films' spectacles, instead distancing and insulating the spectator from these forms of involvement and implication. Surveillance functions as both narrative device and as a trope linking the films' model of spectatorship to dominant ideologies of the post-9/11 United States, in which citizens are compelled to relinquish privacy and civil liberties because "if you have nothing to hide, you have nothing to fear."

The *Saw* films exemplify the principle identified by Linda Williams wherein the "body genres" of horror, melodrama, and pornography aim to provoke a relation of mimicry between the body on screen and the body of the spectator. In this sense, the films create for viewers a feeling of over-proximity. Despite her shift from psychoanalytic theory's emphasis on voyeuristic distance as a fundamental component of spectatorship to a model emphasizing proximity and bodily response, Williams's analysis of spectatorial "mimicry" maintains that such responses are rooted in structures of fantasy articulated in psychoanalytic theory: the fantasy of seduction for pornography, of castration for horror, and the origin fantasy for melodrama.[1]

In her influential analysis of the slasher horror film, Carol Clover also suggests alternatives to models of spectatorship developed in psychoanalytic and apparatus theory that describe a position of distanced mastery over the image. The slasher is a sub-genre of film that would, on the surface, seem to exemplify the qualities of voyeuristic and sadistic male gazing identified by these theories. Clover argues, however, that the slasher film promotes an unconventional male-to-female form of cross-gender identification and a masochistic, "reactive" gaze that ultimately undermines and takes priority over the sadistic—both for the characters in the film and for the specta-tor.[2] However, Clover still situates these transgressions of conventional viewing positions in a psychoanalytic framework, arguing that they remain responses to fantasies of castration. The spectator is engaged by a sadomas-ochistic fantasy that ultimately resolves castration anxiety by eliminating the early female victims and then reconstituting the "Final Girl" (locus of viewer identification) as masculine.[3]

In Williams's and Clover's analyses, spectators' affective and bodily responses implicate them at deeper psychological levels; body genres, like slasher horror films, tap into structures of fantasy rooted in the formation of the subject in the bourgeois family. These films produce their ideological effects (in slasher horror, a moderate transgression of conventional gender roles, which are then recuperated by the resolution of castration anxiety) by tethering bodily response to modes of identification with characters. I have argued elsewhere that the most notable films of the "torture porn" cycle other than the *Saw* series—Eli Roth's *Hostel* (2005) and *Hostel II* (2007)—derive certain of their themes and conventions from earlier slashers. Like the influential slasher *The Texas Chainsaw Massacre* (Tobe Hooper, 1974), they must be interpreted as allegories of broader sociopolitical anxieties—as forms of cultural problem solving.[4] While, in Williams's analysis, the body genres also represent modes of cultural problem solving, she frames these questions in broad terms that encompass the individual psychological along with the social: the problem of sex itself, the problem of violence related to sexual difference, and the problem of the pathos of loss.[5]

In my argument, *Hostel* follows iconic horror films like *Texas Chainsaw* in depicting the horrific return of the repressed in social terms, rather than simply as a matter of individual psychology. Where *Texas Chainsaw* the-matizes the horrific unrepression of a mode of commodity production that middle-class society would prefer to keep out of sight and mind, *Hostel* adapts this structure of reversal for the context of the "war on terror" and the positions of torturer and tortured. In *Texas Chainsaw*, the working-class labor of meat production represents the repressed; the analogous object in the thematics of *Hostel* is the United States' "renditions" program and other dirty business in the "war on terror."[6] The films, in certain respects, present a critical perspective on US political and cultural imperialism. Both *Hostel* films follow the slashers in performing their cultural problem solv-ing via modes of viewer identification with characters; indeed, both rework conventions of the "Final Girl" in differing ways. In *Hostel,* the spectacle of young, middle-class white American males subjected to abduction and torture in foreign nations dramatizes the exceptionalism accorded to the "ordinary American" in the discursive regimes of the "war on terror," and identification with these characters constructed for the film's ideal (young male) spectator provokes critical reflection on this exceptionalism. Ulti-mately, however, identification with the protagonist Paxton's acts of brutal vengeance in the film's closing sequence helps to contain this criticism and reaffirm a "(neo)conservative view of the necessity for American aggression in what is represented as a corrupt and dangerous world."[7]

However, unlike the *Hostel* films, the *Saw* films' visual and narrative strategies work to severely attenuate the prospects for viewer identification with any of their multiple characters—killer and accomplices, cops, and various victims. The films invite viewer involvement in suspenseful narratives premised upon concealment, misdirection, and the gradual revelation of story information, and provoke moments of intense affective and bodily viewer response to the often brutal and gruesome trials of the bodies onscreen. Nevertheless, these forms of bodily and affective intimacy are mediated by the films' distancing strategies: Specifically, the films displace conventional devices fostering viewer identification with characters, and privilege dramatic spectacles of bodily suffering, narrative puzzles, and reflexive gestures. The resulting form of what I term "intimate distance" for the spectator suggests a way of understanding the films' political resonances and ethical implications.

Catherine Zimmer argues that while the films are not marked by explicit political commentary, they do address, in a somewhat haphazard fashion, various themes relevant to war on terror-era politics—even if their political thematics "often seem [. . .] less like a jigsaw puzzle and more like a game of pickup sticks."[8] However, I argue that through its construction as intimate distance, the film's *model of spectatorship*—rather than any given component of its plot or characterizations—allegorizes key features of post-9/11 American citizenship. If, as the adage goes, every era gets the monster it deserves (that is, each era's monsters tap into period-specific anxieties), the *Saw* films can be understood more expansively as offering not just a killer appropriate to the war on terror era, but also a mode of spectatorship that instantiates a subjectivity characterized simultaneously by proximity and distance, fascination and insulated remove.

My analysis of spectatorship of the *Saw* films is shaped by, and in turn contributes new insights to, Michele Aaron's model of an ethics of film spectatorship. She reviews a familiar distinction between ethics and morality, in which ethics calls for "recognition, realization, and reflection—the stuff of agency—over (moral) prescription, proclamation, and punishment—the stuff of ideology." If ethics is about "thinking through one's relationship to morality rather than just adhering to it," then Aaron suggests that "some films nurture reflection, recognition, and responsibility, and some prevent it."[9] More specifically, Aaron argues that an ethics of spectatorship does not attempt to polarize films with or without a moral framework, but rather directs us to think about films that require us to reflect on our own moral framework. Especially pertinent to my analysis of *Saw*, Aaron examines the opening sequence of Spielberg's *Saving Private Ryan* (1998) to suggest that its investment in *moving* the spectator at bodily and emotional levels "marks the experience as moral but not ethical: involuntary emotion is the opposite of reflection and implication."[10] Instead, Aaron argues, moving the spectator through involuntary emotion creates a form of "spectatorial insulation" and "collective absolution" of responsibility for the suffering of others.[11]

This doesn't mean that this analysis, which applies to films such as *Saving Private Ryan* that present an explicitly moral framework, can simply be transposed to an explanation of the ethics of spectatorship for the *Saw* films. However, Aaron's valuable concept of "spectatorial insulation" does point us in the right direction. The *Saw* films present a blunt moral framework of sorts as their basic premise: The killer, Jigsaw, has survived his own suicide attempt following a fatal cancer diagnosis. Transformed by the experience to recognize the preciousness of life, he embarks on a campaign of trying to shock people who are in some way "wasting or abusing their lives"[12] into a similar epiphany. Jigsaw creates elaborate and sadistic trials or traps that his victims must try to solve or suffer gruesome deaths. Given the obvious incommensurability between his victims' wrongdoings (ranging from drug abuse to working as an informant to attempting suicide themselves) and their ordeals (such as being forced to attempt to escape death by entombment by crawling naked through a tangle of razor wire within a time limit), it is clear that the films intend the moral framework only as a pretext for a series of increasingly baroque and spectacular death scenes.

The films' version of "moving" the spectator occurs at a superficially visceral level—a cringe or recoil at the implication or sight of bodily suffering, rather than even the kind of involuntary emotional response described by Aaron. In other words, the *Saw* films present neither a moral nor an ethical framework: There is no implication of the spectator in or by the image, no space for reflection on one's own moral framework. By opening up a space for critical reflection on the logic of American exceptionalism in war on terror ideology, *Hostel* initially offers the prospect of an ethical form of spectatorship (despite its ultimately conservative narrative and thematic resolution that forecloses these critical possibilities). The same could be said for more conventional slasher films, which often disrupt conventional gender binaries and modes of viewer identification, but ultimately offer relatively safe and reassuring masculinist fantasies. The *Saw* films, on the other hand, never open up a space for implication and reflection at all, instead offering intense moments of involuntary bodily response experienced from within a space of "spectatorial insulation" from ethical considerations—intimate distance.

If *Hostel* thematizes torture, then *Saw* responds to the dramatically increased presence of government surveillance in the name of homeland security following the passage of the USA Patriot Act, a ubiquity that is redoubled by the forms of corporate surveillance that likewise pervade the American every day. Surveillance functions in the *Saw* films as both a central visual motif and narrative device; hidden cameras and monitors allow characters to spy upon one another for various purposes. It is the trope that connects these films to the real-world political domain, as torture is in *Hostel*.[13] However, the connection is not so simple as to merely align the villain with the agent of government surveillance; nor does the film offer a symbolically critical reversal of power, as in *Hostel*. Rather, especially in the first *Saw*, surveillance functions to draw equivalences among the different characters—cops, villains, and victims.

Throughout the film, a transition between scenes will occur when our perspective on a scene is replaced by that of a diegetic surveillance camera, and we realize that the entire scene we have been watching has also been observed by another character in the film. This device combined with the films' narrative puzzles train viewers to avoid assumptions about the story information or attachments to the characters, as the films' continually shifting points of view and ongoing plot twists and revelations destabilize such assumptions and attachments. As Zimmer notes, "It would be reasonable to suggest that the films posit every character as both guilty and innocent."[14] The exception to this rule, I argue, is the viewer. In contrast to *Hostel*, in which the films' ideological work is premised upon structures of identification that implicate the viewer, *Saw* insulates viewers from implication in the films' spectacles of guilt and punishment and their ostensible moral frameworks.

If the trope of surveillance most directly links the films' diegesis to post-9/11 American society, this model of spectatorship reproduces the logic by which the figure of the citizen is dramatically reconfigured in this period. As Donald Pease writes, the US Patriot[15] Act "effected the most dramatic abridgment of civil liberties in the nation's history. [It] subordinated all concerns of ethics, human rights, due process, constitutional hierarchies, and the division of power to the state's monopoly over the exception."[16] Pease analyzes the logic of the Patriot Act's provisions as a conversion of the public into spectators offered a dramatic spectacle of the violation of the rights of other sovereign states. This spectacle substituted for and reinforced the relinquishment of the public's individual and collective rights and civil liberties. Further, "[b]ecause the spectators could not enjoy the state's spectacles without dissociating from the assumptions that would have rendered them unimaginable as American spectacles," such spectacles insulated the "spectatorial publics from the national forms of life."[17] While dis-empowering its citizens and separating them from participation in public life, "[t]he spectacle encouraged the public's belief that it shared in the state's power because it shared in the spectacle through which the state gave expression to its power."[18]

Perhaps the most prominent rhetorical commonplace in support of the US Patriot Act and similar legislation in ally nations, such as the United Kingdom, was the claim that the legislation was no cause for concern because "I've got nothing to hide."[19] According to this logic, the individual citizen's presumed innocence of the offenses ostensibly under surveillance makes acceptable the intimacy and proximity (via cameras and phonetaps) between state authority and our private lives. This logic represents one form of "intimate distance": citizens are intimate with the apparatus of state

authority and punishment, but feel distanced from the potential for implication in this apparatus. In war on terror America, people are marked as
having "something to hide" largely on the grounds of ethnicity, religion, and
national citizenship. *Saw*'s imaginary transposition of this political reality
to its diegesis presents victims who have something to hide because of how
they choose to live their lives—they are subject to surveillance and punishment due to supposed moral failings, apathy, or insufficient or unproductive
affective states.

In the post-9/11 United States, saying you have "nothing to hide"
implicitly posits the presence in the national body of people who *do* have
"something to hide." No one in the *Saw* films ever has nothing to hide;
everyone is guilty of something. The *Saw* films thus offer the spectator a
reinforcement of the logic behind the claim of nothing to hide: the films'
signature narrative twists and revelations offer us the pleasure of finding
out the source of the guilt, and the visuals offer spectacles of punishment.
Like the post-9/11 US citizen of Pease's account, *Saw*'s spectator witnesses a
spectacle of punishment from which he or she feels insulated.

The first *Saw* film opens with two men waking from drug-induced uncon-
sciousness to find themselves chained to either end of a decrepit, abandoned
industrial bathroom. A dead body with a tape recorder and gun lies in the
middle of the floor between them. The film bases its suspense in part upon
the classic cinematic device of a narrative deadline. Through various bits of
information made available in recorded and written messages, Dr. Lawrence
Gordon learns that his wife and daughter have been kidnapped and he must
find a way to save them by a certain hour. Moreover, some of the notes that
he reads privately intimate that killing his counterpart, Adam, will provide
his way out. In the first half hour of the film, we see the two men struggle to
free themselves and to make sense of their predicament. Finally, Dr. Gordon
reveals that he thinks he knows who may be behind it all. In flashback scenes
that accompany Gordon's explanation, we learn about the serial killer, Jigsaw, and his methods, and meet his one surviving victim as well as two police
officers pursuing him—Detectives David Tapp and Steven Sing.

This flashback sequence shifts the viewer's perspective on Dr. Gordon's
character. Prior to this point, he has been characterized as the calm and
responsible doctor who tries to take a rational approach to the situation,
where Adam is presented as youthful, hot-tempered, and somewhat lout-
ish. The flashback sequence, however, suggests that Gordon may have some
culpability for their predicament. The police find his penlight at the crime
scene of a Jigsaw killing, and he is taken to headquarters for questioning.
Gordon's alibi points toward a different form of guilt, however: Away from
home that night, he was in fact meeting up at a cheap hotel with a younger
female intern from his hospital. Scenes from the flashback also emphasize

Gordon's arrogant and insensitive behavior toward a patient, an orderly in the hospital (both of whom will later emerge as key characters in the film), and the police, distancing the viewer from him as a potential point of identification.

An important component of the film's narrative is to gradually reveal how the various characters are connected to one another in ways not initially apparent to the viewer or to themselves, and to emphasize how these connections are manifested in interlocking chains of mutual surveillance and culpability. We learn that Adam is a scandal photographer-for-hire, who makes his living by documenting extramarital affairs and so on. He has been hired to follow and photograph Doctor Gordon. A further twist reveals that the man who has hired Adam to do this is in fact former detective David Tapp. As we learn in subsequent flashbacks, following an unsuccessful raid on Jigsaw's lair in which his partner was killed, Tapp becomes obsessed with Jigsaw to the point of madness and is forced to leave the police force. At one of the film's transitions in which a scene cuts to its own diegetic representation via surveillance footage, we find Tapp unkempt and muttering to himself in a tiny apartment overstuffed with newspaper clippings and other records on the killer, monitoring Gordon's house obsessively.

Recursively depicting forms of mutual surveillance among the characters and suggesting they share a kind of contagion of guilt and pathology, the film offers viewers occasional moments of potential identification and sympathy with each, only to distance us from them with the subsequent revelation of additional story information. The moments in which the film cuts from a scene to the same scene depicted in low-resolution black and white surveillance footage on a monitor serves as a visual figuration of this process of spectatorial distancing: Just as we think we have come to know a character or characters, we are placed at a remove from them and compelled to see them from a different point of view. All characters that engage in surveillance activities are linked to the killer's pathologies; as one of the detectives points out in discovering a peephole to the chamber of a murder site: "Looks like he likes to give himself a front row seat to his own sick little games" (along with indications that he trails and photographs his victims in preparation for their tribulations).

Following the first flashback scene in which we learn about Gordon's connection to the Jigsaw killer, he and Adam discover the surveillance camera that is recording their ordeal. Gordon tries to stop Adam from attempting to destroy the camera by hurling objects at it, in an exchange of dialogue that reflexively describes the intended reaction of the spectator to the film itself. He argues: "Well, you won't stop it. That's why we can't cut through these chains, why you won't break that glass—every possible angle has been pre-thought out by him." Adam comments, "You sound like you admire this prick!"—and, indeed, the viewer's admiration of the ingenuity of the cinematic construction is precisely the goal here. The film works overtime to demonstrate how "every possible angle" of its story has been "pre-thought out" to provide the maximum possible number of revelations, twists, and surprises, leaving no loose ends.

Adam Lowenstein has convincingly drawn a connection between the cycle of American horror films exemplified by the *Hostel* and *Saw* franchises and Tom Gunning's highly influential analysis of early film as a "cinema of attractions." Lowenstein argues that the "torture porn" label that commonly describes this cycle should be replaced by what he proposes as a more theoretically fitting term: "spectacle horror."[20] He defines spectacle horror as "the staging of spectacularly explicit horror for purposes of audience admiration, provocation, and sensory adventure as much as shock or terror, but without necessarily breaking ties with narrative development or historical allegory."[21] Lowenstein rightly suggests that viewer identification (with either victim or killer) is "not the exclusive form of viewer engagement with the film," noting that much important scholarship in horror studies has maintained a primary focus on identification.[22] Lowenstein cites Gunning to demonstrate the resonances between "spectacle horror" and the "aesthetic of astonishment" in early cinema—in which the film addresses the audience directly and "an attraction is offered to the spectator by a cinema showman . . . its energy moves outward towards an acknowledged spectator rather than inward towards the character-based situations essential to classical narrative."[23] Lowenstein is correct in identifying this impulse within this cycle of American horror films, and he does suggest that *Hostel* (the focus of his essay) does not void spectator identification altogether, but rather promotes forms of attraction that exceed structures of identification. Moreover, he argues that "spectacle horror" can be compatible with "feeling history" (or an allegorical narrative function)—an argument that supports my own more extensive analysis of *Hostel* as a form of cultural problem solving.

The *Saw* films, however, provide a more useful model for thinking through this horror cycle as a contemporary cinema of attractions. In my analysis, the *Hostel* films' allegorical meanings are deeply rooted in their deployment and manipulation of modes of viewer identification rooted in slasher film conventions. On the other hand, Dr. Gordon's stated "admiration" for how every detail has been "pre-thought out" neatly expresses how the *Saw* films stage themselves as "attraction[s] . . . offered to the spectator by a cinema showman."[24] Many scenes in the *Saw* films function primarily as spectacle and attractions, particularly moments that "move outward towards an acknowledged spectator" to produce the forms of affective and bodily mimicry described by Linda Williams—the cringing responses of disgust and horror. Such moments extend or exceed narrative necessity and causality.

For example, early in the film, Adam must reach into a decrepit toilet full of brown-green filth to try to retrieve a key. The film lingers on a close-up shot of Adam's hand rooting around in the bowl while we hear him suppressing gags—clearly the intended response for the viewer, as well—only to then reveal that the key was hidden elsewhere. The flashback scenes that depict the deaths of Jigsaw's earlier victims are also quite showy and exhibitionistic, marked by distinctly different filming and editing styles from other scenes in the film. In David Fincher's *Se7en* (1995)—clearly the foremost influence on the *Saw* films—the baroque murders are never shown, but implied by images of their aftermath and descriptive dialogue that leaves visualization to the viewer's imagination. By contrast, the *Saw* films display the killings in graphic and spectacular fashion, accentuated by devices including extreme fast motion in the cinematography, quick zooms and frenetic camera movement, and rapid-fire editing.

Gunning argues that despite being an aesthetic primarily present in early cinema, "The cinema of attractions persists in later cinema, even if it rarely dominates the form of a feature film as a whole. It provides an underground current flowing beneath narrative logic and diegetic realism."[25] In the *Saw* films, however, rather than spectacle being submerged under narrative logic and realism (or creating rupture or tension with them), narrative itself becomes a form of "attractions." The films' narratives continually gesture "outward" to astonish and impress the spectator with their twists, turns, and final revelations of how all the pieces fit together. The spectator's involvement in the film is premised upon a combination of visceral thrills at the disgusting and violent spectacles, and homologous thrills of curiosity and astonishment at the narrative contortions. Indeed, the spectacular style of the flashback scenes to the Jigsaw murders reaches its apotheosis in the film's climax, which is also the moment in which all of the narrative threads are brought together in a final twist ending and the full set of causal connections in the story made clear to the viewer.

The film makes a point to grant the viewer access to certain story information unavailable to Dr. Gordon and Adam, implying that the hospital orderly, Zep, is in fact the Jigsaw killer. The film's climax reveals that this information has been misleading; the characters and viewer are equally surprised when the ostensibly dead body on the bathroom floor rises up, alive, and reveals himself to be the Jigsaw killer. Where we have previously encountered Jigsaw indirectly through his actions, and in one flashback sequence in which his hooded face remains obscured from view, here he emerges as the ultimate causal agent in the narrative and the locus of narrative coherence. The viewer's pleasure in understanding how all the plot pieces fit together corresponds with recognition that everything has transpired precisely according to this character's plan—"every possible angle has been pre-thought out by him."

The final minutes of the film are scored with a repetitive, dramatic orchestral motif that builds in intensity as the erstwhile corpse rises slowly from the floor before Adam's incredulous eyes. The use of this same piece of music, titled "Hello Zepp," at the ending of subsequent *Saw* films demonstrates the consistent centrality of major narrative revelations to the films' "attractions." The music creates an almost triumphal feeling as it underscores increasingly rapid editing (evoking the style of the flashback scenes depicting the deaths of Jigsaw's previous victims) that reviews significant scenes and moments from throughout the film, now assembling these various puzzle pieces together into a causally coherent chain of events. Finally, the editing increases to a breakneck pace with each image held for just a split second, converting the editing's function as display of narrative virtuosity into simply a set of visual pyrotechnics that abruptly flame out as the film draws to an end. In other words, the editing here demonstrates the isomorphism between narrative and spectacle: The viewer is meant to be astonished at seeing how all the narrative strands fit together through the agency of this character that rises from the bathroom floor. Then, the radically increased pace of the editing converts the series of flashback images from a display of narrative coherence into a sensory assault, in which these same images are unmoored from their narrative context and function as pure, visceral spectacle.[26]

Present mainly onscreen as a *faux* corpse, with little dialogue or psychological development, the Jigsaw figure is hardly a character at all, much less one who might engender some form of viewer identification. Rather, Jigsaw stands in at a diegetic level for Gunning's "cinema showman"—the agency behind the film itself, which "solicits spectator attention" through theatrical displays of "shock or surprise."[27] The difference between Gunning's formulation and this contemporary instantiation of a "cinema of attractions" is that the *Saw* films disarticulate the necessity of viewer identification with characters from viewer investment in narrative situations. As I have argued, the films convert narrative itself into a form of spectacle soliciting viewer astonishment and admiration.

In this sense, the *Saw* films are not simply "post-classical" cinema, but in some respects invert the modes of spectatorship solicited by classical narrative form. Nick Browne's influential essay on *Stagecoach* (John Ford, 1939) argues that in the classical system "the film is directed in all its structures of presentation toward the narrator's construction of a commentary on the story and toward placing the spectator at a certain 'angle' to it."[28] Through identification with characters, the spectator is placed "inside the fictional space . . . his presence integral and constitutive of the structure of views." Narrative authority is masked and displaced through this spectator placement and viewer identification with characters; the cumulative effect is that the spectator is introduced "into what might be called the moral order of the text," or its perspective on the social issues raised in the story.[29] Rather than masking and displacing narrative authority, the *Saw* films flaunt it and convert it into a major component of the films' attractions: The central figure, Jigsaw, is ultimately less a character than a diegetic placeholder for this very narrative authority. Instead of placing the spectator into the text to foster, as Browne puts it, "the exposition of a moral idea," the *Saw* films' modes of exhibitionistic display gesture outward toward the spectator, folding narrative into spectacle and delimiting the prospects for an implication of the spectator that would enable the exposition of a moral (or ethical) idea.

———

Saw II and *III* shape the conventions and mode of spectator address in the first film into a formula that has now been repeated across six sequels, one released each year since the original to consistent box office success. The first *Saw* opens with the two central characters and narrative exposition: They awaken in the bathroom, and must figure out how they got there and what is being done to them. The opening of *Saw II*, by contrast, demonstrates how the scenes of overt spectacle depicting Jigsaw's traps now take pride of place in the films. *Saw II* begins *in medias res*, with a character that awakens to find himself placed in one of Jigsaw's traps. We know nothing about this character and his backstory is sketched out in only the briefest of terms by the killer's recorded monologue. Accused by Jigsaw of some vaguely explained crimes involving voyeurism, he must cut out his own eyeball to retrieve a key that the killer has surgically implanted behind it. If he fails to cut out his eye within sixty seconds, one of Jigsaw's elaborate constructions (modeled on a Venus flytrap of sorts) will snap shut on his head, killing him. This opening announces how the narrative of *Saw II* will be structured around the presentation of these spectacular death scenes, rather than embedding them in narrative flashbacks as in part one. It moves the film closer than the original to the overt privileging of "number" over narrative often found in musicals—a genre of narrative feature film in which Gunning sees the persistence of an "aesthetic of attractions."[30]

One significant difference in the film's sequel is the emergence of Jigsaw as a full-fledged character in the narrative action. Sustaining the original's distribution of guilt and culpability among the various characters, the sequel is even more blunt in demonstrating similarities in behavior and character traits among Jigsaw himself, Detective Eric Matthews (the film's central protagonist), and the assorted victims—all of them convicted criminals, including Matthews's son—whom Jigsaw has assembled in a trap-laden house (monitored, of course, by surveillance cameras). One character introduced in the first film that plays a significant role in the sequels is a drug addict named Amanda. Having survived one of Jigsaw's traps (shown in one of the first film's spectacular flashback sequences), she explains in the sequel that she has now become his disciple. Amanda describes how she was "guilty," but then her life was "saved" by Jigsaw, and calls him a "leader" and a "father."

Amanda represents Jigsaw's success story, following his own model of near-death and redemption. Describing in *Saw II* his terminal diagnosis and survival of a suicide attempt, Jigsaw suggests that, "knowledge of death changes everything . . . it shatters your world completely." The language he uses to describe his conversion experience echoes the ubiquitous phrase surrounding the attacks of September 11, 2001: They "changed everything." I have argued that through the visual and narrative device of surveillance and the creation of an "intimate distance" for the spectator that privileges spectacular forms of bodily suffering and attenuates viewer identification with characters, the *Saw* films construct a model of cinematic spectatorship that allegorizes conditions of post-9/11 US citizenship. Supported by an ideology that claims the individual has "nothing to fear because he/she has nothing to hide," the citizen becomes, as Pease argues, a spectator to the state's violent retribution toward other sovereign nations and repression of internal "others," while insulated from ethical implication in these spectacles. In conclusion, I wish to point out a further way in which Jigsaw's motivations and rhetoric thematize dominant ideologies articulated in the war on terror era.

Jigsaw's victims are not always criminals, but often simply people whose affective states block them in some way from active, productive participation in society and their family lives. In *Saw III* (Darren Lynn Bousman, 2006), the central subject of Jigsaw's trials is an ordinary man, Jeff, who has lost his beloved son to a drunk driver. Unable to move on—to pass through what Freud terms "mourning" rather than experience perpetual "melancholia"— he ignores the daughter who still needs him and lets his marriage fall apart.[31] A secondary victim-character, Lynn, is a doctor ostensibly kidnapped to keep Jigsaw alive. She is presented in parallel fashion to Jeff as affectively deadened; as Jigsaw puts it in one of his rants, "the kind of person who turns their back on their husband, neglects their child, swallows antidepressants to hide the pain." The charge of insufficient or counterproductive affect is also directed at Dr. Gordon in part one. He is never depicted as a bad man, but rather, as cold and detached. In one flashback his frustrated wife demands that he just express some emotion, whether positive or negative.

George W. Bush's rhetoric following the attacks of 9/11 often turned upon the importance of mobilizing the grief Americans felt toward particular forms of action. On the one hand, of course, Bush tapped into Americans' grief and anger to garner support for the invasions of Afghanistan and Iraq. Additionally, however, a major focus of the president's speeches was to redirect citizens from a nonproductive melancholia toward (economically) productive forms of "enjoyment." As he stated in a speech on September 27, 2001, at O'Hare International Airport in Chicago, "It's to tell the traveling public: Get on board. Do your business around the country. Fly and enjoy America's great destination spots. Get down to Disney World in Florida. Take your families and enjoy life, the way we want it to be enjoyed."[32] Defiantly claiming that America would never be intimidated, he described the response of an ideal citizen in terms of a list of religious and leisure activities[33]: "People are going about their daily lives, working and shopping and playing, worshiping at churches and synagogues and mosques, going to movies and to baseball games."[34] Perhaps most concisely, in his address to the nation on September 20, he noted that in the face of such fear, Americans are asking, "What is expected of us?" Bush's response to this question was simple and straightforward: "I ask you to live your lives and hug your children."[35] This message actually summarizes quite well what all of Jigsaw's contraptions are aimed toward forcing his victims to do. As he explains in *Saw III*, adversity will make it plain to people how they should feel lucky, should in fact feel privileged, to be alive.

My point is not to align Bush with Jigsaw (however tempting that might be), or simply to point out parallels between Jigsaw's rhetoric and Bush's post-9/11 speeches. It is to suggest that if every generation gets the monster it deserves, then Jigsaw is a monster perfectly tailored to the dominant ideology of the post-9/11 period in the United States. In his influential essay, "The American Nightmare," Robin Wood draws a distinction between "progressive" and "reactionary" horror based upon a number of factors—particularly a given film's representation of the relationship between the monster and the normal society threatened or disrupted by the monster.[36] Conservative or reactionary horror films encourage spectators to root for the restoration of social order. Progressive horror films (including *Texas Chainsaw Massacre*) present the threatened normality in a critical light, even in a state of "extreme cultural crisis and disintegration."[37] Where, to put it in Wood's terms, the *Hostel* films offer a progressive gesture that is then contained by a reactionary resolution, the *Saw* franchise could be seen to fall even further to the right than Wood's "reactionary" category. The monster here does not even threaten an admirable social order that the viewer wishes to see restored; the monster is in fact the agent of this restoration, coercively correcting forms of deviance, pathology, or simply prolonged grief and other "unproductive" affects.

Accordingly, one scene in the first *Saw* film actually aligns the visceral form of spectatorial mimicry with a more conventional mode of viewer identification with a character (rather than substituting the former for the latter). It is the moment just prior to the narrative revelations of the film's climax, when a desperate and emotionally distraught Dr. Gordon finally stops trying to outwit the game designed by Jigsaw, and plays along by sawing off his own foot to escape from the room and rescue his abducted wife and daughter. In the third act of the film the viewer has been increasingly encouraged to sympathize with Gordon, because he seems to start feeling genuine regret about his coldness toward his wife, agonizes over the predicament of his family, but resists the opportunity to kill Adam as a means of escape (instead trying to work with Adam to deceive their unseen captors).

Bodily mimicry and psychological identification are uniquely complementary at this moment: As we cringe and shudder through the spectacle of Gordon cutting through his own flesh and bone, the scene drives home the point of how much he cares for his family and how far he is willing to go in an attempt to protect them. His coldness is transformed into passionate, goal-driven affect, and he comes across as a different man as he courageously drags himself across the floor, issues what seems a sincere promise to Adam to return to help him, and escapes from the room. It is only by finally submitting to Jigsaw's authority and the logic of his horrific schemes to shock people from their complacency that Gordon is able to serve as a point of viewer identification. Nevertheless, this moment of identification does not threaten the film's dominant mode of spectatorship as "intimate distance" insulated from ethical implication in its violent spectacles. It simply offers a complementary spectacle of redemptive sacrifice and suffering, a scene of productive affect and the will to "do what it takes" equally consonant with dominant post-9/11 ideology in the United States.

NOTES

1. Linda Williams, "Film Bodies: Gender, Genre, Excess," in *Film Genre Reader III,* ed. Barry Keith Grant (Austin: University of Texas Press, 2003), 155. Williams's arguments connect to Steven Shaviro's analysis of spectatorship and corporeality, which shifts the paradigm even further away from psychoanalytic models that posit spectatorship as an experience of distance premised upon a structuring lack. Shaviro calls for an understanding of film viewing as "masochistic, mimetic, and corporeal," acknowledging "a continuity between the physiological and affective responses of my own body and the . . . bodies and images on screen." Steven Shaviro, *The Cinematic Body* (Minneapolis: University of Minnesota Press, 1993), 56, 254–255.
2. Indeed, citing David Rodowick's analysis of the foundational psychoanalytic theories of film spectatorship in Christian Metz, she suggests that the psychic formation of distance and mastery described by Metz in fact *proceeds from* the passive, introjective gaze rooted in the primal scene. Carol Clover, *Men, Women, and Chainsaws: Gender in the Modern Horror Film* (Princeton, NJ: Princeton University Press, 1992), 168–181, 207.
3. Ibid., 49–53.
4. Jason Middleton, "The Subject of Torture: Representing the Pain of Americans in *Hostel,*" *Cinema Journal* 49.4 (2010): 1–24.
5. Williams, "Film Bodies," 153.
6. Middleton, "The Subject of Torture," 9.
7. Ibid., 1.
8. Zimmer suggests that these themes include, "the morality or efficacy of torture, definitions of life, fundamentalist belief systems, and bodily and psychological experiences of violence." Catherine Zimmer, "Caught on Tape? The Politics of Video in the New Torture Film," in *Horror After 9/11,* ed. Aviva Briefel and Sam J. Miller (Austin: University of Texas Press, 2011), 85.
9. Michele Aaron, *Spectatorship: The Power of Looking On* (London: Wallflower Press, 2007), 109.
10. Ibid., 116.
11. Ibid., 116.
12. Zimmer, "Caught on Tape?," 85.
13. Catherine Zimmer makes this point about surveillance in the *Saw* films, as well (ibid., 86).
14. Ibid., 85.
15. An acronym for Uniting and Strengthening America by Providing Appropriate Tools to Intercept and Obstruct Terrorism.
16. Donald Pease, "The Global Homeland State: Bush's Biopolitical Settlement," *boundary 2* 30.3 (2003): 1–18, 7.
17. Ibid., 9–10.
18. Ibid., 11.
19. See Daniel J. Solove, "Why Privacy Matters Even if You Have 'Nothing to Hide,'" *The Chronicle Review*, May 15, 2011, accessed July 5, 2013, https://chronicle.com/article/Why-Privacy-Matters-Even-if/127461/.
20. Adam Lowenstein, "Spectacle Horror and *Hostel*: Why 'Torture Porn' Does not Exist," *Critical Quarterly* 53.1 (2011): 42–60, 42.

21. Ibid., 42.
22. Lowenstein specifically refers here to the work of Carol Clover and Jeffrey Sconce. (Lowenstein, "Spectacle Horror and *Hostel*," 43).
23. Cited in Lowenstein, "Spectacle Horror and *Hostel*," 44.
24. Ibid.
25. Tom Gunning, "An Aesthetic of Astonishment: Early Film and the (In)Credulous Spectator," in *Film Theory and Criticism: Introductory Readings,* fifth edition, ed. Leo Braudy and Marshall Cohen (New York: Oxford University Press, 1999), 826–827.
26. Zimmer argues that the formal closure here is "as much about the systematic reproduction of violence as about narrative resolution," suggesting how Jigsaw's games are not simply the work of a lone deviant, but express "a politics of surveillance and torture." ("Caught on Tape?," 92).
27. Cited in Lowenstein, "Spectacle Horror and *Hostel*," 44.
28. Nick Browne, "The Spectator-in-the-Text: The Rhetoric of *Stagecoach,*" in *Film Theory and Criticism: Introductory Readings,* fifth edition, ed. Leo Braudy and Marshall Cohen (New York: Oxford University Press, 1999), 161.
29. Browne, "Spectacle Horror and *Hostel*," 161–162.
30. Gunning, "An Aesthetic of Astonishment," 826. See also Linda Williams's transposition of the "narrative and number" convention in film musicals to her analysis of feature-length hardcore pornography, in *Hard Core: Power, Pleasure, and the 'Frenzy of the Visible'* (Berkeley: University of California Press, 1989), especially chapter five, "Generic Pleasures."
31. Sigmund Freud, "Mourning and Melancholia," in *General Psychological Theory,* trans. M.N. Searl (New York: Macmillan, 1963), 164–179.
32. Tom Murse, "Did George Bush Really Tell Americans to 'Go Shopping' After 9/11?," *about.com*, accessed July 5, 2013, http://usgovinfo.about.com/od/thepresidentandcabinet/a/did-bush-say-go-shopping-after-911.htm.
33. That is, as opposed to forms of political action. Citizen participation in politics was framed by the administration at that point primarily in terms of "supporting the troops" and the government's war efforts.
34. Tom Murse, "Did George Bush Really Tell Americans to 'Go Shopping' After 9/11?," *about.com*, accessed July 5, 2013, http://usgovinfo.about.com/od/thepresidentandcabinet/a/did-bush-say-go-shopping-after-911.htm.
35. Frank Pelligrini, "The Bush Speech: How to Rally a Nation," *Time*, September 21, 2001, accessed July 5, 2013, http://www.time.com/time/nation/article/0,8599,175757,00.html.
36. Robin Wood, *Hollywood from Vietnam to Reagan* (New York: Columbia University Press, 1986), 77 and *passim*.
37. Ibid., 84.

Part IV

Ethics and the Images of Nature

12 Community Engagement and Film

Toward the Pursuit of Ethical Goals through Applied Research on Moving Images

Mette Hjort

Film scholarship has a well-established tradition of being attuned to moral, political, and social values. Contributing to such values has often been a matter of developing interpretations of films, many of them highly critical of a given social order. While such critiques may have a certain efficacy within the classroom or amongst scholars, it is not clear that their effects extend into the spheres where change is actually being worked toward or achieved. It is well worth asking whether the aspiration to promote ethical values and social progress through film scholarship requires a different approach, one involving interdisciplinary research teams, partnerships with practitioners of various sorts, and institution-building across the boundaries of academe. Such an approach may not evoke the sorts of dramatic changes that are sometimes wished for in film interpretation, but it might be able to deliver concrete change of the sort that counts as ethically worthwhile.

The academic world is a rapidly changing one, and some of the tendencies make the prospect of exploring a more "applied" approach to film scholarship appealing. Many of the world's film scholars are charged with teaching and carrying out research in the context of university environments where the emphasis increasingly is on providing evidence of the *value* of scholarly efforts to society, preferably through various forms of knowledge transfer. In response to such developments it makes sense to ask whether, and if so how, research efforts can be developed that contribute, not merely to scholarly debates and the archive of film-historical learning, but to the well-being and development of a given society, or to sectors within it.

Let me be clear. The aim here is not to suggest that the methodologies that have defined film studies to date should be jettisoned. Rather, the point is to invite reflection on the ways in which the film scholar's role might be *expanded* by approaching the requirement of social relevance, embedded within various calls for accountability and knowledge transfer, with a positive mind-set.[1] That the requirement in question need not be cause for despondency is clearly suggested by teaching examples drawn from one of Asia's leading Liberal Arts institutions, Lingnan University, where service learning is a major institutional commitment.[2] Defined neither as community work, nor as a form of internship, service learning has affinities with both, for it is a matter of students and scholars putting their conceptual and historical (or generally academic and scholarly) knowledge to work in a particular context of need, under expert supervision, and with an eye to both cognitive gains and social benefits or contributions.

It is worth noting that at Lingnan University, successful service learning projects have been developed, not only in the context of the institution's traditionally more pragmatically oriented disciplines, but also in the context of such fields as visual studies and cultural studies. Students taking visual studies courses such as Environmental Aesthetics and Non-fiction Film have been afforded opportunities to apply, test, and deepen their historical and conceptual learning through partnerships with carefully selected groups or organizations that are linked to the university through a larger network of affiliations associated with Hong Kong's emerging civil society.

In the case of the Non-fiction Film course, the partner organization was the Dragon Garden Charitable Trust, created by Cynthia Lee, who became a heritage activist when the Chinese garden built by her grandfather in the 1950s—where *The Man with the Golden Gun* (1974) was later partially shot—was threatened by demolition at the hands of developers.[3] Lee brought students into her sphere of influence, thereby helping them to gain insight into the historical as well as legal dimensions of the struggle for heritage conservation in Hong Kong. At the same time, the academic content of the Non-Fiction Film course provided an awareness of different types of documentary film, and of the various ethical issues that tend to arise in connection with each of them. Working as a group,[4] and under the guidance of then PhD student Cheung Tit-leung, a documentary filmmaker who served as the teaching assistant for the course, students produced a short documentary film, combining elements of direct cinema and interactive filmmaking, about Dragon Garden, near Tuen Mun in the New Territories, and the Blue House in Wanchai, on Hong Kong Island. Entitled *The Preservationist* (2011), the film developed a nuanced argument reflecting students' views on aspects of the heritage debate in Hong Kong. Making the film thus facilitated students' understanding of concepts and approaches that are central to documentary film practice, but also fostered a commitment on their part to being active participants in Hong Kong's civil society debates and activities. Eschewing the expository type of documentary film that Lee and her colleagues at the Dragon Garden Charitable Trust initially expected to see implemented, the students' filmmaking efforts also proved to be a learning experience for the partner organization. Combined with a series of individually authored reflections on the filmmaking process, the film provided a means of assessing students' performance while also producing something of value to those who seek a vigorous, open, and fair-minded discussion of heritage issues in Hong Kong.

My point is this: The experience with service learning at a leading liberal arts university suggests that the call for public accountability, social relevance, and community engagement can be answered in ways that are meaningful and worthwhile. Initiatives of the kind described here have the potential, through collaborative efforts, to become methodologically innovative, and thus fruitful in terms of the further development of film studies. Changing expectations and understandings of what universities do or should be doing may offer opportunities to pursue tasks that have not traditionally been on the film scholar's agenda. The task of implementing teaching and research with an applied dimension that is broadly ethical in its thrust is, in my view, well worth taking up, and not merely on account of the inherent value attached to the envisaged results. Research initiatives and results offering benefits to a wider community that extends well beyond the confines of academe can only strengthen the institutional ground on which the discipline operates.

IDENTIFYING THE NEEDS

Students of social entrepreneurship are asked, among other things, to iden-tify social needs and to find at once ethically responsible and economically viable ways of responding to them. What if film scholars were to envisage an approach that made entrepreneurial efforts, both teaching- and research-wise, a vehicle, not for economic gains, but for cognitive gains in combination with social and/or ethical gains? In Hong Kong, from where I write, issues having to do with nature loom large on the radar when we begin to think along such lines. The focus here will thus be on moving images of nature and the role that film scholars, drawing on interdisciplinary research exper-tise, as well as partnerships with film and health practitioners, might play in shaping the production and reception of films with the potential to offer ethical benefits. Before we can see moving images as providing a response to community needs arising from challenges having to do with nature, it is necessary briefly to evoke the nature of the challenges in question.

Biophobia

Recent findings by psychologists focusing on mental health in Hong Kong identify biophobia—the fear of nature—as an ever-more prominent feature of young Hong Kong citizens' psychological make-up. Described by Simon Parry as "a little-known affliction . . . suffered by . . . tens of thousands of Hong Kong youngsters," biophobia encompasses symptoms such as "fear, anxiety and, in extreme cases, deep distress and trauma . . . [;] unless treated at an early age, it can last a lifetime." Citing Ruth Wilson, a researcher specializing in childhood development, Parry makes the point that biophobia is a poten-tial factor in the failure to curb ongoing environmental degradation: "When a generation grows up suffering from biophobia, the effect on the natural environment can be devastating and far-reaching."[5] It is common knowledge in Hong Kong that fear of nature intensified considerably in the wake of SARS and the perceived threat of pandemics such as Swine Flu. The result was a clear tendency on the part of parents actively to discourage, and even prohibit children from tactile engagements with nature. Students involved in service learning in connection with the visual studies course Environmental Aesthetics & the Visual Environment reported that the kindergarten in which they tested and applied their theoretical learning by engaging young children in environmental art projects proved to be a challenging space within which to work. The parents, it turned out, discouraged their children from gathering and touching the natural objects—leaves, for example—that figured centrally in the various art projects.

Health Threats

Pollution levels in the Pearl River Delta where Hong Kong is located have been increasing steadily, and are described by such experts as former University of Hong Kong Chair of Community Medicine Anthony Hedley as posing serious threats to the health of Hong Kong citizens. Indeed Hedley and his colleagues estimate that 1,100 Hong Kong citizens die on an annual basis as a result of poor air quality. Mostly imposed by Beijing and mostly unelected by ordinary Hong Kong residents, the government of the Hong Kong SAR (Special Administrative Region) has been mostly unresponsive to its citizens' calls for better air, favoring at all times the interests of the business sector. This may be about to change, with the appointment of Christine Loh Kung-wai, CEO of Civic Exchange and a former legislator, as undersecretary for the environment in the new government led by C. Y. Leung, but at the time of writing, it remains to be seen whether the political will and support from the most influential corners of society, both of which are needed to curb pollution, actually exist to the degree that is necessary.

Urban "Development"

Critics of the status quo in Hong Kong see power collusion as taking the form of high levels of both acknowledged and behind-the-scenes government support for the endeavors of various tycoons, who in turn support the government and often run highly lucrative property development businesses. Driven by a strong desire to maximize the yield of every square foot granted to them at preferential government rates, the Hong Kong developers have overseen the destruction of traditional Chinese gardens, of entire neighborhoods, and of a number of now well-known villages. These areas have mostly been replaced by concrete high-rises featuring ever-smaller apartments sold at ever higher prices, often to property speculators who choose to leave them empty, further aggravating an already acute shortage of afford-able housing in the special administrative region. The result of these various tendencies, among other things, is a significant decrease in ordinary Hong Kongers' *access* to nature. Although Hong Kong boasts some of the most spectacular landscapes in the world and some of the most beautiful country parks, the relevant natural environments are accessible only to those who have the leisure time and the money (needed for transportation) to enjoy them. As nature *within* the urban landscape is destroyed in the pursuit of profit, certain sectors of society are increasingly deprived of opportunities to engage with nature.

Of particular interest in the present context are the poor and elderly, for, as we shall see, theirs is a situation that might well be improved through cross-disciplinary initiatives and partnerships to which film scholars are able to contribute. The plight of the elderly is of considerable concern to those who seek a fairer society in Hong Kong. Elderly Hong Kongers living in poverty created much of the city's prosperity, and having toiled in factories during their working lives, are widely seen as deserving the kind of support that would allow them to live out their old age with dignity. The reality, however, is that many of the individuals in question live in subdivided flats and so-called "cage" homes, for which property speculators charge exorbi-tant per foot rates. Homes for the elderly exist in Hong Kong, many of them privately run and operating to very different standards.[6] Ann Hui's award-winning *A Simple Life* (2011) with Deannie Yip in the role of the elderly servant Ah Tao, provides insight into some of the arrangements in question. In some instances, as in the film, a bed in a cubicle is offered. At the other end of the spectrum are those rare institutions where residents, in addition to private rooms, enjoy some form of access to nature.

The problems evoked above are different in important respects, yet they cannot be seen as unrelated. For example, it is hard not to suspect that the failure to appreciate nature, which finds extreme expression in biophobic attitudes, lends energy to the money-driven endeavors that produce hazard-ous air and/or diminish citizens' access to nature. The issues also appear to be related inasmuch as all three fall within the scope of public health ethics, understood as a field dedicated to "promoting and protecting the health of populations." As a field, public health ethics admits, as is to be expected, of competing approaches, with one influential view being that the "moral foundation of public health" involves "an injunction to maximize welfare, and [. . .] health as a component of welfare." A second influential view sees "social justice" as lying "at the moral foundation of public health," the idea being to "secure a sufficient level of health for all and to narrow unjust inequalities."[7] Both approaches are suggestive in the present context, where the additional point that needs to be made is that health no longer tends to be defined as the mere "absence of disease," but rather more positively, as "a state of complete physical, mental and social well-being."[8] Whereas toxic air contributes to illness, clean air alone does not necessarily lead to well-being, for the latter depends, among other things, on the possibility of engaging mindfully with nature on a regular basis.

In what follows, I look at two distinct ways in which the efforts of film scholars might forge a productive link between community needs and specific sorts of films. The first line of argument focuses on what film has to offer, in the way of health benefits, in contexts where access to nature is radically curtailed. The second draws on debates in environmental aesthetics to make the following point: Carefully selected films have the capacity to counter the kind of biophobic tendencies that undermine health and well-being and foster attitudes at odds with ethical thinking along environmental lines.

Given that the cinematic depiction of nature is central to both of the envisaged lines of argument, it is important to define the term *nature*. Let me underscore that 'nature', as I am using it here, does not refer *only* to picturesque or spectacular landscapes.[9] Cinematic depictions and evocations of nature, as it exists amongst us, in even the densest of urban environments, may warrant attention, alongside more traditionally picturesque depictions of landscapes. For present purposes, environmental aesthetician Glenn Parsons's definition of nature is helpful. According to Parsons, nature cannot be defined as "a pristine refuge" or as a "place unmodified by humanity": "Critics point out [that] the extension of the effects of human civilization (e.g., pollution), if not of human civilization itself, has long since extinguished nature, in this sense. There simply is no place left on the planet that is unmodified by humanity." Adapting a phrase from John Stuart Mill, Parsons proposes to rethink the concept of nature as encompassing "what takes place without the agency, or without the voluntary and intentional agency, of man." Examples of nature, on this definition of the term, are "the clouds in the sky, the motion of the seas and a population of herons [. . .] since such things typically do not come about through the voluntary and intentional agency of human beings."[10] In a Hong Kong context, the feral cattle wandering along the (increasingly busy) roads of Sai Kung in the Eastern New Territories come to mind. The point is that thinking about cinematic depictions of nature and their potential benefits should not be based only on films in which panoramic shots of stunning landscapes feature prominently. Sequences capturing some of the more humble, less dramatic workings of nature may also have a significant role to play.[11]

MOVING IMAGES OF NATURE: THE BENEFITS TO HEALTH AND WELL-BEING AFFORDED BY MEDIATED ACCESS TO NATURAL ENVIRONMENTS

The findings of environmental psychologists, social ecologists, architects, and other professionals clearly suggest that diminished access to nature is a problem with clear implications for health and well-being. The health and well-being of a person, these researchers claim, are linked to the opportunities that this person does or does not have to engage with nature. Engaging with nature can take many forms, including the more or less mindful perception of trees through an office window; the glimpsing of hills in the distance from the windows of a moving car;[12] the full sensory experience of taking a walk in a country park, and so on. As we shall see, the perception of representations of nature—of paintings, photographs, and films—also counts as a form of mediated access, which is crucial in the present context.

The understanding of human beings as having a deep *need* for nature, one that is often thwarted by aspects of modern life, clearly motivates a film such as *Biophilic Design* (2011), which conveys the findings of such researchers as E. O. Wilson, Roger Ulrich, Judith Heerwagen, and Stephen Kellert, among others, to a much wider audience. *Biophilic Design* was produced by Stephen Kellert (the Tweedy Ordway professor of social ecology at Yale University's School of Forestry and Environmental Studies), in partnership with Bill Finnegan (co-founder of Tamarack Media). The description provided on the film's jacket cover effectively suggests how the relevant researchers understand the role of nature in human life:

> Biophilic design is an innovative way of designing the places where we live, work, and learn. We *need* [emphasis added] nature in a deep and fundamental fashion, but we have often designed our cities and suburbs in ways that both degrade the environment and alienate us from nature. [. . .] Together, we will encounter buildings that connect people and nature—hospitals where patients heal faster, schools where children's test scores are higher, offices where workers are more productive, and communities where people know more of their neighbors and families thrive. **Biophilic Design** *points the way toward creating healthy and productive habitats for modern humans.*[13]

Underpinning the concept of a "need" for nature is a psycho-evolutionary perspective that sees human beings as having an "unlearned predisposition to pay attention to and respond positively to"[14] the kinds of natural environments that were once essential to survival. Roger Ulrich, for example, argues that, by virtue of their evolutionary history, human beings have an innate tendency to respond positively to natural environments that are nonthreatening in specific respects; to natural environments, that is, that offer wide views, shelter in the form of trees with high trunks and rich canopies, and a glossiness that is suggestive of water.[15] In the context of discussions of health and well-being, what counts as a positive response, it should be noted, is not merely an appreciative attitude toward nature, but a cluster of "emotional, attentional and physiological" changes that together counteract the effects of various stressors. Relevant stressors include environmental ones, such as "crowding, community noise, [and] air pollution," but also those generated by medical interventions, such as surgery.[16]

Based at Texas A&M, and with strong collaborative ties to such institutions as Lund Institute of Technology, Uppsala University, and the Karolinska Institute of Medicine, Roger Ulrich has played a leading role in two areas of research that are of potential value to any film scholar with an interest in engaging in more applied forms of research. More specifically, Ulrich and his collaborators have conducted empirical studies that point to the beneficial effects that are to be derived from *mediated* encounters with nature in contexts such as hospitals, where access to actual nature tends to be very limited indeed, and where health outcomes are central.[17] Much of Ulrich's work in this area has focused on photography and painting,[18] but moving images or videos are clearly of considerable interest too, as is suggested by a second area of research in which he has been actively involved. Ulrich and his research teams have also sought to determine which kinds of environments are best able to mitigate the effects of stress. Their empirical work in this area has relied heavily on short videos with moving images depicting "natural" as compared with "human-made properties."[19] That is, videos with a specific kind of content were seen as effectively "standing in," so to speak, for the actual environments being depicted. Given the implications for film studies, a brief description of this experiment is in order.

In the article "Stress Recovery During Exposure to Natural and Urban Environments," Ulrich and his colleagues describe their use of videos in two distinct ways, to test their guiding hypothesis: "that exposures to unthreatening natural environments would foster greater recuperation from stress than contacts with various urban settings."[20] In the first phase of the experiment, moving images were used to stress the subjects who were participating in it ("120 undergraduate volunteers," from various fields of study at the University of Delaware).[21]

> Each individual, while seated in a comfortable armchair, viewed two 10 min videotapes on a 19" color monitor having a supplementary speaker and amplifier system that ensured accurate reproduction of sounds. The first videotape was the stressor: this was a black and white film about prevention of work accidents ("It Didn't Have to Happen") [. . .]. The film depicts several serious injuries, with simulated blood and mutilation, that occur to employees in a woodworking shop as a result of their carelessness or disregard of safety procedures.[22]

During the second phase of the experiment, which sought to identify environments that would count as genuine "recovery environments," the same subjects were shown a "second ten minute tape [. . .] that was a color/sound display of one of six different everyday outdoor settings." Two of these settings were classified as "natural" by the researchers, the others as "urban." One of the nature-oriented videos focused, for example, on an environment with "nature vegetation" having the following "visual content": "[a] setting dominated by trees and other vegetation; some openness among trees, occasional light breeze in the background; no people or animals." The sounds accompanying the moving images in question are identified as being those of "birds" and of a "light breeze." One of the urban environments featured "heavy traffic" and visual content focusing on a "commercial street with moderately heavy traffic (24 vehicles per minute) and no pedestrians or animals," among other features. The sounds accompanying those depictions are described as having a "range of dB levels" from 65–93.[23] It is not necessary to discuss the conclusions of the study in any great detail. Suffice it to note that Ulrich and his team see "content differences in terms of natural vs. human-made properties" as apparently "decisive in accounting for the differences in recuperation and perceptual intake."[24] The natural environments—and, we might add, their depictions through moving images—proved best able to foster the processes of restoration following episodes of stress in which the researchers were interested.

An interdisciplinary field of theoretical and applied research devoted to health and moving images would have much to contribute in a Hong Kong context, where access to nature (whether mediated or direct), especially for the poor, elderly, and sick, is very limited indeed. Film scholars—working in partnership with film practitioners with whom they should, ideally, be well placed to interact effectively—have a role to play in this regard, for they are in a position to bring valuable film-related expertise to various research processes, as well as to assist with the devising and implementing of initiatives that are consistent with significant research findings. Small nations (and Hong Kong does count as one, given the "One Country, Two Systems" arrangement that governs the SAR's relation to China) are of special interest when envisaging the possibility of research teams involving interaction amongst scientific researchers, medical professionals, film scholars, and film practitioners. In small-nation contexts, film scholars and film practitioners are, quite simply, far more likely to know each other, and to be open to the kind of collaboration that is needed. This is certainly true of Hong Kong, where film scholars and film practitioners do, in fact, collaborate on a regular basis, and where an entity such as the Centre for Cinema Studies at Lingnan University understands its mission to include the forging of productive and mutually supportive partnerships between the research milieu and independent filmmaking practice.[25]

Moving images with nature-based visual content have the capacity to promote health and well-being. Yet, if such materials are to be brought to the sectors of society where they are needed, then researchers will need to commit to community engagement, and to institution-building reaching well beyond the university. That efforts along these lines are needed should not, however, be cause for pessimism. There is a tendency on the part of governments, arguably on a worldwide basis, to encourage universities to engage in knowledge transfer, and in many instances universities have responded to encouragement or pressure by developing service learning programs (and, indeed, the partnerships that are required to run them). Such developments combine to produce a landscape in which there is every reason to be optimistic about the possibility of extending the benefits of film viewing well beyond the usual sites and pleasures of mere entertainment, and into the domain of public health.

ENVIRONMENTAL AESTHETICS AND FILM STUDIES

I hope that I have made a convincing case for seeing applied film research within the broad area of public health ethics as a promising direction for film scholars to pursue. Drawing on environmental aesthetics, a significant body of analytic work that has been almost entirely overlooked by film scholars,[26] I now offer a second example of how film research can be responsive to community needs. The aim is to make a case for seeing certain cinematic depictions of nature as having the capacity, when engaged with under the right circumstances, to foster appreciative attitudes toward nature. Some films, I claim, have the capacity to "cue" (to use Noël Carroll's term)[27] an appreciative stance toward nature, and thereby to encourage film spectators to reflect on what is involved in the adopting of such a stance. If this claim were to be seen as convincing then we would be warranted in seeing film scholars—in their capacity as teachers, film programmers, advisors to schools, and so on—as having a role to play in the fostering of a *disposition* to appreciate nature. Such a disposition, experts believe, is decisive for the success of conservation and preservation efforts aimed at combating the widespread degradation and despoliation of nature resulting from its neglect as a value in the context of competing values. Convincingly arguing the point that "environmental aesthetics offers much for the protection and preservation of the environment," Allen Carlson and Sheila Lintott cite J. Baird Callicott as follows: "In the conservation and resource management arena, natural aesthetics [that is, the aesthetics of nature] has, indeed, been much more important historically than environmental ethics. Many more of our conservation and management decisions have been motivated by aesthetic rather than ethical values, by beauty instead of duty."[28]

Given the neglect of environmental aesthetics by film scholars, some remarks about the field are in order. In this connection *Nature, Aesthetics, and Environmentalism: From Beauty to Duty,* a comprehensive volume edited by Allen Carlson and Sheila Lintott, is useful. Environmental aesthetics in the West traces its roots to eighteenth-century thought, particularly that of Immanuel Kant, Edmund Burke, Archibald Alison, William Gilpin, Uvedale Price, and Richard Payne Knight. Whereas some of these figures set the terms for understanding the aesthetic appreciation of beautiful and sublime landscapes, others helped to establish the idea of the picturesque landscape as a dominant "aesthetic ideal."[29] The burgeoning field of environmental aesthetics, as a contemporary area of inquiry, finds its impetus in the article "Contemporary Aesthetics and the Neglect of Natural Beauty," published by Ronald W. Hepburn in 1966. In this seminal piece, Hepburn made a strong case for an approach to the appreciation of nature that would "accommodate not only nature's indeterminate and varying character but also our multisensory experiences [. . .] of it."[30]

Broadly speaking, contemporary environmental aesthetics involves a rejection of two models of aesthetic appreciation, each of them derived from the once influential view that nature should be appreciated as somehow "art-like." The "object model," as Carlson and Lintott put it, "pushes nature in the direction of sculpture, and the landscape model treats it as similar to landscape painting." Whereas the object-centered approach involves "mentally or physically extracting" natural objects "from their natural environments and dwelling on their more formal aesthetic qualities, such as balance and proportion,"[31] the landscape approach, "which comes directly from the tradition of the picturesque, proposes that we aesthetically experience nature [. . .] as a series of two-dimensional scenes."[32] That these models have ramifications beyond the domain of aesthetic appreciation becomes clear if we consider the effective history of the landscape model. It is uncontroversial to note, for example, that the landscape model has had implications for conservation, and for the selection of natural environments warranting protection. As the US-based Japanese environmental aesthetician, Yuriko Saito, puts it, "the picturesque [. . .] approach to nature has [. . .] encouraged us to look for and appreciate primarily the *scenically* interesting and beautiful parts of our environment. As a result, those environments devoid of effective pictorial composition, excitement, or amusement (that is, those not worthy of being represented in a picture) are considered lacking in aesthetic values."[33]

Current debates set aside the object and landscape models, focusing instead on three other models that are deemed especially helpful. These models are: the natural environmental model, proposed by Allen Carlson; the engagement model, proposed by Arnold Berleant; and the arousal model, developed by Noël Carroll in response to Carlson.[34] The natural environmental model "holds that just as a serious, appropriate aesthetic appreciation of art requires a knowledge of art history and art criticism, an aesthetic appreciation of nature requires a knowledge of natural history: the knowledge provided by the natural sciences, especially geology, biology, and ecology."[35] The engagement model "stresses the contextual dimensions of nature and [especially] our multisensory experience of it" as we are located and immersed in it.[36] Proposed as a model that complements rather than competes with the natural environmental model, the arousal model emphasizes an emotional engagement with nature, based on patterns of salience that we, as a species, are well equipped to detect. In developing this model, Carroll takes seriously the thought that aesthetic appreciation may be based on states that are "less intellectual [and] more visceral"[37] than those considered central by Carlson. These models are helpful, not only as proposals for how we as human beings should be responding to nature, but as conceptual tools for discerning crucial differences amongst various cinematic depictions of human interactions with, and responses to, nature, and amongst various attitudes that such depictions encourage. If we are convinced by the transparency view of photographic depiction, for which Kendall Walton[38] and others have argued, then cinematic depictions of natural environments can legitimately be seen as offering a kind of contact with nature. What is more, films in which such depictions figure centrally have a role to play in fostering the dispositions required properly to appreciate nature, for they have the capacity, among other things, vividly to *represent* a particular mode of aesthetic appreciation that may *cue* spectators' actual engagement with nature.

It should be acknowledged that each of the proposed models has generated its share of criticisms: Carlson's approach to the aesthetic appreciation of nature has been charged with collapsing the boundary between the aesthetic and the nonaesthetic as a result of his emphasis on ever-deeper and more detailed natural scientific knowledge and understanding in the process of aesthetic appreciation. Berleant's less cognitive approach has been similarly charged with failing to establish a clear aesthetic/nonaesthetic boundary on account of his rejection of disinterestedness and emphasis on multisensory engagement. In addition, there are worries about how Carroll's intervention, "On Being Moved by Nature: Between Religion and Natural History," articulates with his proposals regarding aesthetic experience more generally.[39] Yet, beyond the quibbles and disputes lies a genuine and lasting contribution; ultimately, a convincing case has been made for seeing nature, and not just art, as the source of aesthetic value, and as a genuine basis for aesthetic experience and appreciation. From the point of view of the film scholar who is interested in understanding how films might shape attitudes toward nature, it is this contribution, and not the quibbles that accompany it, that ultimately matters.

Nevertheless, which films, we might ask, are best able to foster an appreciative stance towards nature? The nature-focused dimension of cinematic depictions admits, as we know, of considerable variety. There are canonized experimental films such as Michael Snow's now classic *La Région Centrale* (1971),[40] and more recent, less well-known works by Pamela Robertson-Pearce (*Borderline*, 2009) and Melissa Bliss (*Hinterland*, 2009). Whereas Robertson-Pearce relies on static framings of long duration to produce a meditative engagement with natural scenes, Bliss's work, described as a "scratch and sniff film," offers audiences a fuller sensory experience, with certain smells being released at precise, visually relevant moments in the film. Documentaries focusing on human beings' appreciative relationship to a given pristine natural environment or to urban environments in which nature (as defined by Parsons), is present, appear to merit attention. Werner Herzog's *Grizzly Man* (2005) comes to mind as an example of the former, and *My Playground* by Kasper Astrup Schröder (2010), focusing on the Parkour or Freerunning phenomenon, as an example of the latter. Films belonging to the "nature genre," such as BBC's *Planet Earth*, would no doubt repay scrutiny. Heritage films such as *Hip hip hurra!* by Kjell Grede (1987) or *Barbara* (1997) by Nils Malmros also appear to be relevant, given their emphasis on a visual style that draws on nature-based visual content to produce a picturesque look. Many other types and categories of films could be mentioned. The approach taken here is to set aside the task of charting the comparative merits of different types of films in the context of considerations arising from environmental aesthetics and ethics. Instead, a single example of a film is provided, one consistent with the thrust of arguments developed by leading environmental aestheticians.

A point that needs to be acknowledged is that gauging the effects of cinematic mediations of nature, in terms of the fostering of dispositions, requires formal analysis, but also empirical research. Analysis of a work's features—of the ways in which it "cues" spectators' responses—is necessary, but so is the study of spectators' actual responses in precise contexts of reception. The latter approach offers opportunities to consider the role played by different formats and platforms in shaping spectators' responses to mediated experiences of nature. It may well be, for example, that one and the same heritage film in which nonthreatening landscapes are made salient through a picturesque style differs in terms of its effects, depending on the size of the screen on which it is seen. A question worth asking is whether the benefits potentially afforded by cinematic mediations of nature can be achieved on a small screen, or whether they depend on a large-screen experience. In discussing the Norwegian "docu-musical" *Heftig og begeistret* (*Cool and Crazy*, 2001), which I propose to see as a paradigmatic instance of a film cuing an appreciate stance toward nature, I focus on the work's formal features and on the intentions that informed its making.

WONDROUS EVER TO BEHOLD: ON BEING MOVED BY NATURE

Released in 2001, Knut Erik Jensen's *Cool and Crazy* was expected by producers to get an audience of somewhere between 10,000 and 15,000 Norwegian viewers. Instead, the film was seen by 600,000 Norwegians within a few months and went on to become something of a hit on the international festival circuit; so much so, in fact, that a sequel, *På sangens vinger* (*Cool and Crazy on the Road*), was released in 2002.[41] *Cool and Crazy* has an unlikely focus: the singing of the all-male Berlevåg choir, with singers ranging from 29 to 96 years of age. A fishing village with a population of about 1,200 people, Berlevåg is situated at 70 degrees latitude, near the North Cape, where the polar day (24 hours of continuous sun) and polar night (24 hours of continuous darkness) are defining features of the landscape. Berlevåg is also part of Finnmark, and thus home to Norway's indigenous people, the Saami. The Finnmark Act from 2005 brought recognition for the Saami way of life, and acknowledges the Saami's right to sustain their language, culture, and society.

The Director's Statement on the DVD is worth quoting at some length, for it provides a key to the film's success, while also clarifying the film's significance in the present context. Knut Erik Jensen describes his first encounter with the choir as follows:

> It was during a late autumn day in Berlevåg on the shoot of the feature film *Passing Darkness*. A cold northwestern wind swept snow horizontally through the streets of the small town. I was on my way to a concert at the community centre. I was going to hear the Berlevåg male choir. From the very first note I was carried away. Here, at the very edge of the world, a motley group of grown men stood singing—gravely, and powerfully and passionately. Furrowed faces which had withstood turbulent seas and ice cold winds, had basked in the midnight sun and wondered at the awesome stillness of the ocean, softened through this encounter with music and poetry. Through the choir these men had sought refuge from the daily grind into a world of ballads, hymns and full blown marches—into the song of Berlevåg.

In an interview with BBC Four, Knut Erik Jensen makes it clear that a kind of politics of recognition, one drawing attention to the value of a neglected Nordic culture, is at work in the film:

> What goes on in this very remote area has never really been understood or been of any interest to the southern part of Norway. This [film] is one of the first times that people from up there could perform their own way, to show their diversity, and what they are about.

The film, according to the director, is also about the disappearance of a whole way of life, one lived at the very edges of the world:

> A lot of young people leave these small places. They don't get in touch with their culture. . . . They are listening to Anglo-Saxon music and want to go to European cities.

In his response to the interviewer's question as to why he did not choose to record a standard concert performance, the director highlights the question of nature and of the choir members' place within it:

> I wanted to show that the people belonged to nature and that they are singing towards the sea. The song at the beginning of the film is emerging from the sea. These people's lives are based on the sea and the songs and the way they behave is directly related to that. That simplicity gives several dimensions to the songs. The contrast between the old men's faces and the context of the songs and the places where they sing means it can be very emotional.[42]

The film, to put it differently, documents a deep appreciation of an extreme Nordic nature, not as an isolated, discrete aesthetic object or as a landscape to be merely viewed, but as an *environment* that changes according to knowable and known natural rhythms, invites multisensory and multivalent engagement, and prompts strong emotions comprising both cognitive and physiological elements. Again and again, the film shows the men's knowledgeable appreciation of nature's forces, their multisensory engagement with it, and their emotional responses to it, in a way that brings to mind aspects of the natural environmental model, the engagement model, and the arousal model of Carlson, Berleant, and Carroll, respectively. In some instances, as in the 'Midnight Sun' sequence, the natural forces produce a gentle beauty that correlates, we may suppose, with the pleasures of being in and surrounded by nature. Much of the film, however, emphasizes the severity of winter, with the men singing to (and in) blizzards that can only be a source of considerable discomfort, of pain that is somehow overcome through the songs and the deep appreciation of Finnmark that they express. The film shows us the natural environment as changing of its own accord, a feature that Carlson deems central to the appreciation of nature as nature.[43] The film also shows how a peripheral part of the world, one shaped by extreme natural forces, can be thought of as home, and as a legitimate intentional object for a whole range of positive emotions. Inasmuch as the film is a documentary, it invites viewers to recognize the filmmaker's implicit assertoric stance (to use Noël Carroll's term),[44] and to entertain the film's argument and constitutive assertions as true. Let us now look at that argument in terms of specific images and cinematic techniques.

Nature, and the choir members' place within it, are established as the film's focus as early as the first scene, and this by both visual and auditory means. The film opens with a shot of a wintry sea and with the sounds of gulls and waves on the soundtrack. The soundtrack then gives way to a song (being sung by the choir) honoring the extreme nature of Finnmark and those who have made their lives within it. As the words become clear, the choir walks into the snow-filled frame, the roaring waves in the background. Eschewing seamless editing, in this opening scene, Knut Erik Jensen makes use of an approach to editing that is a feature of the film as a whole, and an important part of the participatory and multisensory appreciation that it depicts and cues. A frontal shot of the choir, taken from some distance, gives way to a close-up of the members' faces in profile. Again and again, the editing juxtaposes shots of the same scene from different angles and from varying distances. Whereas the long shots emphasize the choir's location in nature, the close-ups provide evidence of members' immersion in nature, of the ways in which they are affected by it. One of the most moving images in the film is the closing shot of the men's weather-beaten faces, ice hanging from some of them as they sing to nature.

In the greenest of forest vales.

Figure 12.1   Frame grab from Knut Erik Jensen's *Heftig og begeistret (Cool and Crazy)*.

The appreciation of nature is fully conveyed, among other things, through the songs, their contexts, and the editing patterns, but it is also explicitly developed as a theme in the film, in connection, for example, with the choir's trip to Murmansk, where its members are scheduled to perform. As their bus travels through a landscape left desolate by human despoliation, we watch the men's horrified responses, and hear them utter phrases such as: "Look at that. You can't do that to nature." Through their songs, through the natural contexts in which they sing them, and through their conversations, the men repeatedly convey a sense of being part of, and moved by, the many diverse manifestations of an extreme nature, one governed by forces that they take themselves to understand well. In the hearts and minds of the men, that extreme natural environment is also a natural home worthy of respect and appreciation.

Cinematic depictions of nature will always remove us from nature, even as they bring us into contact with it. Such is the nature of the medium, and of the cinematic experience. Yet, whereas in some cases nature serves instrumental (or even exploitative purposes) in films, in other cases what is both depicted and targeted is an appreciative stance toward nature. In the case of *Cool and Crazy*, the depicted stance explains an actual, real-world attachment to nature that is clearly framed as scientifically informed, moving. A worthy task for film scholars is to ensure that *Cool and Crazy*, and other films like it, are more widely seen, and in contexts that encourage thoughtful debate about attitudes toward nature.

CONCLUSION

With universities increasingly being asked to demonstrate their value for, and responsiveness to society, there are good pragmatic reasons for developing applied forms of film research. More interesting, however, are the broadly ethical goals that can be pursued by film scholars when priority is given to community engagement, knowledge transfer, and research collaboration spanning various disciplines, as well as the theory/practice divide. There is a place for filmmakers' depictions of nature in social programs motivated by ethical concerns, whether the aim is to help the elderly to live a dignified life, or to foster attitudes that support a more caring relation to nature. The relevant potential of moving images will only be realized, however, if film scholars are willing to expand their activities beyond the more traditional tasks associated with research in film.

ACKNOWLEDGEMENT

I am grateful to my colleague Sophia Law, a former nurse, for discussions regarding the plight of, and available care for, the elderly in Hong Kong.

NOTES

1. For an interesting discussion of "soft" forms of Knowledge Transfer relevant to Arts and Humanities fields, see Aldo Geuna and Alessandro Musicio, "The Governance of University Knowledge Transfer," SEWPS/SPRU electronic working paper series 173 (2008).
2. For more information about service learning at Lingnan University, see "Office of Service Learning," accessed July 5, 2013, http://www.ln.edu.hk/osl/.
3. The Dragon Garden website includes information about the history of the garden and the challenges involved in preserving it. It also includes a clip from the James Bond film showing the garden in all of its earlier splendor. See: "Dragon Garden," accessed July 5, 2013, http://dragongarden.hk/?page_id=18.
4. The student filmmakers were: Chriz Chan, Frieda Luk, Sophie Cabon, Terence Choi, Tina Yao, and William Seung.
5. Simon Parry, "Battling Biophobia," *South China Morning Post,* May 19, 2009, A12.
6. David Briggs, "Accreditation and the quality journey in aged care," *Asian Journal of Gerontology & Geriatrics* 1.1 (2006): 163–169. I am grateful to Derrick Au for having brought the work of Briggs to my attention.

7. Ruth Faden and Sirine Shebaya, "Public Health Ethics," *Stanford Encyclopedia of Philosophy,* accessed April 12, 2010, http://plato.stanford.edu/entries/publichealth-ethics/.
8. WHO 1948, cited in Dominic Murphy, "Concepts of Disease and Health," *Stanford Encyclopedia of Philosophy*, accessed July 5, 2013, http://plato.stanford/edu/entries/health-disease/.
9. Film scholars have written extensively about landscape in film in recent years. See Giorgio Bertellini, *Italy in Early American Cinema: Race, Landscape, and the Picturesque* (Bloomington: Indiana University Press, 2009); Henrik Gustafsson, *Out of Site—Landscape and Cultural Reflexivity in New Hollywood Cinema 1969–1974* (Saarbrücken: VDM Verlag Dr Müller, 2008); Graeme Harper and Jonathan Rayner, eds., *Cinema and Landscape* (Bristol: Intellect, 2010), David Melbye, *Landscape Allegory in Cinema: From Wilderness to Wasteland* (Basingstoke: Palgrave Macmillan, 2010), and Laraine Porter and Bryony Dixon, eds., *Picture Perfect: Landscape, Place and Travel in British Cinema before 1930* (Exeter: University of Exeter Press, 2007).
10. Glenn Parsons, *Aesthetics and Nature* (New York: Continuum, 2008), 2.
11. Hong Kong new media artist Zoie So makes a similar point in her artwork produced for the Visual Studies conference "What Environment Do We Want?: Environmental Aesthetics and Its Implications" (Lingnan University, November 17–20, 2011). See the *placemarks* catalogue produced for the exhibition that was an integral part of the conference.
12. Russ Parsons et al., "The View From the Road: Implications for Stress Recovery and Immunization," *Journal of Environmental Psychology* 18 (1998): 113–140.
13. See also Stephen Kellert et al., *Biophilic Design: The Theory, Science and Practice of Bringing Buildings to Life* (New York: John Wiley & Sons, 2008).
14. Roger Ulrich et al., "Stress recovery during exposure to natural and urban environments," *Journal of Environmental Psychology* 11 (1991): 205.
15. Roger Ulrich, "Biophilia, Biophobia, and Natural Landscapes," in *The Biophilia Hypothesis,* ed. Stephen R. Kellert and Edward O. Wilson (Washington DC: Island Press, 1993).
16. Ulrich et al., "Stress Recovery," 201.
17. For Ulrich's work on the relation between engaging with nature and faster recovery rates, lower dependence on pain relief medication etc., see "Effects of Health Facility Interior Design on Wellness: Theory and Recent Scientific Research," *Journal of Health Care Design* 3 (1991): 97–109; "How Design Impacts Wellness," *Healthcare Forum Journal* 20 (1992): 20–25; "A Theory of Supportive Design for Healthcare Facilities," *Journal of Healthcare Design* 9 (1997): 3–7, discussion 21–24; "Effects of Gardens on Health Outcomes: Theory and Research," in *Healing Gardens: Therapeutic Benefits and Design Recommendations,* ed. Clare Cooper Marcus and Marni Bates (New York: John Wiley & Sons, 1999): 27–86.
18. Roger Ulrich et al., "Effects of exposure to nature and abstract pictures on patients recovering from heart surgery," paper presented at the Thirty-Third Meeting of the Society for Psychophysiological Research, Rottach-Egern, Germany, abstract published in *Psychophysiology* 30 [1993], supplement 1: 7.
19. Ulrich et al., "Stress recovery," 201.
20. Ibid., 209.
21. Ibid., 210.
22. Ibid.
23. Ibid., 211.
24. Ibid., 201.

25. The Centre for Cinema Studies at Lingnan University has linked teaching initiatives mounted by documentary filmmaker Tammy Cheung, Augustine Lam, and social workers from Caritas, with courses taught by the departments of Visual Studies, Chinese, and Translation. The aim was to facilitate experiential learning focused on social needs arising in nearby Tin Shui Wai, dubbed "city of sadness" on account of poverty and related problems.
26. The exceptions are P. Adams Sitney, "Landscape in the cinema," in *Landscape, Natural Beauty and the Arts*, ed. Salim Kemal and Ivan Gaskell (Cambridge: Cambridge University Press, 1993), 103–126; and Noël Carroll, "On Being Moved by Nature: Between Religion and Natural History," in *Landscape, Natural Beauty and the Arts*, ed. Salim Kemal and Ivan Gaskell (Cambridge: Cambridge University Press, 1993), 244–266.
27. Noël Carroll, *The Philosophy of Horror: Or, Paradoxes of the Heart* (London: Routledge, 1990).
28. Cited by Allen Carlson and Sheila Lintott, "Introduction: Natural Aesthetic Value and Environmentalism," in *Nature, Aesthetics, and Environmentalism: From Beauty to Duty*, ed. Allen Carlson and Sheila Lintott (New York: Columbia University Press, 2008), 1.
29. Ibid., 4.
30. See Ronald W. Hepburn, "Contemporary aesthetics and the neglect of natural beauty," in *British Analytical Philosophy*, ed. Bernard Williams and Alan Montefiore (London: Routledge and Kegan Paul, 1966); discussed by Carlson and Lintott, "Introduction," 7.
31. Carlson and Lintott, "Introduction," 8.
32. Ibid., 8–9.
33. Cited in ibid., 13.
34. See "Appreciating Art and Appreciating Nature," in *Landscape, Natural Beauty and the Arts*, ed. Kemal and Gaskell; and *Aesthetics and the Environment: The Appreciation of Nature, Art and Architecture* (London: Routledge, 2000). Arnold Berleant, *Aesthetics and Environment: Variations on a Theme* (Aldershot: Ashgate, 2005). Noël Carroll, "On Being Moved by Nature."
35. Carlson and Lintott, "Introduction," 9.
36. Ibid., 10.
37. Ibid., 10.
38. Kendall L. Walton, "Transparent Pictures: On the Nature of Photographic Realism," *Critical Inquiry* 11 (1984): 246–276.
39. Robert Stecker, "Aesthetic Experience and Aesthetic Value," *Philosophy Compass* (2006), accessed July 5, 2013, http://www.blackwell-compass.com/subject/philosophy/article_view?article_id=phco_articles_bpl007. Thanks to Paisley Livingston for this reference.
40. It could be argued that this work is really about the strange camera movements that the machine set-up produces.
41. Gunnar Iversen, "The Old Wave: Material History in *Cool and Crazy* and the New Norwegian Documentary," in *Northern Constellations: New Readings in Nordic Cinema*, ed. Claire Thomson (Norwich: Norvik Press, 2006).
42. BBC Four. 2002. "Knut Erik Jensen," accessed December 9, 2002, http://www.bbc.co.uk/bbcfour/documentaries/storyville/jensen-interview.shtml.
43. Carlson, *Aesthetics and the Environment*, xviii.
44. Noël Carroll, "Fiction, Non-fiction, and the Film of Presumptive Assertion: A Conceptual Analysis," in *Film Theory and Philosophy*, ed. Richard Allen and Murray Smith (Oxford: Clarendon Press, 1999), 173–202.

13 Animal-Borne Imaging
Embodied Point-of-View and the Ethics of Identification

Ruth Erickson

"Contact with animals turns human beings into others, effecting a metamorphosis. Animality is, in this sense, a kind of seduction, a magnetic force or gaze that brings humanity to the threshold of its subjectivity."

—Akira Lippit, *Electric Animal*[1]

THE BIRTH OF A SENSATION

Following practices established by his father in the mid-nineteenth century, Julius Neubronner used carrier pigeons to ferry prescriptions and medicaments to and from his family apothecary shop in Kronberg, Germany. One day, as the story has been told, a pigeon, normally "quite punctual," disappeared for a month. Perplexed by this unlikely behavior, Neubronner sought to discover where the pigeon had gone, and so he devised, and in 1907 patented, a small photographic camera outfitted with a timer to strap to the body of a pigeon.[2] As the pigeon ascended into the sky, the camera's shutter was triggered, and the corresponding physical indexes of film and animal body promised to disclose the pigeon's location and to plumb the mysteries of animal behavior.

Neubronner's experiments in southwestern Germany in the first decade of the twentieth century are the earliest known attempts to derive images from cameras mounted on the bodies of animals, a practice that continues up to the present. By combining photographic and animal capabilities—indexical image-making and flight—Neubronner aimed to move beyond his human limitations and to gain proximity to perspectives that eluded his access. The concept of perspective implies both a spatial position—often located via the systematic arrangement of space by, for instance, linear perspective—and a subjective position, meaning a subject's perception, which is shaped by innumerable cultural, political, psychological, and physiological factors. Drawing on these two aspects of perspective, animal-borne imaging displaces the "camera eye"—a system of lenses developed according to human optics—onto the animal, which occupies a physical space and subjective state largely inaccessible to humans. A desire to make such ulterior perspectives visible and, thereby, somehow perceptible or possibly even controllable has compelled inventors, artists, filmmakers, scientists, and, more recently, pet owners (companions) to mount cameras on animals throughout the twentieth century.

A brief foray into recent press uncovers numerous articles about experiments marrying cameras and animals. From a backyard project with the family cat in Seattle to a Dutch artist's film made with pigeons to a twelfth-story camera trained on the nest of two red-tailed hawks in downtown New York City, these stories reveal human infatuation with the animal other.[3] In April 2011, the live-stream feed of eaglets hatching in Iowa crashed the website of the Raptor Resource Project, a nonprofit that manages numerous live-feed, nest cameras across the state.[4] An ABC news report on the "Internet sensation" cited over 11 million views from 130 countries of the eagle cam and also mentioned the even more impressive 26 million views of a Shiba Inu puppy cam in the summer of 2010 (up to 63 million as of June 2013 according to the live-stream website).[5] In June 2011, when a macaque monkey took the camera of the British nature photographer Nathan Slater and captured photographs of herself, a suite of articles debating the copyright of the photographs triggered a passionate, and at times hilarious, discussion about the definition of "creative contribution" and the existence of nonhuman animal consciousness and rights.[6] While incredibly diverse, these examples, and there are many more, reveal a profound human desire to gain proximity to animals through media and fascinating questions about the legal and ethical status of the resulting documentation. Whether selling photographs captured during the neighborhood walkabouts of a family cat or understanding nesting behavior of endangered bald eagles, these practices pose novel questions for media historians and theorists.

By beginning with a brief discussion of Neubronner's pigeon-camera within the context of turn-of-the-century technology and then moving on to more recent examples of animal-borne imaging produced within the spheres of science, art, and mass entertainment, I aim to address a series of questions: What does animal-borne imaging reveal about changing conceptions of animals and technology in the twentieth century? How do animal-camera arrangements throw into question issues of agency, subjectivity, and interpretation? How do images initiate identification and alienation? What do these experiences suggest about the media, exhibition contexts, and material and immaterial qualities of photography and film? Within film studies, animal and wildlife films have increasingly received attention, but this research deals primarily with the display of animals on film as opposed to the dual position of animals as the physical support of the camera and, therefore, as represented, or evoked, through images largely devoid of their bodies.[7] This distinction requires adjusting certain interpretive approaches, such as formalism, ideologies of framing, and authorial motivation, and to concentrate more closely on modes of participatory seeing and spectatorial engagement. In scientific literature, animal-borne imaging has been discussed either as a series of technological feats leading to progressively more precise footage for data accumulation or, in promotional literature, as opportunities to cross over to the animal world. By critically addressing animal-borne imaging, I want to take seriously the claims of its body-camera arrangement—the possibility of identifying with radical others—in ways that resist both the facile rejection and the celebration of ecstatic media experiences. My argument is twofold: First, I suggest that the marriage of animal and camera mark ongoing efforts to colonize or concretize the limits of what constitutes humanity, insofar as the animal and technology are so often invoked at its borderlines. Second, I suggest that the resulting images divulge the difficulty of delimiting human subjectivity by inviting empathetic readings and yet failing to communicate coherent experiences. It is this enticement and resistance to identification that demarcates an ethics of animal-borne imaging.

What Is It Like to Be a Pigeon?

In his foundational essay of 1974, "What is it like to be a bat?" Thomas Nagel establishes an important train of thought in animal studies and cognitive psychology by rejecting human capacity to know or to represent animal experience. "An organism," he writes, "has conscious mental states if and only if there is something that it is like to *be* that organism—something it is like *for* the organism."[8] The "what it is like" aspect of consciousness stipulates its subjective character, and with this assertion of subjectivity, Nagel counters the idea that learning about the structure of animal bodies could provide means to understand animal experience. For Nagel, to know the experience of an animal, one must occupy the subjective position of that animal, and so, he queries "What is it like for a bat to be a bat?"[9] Bats, as Nagel explains, perceive distance, shape, motion, and so forth using sonar, or echolocation, which operates through the correlation of outgoing shrieks and subsequent echoes. The sheer disparity between such a sensing system and that of human beings underscores Nagel's point that imaginative identification of animal consciousness will always come up against the restricted resources of human experience. Only a schematic conception of what it is like for "*me* [as human] to behave as a bat behaves" is ever accessible because mental states are available only to those already acquainted. While opening subjectivity to nonhuman species, Nagel shuts out the possibility of intersubjectivity. His propositions rightly warn against proposals of gaining total knowledge, and I fundamentally agree that an abyss will always stretch between what it is to be human *or* animal. Nevertheless, I resist his disregard for representational (or presentational) realms and alternate models of subjectivity, particularly because animal-borne imaging engenders awareness of the limits of understanding.

For Neubronner in the early twentieth century, the pigeon-camera translated impossible bodily experiences into distorted and blurred photographs. At the time, getting airborne was an active area of research. Alfred

Hildebrandt's 1907 book *Airships Past and Present* captures the transitional nature of the technological moment, when wireless telegraphy and airplanes were beginning to eclipse pigeon carriers and aerial balloon photography. While Hildebrandt celebrates the pigeon for its valiant "defense of the nation" and its uncanny capacity for orientation, he details the disastrous early experiments of "flying machines" and dismisses the Wright brothers' reports as "exaggerated."[10] He was particularly suspicious of early airplanes with movable wings due to their "slavish imitation of the bird-mechanism." According to Hildebrandt, the flight of birds was impossible to replicate because, as experiments by Buttenstedt and Marey showed, "the essential feature in the flight of a bird lies in the state of tension, succeeded by a corresponding state of relaxation" in the bird's body and feathers.[11] The malleable and reactive form of the natural body could not be sufficient rendered by industrial and mechanical means. Hildebrandt's negotiation between old and new technologies evidences preoccupations of the period. Gradually, the advancement of airplanes and aerial photography would render the pigeon anachronistic, but even through World War I, England, Germany, France, and the United States maintained "Pigeon Corps," which had the beguiling ability to get behind enemy lines and move about unnoticed.[12] Rather than positioning the pigeon-camera as an anomalous and minor step from old to new technologies, I want to underline its historical, technological, and aesthetic specificity.[13] The sheer ability to get airborne in addition to characteristics such as chance, freedom, and mystery distinguished the pigeon-camera hybrid from contemporaneous technologies and machines. It made possible what was not yet humanly possible, and the photographs visually manifest this nonhuman experience.

Compared to the stability and clarity of conventional "bird's eye view" images, extant photographs from pigeon cameras are distorted and blurred, redolent with the activity of their own making.[14] Due to both the placement of the camera on the pigeon's breast and the small size of the lenses, the photographs often display askew angles, truncated views, and highly abstracted scenes.

These compositional and stylistic qualities, many of which are side effects of technology and circumstance, endow the photographs with a sense of groundlessness and vertiginous careening quite distinct from contemporaneous aerial photographs. Without vertical orientation or visible horizon lines, the photographs disrupt visual norms of sense-making for human viewers and, in so doing, open up symbolic and imaginative spaces where the mapping of human/animal and of object/subject loses binary stability. The photographs also resist dematerialization into empathetic readings or intersubjective exchanges on account of their clunky materiality and the radical difference of their participating "subjects." Neubronner assembled the pigeon-camera apparatus and then trained the animal and dictated its release. The camera lens does not replicate the multiple visual fields of "bifoveate" pigeon vision but rather recreates the singular visual field of binocular

Figure 13.1   Julius Neubronner, pigeon photographs, c. 1907, silver gelatin print, 8 cm × 3 cm. Copyright Deutsches Museum, Munich.

human vision.[15] At the same time, however, animals equipped with representational means gain new visibility as subjects rather than only objects of the apparatus. Animal-borne imaging, if not suspending human consciousness, generates, through familiar media, visual experiences of space and time radically different from those of everyday human life.

What then is it like to be a pigeon? The photographs reveal very little. I do not know how pigeons perceive the houses below, only how a particular lens and film reacted to light waves at a moment. I find it hard to imagine their split fields of vision in the single rectangular field of the photograph. I have no idea what prompted this flight or even if pigeons have "minds" that might have been occupied by thoughts or ideas, and I doubt every pigeon has the same experience. However, in 1907, to be airborne was a collective dream; the camera captures a view from this unattainable bodily position. Visual cues indicate the release of the ground and a body navigating space without familiar coordinates. Through embodied spectatorship, viewers have the potential to become enmeshed in these alternate bodily experiences of movement. While Neubronner initially attached cameras to pigeons to track their whereabouts, this disciplinary impulse intersected with a yearning for flight, and through the physical proximity of camera to animal, he initiated an experiential venture. Filmmakers over the last three decades have extended Neubronner's animal-camera model into the depths of the ocean and jungle, but they cast their projects within new frameworks of environmental awareness and advocacy. By examining these recent examples, I will suggest that the ethics of animal-borne imaging hinges on a relay of sympathetic and unsympathetic relations between camera-bearing animal and human viewer.

ANIMAL-BORNE ACTIVISM

The animal-borne imaging projects initiated by Greg Marshall, Sam Easterson, and John Downer over the last twenty-five years share a common general aim: to forge greater human understanding of and respect for animals. Like Neubronner at the beginning of the twentieth century, these filmmakers invest in technological ingenuity to gain knowledge by making visible animal life, but in the late-twentieth century this endeavor is framed within the rhetoric of environmentalism. Greg Marshall was inspired to mount cameras on marine animals after witnessing a remora attached to a shark while diving in Belize.[16] In 1989, he successfully attached a camera onto a wild sea turtle on the coast of Saint Croix in hopes of learning about coastal nesting patterns. Naming the project "Crittercam," Marshall eventually garnered support from National Geographic and established the Remote Imaging Laboratory to collect and process footage and data captured from marine animals, which he started making publicly available in 2004 through a television series. Using similar filming techniques to Marshall's, Sam Easterson, an artist and landscape architect, began his own series of animal-borne imaging projects in 1998, and has exhibited the short videos in art exhibitions at venues such as the Whitney Museum of American Art, Mass MoCA, and Documenta 13. The videos, Easterson hopes, might "show people what they haven't seen before, trying to bring a new perspective—a real physical perspective—of how they might see things."[17] In 2009, he created an online archive, the Museum of Animal Perspectives, of his films.[18] John Downer, a wildlife filmmaker, began pioneering innovative techniques in filmmaking in the mid-1980s to gain proximity to animals. For *In-Flight Movie* (1987), he reared a duck from birth so that he could film the flying bird while gliding next to it with a parasail, a method repeated in Jacques Perrin's *Winged Migration* (2001). In 2008, for a BBC series called *Tiger: Spy in the Jungle*, Downer trained elephants to carry cameras into an Indian jungle, as his production company's website explains: "To enter the world of this tiger family, Downer and his wizard team [. . .] deploy the ultimate all-terrain camera vehicles—elephants—kitted out with the latest high-definition 'secret weapons' of wildlife filmmaking—trunk-cam, tusk-cam and log-cams."[19] Elephants serve as unassuming interlopers in a group

of tigers and thereby as interspecies mediators. In all three projects, environmental claims are founded on the understanding and experiences afforded
by animal-borne imaging's unparalleled proximity to animals.

An implicit empathetic relation between human and animal lies at the
heart of the filmmakers' objectives to affect environmental change. In the
process of viewing, the animal's space and time as well as that of the film
medium and the viewer overlap, and this spatial and temporal unity afforded
by the medium facilitates, in the terms set out by the filmmakers, identification between human viewer and animal. As Sam Easterson quips, "If you're
able to see from the perspective of these animals, you're far less likely to
harm them or their habitats."[20] Environmental activism hinges on spectatorial engagement with the animal experience as communicated through
image, movement, sound, montage, and so on. However, the possibility
and efficacy of shaping human sensitivity hinges on a highly nuanced filmic
experience, constituted not only by the filmmakers, film, and environment
but also by spectators' communal and individual projections. Furthermore,
"the animal" of this exchange is not an organic unity, but rather a tech-
nologically and culturally constructed one. The three sets of animal-borne
films diverge dramatically according to their conditions of production and
consumption, specifically in the filmic means and codes employed to inscribe
subject positions and make them readable. In contrast to environmental
activism based on gathering facts and assuring understanding, Easterson's
films offer an alternative and more radical activism by encouraging viewers
to recognize the very limits of fully knowing about themselves or others.
The divergent approaches to understanding animal-borne entail important
ethical ramifications.

POINT-OF-VIEW: "ANYTHING CAN HAPPEN WHEN AN ANIMAL IS YOUR CAMERAMAN"[21]

Animal-borne films constitute animal subjectivity by exploiting a number
of cinematic devices and filmic codes associated with subjective and narrative cinema. The most obvious is the point-of-view (POV) shot, which
these films make radical use of. In his study of POV (and point-of-view
as more than the cinematic device), Edward Branigan connects the structural arrangement of POV directly to subjectivity: "Subjectivity in film
depends on linking the framing of space at a given moment to a *character*
as origin."[22] The camera occupies the spatial position of a character, showing viewers what that character sees and, in consequence, a host of other
psychological, emotional, and sensory phenomena derived from that character. Branigan contends, however, that the communication of subjectivity
demands "something more–beyond the merely formal": "The difficulty
of equating optical (perceptual) POV with the experience of *being that
character* (feeling the character's feelings) leads critics toward attitude,

identification, or language as additional conditions of subjectivity."[23] In animal-borne footage, an animal replaces a human (and, one could even say, man) as at the origin of the POV shot and thus capitalizes on its claim of identification and subjectivity. Other formal devices associated with subjective and auteur cinema, such as eye-line matches and overexposed or blurry sequences, contribute to the subjective and individual character of the animal-borne films. The idea of the "animal cameraman" consolidates both author position and subjective character, so that movements, manipulations to footage, and accidents serve as indicators of an animal's subjective experience, if not creative mark.[24]

The nature of identification, however, between two humans differs qualitatively from that between human viewers and animal subjects. Viewers do not expect a turtle to have complex intentions for its turn to the right, even though it might. Animal-borne imaging, therefore, takes on POV as a cinematic device tied to a subject and inscribed with learned modes of spectatorship, and it exploits the delimited subjectivity of this formal device. Viewers are potentially more willing to accept discontinuities and aporia in animal-borne films, as they also exist in human understanding of animals. The animal-borne filmic point-of-view is the unthinking cameraman whose recorded movement opens a time and space for subjective identification and disidentification. Marshall, Downer, and Easterson treat their POV footage, however, in strikingly different ways in response to their animal subjects, production teams, audiences, and exhibition venues. Variations in editing and narration, in particular, distinguish their projects and alter POV's affective possibilities by prescribing forms of identification and subjectivity.

PRODUCING (MIS)UNDERSTANDING

The filmmakers' different areas of production and consumption—art, science, and mass entertainment—directly influence the filmmakers' narrative and explanatory structures. Easterson works with a small crew that includes a veterinarian, animal handler, and technical assistant and initially funded his projects through gallery and museum commissions, often selecting animals in the geographical region of the exhibition venue. His animal specimens range from bison, sheep, frogs, hawks, armadillos, and snails to a range of insects, constituting a broader and less exotic scope of species than Marshall's and Downer's. Because Marshall usually deploys his "crittercams" as part of ongoing scientific studies of threatened species, his specimens tend to be larger and more exotic animals—penguins, sharks, sea turtles, lions, and bears—and each project includes a complex system of tracking and data gathering through expensive technical outfits. Downer's most recent productions produced for the BBC and Discovery networks have focused on large felines in jungles and savannahs in Africa and India, animals that attract the greatest attention at zoos and in safaris and are particularly suitable for broadcast television. Downer's state-of-the-art technology costs "as much as a small house," as the narrator explains in one episode. These variations in the production scales and in the casts of animals depend on the projects' contexts. Likely with regard for their television audiences and the preset length of the television segment, Marshall and Downer insert their animal-borne footage into fast-paced narratives and heavily interpret the footage for their audiences. Easterson's films, on the other hand, lack significant narrative and editing, which imbues the films with an opaqueness, boredom, and sense of suspended time and space, shifting attention to formal aspects—quality and speed of movement, depth of field, and frame of vision. By resisting conventional modes of sense-making—narrative, editing, camera angles—Easterson's films demonstrate that consciousness-raising may not take place through explanation, narration, and identification with others but rather through viewers' recognition of their own blindness.

One of the most striking aspects of the *Crittercam* television episodes is how little animal-borne footage they actually include. Most often, murky point-of-view shots from the fin of a shark or back of a turtle follow the end of long narrative sequences, thereby inscribing animal-borne footage within the diegesis. The first episode of *Crittercam* exemplifies what I see as the colonization of the animal body by systems of physical, narratological, and virtual capture. It begins with a hunt for the desired animals by a group of intrepid scientists. Once the group locates the bull sharks with the help of local fishermen off the coast of Mexico, multiple cameras in the water and on the boat record failed attempts to wrangle the animals. Events in the wild, however, rarely follow scripts, and as if on morbid cue, a shark, aggravated by the pursuit, attacks a cameraman in the water. Footage shows the camera falling to the sea floor in a cloud of sand, and the film quickly cuts away to a fast-paced rescue operation. The story, seemingly undeterred, quickly returns to the pursuit and successful capture of a bull shark, to which the team attaches a torpedo-shaped camera using a dart that punctures the shark's skin. While the narrator assures viewers that the camera is "noninvasive," the physical penetration of the shark's skin and visual penetration of its environment seem like retaliation tactics following the shark's attack. A short clip depicts the shark gliding away from the boat pulling the camera next to its dark body. The episode ends with the retrieval of the camera, and the crew gathering around a monitor to watch the collected footage. Shots from the shark camera are intercut with the smiling, huddled group as an upbeat piano soundtrack overlays Marshall's affirmations—"fantastic, fantastic"—to cue success.

The episode contains less than a minute of animal-borne footage. In it, a seemingly endless deep blue environment extends beyond the shark's gray body, which fills the bottom portion of the frame. There is a sense of weightless floating as the camera shifts rhythmically from side to side like a pendulum with the shark's dorsal fin keeping time. The footage would likely seem monotonous and even boring if not for the dramatic build-up, intercut segments, and forward momentum of the narrative, which jerks viewers back into the story. The narrator ends the episode by stating what the mysterious footage revealed: Bull sharks prefer to stay close to the ocean floor to hunt except when they perceive danger. I cannot assess the importance of this revelation or its impact on environmental work, but this interpretation assigns a definable value to the footage. Rather than probing the incommunicability of the animal-POV or even alternative forms of engagement, the series consigns the animal within familiar ideological structures and, thus, rearticulates positions of mastery from which humans so often approach their animal counterparts.[25]

Like *Crittercam* television series, the three-part *Tiger: Spy in the Jungle* series tells a rather conventional story and reaffirms existing animal/human relations. Downer uses the camera-bearing elephants and camouflaged technology to penetrate this "wild" environment.

The three episodes follow a litter of tiger cubs to adulthood, and the narrative hits all the familiar milestones of growing up: from the protective mother tiger's watchful eye to the young tigers' first hunt to "leaving home." Elephants tricked out as "spies" afford unparalleled access and proximity to the tigers and, thereby, confirm the series' appeal to the natural order of things. The opening credit sequence cuts quickly between elephants and tigers as a dramatic voiceover set to percussive drum sequences announces: "They enter the tigers' world armed only with spy cameras. [. . .] They are

Figure 13.2 John Downer, production shots from *Tiger: Spy in the Jungle*, 2008, digital photographs. Copyright John Downer Productions.

our spies in the jungle [and] bring us closer than ever before." The series proposes two interrelated forms of viewer identification: First, with the "tiger family," as the pride is often referred to, through familiar narratives and, second, with the camera's surveying eye through the naturalized act of spying. "Naturalized" refers to Downer's elaborate camouflage tactics, which aim to visually minimize the technological intrusion, and to the elephants' status as unmediated, insider viewers.[26] In fact, Downer underlies the story of the growing tiger cubs with another narrative about his seamless integration of animal, environment, and technology. The two narratives work to corroborate one another, so that technological ingenuity authenticates the untainted representation of the wild tigers. Downer's jungle is totally mediated with elephants carrying high-definition cameras outfitted with suspension systems to reduce jerkiness and remote-controlled cameras embedded in faux logs and rocks. Animals and technology become interconstitutive, whereby technology affirms the nature of the tigers and elephants and the animals demonstrate the ever-expanding reach of technology.

Downer positions his animal films as opportunities to interpret "through new eyes" in hopes of learning to achieve a more sustainable balance between human, animal, and agricultural life.[27] A number of clues—including a credit sequence, placement of cameras, and the tigers' names—suggest that Downer filmed *Tiger: Spy in the Jungle* on a nature preserve, a demarcated space for animals to live out of harm's way. This delimitation of space sustains animal life in a modern age, and Downer's total mediation of this already bordered environment enacts supplementary forms of control and of preservation. As we know, the livelihood of the animal increasingly relies on human awareness and behavioral modification, if not on direct aid. Situated in the environment, human viewers learn, through editing and narration, that tigers' lives are much like their own. Whether or not this sense of familiarity leads to greater sustainability or rather validates and extends human control over the earth and its life remains an open question. However, by positing the very possibility of understanding animal life and displaying total access to it through technological ingenuity, Marshall and Downer confirm human domination over animals while also justifying their expensive endeavors to scientific and television audiences.

The contemporary art gallery sets up its own conditions for Easterson's comparatively modest films, which resist many filmic codes and offer different viewer experiences. Usually exhibited as looped short films just a few minutes in length, the clips lack significant modification apart from Easterson's initial selection. The only intelligible narrative is the simple title cards that Easterson inserts to introduce the species of animal bearing the camera. Rather than including processes of attachment or detachment, Easterson opts for sections of film during which little occurs; the animals generally just move forward, occasionally pausing, sniffing, or turning. The titles—"Armadillo," "Mole," or "Sheep"—assist in locating viewers conceptually as well as spatially as they project their knowledge of the animal's anatomy to determine the camera's location and the animal's mode of movement. Suitable to viewing practices in galleries and museums, the sequences repeat *ad nauseum*, delaying any conclusion and producing a strange temporal state of constant presence anathema to narrative duration. The gallery environment fits Easterson's reduction of his films to short, unedited, and looped passages of animal-borne footage. Rather than focusing on unfolding narrative and technological dramas, the films draw attention to the visual, aural, and material substance of the filmic image. By diminishing interpretative frames, Easterson's films enable animals' spatial and temporal experiences— as captured and structured through the apparatus's field of view, distortion, and motion—to open onto spectators' spatial and temporal experiences of viewing. These visual elements come to the fore as narrative falls to the background. Released from demands for closure and conclusive findings, Easterson's films erupt with incoherent, mundane, and yet fascinating visual experiences, proposing an alternative form of environmental activism based on inaccessibility and incomprehension rather than understanding.

TRAJECTIVE, INTERSUBJECTIVE, AND THE END OF TERMINOLOGY

By limiting editing to a single cut and sound to ambient noise, Easterson draws attention to the multifarious visual oddities of animal-borne imaging while establishing relations between animals and viewers. In almost all of the films, one or more edges of the frame intersect with the animal's body, so that, in the case of an armadillo, a gray-brown body and two alert ears cross the bottom of the frame, and these partial bodies invite imaginative completion by viewers.

His films also include dramatic visual shifts—blurring, abstractions, and shallow focal points—that are products of camera lenses and positions as well as animal movement. For instance, miniature cameras used to outfit

Figure 13.3   Sam Easterson, "Armadillo Cam" and "Pheasant Cam," video stills from animal-borne imaging, c. 1998–2008. Copyright Sam Easterson.

small animals produce warped visual spaces, shallow depths of field, and pixilated images. As in Neubronner's photographs, the horizon line in many films disappears entirely, collapsing space, dispersing viewers' attention laterally, and troubling visual orientation. Whether or not they are "technical accidents," these warped and imperfect attributes of the films trigger affective experiences insofar as they disassemble anticipated viewing relationships and associated codes.

The fixed camera vision focuses attention most pointedly on motion, and camera motion, unlike camera vision, appears to replicate animal motion exactly, constituting experiences of travel for viewers. Lumbering from side to side, the bison-camera sways gently in a seesaw motion with abrupt transitions as the massive animal's shifting weight shakes the camera. An alligator-camera glides in smooth intervals with abbreviated pauses, and a turkey-camera pitches forward in spastic and irregular bursts. The fixed, visible portion of an animal's body contrasts with the rapidly shifting environment to produce a sense of being moved through space. But the animals' particularized movements take place without any discernible intentionality or progress toward conclusion; the animals just seem to go, driven by the fact of their own locomotion rather than by a plot. The looped films prolong this seemingly endless pure movement immanent to the bodies and beings of the animals. In Easterson's films, viewers behold movement—the vectorial aspects of species—without intention or even orientation from point A to B. Even more than "behold," viewers partake imaginatively in that movement just as the medium of film participates materially. The films trigger experiences of motion that begin to erode clear distinctions between apparatus, animal, and viewer, so that subjectivity in animal-borne imaging becomes mutually constituted by film, animal, and humans in spectatorship. This description coincides in various ways with Vivian Sobchack's model of intersubjective spectatorship, which offers a compelling means of conceptualizing animal-borne imaging's appeals for identification.

Recasting the space of cinema, Sobchack proposes that multidirectional exchanges take place among film, filmmaker, and viewer through "embodied vision." Arguing for sensory and bodily experiences of film, she writes, "We do not experience any movie only through our eyes. We see and comprehend and feel films with our entire bodily being, informed by the full history and carnal knowledge of our acculturated sensorium."[28] Her model emphasizes the materiality of bodies while anticipating a release from the boundaries of individual bodies in the film experience. In her pioneering book *The Address of the Eye* (1992), she writes, "[the film experience] names a *transitive relationship* between two or more objective body-subjects, each materially embodied and distinctly situated, yet each mutually enworlded. Constituted from this transitive relation is a third, *transcendent space*, that is, a space exceeding the individual body and its unique situation yet concretely inhabited and *intersubjective*."[29] According to Sobchack's proposed schema, the camera-bearing animal's physical body, which is a central material component, maintains a concrete presence while also opening its contours to interpenetration through the film experience. With their dramatic appeal to the body of the spectator, animal-borne imaging makes palpable Sobchack's embodied vision. In fact, animals as well as cyborgs, prosthetics, and a host of other marginally human forms frequently crop up in her more recent work as means of thinking relationality.[30] In the final essay of *Carnal Thoughts* (2004), for instance, she writes, "I want to begin to describe and understand how it is possible that material objects in the world are not only *sensible* to our flesh but how they also can make us devoted and *responsible* to the flesh of the world and others."[31] Sobchack powerfully describes the ethics of interobjectivity and intersubjectivity: That humans recognize themselves as deeply connected—in the flesh—to others in the world.

Despite all of the evocative structural, technological, intellectual, experiential, and sensorial associations constituted by animal-borne imaging between animals and humans, Easterson's films retain an abiding opaqueness and inaccessibility that requires retreating somewhat from Sobchack's claims or, rather, my claims on behalf of her model. As much as his films invite identification, they resist it through their refusal to be written into narrative codes and to relate to rational and intentional human experience. As films, they are difficult because while they beg for intersubjective identification through their POV structures and conceptual imperatives, they do not readily lend themselves to identification due to their rejection of means of sense-making, such as camera orientation, editing, and narrative. As opposed to environmental activism based on gathering facts and assuring understanding, Easterson's films proffer a more radical form of activism by encouraging viewers to recognize the very limits of fully knowing about and connecting with others and themselves. In *Giving an Account of Oneself* (2005), Judith Butler proposes such a theory of subject, "one that acknowledges the limits of self-knowledge." Because the "I" is always relational to an "Other," any attempt to give an account of oneself always includes "moments of unknowingness about oneself" because of this constitutive relation to others. "[T]hese relations," she continues, "call upon primary forms of relationality that are not always available to explicit and reflective thematization." She writes later, "'I' is the moment of failure in every narrative effort to give an account of oneself." The self's resistance to "reflective thematization," which includes representation and narrativization, means that the subject is opaque to itself (on account of its dependence on others), and this opacity, Butler claims, sustains the subject's ethical bonds to others. Easterson's films encourage viewers to interact imaginatively with animals and, through that experience, to recognize the limits of knowing. It is the impossibility to understand fully and the failure to identify with the animal point-of-view that distinguishes Easterson's films from those by Marshall and Downer. This incapacity to define the animal and, thus, the human marks the ethics of animal-borne imaging.

CONCLUSION

In the only piece of serious and critical writing on animal-borne imaging that I know of, Donna Haraway describes the co-adaptation of animals, humans, machines, and technologies in *Crittercam* to explore the reciprocal demands of these bodies.[32] Drawing on her theorization of cyborgian compounds, the article elaborates *Crittercam*'s hybrid relationships, where every part is actively engaged with every other part of the apparatus in "relentless fleshy entanglements of [the] techno-organic world."[33] She describes how in "contact zones" material entities of nature enmesh with representational technologies of culture. While intrigued by the apparent symmetries among humans, animals, and technologies in these contact zones, she concludes, "[T]he contents of the demands are not symmetrical at all."[34] What does "the contents of the demands" mean exactly? Haraway is most likely referring to the imbalances in what humans as compared to animals get out of—or at least expect to get out of—their "enfoldings." In the case of *Crittercam*, human mediation of animal bodies and habitats (this would be the "demands" in Haraway formulation) promises virtual proximity and intellectual possession (the "contents").

From Neubronner's pigeon photographs at the beginning of the twentieth century to Easterson's farmyard films at the end of the century, an abiding desire to access through representation and possess through understanding that which resides outside of human experience compels these diverse animal-borne imaging projects. In all four projects, animals, or animal experiences, constitute that outside, a boundary constantly fluctuating according to various historical, economic, technological, and social conditions. By attaching cameras to animals, these men produced unusual sets of images that appear illegible as much as intelligible. This illegibility fascinates me because it seems to contradict the very aim of these projects—"the contents of the demands"—to make known an "outside." Interpretation, narrative, and editing serve as powerful means of taming the unruly realm of the visual and the indecipherability of "contact zones." However, these tools diminish those very characteristics that compel viewers to reflect on their own incapacity to always make sense of the world. Harraway writes near the end of her essay, "The privilege of people accompanying animals depends on getting these asymmetrical relationships right."[35] To do so, we must recognize not only what we might know about animals, but also what is impossible to know. Animal-borne imaging offers embodied points-of-view that implicate human viewers in a radical relation with an animal other. The ethics of this relation comprise the immense difficulties of accounting for oneself and for others.

NOTES

1. Akira Lippit, *The Electric Animal* (Minneapolis: University of Minnesota Press, 2000), 51.

2. Dates range from 1903 to 1910, with most sources citing 1907 or 1908 as the year that Neubronner patented his device. Neubronner mentions successful experiments in 1903. An exhibition of pigeon photographs at the Internationale Photographische Ausstellung in Dresden in 1909 brought Neubronner increased recognition. See Julius Neubronner, *Die Photographie mit Brieftauben* (Berlin: J. Springer, 1909): 77–96; and Alfred Gradenwitz, "Pigeons as Picture-Makers," *Technical World Magazine* 10 (1908): 485–487.

3. About the cat, see Emma Allen, "Is this Cat a Great Photographer? The Seattle Art Scene's Feline Phenomenon," *Huffington Post*, May 22, 2011, accessed July 5, 2013, http://www.huffingtonpost.com/artinfo/cooper-the-cat-photographer_b_863555.html. Gerco de Ruijter's and Michel Banabila's film made with pigeons "Loslaten" ("Letting Go") is available at http://vimeo.com/26201659. See Geoff Manaugh, "Bird's Eye View," *BLDGBLOG* (blog), July 21, 2011, accessed July 5, 2013, http://bldgblog.blogspot.com/2011/07/birds-eye-view.html. About the red-tailed hawk, see Andy Newman and Emily Rued, "Hawk Cam, Watching Bobby and Violet," *New York Times*, April 6, 2001, accessed July 5, 2013, http://cityroom.blogs.nytimes.com/2011/04/06/hawk-cam-watching-bobby-and-violet/.

4. See the Raptor Resource Project's website, accessed July 5, 2013, http://www.raptorresource.org. The Cornell Lab of Ornithology has archived hundreds of nest-cam films, accessed July 5, 2013, http://www.birds.cornell.edu.

5. AP, "Live Eagle Cam: Thousand Watch On Internet as Eggs Hatch," *Huffington Post*, April 4, 2011, accessed July 5, 2013, http://www.huffingtonpost.com/2011/04/04/live-eagle-cam-2011-video_n_844582.html. For the Siba Inu stream, accessed July 5, 2013, see http://www.ustream.tv/sfshiba.

6. Ben Davis, "Could the Cindy Sherman of Monkeys Accidentally Revolutionize Copyright Law for Artists?" *Huffington Post,* July 17, 2011, accessed July 5, 2013, http://www.huffingtonpost.com/artinfo/could-the-cindy-sherman-o_b_899866.html. Partial resolution was found in the U.S. copyright law 503.03 (a), which states, "In order to be entitled to copyright registration, a work must be the product of human authorship."

7. See Gregg Mitman, *Reel Nature: America's Romance with Wildlife on Film* (Cambridge, MA: Harvard University Press, 1999); Derek Bousé, *Wildlife Films* (Philadelphia: University of Pennsylvania Press, 2000); and Nigel Rothfels, ed. *Representing Animals* (Bloomington and Indianapolis, IN: Indiana University Press, 2002).

8. Thomas Nagel, "What Is It Like to Be a Bat?" *The Philosophical Review* 4 (1974): 436.

9. Ibid., 439.

10. In the 1870 siege of Paris during the Franco-Prussian war, telegraph wires were cut and balloons shot down. The government established a pigeon post to ensure communication and equipped pigeons with hundreds of letters using microphotography. Alfred Hildebrandt, *Airships Past and Present*, trans. W. H. Story (London: Archibald Constable and Company, 1908), 343–357.

11. Ibid., 91–93.

12. See A. H. Osman, *Pigeons in the Great War: A Complete History of the Carrier-Pigeon Service during the Great War, 1914 to 1918* (London: The "Racing Pigeon" Publishing Co., 1928); and United States Army (Army Single Corps), *The Homing Pigeon (War Department)* (Washington, DC: Government Print Office, 1945).

13. As opposed to Paul Virilio's teleological history of aerial reconnaissance, which quickly passes over "camera-pigeons," "camera-kites," and "camera-balloons" to focus on the airplane. See Paul Virilio, *War and Cinema: The Logistics of Perception* (London: Verso, 1989), 11.

14. Neubronner's extant photographs mostly date from 1910 and were made using his Doppel-Sport Panoramic Camera. A large number of pigeon photographs initiated by a Swiss clockmaker named Adrian Michel who adapted Neobronner's apparatus were recently recovered for the 2007 exhibition *Des pigeons photographes?* at the *Musée Suisse de l'appareil photographique* in Vevey.
15. "Pigeons have two visual axes in each eye—a principle axis that lies close to the optic axis and projects to a central fovea, and a second visual axis that projects to a fovea lying in the temporal retina." See Ian Howard and Brian Rogers, "Binocular and Stereoscopic Vision in Animals," *Binocular Vision and Stereopsis, Oxford Psychology Series* 29 (New York: Oxford University Press, 1995): 645–657.
16. As told on *Crittercam* website, accessed July 5, 2013, http://animals.nationalgeographic.com/animals/crittercam-about/#b.
17. "Sam Easterson: Animal, Vegetable, Video: Where the Buffalo Roam," *Creative Capital*, accessed July 5, 2013, http://creative-capital.org/project_contexts/view/132/project:172. See Nato Thompson, *Becoming Animal* (North Adams, MA: MASS MoCA Publishers, 2005), 54–59.
18. The "Museum of Animal Perspectives" is no longer available, but his videos made from cameras mounted on animals and placed in burrows and nests are available for preview at the "Animal-Cams" on the "Video Data Bank," accessed July 5, 2013, http://www.vdb.org/titles/animal-cams. For printed stills, see Sam Easterson, "Readings" *Harper's Magazine*, February 2010, 30.
19. See John Downer Productions website, accessed July 5, 2013, http://www.jdp.co.uk/programmes/Tigers-Spy-in-the-Jungle.
20. Nato Thompson, *Becoming Animal,* 54.
21. This quotation is from a *Crittercam* Advertisement. Quoted in Donna Harraway, *When Species Meet* (Minneapolis: University of Minnesota Press, 2007), 249.
22. Edward Branigan, *Point of View in the Cinema: A Theory of Narration and Subjectivity in Classical Film* (Berlin: Mouton Publishers, 1984), 73.
23. Ibid., 7. Branigan cites the example of Robert Montgomery's *Lady in the Lake* (1946), which shows all of the actions and movement of the main character Detective Marlowe as traveling POV shots. The smooth camera movement and lack of apparent affect renders a shell of a person.
24. Creativity has increasingly debated studies of animal consciousness. See Donald R. Griffin, *Animal Minds: Beyond Cognition to Consciousness* (Chicago: University of Chicago Press, 2001); Clive Wynne, *Do Animals Think?* (Princeton, NJ: Princeton University Press, 2004); and Martin Schönfeld, "Animal Consciousness: Paradigm Change in the Life Sciences," *Perspectives on Science* 14.3 (2006): 354–381.
25. The compulsion to decode animal-borne footage carries over into the academic realm, where graphs, charts, maps, and other devices identify and extract what is important. See the proceedings of a national academic conference convened in 2007 by National Geographic and *Crittercam*, accessed July 5, 2013, http://www.nationalgeographic.com/abis/.
26. On media's relationship to camouflage, see Hanna Rose Shell, *Hide and Seek: Camouflage, Photography, and the Media of Reconnaissance* (New York: Zone Books, 2012).
27. See Downer's books written to accompany other television series *Supersense: Sixth Sense* (London: BBC Books, 1989); and *Lifesense: Our Lives Through Animal Eyes* (London: BBC Books, 1991).

28. Vivian Sobchack, *Carnal Thoughts: Embodiment and Moving Image Culture* (Berkeley: University of California Press, 2004), 63.
29. Vivian Sobchack, *The Address of the Eye* (Princeton: Princeton University Press, 1992), 25.
30. See Vivian Sobchack, *Screening Space: The American Science Fiction Film* (New Brunswick: Rutgers University Press, 1998); and Vivian Sobchack, "Toward a Phenomenology of Non-Fictional Experience," in *Collecting Visible Evidence,* ed. Michael Renov and Jane Gaines (Minneapolis: University of Minnesota Press, 1999), 241–254.
31. Sobchack, *Carnal Thoughts: Embodiment and Moving Image Culture*, 295.
32. Donna Harrawy, "Crittercam: Compounding Eyes in Nature Cultures," *When Species Meet* (Minneapolis: University of Minnesota Press, 2008), 249–263.
33. Ibid., 262.
34. Ibid., 263.
35. Ibid.

Contributors

Vincent Bohlinger is associate professor of English and serves as the director of the Film Studies Program at Rhode Island College. He is currently working on a book exploring film style in the Soviet Union from the late twenties through mid-thirties.

Noël Carroll is a distinguished professor of philosophy at the Graduate Center of the City University of New York. His most recent books were *On Criticism* and *Art in the Three Dimensions*. He has just completed *A Very Short Introduction to Humour* for Oxford University Press. He is a past president of the American Society for Aesthetics, a Guggenheim Fellow, and the author of five documentaries.

Jinhee Choi is senior lecturer in film studies at King's College London. She is the author of *The Korean Film Renaissance: Local Hitmakers, Global Provocateurs* (Wesleyan University Press, 2010) and the co-editor of *Horror to the Extreme: Changing Boundaries in Asian Cinema* (Hong Kong University Press, 2009) with Mitsuyo Wada-Marciano and *Philosophy of Film and Motion Pictures* (Blackwell, 2006) with Noël Carroll. She is currently completing her book manuscript on sensibility.

Robert A. Clift is assistant professor in the Department of Communication at Southern Oregon University. In addition to writing about documentary, he is also a documentary producer and director. His most recent film, *Blacking Up: Hip-Hop's Remix of Race and Identity*, was funded by the Independent Television Service (ITVS), premiered on PBS in January 2010, and was named by the American Library Association (ALA) as one of the most notable nonfictional films of 2010. He received his Ph.D. from Indiana University, Bloomington, where he wrote his dissertation on the relationship between performance and authority in documentary film and video. Currently, he is in preproduction on a film about his family, centered on the actor Montgomery Clift.

Ruth Erickson is a Ph.D. candidate in the history of art at the University of Pennsylvania, where she is completing a dissertation on the intersection of art and the social sciences in France after May 1968. She is the recipient of research fellowships from Fulbright, Kress, Mellon, and the Council for European Studies, and she has published articles on contemporary art in *Framework*, *Art Papers*, the architecture journal *via*, and the forthcoming volume *Critical Landscapes* (2014). In 2008, she co-organized an interdisciplinary conference on animal studies in the humanities at the University of Pennsylvania.

Mattias Frey is senior lecturer in film at the University of Kent (UK). He has published extensively on German and Austrian cinema, film criticism and theory, and the history of film culture in journals such as *Cinema Journal*, *Screen*, *New German Critique*, *Quarterly Review of Film and Video*, *Artforum*, *Jump Cut*, and *Framework*. He is the author of *Postwall German Cinema: History, Film History, and Cinephilia* (Berghahn, 2013) and an editor of the journal *Film Studies*.

Mette Hjort is associate vice president (academic quality assurance) and chair professor of visual studies at Lingnan University, where she is also director of the Center for Cinema Studies. A foundation fellow of the Hong Kong Academy of the Humanities, Mette Hjort is an affiliate professor of Scandinavian studies at the University of Washington, Seattle, and an adjunct professor at the Centre for Modern European Studies, University of Copenhagen. Her publications include Lone Scherfig's *Italian for Beginners* (2010) and the edited volumes *Film and Risk* (2012) and *Creativity and Academic Activism* (with Meaghan Morris, 2012).

Alasdair King is senior lecturer in German and film studies at Queen Mary University of London. He is the author of *Hans Magnus Enzensberger: Writing, Media, Democracy* (2007), as well as numerous articles on German cinema and on the interaction of film and philosophy.

Jason Middleton is assistant professor in the English department and the graduate program in visual and cultural studies, and director of the film and media studies program, at the University of Rochester. He is the author of *Documentary's Awkward Turn: Cringe Comedy and Media Spectatorship* (Routledge, 2014) and has published essays in journals including *Cinema Journal*, *Quarterly Review of Film and Video*, *Afterimage*, and *The Velvet Light Trap*.

Annelies van Noortwijk is senior lecturer for the arts, culture, and media studies department and the Roman languages and culture department at the University of Groningen (the Netherlands). She teaches film studies, literature, and art history and theory. Her research concentrates on contemporary Hispanic documentary, literature, and journalism with a specific interest in questions of engagement, resistance, and ethics and the penetration of the artistic discourse into nontraditional forms of art. She is currently working on a project on (auto)biographical discourse in contemporary documentary.

Trevor Ponech, associate professor of English at McGill University, is the author of *What Is Non-Fiction Cinema?* (Boulder: Westview Press, 1999). His recent work on the philosophy of cinema appears in *The Journal of Aesthetics and Art Criticism, The British Journal of Aesthetics, The Routledge Companion to Philosophy and Film* (ed. Paisley Livingston and Carl Plantinga), and *Film and Risk* (ed. Mette Hjort).

D. N. Rodowick is Glen A. Lloyd Distinguished Service Professor in Cinema and Media Studies at the University of Chicago. His books include: *The Virtual Life of Film* (Harvard University Press, 2007); *Reading the Figural, or, Philosophy after the New Media* (Duke University Press, 2001); *Gilles Deleuze's Time Machine* (Duke University Press, 1997); *The Difficulty of Difference: Psychoanalysis, Sexual Difference, and Film Theory* (Routledge, 1991); and *The Crisis of Political Modernism: Criticism and Ideology in Contemporary Film Theory* (University of Illinois Press, 1989; 2nd edition, University of California Press, 1994). Two new books, *Elegy for Theory* and *Philosophy's Artful Conversation*, will be published by Harvard University Press in 2013 and 2014, respectively.

Jane Stadler is associate professor of film and media studies for the School of English, Media Studies and Art History at the University of Queensland. She is the author of *Pulling Focus: Intersubjective Experience, Narrative Film and Ethics* (2008), co-author of *Screen Media* (2009) and *Media and Society* (2012), and co-editor of an adaptation studies anthology, *Pockets of Change: Adaptation and Cultural Transition* (2011).

References

Aaron, Michele. *Spectatorship: The Power of Looking On.* London: Wallflower Press, 2007.

Abel, Marco. "Imaging Germany: The (Political) Cinema of Christian Petzold." In *The Collapse of the Conventional: German Film and Its Politics at the Turn of the Twenty-First* Century, edited by Jaimey Fisher and Brad Prager, 258–284. Detroit: Wayne State University Press, 2010.

Ahmed, Sara. *The Cultural Politics of Emotion.* Edinburgh: Edinburgh University Press, 2004.

Altman, Rick. *Film/Genre.* London: British Film Institute, 1999.

———. "A Semantic/Syntatic Approach to Genre." *Cinema Journal* 23.3 (1984): 6–18.

Anderson, Linda. *Autobiography.* London: Routledge, 2001.

Angel, Maria. "Seeing Things: Image and Affect." *Cultural Studies Review* 15.2 (2009): 133–146.

Aristotle. *Nichomachean Ethics.* Translated by Martin Ostwald. New York: Macmillan, 1962.

Armitage, John, ed. *Paul Virilio: From Modernism to Hypermodernism and Beyond.* London: Sage, 2000.

Bach, Steven. *Leni: The Life and Works of Leni Riefenstahl.* New York: Vantage, 2007.

Badiou, Alain. *Ethics: An Essay on the Understanding of Evil.* London: Verso, 2001.

Bainbridge, Caroline. "The Trauma Debate: Just Looking? Traumatic Affect, Film Form and Spectatorship in the Work of Lars von Trier." *Screen* 45.4 (2004): 391–400.

Balio, Tino. *The American Film Industry.* Madison: University of Wisconsin Press, 1976.

———. "Hollywood Production Trends in the Era of Globalisation." In *Genre and Contemporary Hollywood,* edited by Steve Neale, 165–184. London: British Film Institute, 2002.

Barker, Jennifer. *The Tactile Eye: Touch and the Cinematic Experience.* Berkeley: University of California Press, 2009.

Barthes, Roland. *Camera Lucida.* Translated by Richard Howard. New York: Hill and Wang, 1981.

Baudry, Jean-Louis. "Ideological Effects of the Basic Cinematographic Apparatus." In *Narrative, Apparatus, Ideology,* edited by Philip Rosen, 286–298. New York: Columbia University Press, 1986.

Berleant, Arnold. *Aesthetics and Environment, Theme and Variations.* Aldershot: Ashgate, 2005.

Bernhardt, Boris and Tania Singer. "The Neural Basis of Empathy." *Annual Review of Neuroscience* 35 (2012): 1–23.

Bertellini, Giorgio. *Italy in Early American Cinema: Race, Landscape, and the Picturesque.* Bloomington: Indiana University Press, 2009.

Beugnet, Martine. "Cinema and Sensation: Contemporary French Film and Cinematic Corporeality." *Paragraph* 31.2 (2008): 173–188.

Björkman, Stig. "The Idiots." In *Trier on von Trier,* translated by Neil Smith and edited by Stig Björkman, 201–218. London: Faber and Faber, 2003.

Blum, Lawrence A. *Moral Perception and Particularity.* Cambridge: Cambridge University Press, 1994.

Bogue, Ronald. "To Choose to Choose—to Believe in This World." In *Afterimages of Gilles Deleuze's Film Philosophy,* edited by D. N. Rodowick, 115–132. Minneapolis: University of Minnesota Press, 2010.

Booth, Wayne. *The Company We Keep: An Ethics of Fiction.* Berkeley: University of California Press, 1988.

Bourdieu, Pierre. *Distinction: A Social Critique of the Judgement of Taste.* Translated by Richard Nice. London: Routledge, 2010.

———. *Free Exchange.* Translated by Randal Johnson and Hans Haacke. Stanford, CA: Stanford University Press, 1995.

Bourriaud, Nicolas. *Relational Aesthetics.* Paris: Presses du Réel, 2002.

Bousé, Derek. *Wildlife Films.* Philadelphia: University of Pennsylvania Press, 2000.

Branigan, Edward. *Point of View in the Cinema: A Theory of Narration and Subjectivity in Classical Film.* Berlin: Mouton Publishers, 1984.

Briggs, David. "Accreditation and the Quality Journey in Aged Care." *Asian Journal of Gerontology & Geriatrics* 1 (2006): 163–169.

Browne, Nick. "The Spectator-in-the-Text: The Rhetoric of *Stagecoach.*" In *Film Theory and Criticism: Introductory Readings.* Fifth edition. Edited by Leo Braudy and Marshall Cohen, 148–163. New York: Oxford University Press, 1999.

Brunette, Peter. "Art Films Offer Unflinching Look." *Boston Globe,* March 9, 2003.

Bruzzi, Stella. *New Documentary: A Critical Introduction.* Second revised edition. London: Routledge, 2006.

Butler, Judith. *Giving an Account of Oneself.* New York: Fordham University Press, 2005.

Caillois, Roger. *Man, Play, and Games.* Translated by Meyer Barash. New York: Free Press, 1961.

Carel, Havi. "A Phenomenology of Tragedy: Illness and Body Betrayal in *The Fly.*" *Scan* 4.2 (2007). Accessed November 23, 2012. http://scan.net.au/scan/journal/display.php?journal_id=95.

Carlson, Allen. *Aesthetics and the Environment: The Appreciation of Nature, Art and Architecture.* London: Routledge, 2000.

———. "Appreciating Art and Appreciating Nature." In *Landscape, Natural Beauty and the Arts,* edited by Salim Kemal and Ivan Gaskell, 199–227. Cambridge: Cambridge University Press, 1993.

Carlson, Allen, and Sheila Lintott, eds. *Nature, Aesthetics, and Environmentalism: From Beauty to Duty.* New York: Columbia University Press, 2008.

Carr, Edward Hallett. *What Is History?* New York: Vintage, 1961.

Carroll, Noël. "Art and Ethical Criticism: An Overview of Recent Directions in Research." *Ethics* 110.2 (2000): 350–387.

———. "Art and the Moral Realm." In *The Blackwell Guide to Aesthetics,* edited by Peter Kivy, 126–151. Malden, MA: Blackwell, 2004.

———. "Ethics and Aesthetics: Replies to Dickie, Stecker, and Livingston," *British Journal of Aesthetics* 46.1 (2006): 82–95.

———. "Fiction, Non-fiction, and the Film of Presumptive Assertion: A Conceptual Analysis." In *Film Theory and Philosophy,* edited by Richard Allen and Murray Smith, 173–202. Oxford: Clarendon Press, 1999.

———. "Film, Emotion, Genre." In *Philosophy of Film and Motion Pictures: An Anthology*, edited by Noël Carroll and Jinhee Choi, 217–233. Malden, MA: Blackwell, 2006.

———. "Film, Rhetoric, and Ideology." In *Theorizing The Moving Image*, 175–189. Cambridge: Cambridge University Press, 1996.

———. "Moderate Moralism." *British Journal of Aesthetics* 36.3 (1996): 223–238.

———. "The Movies and the Moral Emotions." In *Minerva's Night Out: Philosophy, Motion Pictures, and Popular Culture*. Malden, MA: Wiley-Blackwell, forthcoming.

———. "On Being Moved by Nature: Between Religion and Natural History." In *Landscape, Natural Beauty and the Arts*, edited by Salim Kemal and Ivan Gaskell, 244–266. Cambridge: Cambridge University Press, 1993.

———. *The Philosophy of Horror: Or, Paradoxes of the Heart*. London: Routledge, 1990.

———. *A Philosophy of Mass Art*. Oxford: Oxford University Press, 1998.

———. "Recent Approaches to Aesthetic Experience." *Journal of Aesthetics and Art Criticism* 70.2 (2012): 165–177.

Cavell, Stanley. *The World Viewed*. New York: Viking Press, 1971.

———. *The World Viewed: Reflections on the Ontology of Film*. Enlarged edition. Cambridge, MA: Harvard University Press, 1979.

Chartrand, Tanya, and Jessica Lakin. "The Antecedents and Consequences of Human Behavioral Mimicry." *Annual Review of Psychology* 64.18 (2013): 1–24.

Cheshire, Godfrey. "How to Read Kiarostami." *Cineaste* 25.4 (2000): 8–15.

Choe, Steve. "Kim Ki-duk's Cinema of Cruelty: Ethics and Spectatorship in the Global Economy." *Positions* 15.1 (2007): 65–90.

Christensen, Ove. "Spastic Aesthetics: *The Idiots*," *P.O.V.: A Danish Journal of Film Studies* 10 (2000): 35–60.

Chung, Hye Seung. *Kim Ki-duk*. Urbana: University of Illinois Press, 2012.

Classen, Eefje. *Author Representations in Literary Reading*. Amsterdam: John Benjamins, 2012.

Clover, Carol. *Men, Women, and Chainsaws: Gender in the Modern Horror Film*. Princeton, NJ: Princeton University Press, 1992.

Colman, Felicity. *Deleuze and Cinema: The Film Concepts*. Oxford: Berg, 2011.

Coplan, Amy. "Will the Real Empathy Please Stand Up? A Case for a Narrow Conceptualization." *The Southern Journal of Philosophy* 49 (2011): 40–65.

Corrigan, Timothy. *The Essay Film: From Montaigne, After Marker*. Oxford: Oxford University Press, 2011.

Currie, Gregory. *Image and Mind: Film, Philosophy, and Cognitive Science*. Cambridge: Cambridge University Press, 1995.

Dabashi, Hamid. *Close Up: Iranian Cinema, Past, Present and Future*. London: Verso, 2001.

———. *Conversations with Mohsen Makhmalbaf*. London: Seagull Books, 2010.

———. "Mohsen Makhmalbaf's *A Moment of Innocence*." In *Life and Art: The New Iranian Cinema*, edited by Rose Issa and Sheila Whitaker, 115–128. London: British Film Institute, 1999.

Daly, Janis J., and Jonathan R. Wolpaw. "Brain–Computer Interfaces in Neurological Rehabilitation." *Lancet Neurology* 7 (2008): 1032–1043.

Damasio, Antonio. *Self Comes to Mind: Constructing the Conscious Brain*. London: William Heinemann, 2010.

Dargis, Manohla. "Sometimes Blood Really Isn't Indelible." *New York Times*, March 3, 2005.

Daston, Lorraine, and Gregg Mitman, eds. *Thinking with Animals: New Perspectives on Anthropomorphism*. New York: Columbia University Press, 2005.

Davis, Colin. *Critical Excess: Overreading in Derrida, Deleuze, Zizek, and Cavell.* Stanford: Stanford University Press, 2010.

Deleuze, Gilles. *Cinema 1: The Movement-Image.* Translated by Hugh Tomlinson and Barbara Habberjam. London: Continuum, 2005.

——. *Cinema 2: The Time-Image.* Translated by Hugh Tomlinson and Robert Galeta. London: Continuum, 2005.

——. *Negotiations 1972–1990.* Translated by Martin Joughin. New York: Columbia University Press, 1995.

Del Río, Elena. *Deleuze and the Cinemas of Performance: Powers of Affection.* Edinburgh: Edinburgh University Press, 2008.

De Luca, Tiago. "Sensory Everyday: Space, Materiality, and the Body in the Films of Tsai Ming-liang." *Journal of Chinese Cinemas* 5.2 (2011): 157–179.

De Sousa, Ronald. *Emotional Truth.* Oxford: Oxford University Press, 2011.

Des pigeons photographes? Vevey: Musée suisse de l'appareil photographique, 2007.

Devereaux, Mary. "Beauty and Evil: The Case of Leni Riefenstahl's *Triumph of the Will.*" In *Philosophy of Film and Motion Pictures: An Anthology,* edited by Noël Carroll and Jinhee Choi, 347–361. Malden, MA: Blackwell, 2006.

——. "Moral Judgments and Works of Art: The Case of Narrative Literature." *The Journal of Aesthetics and Art Criticism* 62.1 (2004): 3–11.

Didi-Huberman, Georges. "How to Open Your Eyes." In *Harun Farocki: Against What? Against Whom?,* edited by Antje Ehmann and Kodwo Eshun, 39–50. London: Raven Row, 2009.

Diedrich, Lisa. "Breaking Down: A Phenomenology of Disability." *Literature and Medicine* 20.2 (2001): 209–230.

Donald, Merlin. *Origins of the Modern Mind: Three Stages in the Evolution of Culture and Cognition.* Cambridge, MA: Harvard University Press, 1993.

Downing, Lisa, and Libby Saxton. *Film and Ethics: Foreclosed Encounters.* Oxon: Routledge, 2009.

Dudzinski, Denise. "The Diving Bell Meets the Butterfly: Identity Lost and Remembered." *Theoretical Medicine* 22 (2001): 33–46.

Dutton, Denis. "Artistic Crimes: The Problem of Forgery in the Arts." *The British Journal of Aesthetics* 19.4 (1979): 302–341.

Eaton, A. W. "Robust Immoralism." *Journal of Aesthetics and Art Criticism* 70.3 (2012): 281–292.

Edelstein, David. "Now Playing at Your Local Multiplex: Torture Porn." *New York Magazine,* February 6, 2006.

Eder, Jens. "Ways of Being Close to Characters." *Film Studies: An International Review* 8 (2006): 68–80.

Egan, Eric. *The Films of Makhmalbaf: Cinema, Politics & Culture in Iran.* Washington, DC: Mage, 2005.

Eisenberg, Nancy. "Emotion, Regulation, and Moral Development." *Annual Review of Psychology* 51 (2000): 665–697.

Ekman, Paul. *Emotions Revealed: Understanding Faces and Feelings.* Second edition. London: Weidenfeld and Nicholson, 2007.

Elsaesser, Thomas. "Holocaust Memory as the Epistemology of Forgetting? Rewind and Postponement in *Respite.*" In *Harun Farocki: Against What? Against Whom?,* edited by Antje Ehmann and Kodwo Eshun, 58–68. London: Raven Row, 2009.

Epstein, Mikhail N., Alexander Genis, and Slobodanka Vladiv-Glover. *Russian Postmodernism: New Perspectives on Post-Soviet Culture.* New York: Berghahn Books, 1999.

Erll, Astrid and Ansgar Nünning, eds. *Cultural Memory Studies: An International and Interdisciplinary Handbook.* Berlin: De Gruyter, 2008.

Erlmann, Veit. *Reason and Resonance: A History of Modern Aurality.* Cambridge, MA: MIT Press, 2010.

Eshelman, Raoul. "Performatism, or the End of Postmodernism." *Anthropoetics* 6.22 (2000/2001). Accessed April 16, 2012. http://www.anthropoetics.ucla.edu/ap0602/perform.htm.

———. *Performatism, or the End of Postmodernism.* Washington: Library of Congress, 2008.

Faden, Ruth, and Sirine Shebaya. "Public Health Ethics." *Stanford Encyclopedia of Philosophy,* April 12, 2010. Accessed April 22, 2013. http://plato.stanford.edu/entries/publichealth-ethics/.

Flory, Dan. "Spike Lee and the Sympathetic Racist." In *Thinking through Cinema: Film as Philosophy,* edited by Murray Smith and Thomas E. Wartenberg, 67–80. Malden, MA: Blackwell, 2006.

Foucault, Michel. "About the Beginning of the Hermeneutic Self: Two Lectures at Dartmouth." Translated and edited by Mark Balsius. *Political Theory* 21.2 (1993): 198–227.

———. *Ethics: Subjectivity and Truth: The Essential Works of Michel Foucault, Volume I: 1954–1984.* Translated by Robert Hurley and edited by Paul Rabinow. New York: The New Press, 1994.

———. *The Foucault Reader.* Edited by Paul Rabinow. London: Penguin, 1991.

———. *The Hermeneutics of the Subject: Lectures at the Collège de France, 1981–1982.* Translated by Graham Burchell and edited by Frédéric Gros. New York: Picador, 2004.

———. *The History of Sexuality, Volume II: The Use of Pleasure.* Translated by Robert Hurley. New York: Random House, 1985.

———. *The History of Sexuality, Volume III: The Care of the Self.* Translated by Robert Hurley. New York: Pantheon, 1986.

———. "Technologies of the Self." In *Technologies of the Self: A Seminar with Michel Foucault,* edited by Luther H. Martin, Huck Gutman, and Patrick H. Hutton, 16–49. Amherst: University of Massachusetts Press, 1988.

Frankena, William K. *Thinking about Morality.* Ann Arbor: University of Michigan Press, 1980.

Freud, Sigmund. "Mourning and Melancholia." In *General Psychological Theory,* translated by M. N. Searl, 164–179. New York: Macmillan, 1963.

Frey, Mattias. "A Cinema of Disturbance: The Films of Michael Haneke in Context." Second revised edition. *Senses of Cinema* 57 (2010). Accessed December 12, 2012. http://sensesofcinema.com/2010/great-directors/michael-haneke/.

———. "The Message and the Medium: Haneke's Film Theory and Digital Praxis." In *On Michael Haneke,* edited by Brian Price and John David Rhodes, 153–165. Detroit: Wayne State University Press, 2010.

———. "Tuning Out, Turning In, and Walking Off: The Film Spectator in Pain." In *Ethics and Images of Pain,* edited by Asbjørn Grønstad and Henrik Gustafsson, 93–111. New York: Routledge, 2012.

Gans, Herbert J. *Popular Culture and High Culture: An Analysis and Evaluation of Taste.* Second revised edition. New York: Basic Books, 1999.

Gaut, Berys. *Art, Emotion, and Ethics.* Oxford: Oxford University Press, 2007.

———. "The Ethical Criticism of Art." In *Aesthetics and Ethics: Essays at the Intersection,* edited by Jerrold Levinson, 182–203. Cambridge: Cambridge University Press, 1998.

Geuna, Aldo, and Alessandro Musicio. "The Governance of University Knowledge Transfer." *SEWPS/SPRU* Electronic Working Paper Series 173 (2008).

Gibbs, Anna. "After Affect: Sympathy, Synchrony and Mimetic Communication." In *The Affect Theory Reader,* edited by Melissa Gregg, Gregory Seigworth, and Sara Ahmed, 186–205. Durham, NC: Duke University Press, 2010.

Goffman, Erving. *Frame Analysis: An Essay on the Organization of Experience.* New York: Harper & Row, 1974.

———. *The Presentation of Self in Everyday Life.* Woodstock, NY: Overlook Press, 1973.

Goldstein, Richard. "The Tao of Borat." *The Nation,* November 2, 2006. Accessed October 5, 2008. http://www.thenation.com/article/tao-borat.

Gormley, Peter. *The New-Brutality Film: Race and Affect in Contemporary Cinema.* Bristol: Intellect, 2005.

Gradenwitz, Alfred. "Pigeons as Picture-Makers." *Technical World Magazine* 10 (1908): 485–487.

Griffin, Donald R. *Animal Minds: Beyond Cognition to Consciousness.* Chicago: University of Chicago Press, 2001.

Gunning, Tom. "An Aesthetic of Astonishment: Early Film and the (In)Credulous Spectator." In *Film Theory and Criticism: Introductory Readings,* fifth edition, edited by Leo Braudy and Marshall Cohen, 818–832. New York: Oxford University Press, 1999.

Gustafsson, Henrik. *Out of Site—Landscape and Cultural Reflexivity in New Hollywood Cinema 1969–1974.* Saarbrücken: Verlag Dr. Müller, 2008.

Hammer, Espen. *Stanley Cavell: Skepticism, Subjectivity and the Ordinary.* Oxford: Blackwell Publishing, 2002.

Haneke, Michael. "Violence and the Media." Translated by Evan Torner. In *A Companion to Michael Haneke,* edited by Roy Grundmann, 575–579. Malden, MA: Wiley, 2010.

Hanich, Julian. *Cinematic Emotion in Horror Films and Thrillers: The Aesthetic Paradox of Pleasurable Fear.* New York: Routledge, 2010.

———. "Gehört die Gewalt ins Kino, Herr Haneke?" *Der Tagesspiegel,* 10 September 1997.

Harper, Graeme, and Jonathan Rayner, eds. *Cinema and Landscape.* Bristol: Intellect, 2010.

Harraway, Donna. *When Species Meet.* Minneapolis: University of Minnesota Press, 2008.

Hawkins, Joan. "Culture Wars: Some New Trends in Art Horror." *Jump Cut* 51 (2009). Accessed December 12, 2012. http://www.ejumpcut.org/archive/jc51.2009/artHorror/index.html.

———. *Cutting Edge: Art Horror and the Horrific Avant-Garde.* Minneapolis: University of Minnesota Press, 2000.

Hepburn, Ronald W. "Contemporary Aesthetics and the Neglect of Natural Beauty." In *British Analytical Philosophy,* edited by Bernard Williams and Alan Montefiore, 285–310. London: Routledge and Kegan Paul, 1966.

Heusden, Barend van. *Cultuur in de Spiegel.* Accessed January 17, 2013. http://www.cultuurindespiegel.nl/english.

———. "Semiotic Cognition and the Logic of Culture." *Pragmatics and Cognition* 17.3 (2009): 611–627.

Hildebrandt, Alfred. *Airships Past and Present.* Translated by W. H. Story. London: Archibald Constable and Company, 1908.

Hjort, Mette. *Film and Risk.* Detroit: Wayne State University Press, 2012.

———. "The Globalization of Dogma: The Dynamics of Metaculture and Counter-Publicity." In *Purity and Provocation: Dogma 95,* edited by Mette Hjort and Scott MacKenzie, 133–157. London: British Film Institute, 2003.

———. "Lars von Trier." In *Fifty Contemporary Filmmakers,* edited by Yvonne Tasker, 361–370. London: Routledge, 2002.

Hjort, Mette, and Ib Bjondebjerg, eds. *The Danish Directors: Dialogues on a Contemporary National Cinema.* Translated by Mette Hjort. Bristol: Intellect Press, 2001.

Hjort, Mette, and Scott MacKenzie, eds. *Purity and Provocation: Dogma 95.* London: British Film Institute, 2003.

Howard, Ian, and Brian Rogers. "Binocular and Stereoscopic Vision in Animals." In *Binocular Vision and Stereopsis,* edited by Ian Howard and Brian Rogers, 645–657. New York: Oxford University Press, 1995.

Hume, David. "Of the Standard of Taste." In *Essays: Moral, Political and Literary,* edited by Eugene F. Miller, 226–249. Indianapolis: Liberty Fund, 1985.

Iversen, Gunnar. "The Old Wave: Material History in *Cool and Crazy* and the New Norwegian Documentary." In *Northern Constellations: New Readings in Nordic Cinema,* edited by C. Claire Thomson, 175–188. Norwich: Norvik Press, 2006.

Jacobson, Daniel. "In Praise of Immoral Art." *Philosophical Topics* 25.1 (1997): 155–199.

Jakobson, Roman. "On Realism in Art." In *Readings in Russian Poetics: Formalist and Structuralist Views,* edited by Ladislav Matejka and Krystyna Pomorska, 38–46. Cambridge, MA: MIT Press, 1971.

James, Nick. "The Confessions of Lars von Trier." *Sight and Sound,* October 2011, 30–34.

Jones, Ward, and Samantha Vice, eds. *Ethics at the Cinema.* New York: Oxford University Press, 2011.

Juhasz, Alexandra, and Jesse Lerner, eds. *F Is for Phony: Fake Documentary and Truth's Undoing.* Minneapolis: University of Minnesota Press, 2006.

Jun, Nathan, and Daniel W. Smith, eds. *Deleuze and Ethics.* Edinburgh: Edinburgh University Press, 2011.

Kaylan, Melik. "Spoiled Borat." *Wall Street Journal,* November 9, 2006.

Kellert, Stephen, Judith Heerwagen, and Martin Mador. *Biophilic Design: The Theory, Science and Practice of Bringing Buildings to Life.* New York: John Wiley & Sons, 2008.

Kenny, Anthony. *Aristotle on the Perfect Life.* New York: Oxford University Press, 1992.

Kieran, Matthew. "Art and Morality." In *The Oxford Handbook of Aesthetics,* edited by Jerrold Levinson, 451–470. Oxford: Oxford University Press, 2005.

———. "Forbidden Knowledge: The Challenge of Immoralism." In *Art and Morality,* edited by José Bermúdez and Sebastian Gardner, 56–73. New York: Routledge, 2003.

———. "On Obscenity: The Thrill and Repulsion of the Morally Prohibited." *Philosophy and Phenomenological Research* 64.1 (2002): 31–55.

Kirby, Alan. "The Death of Postmodernism And Beyond." *Philosophy Now* 58 (2006). Accessed January 17, 2013. http://philosophynow.org/issues/58/The_Death_of_Postmodernism_And_Beyond.

———. *Digimodernism: How New Technologies Dismantle the Postmodern and Reconfigure our Culture.* New York: Continuum, 2009.

Knudson, Peter Øvig. "The Man Who Would Give Up Control." In *Lars von Trier Interviews,* edited by Jan Lumhold, 117–124. Jackson: University Press of Mississippi, 2003.

Köhler, Margret. "Fremd ist jeder." *Berliner Morgenpost,* February 1, 2001.

Korthals Altes, Liesbeth. *Ethos and Narrative Interpretation, The Negotiation of Values in Fiction.* London: Routledge, forthcoming.

Kracauer, Siegfried. *Theory of Film: The Redemption of Physical Reality.* Princeton, NJ: Princeton University Press, 1960.

Kupper, Joseph H. "Film Criticism and Virtue Theory." In *Philosophy of Film and Motion Pictures,* edited by Noël Carroll and Jinhee Choi, 335–346. Malden, MA: Blackwell, 2006.

Lebeau, Vicky. *Childhood and Cinema*. London: Reaktion, 2008.

Lennsen, Claudia. "'Diese typische BRD-Generation': Interview mit Christian Petzold." *Die Tageszeitung*, 13 February 2003. Accessed July 13, 2011. http://www.taz.de/1/archiv/?id=archiv&dig=2003/02/13/a0182.

Levinas, Emmanuel. *Otherwise than Being or Beyond Essence*. Translated by Alphonso Lingis. The Hague: Martinus Njhoff Publishers, 1981.

Lippit, Akira Mizuta. *The Electric Animal*. Minneapolis: University of Minnesota Press, 2000.

Livingston, Paisley. *Art and Intention: A Philosophical Study*. Oxford: Oxford University Press, 2005.

———. *Cinema, Philosophy, Bergman: On Film as Philosophy*. Oxford: Oxford University Press, 2009.

Lowenstein, Adam. "Spectacle Horror and *Hostel*: Why 'Torture Porn' Does Not Exist." *Critical Quarterly* 53.1 (2011): 42–60.

MacDougal, David. *Transcultural Cinema*. Princeton, NJ: Princeton University Press, 1998.

Malecki, Wojciech. "Borat, or Pessimism: On the Paradoxes of Multiculturalism and the Ethics of Laughter." *Post Script* 28.3 (2009): 123–133.

Malvern, Jack. "Film Director Vows to Remain Silent After Nazi Remarks." *The Times*, October 6, 2011.

Marrati, Paola. *Gilles Deleuze: Cinema and Philosophy*. Translated by Alisa Hartz. Baltimore, MD: Johns Hopkins University Press, 2008.

Matheou, Demetrios. "He'll Hit Her—And Think It Feels Like a Kiss." *The Sunday Times*, May 30, 2010.

McCarthy, Todd. "All That Glitters Not Always Gold." *Variety*, May 19–25, 1997.

McCloskey, Donald N. "Minimal Statism and Metamodernism: Reply to Friedman." *Critical Review: A Journal of Politics and Society* 6.1 (1992): 107–112.

McDonald, Rónán. *The Death of the Critic*. London: Continuum, 2007.

McGill, Hannah. "Inside Out." *Sight and Sound*, June 2010, 40–42.

McNay, Lois. *Foucault: A Critical Introduction*. Cambridge: Polity Press, 1994.

Melbye, David. *Landscape Allegory in Cinema: From Wilderness to Wasteland*. Basingstoke: Palgrave Macmillan, 2010.

Metz, Christian. "The Imaginary Signifier." In *Psychoanalysis and Cinema: The Imaginary Signifier*. Translated by Celia Britton, Annwyl Williams, Ben Brewster, and Alfred Guzzetti, 1–87. Bloomington: Indiana University Press, 1982.

Middleton, Jason. "The Subject of Torture: Regarding the Pain of Americans in *Hostel*." *Cinema Journal* 49.4 (2010): 1–24.

Min, Eunjin, Jinsook Ju, and Hanju Kwak. *Korean Film: History, Resistance and Democratic Imagination*. Westport: Greenwood, 2003.

Mirbakhtyar, Shahla. *Iranian Cinema and the Islamic Revolution*. Jefferson, NC: McFarland, 2006.

Mitman, Gregg. *Reel Nature: America's Romance with Wildlife on Film*. Cambridge, MA: Harvard University Press, 1999.

Morin, Edgar. "Chronicle of a Film." In *Ciné-Ethnography: Jean Rouch*, edited by Steven Feld, 229–265. Minneapolis: University of Minnesota Press, 2003.

Movius, Geoffrey. "An Interview with Susan Sontag." In *Conversations with Susan Sontag*, edited by Leland Poague, 49–56. Jackson: University Press of Mississippi, 1995.

Mulhall, Stephen. *Stanley Cavell: Philosophy's Recounting of the Ordinary*. Oxford: Oxford University Press, 1994

Murphy, Dominic. "Concepts of Disease and Health." *Stanford Encyclopedia of Philosophy*, September 25, 2008. Accessed April 22, 2013. http://plato.stanford/edu/entries/health-disease/.

Naficy, Hamid. *A Social History of Iranian Cinema, Volume 4: The Globalizing Era, 1984–2010.* Durham, NC: Duke University Press, 2012.

Nagel, Thomas. "What Is It Like to Be a Bat?" *The Philosophical Review* 83.4 (1974): 435–450.

Nagib, Lucia. *World Cinema and the Ethics of Realism.* New York: Continuum, 2011.

Neale, Steve. "Art Cinema as Institution." *Screen* 22.1 (1981): 11–19.

Neill, Alex. "Empathy and (Fiction) Film." In *Post-Theory: Restructuring Film Studies,* edited by Noël Carroll and David Bordwell, 175–194. Madison: University of Wisconsin Press, 1996.

Neubronner, Julius. *Die Photographie mit Brieftauben.* Berlin: J. Springer, 1909.

Nichols, Bill. *Blurred Boundaries: Questions of Meaning in Contemporary Culture.* Bloomington: Indiana University Press, 1994.

———. "Discovering Form, Inferring Meaning: New Cinemas and the Film Festival Circuit." *Film Quarterly* 47.3 (1994): 16–30.

———. *Introduction to Documentary.* Bloomington: Indiana University Press, 2001.

———. *Representing Reality: Issues and Concepts in Documentary.* Bloomington: Indiana University Press, 1991.

Noortwijk, Annelies van. "Ars Longis, Vita Brevis, The Importance of Art In Human Life, A Proustian Interpretation Of Honigmann's *Forever.*" *Widescreen* 4.1 (2012). Accessed January 17, 2013. http://widescreenjournal.org/index.php/journal/article/viewArticle/139.

Nussbaum, Martha C. *The Frailty of Goodness: Luck and Ethics in Greek Tragedy and Philosophy.* Revised edition. Cambridge: Cambridge University Press, 2001.

———. *Love's Knowledge: Essays on Philosophy and Literature.* New York: Oxford University Press, 1990.

Oehmke, Philipp, and Lars-Olav Beier. "'Jeder Film vergewaltigt.'" *Der Spiegel,* October 19, 2009.

Osman, A. H. *Pigeons in the Great War: A Complete History of the Carrier-Pigeon Service During the Great War, 1914 to 1918.* London: The "Racing Pigeon" Publishing Co., 1928.

O'Sullivan, Simon. "Lacan's Ethics and Foucault's 'Care of the Self': Two Diagrams of the Production of Subjectivity (and of the Subject's Relation to Truth)." In *Parrhesia* 10 (2010): 51–73. Accessed January 17, 2013. http://www.parrhesiajournal.org/parrhesia10/parrhesia10_osullivan.pdf.

Parry, Simon. "Battling Biophobia." *South China Morning Post,* May 19, 2009.

Parsons, Glenn. *Aesthetics and Nature.* New York: Continuum, 2008.

Parsons, Russ, and Louis G. Tassinary, Roger S. Ulrich, Michelle R. Hebl, Michele Grossman-Alexander. "The View from the Road: Implications for Stress Recovery and Immunization." *Journal of Environmental Psychology* 18 (1998): 113–140.

Pease, Donald. "The Global Homeland State: Bush's Biopolitical Settlement." *Boundary 2* 30.3 (2003): 1–18.

Peña, Richard. "Iranian Cinema at the Festivals." *Cineaste* 31.3 (2006): 40–41.

Pisters, Patricia. *The Matrix of Visual Culture: Working with Deleuze in Film Theory.* Stanford: Stanford University Press, 2003.

Plantinga, Carl. *Moving Viewers: American Film and the Spectator's Experience.* Berkeley: University of California Press, 2009.

———. "The Scene of Empathy and the Human Face on Film." In *Passionate Views: Film, Cognition and Emotion,* edited by Carl Plantinga and Greg M. Smith, 239–255. Baltimore: Johns Hopkins University Press, 1999.

Plotnitsky, Arkady. "Manifolds: On the Concept of Space in Riemann and Deleuze." In *Virtual Mathematics: The Logic of Difference,* edited by Simon Duffy, 187–208. Bolton: Clinamen Press, 2006.

Ponech, Trevor. "Work and Play: The 5-O Game." In *Dekalog 1: On The Five Obstructions,* edited by Mette Hjort, 76–94. London: Wallflower Press, 2008.

Porter, Laraine, and Bryony Dixon, eds. *Picture Perfect: Landscape, Place and Travel in British Cinema before 1930.* Exeter: University of Exeter Press, 2007.

Prinz, Jesse. *The Emotional Construction of Morals.* Oxford: Oxford University Press, 2007.

Quandt, James. "Flesh & Blood: Sex and Violence in Recent French Cinema." *Artforum* 42.6 (2004): 126–132.

Radford, Colin, and Michael Weston. "How Can We Be Moved By the Fate of Anna Karenina?" *Proceedings of the Aristotelian Society,* Supplementary Volumes 49 (1975): 67–93.

Rancière, Jacues. *Dissensus: On Politics and Aesthetics.* Translated by Steven Carcoran. London: Continuum, 2010.

Rascaroli, Laura. *The Personal Camera: Subjective Cinema and the Essay Film.* London: Wallflower Press, 2009.

Reinecke, Stefan. "Das Kino als Versuchsanordnung. Ein Werkstattgespräch mit dem Regisseur Christian Petzold." *epd-film,* October 2, 2003. Accessed July 13, 2011. http://www.filmportal.de/node/263489/material/1020977.

Reynolds, David S. *Mightier Than the Sword: Uncle Tom's Cabin and the Battle for America.* New York: W. W. Norton and Company, 2011.

Ridgely, Steven. *Japanese Counterculture: The Antiestablishment Art of Terayama Shūji.* Minneapolis: University of Minnesota Press, 2010.

Rodowick, D. N. "An Elegy for Theory." *October* 122 (2007): 91–110. Reprinted in *The Film Theory Reader: Debates and Arguments,* edited by Marc Furstenau, 24–37. Oxon: Routledge, 2010.

———. *The Virtual Life of Film.* Cambridge, MA: Harvard University Press, 2007.

———. "The World, Time." In *Afterimages of Gilles Deleuze's Film Philosophy,* edited by D. N. Rodowick, 97–114. Minneapolis: University of Minnesota Press, 2010.

Rose, David. "Evidence Mounts That Violent Videos Desensitise Teenagers." *The Times,* October 19, 2010.

Ross, Andrew. *No Respect: Intellectuals and Popular Culture.* New York: Routledge, 1989.

Rothfels, Nigel, ed. *Representing Animals.* Bloomington: Indiana University Press, 2002.

Rothman, William, and Marian Keane. *Reading Cavell's "The World Viewed": A Philosophical Perspective on Film.* Detroit: Wayne State University Press, 2000.

Rouch, Jean. *Ciné-Ethnography.* Translated and edited by Steven Feld. Minneapolis: University of Minnesota Press, 2010.

Rushton, Richard. *Cinema After Deleuze.* New York: Continuum, 2012.

Sadr, Hamid Reza. *Iranian Cinema: A Political History.* London: I. B. Tauris, 2006.

Saeed-Vafa, Mehrnaz. "Location (Physical Space) and Cultural Identity in Iranian Films." In *The New Iranian Cinema: Politics, Representation and Identity,* edited by Richard Tapper, 200–214. London: I. B. Tauris, 2008.

Sarris, Andrew, ed. *Interviews with Film Directors.* New York: Avon Books, 1967.

Schepelern, Peter. "'Kill Your Darlings': Lars von Trier and the Origins of Dogma 95." In *Purity and Provocation: Dogma 95,* edited by Mette Hjort and Scott MacKenzie, 58–69. London: British Film Institute, 2003.

Schütte, Wolfram. "Eine deutsche Psychose?" *perlentaucher.de,* October 21, 2009. Accessed December 12, 2012. http://www.perlentaucher.de/artikel/5806.html.

Scott, A. O. "Colloquies on the Finer Points of Drooling." *New York Times,* April 28, 2000. Accessed October 20, 2012. http://www.nytimes.com/2000/04/28/movies/film-review-colloquies-on-the-finer-points-of-drooling.html?scp=1&sq=The=Idiots&st=nyt.

Shaviro, Steven. *The Cinematic Body.* Minneapolis: University of Minnesota Press, 1993.

Simons, Jan. *Playing the Waves: Lars von Trier's Game Cinema.* Amsterdam: Amsterdam University Press, 2007.

Sitney, P. Adams. "Landscape in the Cinema: The Rhythms of the World and the Camera." In *Landscape, Natural Beauty and the Arts,* edited by Salim Kemal and Ivan Gaskell, 103–126. Cambridge: Cambridge University Press, 1993.

Smith, Greg M. "Local Emotions, Global Moods, and Film Structure." In *Passionate Views: Film, Cognition and Emotion,* edited by Carl Plantinga and Greg M. Smith, 103–127. Baltimore: Johns Hopkins University Press, 1999.

Smith, Murray. *Engaging Characters: Fiction, Emotion and the Cinema.* Oxford: Clarendon Press, 1995.

Sobchack, Vivian. *The Address of the Eye.* Princeton, NJ: Princeton University Press, 1992.

———. *Carnal Thoughts: Embodiment and Moving Image Culture.* Berkeley: University of California Press, 2004.

———. *Screening Space: The American Science Fiction Film.* New Brunswick, NJ: Rutgers University Press, 1998.

Solove, Daniel J. "Why Privacy Matters Even if You Have 'Nothing to Hide.'" *The Chronicle Review,* May 15, 2011.

Sontag, Susan. "One Culture and the New Sensibility." In *Against Interpretation,* 293–304. New York: Farrar, Straus & Giroux, 1966.

———. "The Pornographic Imagination." In *A Susan Sontag Reader,* 205–234. New York: Vintage, 1983.

Sorgenfrei, Carol Fisher. *Unspeakable Acts: The Avant-Garde Theatre of Terayama Shūji and Postwar Japan.* Honolulu: University of Hawai'i Press, 2005.

Stecker, Robert. "Aesthetic Experience and Aesthetic Value." *Philosophy Compass,* February 2006. Accessed April 20, 2013. http://www.blackwell-compass.com/subject/philosophy/article_view?article_id=phco_articles_bpl007.

———. *Aesthetics and the Philosophy of Art: An Introduction.* Lanham, MD: Rowman and Littlefield, 2005.

Stevenson, Jack. "Lars von Trier: Pornographer?" *Bright Lights Film Journal* 43 (2004). Accessed October 23, 2012. http://brightlightsfilm.com/43/trier.php.

Stowe, Harriet Beecher. *Uncle Tom's Cabin,* edited by Jean Fagan Yellin. Oxford: Oxford University Press, 1998.

Sullivan, Zohreh T. "Iranian Cinema and the Critique of Absolutism." In *Media, Culture and Society in Iran: Living with Globalization and the Islamic State,* edited by Mehdi Semati, 193–204. London: Routledge, 2008.

Tanner, Michael. "Morals in Fiction and Fictional Morality." *Proceedings of the Aristotelian Society,* Supplementary Volumes 68 (1994): 51–65.

Thompson, Kristin. "Ponds and Performers: Two Experimental Documentaries," 7 October 2011. Accessed January 19, 2013. http://www.davidbordwell.net/blog/2011/10/07/ponds-and-performers-two-experimental-documentaries/.

Thompson, Nato. *Becoming Animal.* North Adams, MA: MASS MoCA Publishers, 2005.

Thorpe, Vanessa. "Outrage as French Couple's Film Judged Too Sexy for Cannes." *The Observer,* May 16, 2010.

Timmer, Nicole. *Do You Feel It Too? The Post-Postmodern Syndrome in American Fiction at the Turn of the Millennium.* Amsterdam: Rodopi, 2010.

Tourraine, Alain. *Beyond Neoliberalism.* Paris: Ecole des Hautes Etudes en Sciences Sociales, 2001.

Trimborn, Jürgen. *Leni Riefenstahl: A Life.* Translated by Edna McCown. New York: Faber & Faber, 2007.

Trouillot, Michel-Rolph. *Silencing the Past: Power and the Production of History.* Boston: Beacon Press, 1995.

Turan, Kenneth. *Sundance to Sarajevo: Film Festivals and the World They Made.* Berkeley: University of California Press, 2002.

Ulrich, Roger. "Biophilia, Biophobia, and Natural Landscapes." In *The Biophilia Hypothesis,* edited by Stephen R. Kellert and Edward O. Wilson, 73–137. Washington, DC: Island Press, 1993.

———. "Effects of Gardens on Health Outcomes: Theory and Research." In *Healing Gardens: Therapeutic Benefits and Design Recommendations,* edited by Clare Cooper Marcus and Marni Barnes, 27–86. New York: John Wiley & Sons, 1999.

Ulrich, Roger. "Effects of Health Facility Interior Design on Wellness: Theory and Recent Scientific Research." *Journal of Health Care Design* 3 (1991): 97–109.

Ulrich, Roger. "How Design Impacts Wellness." *Healthcare Forum Journal* 20 (1992): 20–25.

———. "A Theory of Supportive Design for Healthcare Facilities." *Journal of Healthcare Design* 9 (1997): 3–7.

———. "View Through a Window May Influence Recovery From Surgery." *Science* 224 (1984): 420–421.

Ulrich, Roger, Robert F. Simons, Barbara D. Losito, Evelyn Fiorito, Mark A. Miles, Michael Zelson et al. "Stress Recovery During Exposure to Natural and Urban Environments." *Journal of Environmental Psychology* 11 (1991): 201–230.

Ulrich, Roger, O. Lundén, and J.L. Eltinge. "Effects of Exposure to Nature and Abstract Pictures on Patients Recovering from Heart Surgery." Paper presented at the Thirty-Third Meeting of the Society for Psychophysiological Research, Rottach-Egern, Germany, 1993. Abstract published in *Psychophysiology* 30, Supplement 1 (1993): 7.

United States Army (Army Single Corps). *The Homing Pigeon (War Department).* Washington, DC: Government Printing Office, 1945.

Valdivia, Baselli. "Alberto Ekphrasis como traducción visual y correspondencias literarias en el lenguage pictórico desde museo interior de José Watanabe." *Revista de Literatura Ajos & Zafiros* 7 (2005): 239–255.

van der Vliet, Emma. "Naked Film: Stripping with *The Idiots.*" *Post Script* 28.3 (2009): 14–30.

Vermeulen, Timotheus, and Robin van den Akker. "Notes on Metamodernism." *Journal of Aesthetics and Culture* 2 (15 November, 2010). Accessed January 17, 2013. doi:10.3402/jac.v1i0.5677.

Vincendeau, Ginette. "Sisters, Sex and Sitcom." *Sight and Sound,* December 2001, 18–20.

Virilio, Paul. *War and Cinema.* London: Verso, 1989.

Vogel, Amos. *Film as a Subversive Art.* London: Weidenfeld and Nicolson, 1974.

von Trier, Lars. Dogme 2: Idioterne, manuskript og dagbog. Copenhagen: Gyldendal, 1998.

———. *Les Idiots: Journal intime et scénario.* Translated by Inès Jorgensen. Paris: Atelier Alpha Bleue, 1998.

Walker, John A. *Art and Outrage: Provocation, Controversy and the Visual Arts.* London: Pluto Press, 1999.

Walters, Tim. "Reconsidering *The Idiots:* Dogme 95, Lars von Trier, and the Cinema of Subversion?" *The Velvet Light Trap* 53 (2004): 40–54.

Walton, Kendall. *Mimesis as Make-Believe: On the Foundations of the Representational Arts.* Cambridge, MA: Harvard University Press, 1993.

Walton, Kendall L. "Transparent Pictures: On the Nature of Photographic Realism." *Critical Inquiry* 11 (1984): 246–277.

Welch, David. *Propaganda and the German Cinema 1933–1945*. Revised edition. London: I. B. Taurus, 2001.

Wilinsky, Barbara. *Sure Seaters: The Emergence of Art House Cinema*. Minneapolis: University of Minnesota Press, 2001.

Williams, Bernard. *Truth and Truthfulness: An Essay in Genealogy*. Princeton: Princeton University Press, 2002.

Williams, Linda. "Film Bodies: Gender, Genre, Excess." In *Film Genre Reader III*, edited by Barry Keith Grant, 141–159. Austin: University of Texas Press, 2003.

———. *Hard Core: Power, Pleasure, and the 'Frenzy of the Visible.'* Berkeley: University of California Press, 1989.

Williams, Raymond. "Base and Superstructure in Marxist Cultural Theory." *New Left Review* 82 (1973): 3–16.

Wilson, Emma. *Cinema's Missing Children*. London: Wallflower Press, 2003.

Winston, Brian. *Claiming the Real: The Documentary Film Revisited*. London: British Film Institute, 1995.

Wood, Robin. "The American Nightmare: Horror in the '70s." In *Hollywood from Vietnam to Reagan*, 70–94. New York: Columbia University Press, 1986.

Wynne, Clive. *Do Animals Think?* Princeton, NJ: Princeton University Press, 2004.

Zimmer, Catherine. "Caught on Tape? The Politics of Video in the New Torture Film." In *Horror After 9/11*, edited by Aviva Briefel and Sam J. Miller, 83–106. Austin: University of Texas Press, 2011.

Index